ISBN 978-0-259-50438-2
PIBN 10820440

1 MONTH OF
FREE
READING

at
www.ForgottenBooks.com

By purchasing this book you are eligible for one month membership to ForgottenBooks.com, giving you unlimited access to our entire collection of over 700,000 titles via our web site and mobile apps.

To claim your free month visit: www.forgottenbooks.com/free820440

English
Français
Deutsche
Italiano
Español
Português

www.forgottenbooks.com

Mythology Photography **Fiction**
Fishing Christianity **Art** Cooking
Essays Buddhism Freemasonry
Medicine **Biology** Music **Ancient
Egypt** Evolution Carpentry Physics
Dance Geology **Mathematics** Fitness
Shakespeare **Folklore** Yoga Marketing
Confidence Immortality Biographies
Poetry **Psychology** Witchcraft
Electronics Chemistry History **Law**
Accounting **Philosophy** Anthropology
Alchemy Drama Quantum Mechanics
Atheism Sexual Health **Ancient History**
Entrepreneurship Languages Sport
Paleontology Needlework Islam
Metaphysics Investment Archaeology
Parenting Statistics Criminology
Motivational

The Fate of the Persecutors
of the
Prophet Joseph Smith

Being a compilation of historical data on the personal testimony of Joseph Smith, his greatness, his persecutions and prosecutions, conspiracies against his life, his imprisonments, his martyrdom, his funeral and burial, the trial of his murderers, the sorrow and mourning of his followers, the fate of those who persecuted and killed him, and the attitude of his followers who also endured and passed through many of these experiences.

Compiled by N. B. Lundwall

BOOKCRAFT PUBLISHERS
SALT LAKE CITY, UTAH

LITHOGRAPHED IN U S A
BY

PUBLISHERS PRESS

PP

SALT LAKE CITY, UTAH

JOSEPH SMITH, THE PROPHET

HYRUM SMITH

FOREWORD

The Prophet Joseph Smith was subject to constant persecution from the time of his First Vision until his death. Scores of times he was brought by enemies before the courts of the land but never found guilty of the things for which he was charged. Readers of his tempestuous life constantly wonder about the fate of his persecutors who often made unhappy his life and finally murdered him.

In this book Brother Lundwall has collected all the material bearing on the subject available to him. Much of the collection is found in the History of the Church and in various Church publications, but has not before been assembled under one cover. Some of the material is distinctly new even to experienced students of the life of the Prophet.

The Gospel of the Lord Jesus Christ as taught by the Prophet Joseph Smith is the gospel of love and forgiveness. The material found within this cover does not represent hate of the persecutors of the people but sorrow for them. They serve, however, as a warning to those who without proper investigation allow their prejudices to lead them to actions contrary to the spirit of right and justice.

Certainly this book will be read with challenging interest by the members of the Church and by others. We should be grateful to the compiler for the long hours of tedious work spent in making the compilation.

—JOHN A. WIDTSOE

ACKNOWLEDGMENTS

This Compilation represents some twelve years of research, not, however, continuous application. In collecting these data grateful acknowledgment is hereby expressed to the following:

To Raymond E. Nilson for magnificent assistance in making this publication possible.

To my wife, Josephine F. Lundwall, for the fine cooperation and assistance rendered on this and on all other of my compilations.

To Olof and Lucille Lundwall in assisting in proofreading.

To the following who have so courteously given much of the information that is incorporated in this book:

Ralph D. Thomson, Assistant Librarian, University of Utah.

Leslie E. Bliss, Librarian, Huntington Library.

Dr. Elmer Belt of Los Angeles, Calif.

Mrs. Bertha H. Martin, Santa Rosa, Calif.

Mrs. Edw. M. Bunker, American Fork, Utah.

Mrs. Donald E. Judkins, Mesa, Arizona.

Juanita Brooks, St. George, Utah.

Robert W. Hill, Keeper of Manuscripts, N.Y. Public Library.

George F. Egert, Nauvoo, Ill., (for air photos of Nauvoo).

Ephraim Tolman, Bountiful, Utah, (for photos of Liberty Jail and letter of the Prophet to his wife, Emma).

Hyrum A. Knight, Carthage, Ill. (for photo of Carthage Jail).

Pres. Israel Smith and John Blackmore of Independence, Mo., for courteous willingness to furnish data.

Illinois Public Library, Springfield, Ill.

Earl Olsen, Historian's Office, Salt Lake City, Utah.

To the hundreds who expressed an intense interest in the coming forth of this Compilation from the press.

Gratitude is expressed to Dr. John A. Widtsoe, for reading the page proof and writing the "Foreword" to this book. Dr. Widtsoe has written the book reviews for all former compilations. His genuine friendship, his learning, his humility and greatness are appreciated and prized.

Appreciation is also expressed to Elder Mark E. Petersen for suggestions offered, and for his friendship which was first formed in 1917.

N. B. LUNDWALL,
Compiler and Publisher

CONTENTS

ILLUSTRATIONS

CHAPTER 1

The Prophet Joseph Smith Speaks for Himself

I was born in the year of our Lord one thousand eight hundred and five, on the twenty-third day of December, in the town of Sharon, Windsor County, State of Vermont. My father, Joseph Smith, Sr., left the State of Vermont and moved to Palmyra, Ontario (now Wayne) County, in the State of New York, when I was in my tenth year, or thereabouts. In about four years after my father's arrival in Palmyra, he moved with his family into Manchester, in the same County of Ontario.

Some time in the second year after our removal to Manchester, there was in the place where we lived an unusual excitement on the subject of religion. It commenced with the Methodists, but soon became general among all the sects in that region. Indeed, the whole district seemed affected by it, and great multitudes united themselves to the different religious parties, which created no small stir and division amongst the people, some crying, "Lo here!" and others, "Lo there!" Some were contending for the Methodist faith, some for the Presbyterian, and some for the Baptist.

For notwithstanding the great love which the converts to these different faiths expressed at the time of their conversion, and the great zeal manifested by the respective clergy, who were active in getting up and promoting this extraordinary scene of religious feeling, in order to have everybody converted, as they were pleased to call it, let them join what sect they pleased—yet when the converts began to file off, some to one party and some to another, it was seen that the seemingly good feeling of both the priests and the converts were more pretended than real; for a scene of great confusion and bad feeling ensued; priest contending against priest and convert against convert; so that all good feelings one for another, if ever they had any, were entirely lost in the strife of words and a contest about opinions.

I was at this time in my fifteenth year. My father's family was proselyted to the Presbyterian faith, and four of them joined the church, namely—my mother, Lucy; my brothers, Hyrum and Samuel Harrison, and my sister, Sophronia.

During this time of great excitement, my mind was called up to serious reflection and great uneasiness; but though my feelings were deep and often poignant, still I kept myself aloof from all these parties, though I attended their several meetings as often as occasion would permit. In process of time my mind became somewhat partial to the Methodist Sect, and I felt some desire to be united with them but so great were the confusion and strife among the different denominations, that it was impossible for a person young as I was, and so unacquainted with men and things, to come to any certain conclusion who was right and who was wrong.

My mind at times was greatly excited, the cry and tumult were so great and incessant.

In the midst of this war of words and tumult of opinions I often said to myself, What is to be done? Who of all these parties is right; or, are they all wrong together? If any one of them be right, which is it, and how shall I know it?

While I was laboring under the extreme difficulties caused by the contests of these parties of religionists, I was one day reading the Epistle of James, first chapter and fifth verse, which reads: *"If any of you lack wisdom, let him ask of God, that giveth to all men liberally, and upbraideth not; and it shall be given him."*

Never did any passage of scripture come with more power to the heart of man than this did at this time to mine. It seemed to enter with great force into every feeling of my heart. I reflected on it again and again, knowing that if any person needed wisdom from God, I did; for how to act I did not know, and unless I could get more wisdom than I then had, I would never know; for the teachers of religion of the different sects understood the same passage of scripture so differently as to destroy all confidence in settling the question by an appeal to the Bible.

At length I came to the conclusion that I must either remain in darkness and confusion, or else I must do as James directs, that is, ask of God. I at length came to the determination to ask of God, concluding that if He gave wisdom to them that lacked wisdom, and would give liberally, and not upbraid, I might venture.

So in accordance with this, my determination to ask of God, I retired to the woods to make the attempt. It was on the morning of a beautiful, clear day, early in the spring of eighteen hundred and twenty. It was the first time in my life that I had made such an attempt, for amidst all my anxieties I had never as yet made the attempt to pray vocally.

After I had retired to the place I had previously designed to go, having looked around me, and finding myself alone, I kneeled down and began to offer up the desires of my heart to God. I had scarcely done so, when immediately I was seized upon by some power which entirely overcame me, and had such an astonishing influence over me as to bind my tongue so that I could not speak. Thick darkness gathered around me, and it seemed to me for a time as if I were doomed to sudden destruction.

But exerting all my power to call upon God to deliver me out of the power of this enemy which had seized upon me, and at the very moment when I was ready to sink in despair and abandon myself to destruction—not to an imaginary ruin, but to the power of some actual being from the unseen world, who had such marvelous power as I had never before felt in any being—just at this moment of great alarm, I saw a pillar of light exactly over my head, above the brightness of the sun, which descended gradually until it fell upon me.

It no sooner appeared than I found myself delivered from the enemy which held me bound. When the light rested upon me I saw two personages, whose brightness and glory defy all description, standing above me in the air. One of them spake unto me, calling me by name, and said, pointing to the other—*"This is my Beloved Son, hear Him!"*

My object in going to inquire of the Lord was to know which of all the sects was right, that I might know which to join. No sooner, therefore, did I get possession of myself, so as to be able to speak, than I asked the Personages who stood above me in the light, which of all the sects was right—and which I should join.

I was answered that I must join none of them, for they were all wrong and the Personage who addressed me said that all their creeds were an abomination in His sight, that those professors were all corrupt; that "they draw near to me with their lips, but their hearts are far from me; they teach for doctrines the commandments of men, having a form of godliness, but they deny the power thereof."

He again forbade me to join with any of them; *and many other things did He say unto me, which I cannot write at this time.* When I came to myself again, I found myself lying on my back, looking up into heaven.

THE HEAVENLY VISION

BY ORSON PRATT

(Note: Elder Orson Pratt was very familiar with the home life of the Prophet Joseph. He stayed at the home of the Prophet when in from his missions and knew him as a husband and father, and was intimately associated with him in his private affairs. The following account of the heavenly vision can therefore be relied upon as a true narration of the Prophet to him. This excerpt is taken from a pamphlet issued in Edinburgh in 1840, printed by Ballantyne and Hughes, and entitled: "Interesting Account of Several Remarkable Visions, and of the Late Discovery of Ancient American Records by O. Pratt.")

He, therefore, retired to a secret place, in a grove, but a short distance from his father's house, and knelt down, and began to call upon the Lord. At first, he was severely tempted by the powers of darkness, which endeavoured to overcome him; but he continued to seek for deliverance, until darkness gave way from his mind; and he was enabled to pray, in fervency of the spirit, and in faith. *And, while thus pouring out his soul, anxiously desiring an answer from God, he, at length, saw a very bright and glorious light in the heavens above; which, at first, seemed to be at a considerable distance. He continued praying, while the light appeared to be gradually descending towards him; and, as it drew nearer, it increased in brightness, and magnitude, so that, by the time that it reached the tops of the trees, the whole wilderness, for some distance around, was illuminated in a most glorious and brilliant manner. He expected to have seen the leaves and boughs of the trees consumed, as soon as the light came in contact with them; but, perceiving that it did not produce that effect, he was encouraged with the hopes of being able to endure its presence. It continued descending, slowly, until it rested upon the earth, and he was enveloped in the midst of it. When it first came upon him, it produced a peculiar sensation throughout his whole system; and, im-*

*mediately, his mind was caught away, from the natural objects
with which he was surrounded; and he was enwrapped in a heavenly
vision, and saw two glorious personages, who exactly resembled
each other in their features or likeness. He was informed, that his
sins were forgiven.* He was also informed upon the subjects, which
had for some time previously agitated his mind, viz., that all the
religious denominations were believing in incorrect doctrines; and,
consequently, that none of them was acknowledged of God, as his
church and kingdom. And he was expressly commanded, to go not
after them; and he received a promise that the true doctrine, the
fulness of the gospel, should, at some future time, be made known
to him; after which, the vision withdrew, leaving his mind in a
state of calmness and peace, indescribable.

MORONI'S VISIT

I continued to pursue my common vocations in life until the
twenty-first of September, one thousand eight hundred and twenty-
three, all of the time suffering severe persecution at the hands of all
classes of men, both religious and irreligious, because I continued
to affirm that I had seen a vision.

During the space of time which intervened between the time
I had the vision and the year eighteen hundred and twenty-three—
having been forbidden to join any of the religious sects of the day,
and being of very tender years, and persecuted by those who ought
to have been my friends and to have treated me kindly, and if they
supposed me to be deluded to have endeavored in a proper and
affectionate manner to have reclaimed me—I was left to all kinds
of temptations; and mingling with all kinds of society, I frequently
fell into many foolish errors, and displayed the weakness of my
youth, and the foibles of human nature; which, I am sorry to say
led me into divers temptations, offensive in the sight of God. In
making this confession, no one need suppose me guilty of any great
or   a   a   sins. A disposition to commit such was never in my
natmrdign nt

In consequence of these things, I often felt condemned for my
weakness and imperfections; when, on the evening of the above
mentioned twenty-first of September, after I had retired to bed
for the night, I betook myself to prayer and supplication to
Almighty God for forgiveness of all my sins and follies and also
for a manifestation to me, that I might know of my state and standing before Him; for I had full confidence in obtaining a divine
manifestation, as I previously had done.

While I was thus in the act of calling upon God I discovered
a light appearing in my room, which continued to increase until
the room was lighter than at noonday, when immediately a personage appeared at my bedside, standing in the air, for his feet did
not touch the floor.

He had on a loose robe of most exquisite whiteness. It was a
whiteness beyond anything earthly I had ever seen; nor do I believe
that any earthly thing could be made to appear so exceedingly white
and brilliant. His hands were naked, and his arms also, a little

above the wrists; so, also, were his feet naked, as were his legs, a little above the ankles. His head and neck were bare. I could discover that he had no other clothing on but this robe, as it was open, so that I could see into his bosom.

Not only was his robe exceedingly white, but his whole person was glorious beyond description, and his countenance truly like lightning. The room was extremely light, but not so very bright as immediately around his person. When I first looked upon him I was afraid, but the fear soon left me.

He called me by name, and said unto me that he was a messenger sent from the presence of God to me, and that his name was Moroni; that God had a work for me to do; and that my name should be had for good and evil among all nations, kindreds and tongues, or that it should be both good and evil spoken of among all people.

He said there was a book deposited, written upon gold plates, giving an account of the former inhabitants of this continent, and the source from whence they sprang. He also said that the fulness of the everlasting Gospel was contained in it; as delivered by the Savior to the ancient inhabitants.

Also, that there were two stones in silver bows—and these stones, fastened to a breastplate, constituted what is called the Urim and Thummim—deposited with the plates; and the possession and use of these stones were what constituted "seers" in ancient or former times; and that God had prepared them for the purpose of translating the book.

After telling me these things, he commenced quoting the prophecies of the Old Testament. He first quoted part of the third chapter of Malachi, and he quoted also the fourth or last chapter of the same prophecy, though with a little variation from the way it reads in our Bibles. Instead of quoting the first verse as it reads in our books, he quoted it thus:

"For behold, the day cometh that shall burn as an oven, and all the proud, yea, and all that do wickedly, shall burn as stubble; for they that come shall burn them, saith the Lord of Hosts, that it shall leave them neither root nor branch."

And again he quoted the fifth verse thus: *"Behold, I will reveal unto you the Priesthood, by the hand of Elijah, the Prophet, before the coming of the great and dreadful day of the Lord."*

He also quoted the next verse differently: *"And he shall plant in the hearts of the children the promise made to the fathers, and the hearts of the children shall turn to their fathers; if it were not so, the whole earth would be utterly wasted at His coming."*

In addition to these he quoted the eleventh chapter of Isaiah, saying that it was about to be fulfilled. He quoted also the third chapter of Acts, twenty-second and twenty-third verses, precisely as they stand in our New Testament. He said that the prophet was Christ, but the day had not yet come when they who would not hear His voice should be cut off from among the people, but soon would come.

He also quoted the second chapter of Joel, from the twenty-eighth verse to the last. He also said that this was not yet fulfilled, but was soon to be. And he further stated that the fulness of the Gentiles was soon to come in. He quoted many other passages of scripture, and offered many explanations which cannot be mentioned here.

Again he told me that when I got those plates of which he had spoken—for the time that they should be obtained was not yet fulfilled—I should not show them to any person; neither the breastplate with the Urim and Thummim; only to those to whom I should be commanded to show them; if I did I should be destroyed. While he was conversing with me about the plates, the vision was opened to my mind that I could see the place where the plates were deposited, and that so clearly and distinctly that I knew the place again when I visited it.

After this communication, I saw the light in the room begin to gather immediately around the person of him who had been speaking to me, and it continued to do so, until the room was again left dark, except just around him, when instantly I saw as it were, a conduit open right up into heaven, and he ascended till he entirely disappeared, and the room was left as it had been before this heavenly light had made its appearance.

I lay musing on the singularity of the scene, and marveling greatly at what had been told to me by this extraordinary messenger, when, in the midst of my meditation, I suddenly discovered that my room was again beginning to get lighted, and in an instant, as it were, the same heavenly messenger was again by my bedside.

He commenced, and again related the very same things which he had done at his first visit, without the least variation; which having done, he informed me of great judgments which were coming upon the earth, with great desolations by famine, sword, and pestilence, and that these grievous judgments would come on the earth in this generation. Having related these things, he again ascended as he had done before.

By this time, so deep were the impressions made on my mind, that sleep had fled from my eyes, and I lay overwhelmed in astonishment at what I had both seen and heard. But what was my surprise when again I beheld the same messenger at my bedside, and heard him rehearse or repeat over again to me the same things as before; and added a caution to me, telling me that Satan would try to tempt me (in consequence of the indigent circumstances of my father's family), to get the plates for the purpose of getting rich. This he forbade me, saying that I must have no other object in view in getting the plates but to glorify God, and must not be influenced by any other motive than that of building His Kingdom, otherwise I could not get them.

After his third visit he again ascended into heaven as before, and I was again left to ponder on the strangeness of what I had just experienced; when almost immediately after the heavenly messenger had ascended from me for the third time, the cock crowed, and I found that the day was approaching, so that our interviews must have occupied the whole of that night.

I shortly after arose from my bed, and, as usual, went to the necessary labors of the day; but, in attempting to work as at other times, I found my strength so exhausted as to render me entirely unable. My father, who was laboring along with me, discovered something to be wrong with me, and told me to go home. I started with the intention of going to the house; but, in attempting to cross the fence out of the field where we were, my strength entirely failed me, and I fell helpless on the ground, and for a time was quite unconscious of anything.

The first thing that I can recollect was a voice speaking to me, calling me by name. I looked up and beheld the same messenger standing over my head, surrounded by light as before. He then again related unto me all that he had related the previous night, and commanded me to go to my father and tell him of the vision and commandments which I had received.

I obeyed; I returned to my father in the field, and rehearsed the whole matter to him. He replied to me that it was of God, and he told me to go and do as commanded by the messenger. I left the field, and went to the place where the messenger had told me the plates were deposited; and owing to the distinctness of the vision which I had concerning it, I knew the place the instant that I arrived there.

MORONI'S INSTRUCTIONS

Upon arriving at the repository, a little exertion in removing the soil from the edges of the top of the box, and a light pry, brought to his natural vision its contents. While viewing and contemplating this sacred treasure with wonder and astonishment, behold! the Angel of the Lord, who had previously visited him, again stood in his presence, and his soul was again enlightened as it was the evening before, and he was filled with the Holy Spirit, and the heavens were opened, and the glory of the Lord shone round about and rested upon him. While he thus stood gazing and admiring, the Angel said, "Look!" And as he thus spake, he beheld the Prince of Darkness, surrounded by his innumerable train of associates. All this passed before him, and the heavenly messenger said, "All this is shown, the good and the evil, the holy and impure, the glory of God, and the power of darkness, that you may know hereafter the two powers, and never be influenced or overcome by that wicked one. Behold, whatsoever enticeth and leadeth to good and to do good, is of God, and whatsoever doth not, is of that wicked one. It is he that filleth the hearts of men with evil, to walk in darkness and blaspheme God; and you may learn from henceforth, that his ways are to destruction, but the way of holiness is peace and rest. You cannot at this time obtain this record, for the commandment of God is strict, and if ever these sacred things are obtained, they must be by prayer and faithfulness in obeying the Lord. They are not deposited here for the sake of accumulating gain and wealth for the glory of this world; they were sealed by the prayer of faith, and because of the knowledge which they contain, they are of no worth among the children of men, only for their knowledge. On them is contained the fulness of the gospel of Jesus Christ, as it was given to his people on this land; and when it shall be brought forth by the power of God, it shall be carried to the Gentiles, of whom many will receive it, and after will the seed of Israel be brought into the fold of their Redeemer by obeying it also. Those who kept the commandments of the Lord on this land, desired this at his hand, and through the prayer of faith obtained the promise, that if their descendants should transgress and fall away, that a record should be kept, and in the last days come to their children. These things are sacred, and must be kept so, for the promise of the Lord concerning them must be fulfilled. No man can obtain them if his heart is impure, because they contain that which is sacred." * * * "By them will the Lord work a great and marvelous work; the wisdom of the wise shall become as naught, and the understanding of the prudent shall be hid, and because the power of God shall be displayed, those who profess to know the truth, but walk in deceit, shall tremble with anger; but with signs and with wonders, with gifts and with healings, with the manifestations of the power of God, and with the Holy Ghost, shall the hearts of the faithful be comforted. You have now beheld the power of God manifested, and the power of Satan; you see that there is nothing desirable in the works of darkness; that they cannot bring happiness; that those who are overcome therewith are miserable; while, on the other hand, the righteous are blessed with a place in the kingdom of God, where joy unspeakable surrounds them. There they rest beyond the power of the enemies of truth, where no evil can disturb them. The glory of God crowns them, and they continually feast upon his goodness, and enjoy his smiles. Behold, notwithstanding you have seen this great display of power, by which you may ever be able to detect the evil one, yet I give unto you another sign, and when it comes to pass then know that the Lord is God, and that he will fulfill his purposes, and that the knowledge which this record contains will go to every nation, and kindred, and tongue, and people under the whole heaven. This is the sign: When these things begin to be known, that is, when it is known that the Lord has shown you these things, the workers of iniquity will seek your overthrow. They will circulate falsehoods to destroy your reputation; and also will seek to take your life; but remember this, if you are faithful, and shall hereafter continue to keep the commandments of the Lord, you shall be preserved to bring these things forth; for in due time he will give you a commandment to come and take them. When they are interpreted, the Lord will give the holy priesthood to some, and they shall begin to proclaim this gospel and baptize by water, and after that, they shall have power to give the Holy Ghost by the laying on of their hands. Then will persecution rage more and more; for the iniquities of men shall be revealed, and those who are not built upon the Rock will seek to overthrow the church; but it will increase the more opposed, and spread farther and farther, increasing in knowledge till they shall be sanctified, and receive an inheritance where the glory of God will rest upon them; and when this takes place, and all things are prepared, the ten tribes of Israel will be revealed in the north country, whither they have been for a long season; and when this is fulfilled will be brought to pass that saying of the prophet: 'And the Redeemer shall come to Zion, and unto them that turn from transgression in Jacob, saith the Lord.' But, notwithstanding the workers of iniquity shall seek your destruction, the arm of the Lord will be extended, and you will be borne off conqueror if you keep all his commandments. Your name shall be known among the nations, for the work which the Lord will perform by your hands shall cause the righteous to rejoice and the wicked to rage; with the one it shall be had in honor, and with the other in reproach; yet, with these it shall be a terror, because of the great and marvelous work which shall follow the coming forth of the fulness of the gospel. Now, go thy way, remembering what the Lord has done for thee, and be diligent in keeping his commandments, and he will deliver thee from temptations and all the arts and devices of the wicked one. Forget not to pray, that thy mind may become strong, that when he shall manifest unto thee, thou mayest have power to escape the evil, and obtain these precious things."

Remarkable Visions—1840 By Orson Pratt.

Continuing the narration of this interview before given, Lucy Mack Smith, mother of the Prophet Joseph, relates:

"Furthermore, the angel told him, at the interview mentioned last, that the time had not yet come for the plates to be brought forth to the world; that he could not take them from the place wherein they were deposited until he had learned to keep the commandments of God—not only till he was willing but able to do it. The angel bade Joseph come to this place every year, at the same time of the year, and he would meet him there and give him further instructions.

"*The ensuing evening, when the family were all together, Joseph made known to them all that he had communicated to his father in the field, and also of his finding the record, as well as what passed between him and the angel while he was at the place where the plates were deposited.* Sitting up late that evening, in order to converse upon these things, together, with over-exertion of mind, had much fatigued Joseph; and when Alvin observed it, he said: 'Now, brother, let us go to bed, and rise early in the morning, in order to finish our day's work at an hour before sunset, then, if mother will get our suppers early, we will have a fine long evening, and we will all sit down for the purpose of listening to you while you tell us the great things which God has revealed to you.'

"*Accordingly, by sunset the next day, we were all seated, and Joseph commenced telling us the great and glorious things which God had manifested to him; but, before proceeding, he charged us not to mention out of the family that which he was about to say to us, as the world was so wicked that when they came to a knowledge of these things they would try to take our lives; and that when we should obtain the plates, our names would be cast out as evil by all people. Hence the necessity of suppressing these things as much as possible, until the time should come for them to go forth to the world.*

"After giving us this charge, he proceeded to relate further particulars concerning the work which he was appointed to do, and we received them joyfully, never mentioning them except among ourselves, agreeable to the instructions which we had received from him. *From this time forth, Joseph continued to receive instructions from the Lord, and we continued to get the children together every evening for the purpose of listening while he gave us a relation of the same. I presume our family presented an aspect as singular as any that ever lived upon the face of the earth —all seated in a circle, father, mother, sons and daughters, and giving the most profound attention to a boy, eighteen years of age, who had never read the Bible through in his life; he seemed much less inclined to the perusal of books than any of the rest of our children, but far more given to meditation and deep study.*

"We were now confirmed in the opinion that God was about to bring to light something upon which we could stay our minds, or that would give us a more perfect knowledge of the plan of salvation and the redemption of the human family. This caused us greatly to rejoice, the sweetest union and happiness pervaded our house, and tranquility reigned in our midst.

"During our evening conversations, Joseph would occasionally give us some of the most amusing recitals that could be imagined. He would describe the ancient inhabitants of this continent, their dress, mode of traveling, and the animals upon which they rode; their cities, their buildings, with every particular; their mode of warfare; and also their religious worship. This he would do with as much ease, seemingly, as if he had spent his whole life among them."   History of Joseph Smith, by Lucy Mack Smith, pp. 81-83.

MANY ANGELS VISITED JOSEPH

I was also informed concerning the aboriginal inhabitants of this country, and shown who they were, and from whence they came, a brief sketch of their origin, progress, civilization, laws, governments, of their righteousness and iniquity, and the blessing of God being finally withdrawn from them as a people was made known unto me. I was also told where there was deposited some plates on which were engraven an abridgment of the records of the ancient prophets that had existed on this continent. The angel appeared to me three times the same night and unfolded the same things. *After having received many visits from the angels of God unfolding the majesty, and glory of the events that should transpire in the last days, on the morning of the 22nd of September, A. D. 1827, the angel of the Lord delivered the records into my hands.*

Excerpts from the Wentworth Letter—Times and Seasons, 3:706-710.

THE PROPHET JOSEPH REPLIES TO A
MODERN POLITICIAN—JAMES ARLINGTON BENNETT

"But, sir, when I leave the dignity and honor I received from heaven to hoist a man into power, through the aid of my friends, where the evil and designing, after the object has been accomplished can look up the clemency, intended as a reciprocation for such favors, and where the wicked and unprincipled, as a matter of course, would seize the opportunity to flintify the hearts of the nation against me for dabbling at a sly game in politics; verily, I say, when I leave the dignity and honor of heaven to gratify the ambition and vanity of man or men, may my power cease, like the strength of Samson, when he was shorn of his locks, while asleep in the lap of Delilah! Truly said the Savior, 'Cast not your pearls before swine, lest they trample them under their feet, and turn again and rend you.'

"Shall I, who have witnessed the visions of eternity, and beheld the glories of the mansions of bliss, and the regions and the misery of the damned, shall I turn to be a Judas? Shall I, who have heard the voice of God, and communed with angels, and spake, as moved by the Holy Ghost, for the renewal of the everlasting covenant, and for the gathering of Israel in the last days, shall I worm myself into a political hypocrite? Shall I, who hold the keys of the last kingdom, in which is the dispensation of the fulness of all things spoken by the mouths of all the holy prophets, since the world began, under the sealing power of the Melchisedec Priesthood—shall I stoop from the sublime authority of Almighty God to be handled as a monkey's catspaw, and pettify myself into a clown to act the farce of political demagoguery? No, verily no! The whole earth shall bear me witness that I, like the towering rock in the midst of the ocean, which has withstood the mighty surges of the warring waves for centuries, *am impregnable*, and am a faithful friend to virtue, and a fearless foe to vice; no odds, whether the former was sold as a pearl in Asia, or hid as a gem in America, and the latter dazzles in palaces, or glimmers among the tombs.

"I combat the errors of ages; I meet the violence of mobs; I cope with illegal proceedings from executive authority; I cut the Gordian knot of powers; and I solve mathematical problems of universities WITH TRUTH—*diamond truth; and God is my 'right-hand man.'* "

Life of Joseph the Prophet, by Geo. Q. Cannon, p. 432.

CHAPTER 2

The Greatness of the Prophet Joseph

By **Eliza R. Snow**: On my return to Kirtland, by solicitation, I took up my residence in the family of the prophet and taught his family school. Again I had ample opportunity of judging of his daily walk and conversation, and the more I made his acquaintance, the more cause I found to appreciate him in his divine calling. His lips ever flowed with instructions and kindness; but, although very forgiving, indulgent and affectionate in his nature, when his god-like intuition suggested that the good of his brethren, or the interests of the kingdom of God demanded it, no fear of censure, no love of approbation, could prevent his severe and cutting rebukes. *His expansive mind grasped the great plan of salvation, and solved the mystic problem of man's destiny; he was in possession of keys that unlocked the past and the future, with its successions of eternities; yet in his devotions he was as humble as a little child. Three times a day he had family worship; and these precious seasons of sacred household service truly seemed a foretaste of celestial happiness.* Women of Mormondom, By E. W. Tullidge, pp. 65-66.

By **Orson Pratt**: I had the great privilege when I was in from my missions, of boarding most of the time at his house, so that I not only knew him as a public teacher, but as a private citizen, as a husband and father. I witnessed his earnest and humble devotions both morning and evening in his family. *I heard the words of eternal life flowing from his mouth, nourishing, soothing and comforting his family, neighbors and friends. I saw his countenance lighted up as the inspiration of the Holy Ghost rested upon him, dictating the great and most precious revelations now printed for our guidance. I saw him translating, by inspiration, the Old and New Testaments, and the inspired Book of Abraham from Egyptian papyrus.* J. D. 7:176.

By **John Taylor**: *No wonder that Joseph Smith should say that he felt himself shut up in a nutshell—there was no power of expansion; it was difficult for him to reveal and communicate the things of God, because there was no place to receive them. What he had to communicate was so much more comprehensive, enlightened and dignified than that which the people generally knew and comprehended, it was difficult for him to speak; he felt fettered and bound, so to speak, in every move he made.* J. D. 10:148.

The principles had placed him in communication with the Lord, and not only with the Lord, but with the ancient apostles and prophets; such men, for instance, as Abraham, Isaac, Jacob, Noah, Adam, Seth, Enoch, and Jesus and the Father, and the apostles that lived on this continent as well as those who lived on the Asiatic continent. He seemed to be as familiar with these people as we are with one another. J. D. 21:94.

By Brigham Young: *Those who were acquainted with him knew when the Spirit of revelation was upon him, for his countenance wore an expression peculiar to himself while under that influence. He preached by the Spirit of revelation, and taught in his council by it, and those who were acquainted with him could discover it at once, for at such times there was a peculiar clearness and transparency in his face.*   *J. D.* 9:89.

Joseph Smith holds the keys of this last dispensation, and is now engaged behind the veil in the great work of the last days. I can tell our beloved brother Christians who have slain the Prophets and butchered and otherwise caused the death of thousands of Latter-day Saints, the priests who have thanked God in their prayers and thanksgiving from the pulpit that we have been plundered, driven, and slain, and the deacons under the pulpit, and their brethren and sisters in their closets, who have thanked God, thinking that the Latter-day Saints were wasted away, something that no doubt will mortify them—something that, to say the least, is a matter of deep regret to them—namely, that no man or woman in this dispensation will ever enter into the Celestial Kingdom of God, without the consent of Joseph Smith. From the day that the Priesthood was taken from the earth to the winding-up scene of all things, every man and woman must have the certificate of Joseph Smith, junior, as a passport to their entrance into the mansion where God and Christ are—I with you and you with me. I cannot go there without his consent. He holds the keys of that kingdom for the last dispensation—the keys to rule in the spirit world; and he rules there triumphantly, for he gained full power and a glorious victory over the power of Satan while he was yet in the flesh, and was a martyr to his religion and to the name of Christ, which gives him a most perfect *victory in the spirit world. He reigns there as supreme a being* in his sphere, capacity, and calling, as God does in heaven. Many will exclaim, "Oh, that is very disagreeable! It is preposterous! We cannot bear the thought!" But it is true.   *J. D.* 7:289.

By John Reid, Lawyer: The first acquaintance I had with Gen. Smith was about the year 1823. He came into my neighborhood, being then about eighteen years of age, and resided there two years; during which time I became intimately acquainted with him. I do know that his character was irreproachable; that he was well known for truth and uprightness; that he moved in the first circles of the community, and he was often spoken of as a young man of intelligence and good morals, and possessing a mind susceptible of the highest intellectual attainments. I early discovered that his mind was constantly in search of truth, expressing an anxious desire to know the will of God concerning His children here below, often speaking of those things which professed Christians believe in. I have often observed to my best informed friends, (those that were free from superstition and bigotry) that I thought Joseph was predestinated by his God from all eternity to be an instrument in the hands of the great Dispenser of all good, to do a great work; what it was I knew not.   *D.H.C.* 1:93.

By Parley P. Pratt: Yes, that extraordinary man, whose innocent blood is yet dripping, as it were, from the hands of assassins and their accessories, in the United States, was the chosen vessel honored of God, and ordained by angels, to ordain other Apostles and Elders, to restore the Church and the Kingdom of God, the gifts of the Holy Spirit, and to be a messenger in the spirit, and power of Elijah to prepare the way of the Lord! "For, behold, he will suddenly come to his temple!"

Like John, who filled a similar mission preparatory to the first advent of the Son of God, he baptized with water unto repentance, for the remission of sins; like him, he was imprisoned; and, like him, his life was taken from the earth; and, finally, like all other true messengers, his message is being demonstrated by its progressive fulfillment—the powers, gifts, and signs following the administration of his message in all the world, and every minute particular of his predictions fulfilling in the order of events, as the wheels of time bring them due.

But in one important point his message differs from all former messages. The science of Theology revived by him will never decline, nor its keys be taken from the earth. They are committed to man for the last time. Their consummation will restore the tribes of Israel, and Judah, overthrow all corrupt institutions. usher in the reign of universal peace and knowledge, introduce tc earth her lawful and eternal king, the crucified Nazarene, the resurrected Messiah, banish darkness and death, sorrow, mourning and tears, from the face of our globe, and crown our race with the laurels of victory and eternal life.

Ages yet unborn will rise up and call him blessed. A thousand generations of countless myriads will laud his name and recount his deeds, while unnumbered nations bask in the light and enjoy the benefits of the institution founded by his instrumentality.

His kindred, the nation that gave him birth, and exulted at his death, nay, his very murderers and their posterity, will yet come bending unto him and seek his forgiveness and the benefits of his labors.

But Oh! the pain! the dark despair! the torments of a guilty conscience! the blackness of darkness in the lower hell, which the guilty wretches will experience before that happy day of deliverance! Oh! the countless myriads of the offspring of innocent and honorable men who will walk the earth, tread on the ashes, or plough and reap over the bones and dust of those miserable murderers and their accomplices who have consented to the shedding of innocent blood, ere the final trump shall sound, which calls up their sleeping dust from its long slumbers in the tomb, and their spirits from the prison of the damned!

And even when this, to them almost interminable, period has rolled away, and they rise from the dead, instead of a welcome exaltation to the presence and society of the sons of God, an eternal banishment awaits them. They never can come where God and Christ dwell, but will be servants in the dominions of the Saints, their former victims.

The Key To Theology, pp. 80-82, 1938 edition.

By **Parley P. Pratt:** *In Philadelphia I had the happiness of once more meeting with President Smith, and of spending several days with him and others, and with the saints in that city and vicinity. During these interviews he taught me many great and glorious principles concerning God and the heavenly order of eternity. It was at this time that I received from him the first idea of eternal family organization and in the eternal union of the sexes in those inexpressibly endearing relationships which none but the highly intellectual, the refined and pure in heart, know how to prize, and which are at the very foundation of everything worthy to be called happiness.* Till then I had learned to esteem kindred affections and sympathies as appertaining solely to this transitory state, as something from which the heart must be entirely weaned, in order to be fitted for its heavenly state. *It was Joseph Smith who taught me how to prize the endearing relationships of father and mother, husband and wife; of brother and sister, son and daughter. It was from him that I learned that the wife of my bosom might be secured to me for time and all eternity; and that the refined sympathies and affections which endeared us to each other emanated from the fountain of divine eternal love. It was from him that I learned that we might cultivate these affections, and grow and increase in the same to all eternity; while the result of our endless union would be an offspring as numerous as the stars of heaven, or the sands of the sea shore. It was from him that I learned the true dignity and destiny of a son of God, clothed with eternal priesthood, as the patriarch and sovereign of his countless offspring. It was from him that I learned that the highest dignity of womanhood was to stand as a queen and princess to her husband, and to reign for ever and ever as the queen mother of her numerous and still increasing offspring. * * * Yet, at that time, my dearly beloved brother, Joseph Smith, had barely touched a single key; had merely lifted a corner of the veil and given me a single glance into eternity.*

Autobiography of Parley P. Pratt, pp. 329-330.

By **David Whitmer:** Before I knew Joseph, I had learned about him and the plates from persons who declared they knew he had them, and swore they would get them from him. When Oliver Cowdery went to Pennsylvania he promised to write me what he should learn about these matters, which he did. He wrote me that Joseph had told him his (Oliver's) secret thoughts, and all he had meditated about going to see him, which no man on earth knew, as he supposed, but himself, and so he stopped to write for Joseph. . . . When I arrived at Harmony, Joseph and Oliver were coming toward me, and met me some distance from the house. Oliver told me that Joseph had informed him when I started from home, where I had stopped the first night and how I read the sign at the tavern, where I stopped the next night, etc., and that I would be there that day before dinner, and this was why they had come out to meet me; all of which was exactly as Joseph had told Oliver, at which I was greatly astonished.

Elders' Journal, Vol. 4, No. 16, May 15, 1907.

By **Parley P. Pratt:** I bear this testimony this day, that Joseph

Smith was and is a Prophet, Seer'and Revelator—an Apostle holding the keys of this last dispensation and of the kingdom of God, under Peter, James and John. And not only that he was a Prophet and Apostle of Jesus Christ, and lived and died one, but that he now lives in the spirit world, and holds those same keys to usward and to this whole generation. Also that he will hold those keys to all eternity; and no power in heaven or on the earth will ever take them from him; for he will continue holding those keys through all eternity, and will stand—*yes, again in the flesh upon this earth, the head of the Latter-day Saints under Jesus Christ, and under Peter, James and John. He will hold the keys to judge the generation to whom he was sent, and will judge my brethren that preside over me; and will judge me, together with the Apostles ordained by the word of the Lord through him and under his administration.*

When this is done, those Apostles will judge this generation and the Latter-day Saints; and they will judge them with that judgment which Jesus Christ will give unto them; and they will have the same spirit and the same mind as Jesus Christ, and their judgment will be His judgment, for they will be one.

J. D.   5:195-6.

By Wilford Woodruff: I have seen men in the days of Joseph bring up principles, and read and teach, and advocate theories, when the Prophet would say: "It is not right to do so; they are not true." Those men would still argue, maintain their position, and they would write in defence of their theories when the Prophet condemned them, and they would say: "We have no faith in your theory, nor in the system you present." The very moment a man does that he crosses the path of the servant of God who is set to lead the way to life and salvation. This is one thing that the Elders should carefully avoid. The fact is, there are a great many things taught in the building up of this kingdom which seem strange to us, being contrary to our traditions, and are calculated to try men. *Brother Joseph used a great many methods of testing the integrity of men; and he taught a great many things which, in consequence of tradition, required prayer, faith, and a testimony from the Lord, before they could be believed by many of the Saints. His mind was opened by the visions of the Almighty, and the Lord taught him many things by vision and revelation that were never taught publicly in his days; for the people could not bear the flood of intelligence which God poured into his mind.*   J. D. 5:83.

By Heber C. Kimball: Nearly twenty years ago, I was in a place in England in which I felt very curious; but I did not know at the time what it meant. I went through a town called Chadburn, beyond Clithero. Before I went there, some persons told me that there was no use in my going, and asked me what I wanted to go to Chadburn for, saying it was the worst place in the country; for the sectarian priests had preached there faithfully thirty years without making any impression. Notwithstanding that, I went, and preached once and baptized twenty-five persons, where the priests had not been able to do a thing.

I went through the streets of that town feeling as I never before felt in my life. My hair would rise on my head as I walked through the streets, and I did not then know what was the matter with me. I pulled off my hat, and felt that I wanted to pull off my shoes, and I did not know what to think of it. When I returned, I mentioned the circumstances to brother Joseph, who said: "Did you not understand it? That is the place where some of the old Prophets traveled and dedicated that land, and their blessing fell upon you."   J. D. 5:22.

Blessing given to Joseph the Prophet by his father: A marvelous work and a wonder has the Lord wrought by thy hand, even that which shall prepare the way for the remnants of his people to come in among the Gentiles, with their fulness, as the tribes of Israel are restored. I bless thee with the blessings of thy fathers Abraham, Isaac and Jacob; and even the blessings of thy father Joseph, the son of Jacob. Behold, he looked after his posterity in the last days, when they should be scattered and driven by the Gentiles, and wept before the Lord; he sought diligently to know from whence the Son should come who should bring forth the word of the Lord, by which they might be enlightened, and brought back to the true fold, and his eyes beheld thee, my son; his heart rejoiced and his soul was satisfied and he said: As my blessings are to extend to the utmost bounds of the everlasting hills; as my father's blessings prevailed over the blessings of his progenitors, and as my branches are to run over the wall, and my seed are to inherit the choice land whereon the Zion of God shall stand in the last days, from among my seed, scattered with the Gentiles, shall a choice Seer arise, whose bowels shall be a fountain of truth, whose loins shall be girded with the girdle of righteousness, whose hands shall be lifted with acceptance before the God of Jacob to turn away his anger from his anointed, whose heart shall meditate great wisdom, whose intelligence shall circumscribe and comprehend the deep things of God, and whose mouth shall utter the law of the just and he shall feed upon the heritage of Jacob his father. Thou (Joseph Smith, Jr.) shall hold the keys of this ministry, even the presidency of this Church, both in time and in eternity, and thou shall stand on Mount Zion when the tribes of Jacob come shouting from the north, and with thy brethren, the Sons of Ephraim, crown them in the name of Jesus Christ.

Genealogy Lessons for 1948.

THE PERSONALITY AND CHARACTER OF THE PROPHET JOSEPH SMITH

President Joseph Smith was in person tall and well built, strong and active; of a light complexion, light hair, blue eyes, very little beard, and of an expression peculiar to himself, on which the eye naturally rested with interest, and was never weary of beholding. His countenance was ever mild, affable, beaming with intelligence and benevolence; mingled with a look of interest and an unconcious smile, or cheerfulness, and entirely free from all restraint or affectation of gravity; and there was something connected with the serene and steady penetrating glance of his eye, as if he would penetrate the deepest abyss of the human heart, gaze into eternity, penetrate the heavens, and comprehend all worlds.

He possessed a noble boldness and independence of character; his manner was easy and familiar; his rebuke terrible as the lion; his benevolence unbounded as the ocean; his intelligence universal, and his language abounding in original eloquence peculiar to himself, not polished, not studied, not smoothed and softened by education and refined by art; but flowing forth in its own native simplicity, and profusely abounding in variety of subject and manner. He interested and edified, while, at the same time, he amused and entertained his audience; and none listened to him that were ever weary with his discourse. I have even known him to retain a congregation of willing and anxious listeners for many hours together, in the midst of cold or sunshine, rain or wind, while they were laughing at one moment and weeping the next. Even his most bitter enemies were generally overcome, if he could once get their ears.

I have known him when chained and surrounded with armed murderers and assassins who were heaping upon him every possible insult and abuse, rise up in the majesty of a son of God and rebuke them, in the name of Jesus Christ, till they quailed before him, dropped their weapons, and, on their knees, begged his pardon, and ceased their abuse.

In short, in him the characters of a Daniel and a Cyrus were wonderfully blended. The gifts, wisdom and devotion of a Daniel were united with the boldness, courage, temperance, perseverance and generosity of a Cyrus. And had he been spared a martyr's fate till mature manhood and age, he was certainly endued with powers and ability to have revolutionized the world in many respects, and to have transmitted to posterity a name associated with more brilliant and glorious acts than has yet fallen to the lot of mortal. As it is, his works will live to endless ages, and unnumbered millions yet unborn will mention his name with honor, as a noble instrument in the hands of God, who, during his short and youthful career, laid the foundation of that kingdom spoken of by Daniel, the prophet, which should break in pieces all other kingdoms and stand forever.   *Autobiography of Parley P. Pratt, pp. 47-48.*

L. O. LITTLEFIELD MEETS JOSEPH THE PROPHET

I had read some in the scriptures and heard men often talk about the prophets and apostles of the days of the Savior and had formed an idea, of course, that they must have been remarkable and good men, and the thought that I was to look upon a prophet of God in my day—that I was, indeed, in the flesh, to behold a person who stood in that near and familiar relationship to God, that His will was made manifest to him—was something that awakened reflections that my young mind could not well fathom or reconcile. But the opportunity came, and I first beheld him a tall, well-proportioned man, busily mingling with the members of Zion's Camp, shaking hands with them, meeting them with friendly greetings and carefully seeing to their comforts. His familiar, yet courteous and dignified manner, his pleasant and intelligent countenance, his intellectual and well-formed forehead, the expressive and philanthrophic facial lineaments, the pleasant smile and the happy light that beamed from his mild blue eyes; all these were among the attractive attributes that at once awakened a responsive interest in the mind of every kindly beholder, which increased in intensity as the acquaintance continued. With his most familiar friends he was social, conversational and often indulged in harmless jokes; but when discoursing upon complicated topics that pertained to the welfare of individuals or the progressiveness of communities, his elucidations were clear and so full of common sense and genuine philosophy that the candid and fair-minded felt interested by his views, though they might decline to entertain or promulgate all of the self-evident truths he originated.

Juvenile Instructor, Vol. 27:56.

HOSPITALITY OF THE PROPHET JOSEPH

I often wonder, when I hear brethren and sisters complain at the trifling inconveniences which they have to suffer in these days, and I think to myself that salvation is worth as much now as it was in the commencement of the work. But "all like the purchase, few the price would pay." How often I have parted every bed in the home for the accommodation of the brethren, and then laid a single blanket on the floor for my husband and myself, while Joseph (the Prophet-N.B.L.) and Emma slept upon the same floor, with nothing but their cloaks for both bed and bedding.

Life of Joseph Smith the Prophet, by Lucy Smith, pp. 203-4.

NONE COULD COMPREHEND THE PROPHET JOSEPH

By George Q. Cannon

There are many, perhaps all of us, that have more or less of a desire to conform to the ideas which prevail in the world. These ideas we have inherited, and they come natural to us; and not having progressed sufficiently to overcome them, we naturally lean toward them. We do this in politics, in finance, in trading, in almost everything. It seems to be right to us, because all of our inherited tendencies are in that direction. If we could have a glimpse of heaven, and understand things as they are, we might be able to do better; but this is not God's way of doing things. He wants us to work out our own development, and to exert the powers we have inherited from Him in conquering the wrong tendencies we have inherited from our fathers. He gives us line upon line, precept upon precept, here a little and there a little; but He does not reveal it all at once. At the same time He would like us to comprehend more than we do. I have sometimes thought that the Prophet Joseph, with the knowledge he possessed and the progress he had made could not stay with the people, so slow were we to comprehend things and so enshrouded in our ignorant traditions. The Saints could not comprehend Joseph Smith; the Elders could not; the Apostles could not. They did so a little towards the close of his life; but his knowledge was so extensive and his comprehension so great that they could not rise to it. It was so with President Young; and I may say it is so with the leaders of the Church now. It is a continual labor on their part to lift the people up to the comprehension of the will of God and His purposes connected with this work. The people are bound down by their traditions, and because of this it is rarely that you can get even the Elders to see the propriety of certain things.

Millennial Star, 61:629.

THE PROPHET JOSEPH'S BROTHER, WILLIAM, TESTIFIES

Before William Smith, brother of Joseph and Hyrum Smith, died he was visited by J. W. Peterson. That gentleman has written an account of the interview with father Smith, to Zion's Ensign, a paper published at Independence, Missouri. It is written from Bradtville, Wisconsin, and is as follows: Brother Briggs and I visited him next day after he returned from St. Paul, it being about two weeks before his death. We found him able to be about the house and quite willing to talk. After passing the time of day, Brother Briggs and he spoke of former meetings and finally drifted on to the subject of Brother Smith's early boyhood and his knowledge of the rise of the Church, Book of Mormon, etc.

Brother Briggs then handed me a pencil and asked Brother Smith if he ever saw the plates his brother had had, from which the Book of Mormon was translated.

He replied: "I did not see them uncovered, but I handled them and hefted them while wrapped in a tow frock and judged them to have weighed about sixty pounds. I could tell they were plates of some kind and that they were fastened together by rings running thru the back. Their size was as described in mother's history."

Brother Briggs then asked: "Did any others of the family see them?"

"Yes," said he, "father and my brother Samuel saw them as I did while in the frock. So did Hyrum and others of the family."

"Was this frock one that Joseph took with him especially to wrap the plates in?"

"No, it was his every-day frock such as young men used to wear then."

"Didn't you want to remove the cloth and see the bare plates?" said Brother Briggs.

"No," he replied, "for father had just asked if he might not be permitted to do so, and Joseph, putting his hand on them said: 'No, I am instructed not to show them to any one. If I do, I will transgress and lose them again.' Besides we did not care to have him break the commandment and suffer as he did before."

"Did you not doubt Joseph's testimony sometimes?" said Brother Briggs.

"No," was the reply. "We all had the most implicit confidence in what he said. He was a truthful boy. Father and mother believed him, why should not the children? I suppose if he had told crooked stories about other things we might have doubted his word about the plates, but Joseph was a truthful boy. That father and mother believed his report and suffered persecution for that belief shows that he was truthful. No sir, we never doubted his word for one minute."

"Well," said Brother Briggs, "it is said that Joseph and the rest of the family were lazy and indolent."

"We never heard of such a thing until after Joseph told his vision, and not then, by our friends. Whenever the neighbors wanted a good day's work done they knew where they could get a good hand and they were not particular to take any of the other boys before Joseph either. We cleared sixty acres of the heaviest timber I ever saw. We had a good place. We also had on it from twelve to fifteen hundred sugar-trees, and to gather the sap and make sugar and molasses from that number of trees was no lazy job. We worked hard to clear our place and the neighbors were a little jealous. If you will figure up how much work it would take to clear sixty acres of heavy timber land, heavier than any here, trees you could not conveniently cut down, you can tell whether we were lazy or not, and Joseph did his share of the work with the rest of the boys."

"We never knew we were bad folks until Joseph told his vision. We were considered respectable till then, but at once people began to circulate falsehoods and stories in a wonderful way."

"Were your folks religiously inclined before Joseph saw the angel?" asked Brother Briggs.

"Yes, we always had family prayers since I can remember. I well remember father used to carry his spectacles in his vest pocket, (feeling in his lower right hand pocket to show us how and where) and when us boys saw him feel for his specs, we knew that was a signal to get ready for prayer, and if we did not notice it mother would say, 'William,' or whoever was the negligent one, 'get ready for prayer.' After the prayer we had a song we would sing. I remember part of it yet:

> Another day has passed and gone,
> We lay our garments by.

"Hyrum, Samuel, Catharine and mother were members of the Presbyterian church. My father would not join. He did not like it because a Rev. Stockton had preached my brother's funeral sermon and intimated very strongly that he had gone to hell, for Alvin was not a church member, but he was a good boy, and my father did not like it."

"What caused Joseph to ask for guidance as to what church he ought to join," asked Brother Briggs.

"Why, there was a joint revival in the neighborhood between the Baptists, Methodists and Presbyterians and they had succeeded in stirring up quite a feeling, and after the meeting the question arose which church should have the converts. Rev. Stockton was the president of the meeting and suggested that it was their meeting and under their care and they had a church there and they ought to join the Presbyterians, but as father did not like Rev. Stockton very well. our folks hesitated and the next evening a Rev. Mr. Lane of the Methodists preached a sermon on: 'What church shall I join?' And the burden of his discourse was to ask God, using as a text: 'If any man lack wisdom let him ask of God who giveth to all men liberally.' And of course when Joseph went home and was looking over the text he was impressed to do just what the preacher had said, and going out into the woods with child-like simple trusting faith, believing that God meant just what He said, he kneeled down and prayed; and the time having come for the reorganization of His church, God was pleased to show him that he should join none of these churches, but if faithful he should be chosen to establish the true Church."   *Millennial Star,* 56:132-134.

THE GREATNESS OF THE PROPHET JOSEPH
By Dr. John A. Widtsoe

Since I struggled as a boy to find the Church and the message of Joseph Smith, I have been overwhelmed by the greatness of the Prophet. He towers above all men by his great teachings. Of course, he was a man with the frailties of the flesh, but he so lived that God spoke to men through him. Indeed, he is the biggest man in the history of the world since the Savior lived among men nearly two thousand years ago. He was a magnificent type of man. The Prophet stands unique among the religious leaders of the world, for in practically all of his work in the restoration he had witnesses. Mohammed, Buddha, Confucius, as examples, each established his work without witnesses, but not so Joseph Smith. There were witnesses to the Gold Plates and the Book of Mormon, in the visitation of heavenly personages, and in the receiving of many of the revelations. His work was inaugurated not by himself alone, but by and with witnesses. His teachings clear up so many misconceptions, that any man who honestly investigates the Prophet and his work, must come to a conviction that he was *indeed* a Prophet.   Church Section, *Deseret News,* January 30, 1952.

JOSIAH QUINCY'S OPINION OF THE PROPHET JOSEPH

*"It is by no means improbable that some future text book, for the use of generations yet unborn, will contain a question something like this: What historical American of the nineteenth century has exerted the most powerful influence upon the destinies of his countrymen? And it is by no means impossible that the answer to that interrogatory may be thus written: JOSEPH SMITH, THE MORMON PROPHET. And the reply, absurd as it doubtless seems to most men now living, may be an obvious commonplace to their descendants. History deals in surprises and paradoxes quite as startling as this. The man who established a religion in this age of free debate, who was and is today accepted by hundreds of thousands as a direct emissary from the Most High—such a rare human being is not to be disposed of by pelting his memory with unsavory epithets. * * * The most vital questions Americans are asking each other today have to do with this man and what he has left us. * * * * Burning questions they are, which must give a prominent place in the history of the country to that sturdy self-asserter whom I visited at Nauvoo. Joseph Smith, claiming to be an inspired teacher, faced*

adversity such as few men have been called to meet, enjoyed a brief season of prosperity such as few men have ever attained, and, finally, forty-three days after I saw him, went cheerfully to a martyr's death. When he surrendered his person to Governor Ford, in order to prevent the shedding of blood, the Prophet had a presentiment of what was before him. 'I am going like a lamb to the slaughter,' he is reported to have said, 'But I am as calm as a summer's morning. I have a conscience void of offence and shall die innocent.' "   Figures of the Past, **May 15, 1844.**

ADMONITION TO THE YOUNG

Oh, that the children who read this Biography would take his life for an example, imitate his faith, his humility, his love for God and man, his devotion to the truth, his fearlessness in clinging to and upholding the right, his firmness and his perfect obedience in doing the will of God! If they will do so, their lives will be great and useful in the sight of God and man, and their eternal reward will be sure. If they will do so, how ample will be our reward for the time we have spent in writing the incidents of this great and noble life!

When we recollect that Joseph was only thirty-eight years of age at the time he was killed, the work which he was the instrument in the hands of God in accomplishing seems truly wonderful. Alone, with no one to help him but the Lord, he had started out with the determination to obey the commands which he received from heaven. He had not learning, he had not wealth, powerful friends he had none; but he had what were of greater value to him than all these—he had the truth and the authority from God to proclaim it. And the Lord whom he served made him mighty in word and in deed. He performed a marvellous work, and in the face of obstacles, too, that would have frightened the most of men, and which he himself could never have overcome had the Lord not given him help.

Life of Joseph the Prophet by George Q. Cannon, *Instructor,* Vol. 15.

THE NOBILITY OF THE GREATEST SEER
OF ALL TIME

As a son, he was nobility itself, in love and honor of his parents; as a brother he was loving and true, even unto death; as a husband and father, his devotion to wives and children stopped only at idolatry. His life's greatest motto after "God and His Kingdom" was that of "wives, children and friends."

Joseph the Prophet, as a friend was faithful, long suffering, noble and true to that degree that the erring who did love him were reminded that the rod of a friend was better than the kiss of an enemy, "while others who sopped in his dish" but bore not reproof, became his enemies, and like Law, Marks, Foster, Higbee and others who hated him, conspired to his death.

As companion, socially, he was highly endowed; was kind, generous, mirth loving, and at times, even convivial. He was partial to a well supplied table and he did not always refuse the wine that "maketh the heart glad." For amusements, he would sometimes wrestle with a friend, or ofttimes would test strength with others by sitting upon the floor with feet together and a stick grasped between them, but he never found his match. Jokes, rebuses, matching couplets in rhymes, etc., were not uncommon. But to call for the singing of one or more of his favorite songs was more frequent. Of those, "Wives, Children and Friends," "Battle of River Russen," "Soldier's Tear," "Soldier's Dream," and "Last Rose of Summer," were most common. And yet, although so social and even convivial at times, he would allow no arrogance or undue liberties, and criticisms, even by his associates, were rarely acceptable, and contradictions would rouse in him the lion at once, for by no one of his fellows would he be superseded. And while with him in such fraternal, social and sometimes convivial moods, we could not then so fully realize the greatness and majesty of his calling, which, since his martyrdom, has continued to magnify in our view, as the glories of this last dispensation were more fully unfolded to our comprehension.

One small incident, among the many, I will relate to show his playful, familiar, kind and loving nature toward one who to him was as a protege or a younger brother. Soon after the Prophet escaped from Missouri and arrived at Old Commerce, the future Nauvoo, in 1839, I was with him. The people had flocked in from the terrible exposures of the past, and nearly every one was sick with intermittent or other fevers, of which many died. In this time of great sickness, poverty and death, the Prophet called his brother, Don Carlos, and cousin, G. A. Smith, as missionaries to administer to and to comfort the people. And there being there two young Botanic medical students, Doctors Wiley and Pendleton, he called upon them to prescribe medicine, and called on me to follow and take general oversight and care of all the sick, which for weeks, I did, without even one night of respiteful sleep. The forepart of September, Dr. Wiley became sick unto death, which soon occurred, after which the Prophet, too, had a violent attack of the prevailing sickness. As Emma was in no degree able to care for him, it wholly devolved upon me, and both day and night, through a period of little less than two weeks, I was hardly absent from his room; as almost his only food was gruel, and about the only treatment he would accept was a flush of the colon with warm water, perhaps tinctured slightly with capsicum or myrrh, or a little soda and salt, both of which were prepared and administered by me in the room he occupied; and if any sleep came to me it was while lying upon his bed or sitting in my chair. At the termination of this sickness and fasting, he arose from his bed like a lion, or as a giant refreshed with wine. He went to President Rigdon with great reproof, commanding him and his house to repent; and called for a skiff across the river, and finding Elijah Fordham in death's struggle, he commanded him to arise, which he did at once, and was made whole, as were others by his administrations.

Soon after the Prophet's recovery, I too, came apparently nigh unto death through a violent attack of the fever, through which my comfort was kindly looked after by the Prophet.

About the middle of October a letter came to say that my dear mother and young sister were apparently near to death, in Springfield, Illinois, and were anxious for my return. In my anxiety to again see my mother, I procured quinine, which was just becoming known as an antidote for fever, and taking it in large quantities, my fever soon abated, and under it's tonic influence I fancied I had become well, and in great joy and hope hastened preparations to start for the home of my mother and kindred in Springfield. My horse was in the yard ready to mount, but I wished to take leave of the Prophet, with the hope of again receiving his blessings. Of the whole sum I had obtained with which to pay for outfit and passage to England, with the Twelve, when they could start, to which I had been called by the June Conference at Quincy, I had but one ten dollar bill left, and I thought on it at least I would pay a tithing; so going to the Prophet I told him I was ready to leave, and reaching to him the bill, I said, "As this is all I have left, I want to pay a tithe of it." He saw I was weak in body and that my heart was sad in leaving him, so thinking to cheer and arouse me, when putting the nine silver dollars in my hand he playfully knocked my hand upward, scattering the money all over the room. My heart was full of tears, and my emotions must have vent, so forgetting all about the feeling that we were boy companions playing together, I sprang at and grappled him so as to teach him a lesson. But the lesson was all to me, for on making the one grand effort to throw him, I found myself in strength no more than a bullrush as compared with him, and as my strength was fictitious and my real recovery but an illusion, I collapsed and fainted in his arms. He placed me in repose, gathered up the scattered money, and after a period of delay, weak, trembling and desolate, yet determined to start, I led my horse to the outer gate, and as I was passing through, with the bridle on my arm, his hand detained me, and placing his hands upon my head, he seemed to pour out his soul in blessing me. He told the Lord I had been faithful to care for others, but I was now worn and sick, and that on my journey I would need His care, and he asked that a special guardian might go with me from that day and stay with me through all my life. And O! my dear brother, how often have I seen through life the footprints of that angel, and knew that his hand had drawn me back from death.

And then you would have "further truths from the teachings of the Prophet." Where shall I commence, and how shall I write to your understanding, even the little I may have retained in my memory? You will not forget that the march of science through the last seventy years has in many things reversed the world's thought, changed its "modus" and almost its face, and in fact exploded the dogmas of outside theology. Well, the keys to all this knowledge were first committed to the Prophet Joseph, as a part of the gospel, for the world's benefit, for all of which he was derided. He was the first to teach in this age, "substantialism," the eternity of matter, that no part or particle of the great universe could become annihilated or destroyed; that light and life and spirit were one; that all light and heat are the "Glory of

God," which is His power, that fills the "immensity of space," and
is the life of all things, and permeates with latent life, and heat,
every particle of which all works are composed; that light or spirit,
and matter, are the two first great primary principles of the universe, or of Being; that they are self-existent, co-existent, inde-
structible, and eternal, and from these two elements both our spirits
and our bodies were formulated, and he gave us to understand
that there were twelve Kingdoms, or planets, revolving around
our solar system, to which the Lord gave an equal division of His
time or ministry; and that now was His time to again visit the
earth. He taught that all systems of worlds were in revolution,
the lesser around the greater. He taught that all the animal kingdoms would be resurrected, and made us understand that they
would remain in the dominion of those who, with creative power,
reach out for dominion through the power of eternal lives. He
taught us that the saints would fill the great West, and through
Mexico, and Central and South America we would do a great work
for the redemption of the remnant of Jacob. And he taught us
relating to the Kingdom of God, as it would become organized,
upon the earth through "all nations learning war no more," and
all adopting the God-given constitution of the United States as a
Paladium of Liberty and Equal Rights.

But this, of itself, would require a long chapter, which must
wait until the fulfillment of a prediction by the Prophet, relating
to a testimony that I should bear, after I had become hoary with
age, of things which he that day taught to the circle of friends
then around him, of whom I am the only one living. So here I will
leave this subject for your further interrogations, and proceed
to give you, so far as I can, the Prophet's last charge to the
Quorum of the Twelve Apostles.

It was in Nauvoo early in 1844 in an assembly room, common to the meeting of a council, or a select circle of the Prophet's
most trusted friends, including the Twelve, but not all of the constituted authorities of the Church, for Presidents Rigdon, Law
or Marks, the High Council, or presidents of quorums were not
members of that council, which at times would exceed fifty in
number. Its sittings were always strictly private, and all its rules
were carefully and promptly observed and though its meetings
were at times oftener than monthly, and my home at Ramus over
twenty miles distant, I was present at every session, and being
about the youngest member of that council, I was deeply impressed with all that transpired, or was taught by the Prophet.

Criticism had already commenced by those near him in authority with regard to his teachings and his doings. And we
began now, in a degree, to understand the meaning of what he
had so often publicly said, that, should he teach and practice the
principles that the Lord had revealed to him, and now requested
of him, that those then nearest him in the stand would become
his enemies and the first to seek his life; which they soon did, just
as he had foretold. And to show you that under conditions then
existing that the Prophet did not really desire longer to live, and
that you may see how my mind was in a degree prepared for after

results, I will briefly relate an incident that occurred at his last visit to us at Ramus.

After he had that evening preached with great animation to a large congregation, and had blessed nineteen children, he turned to me and said, "Benjamin, I am tired, let us go home," which only a block distant, we soon reached, and entering we found a warm fire with a large chair in front, and my wife sitting near with her babe, our eldest, upon her lap, and approaching her, I said, "Now, Melissa, see what we have lost by your not going to meeting. Brother Joseph has blessed all the children in the place but ours, and it is left out in the cold." But the Prophet at once said, "You shall lose nothing," and he proceeded to bless our first born, and then, with a deep drawn breath, as a sigh of weariness, he sank down heavily in his chair, and said, "O, I do get so tired and weary, that at times I almost yearn for my rest," and then proceeded to briefly recount to us some of the most stirring events of his life's labors, sufferings and sacrifices, and then he said, "I am getting tired and would like to go to my rest."

And now returning to the council and the last charge. Let us remember that by revelation he had organized the Holy Priesthood, and that by command of the Lord (D. & C. 124 and 125) had taken from the First Presidency his brother Hyrum to hold as Patriarch, the sealing power, the first and highest honor due to priesthood; that he had returned the keys of endowments, to the last anointing, and sealing, together with the keys for the salvation for the dead, with the eternity of the marriage covenant and the power of endless lives. All these keys he held, and under these then existing conditions he stood before that association of his select friends, including all of the Twelve, and with great feeling and animation he graphically reviewed his life of persecution, labor and sacrifice for the church and the kingdom of God, both of which he declared were now organized upon the earth, the burden of which had become too great for him longer to carry, that he was weary and tired with the weight he had so long borne, and he then said, with great vehemence: "And in the name of the Lord, I now shake from my shoulders the responsibility of bearing off the Kingdom of God to all the world, and here and now I place that responsibility, with all the keys, powers and privileges pertaining thereto, upon the shoulders of you the Twelve Apostles, in connection with this council; and if you will accept this, to do it, God shall bless you mightily and shall open your way; and if you do it not you will be damned. I am henceforth free from this responsibility and I now shake my garments clear and free from the blood of this generation and of all men"; shaking his shirt with great vehemence he raised himself from the floor, while the spirit that accompanied his words thrilled every heart as with a feeling that boded bereavement and sorrow.

And now, my dear brother, after 60 years have passed, at 85 year's in age, I bear to you and to all the world a solemn testimony of the truth and veracity of what I have written above, for although so many years have intervened, they are still in my mind, as fresh as when they occurred; no doubt as a part fulfillment of a prediction by the Prophet relating to "testimonies I should bear of his teachings, after I had become hoary with age."

There were, my dear brother, other teachings to that council, of which I am not at full liberty to write, but if I had your ear, I would remember that the Prophet once said to me: "Benjamin, in regard to those things I have taught you privately, that are not yet for the public, I give you right when you are so led, to commit them to others, for you will not be led wrong in discerning those worthy of your confidence."

Of Brigham Young as President of the Church, I will again bear this as a faithful testimony that I do know and bear record that upon the head of Brigham Young as chief, with the Apostleship in full, was by the voice of the Prophet Joseph, in my hearing, laid the full responsibility of bearing off the kingdom of God to all the world. And I do further bear this as a testimony, faithful and true, to the Church and to all the world, that at a conference of the whole Church, at Nauvoo, subsequent to the Prophet's death and before the return of the absent Apostles, that I sat in the assembly near President Rigdon, closely attentive to his appeal to the conference to recognize and sustain his claim as "Guardian for the Church." And was, perhaps, to a degree, forgetful of what I knew to be the rights and duties of the apostleship, and as he closed his address and sat down, my back was partly turned to the seats occupied by Apostle Brigham Young and other Apostles, when suddenly, and as from Heaven, I heard the voice of the Prophet Joseph, that thrilled my whole being, and quickly turning around I saw in the transfiguration of Brigham Young, the tall, straight and portly form the Prophet Joseph Smith, clothed in a sheen of light, covering him to his feet; and I heard the real and perfect voice of the Prophet, even to the whistle, as in years past caused by the loss of a tooth said to have been broken out by the mob at Hiram. This view, or vision, although but for seconds, was to me as vivid and real as the glare of lightning or the voice of thunder from the heavens, and so deeply was I impressed with what I saw and heard in the transfiguration, that for years I dared not tell what was given me of the Lord to see. But when in later years I did publicly bear this testimony, I found that others had testified to having seen and heard the same. But to what proportion of the congregation that were present, I could never know. But I do know that this, my testimony, is true.

The Prophet's lost tooth, to which I allude, was, as generally understood, broken out by the mob at Hiram while trying to pry open his mouth to strangle him with acid, from which time, until the tooth was replaced by a dentist neighbor, a year or two previous to his death, there had been a whistle-like sound to accompany all his public speaking which I again plainly heard at the time of which I write.   Excerpt from letter of Benjamin F. Johnson to George S. Gibbs.

THE SEER

The Seer—the Seer—Joseph the Seer—
I'll sing of the Prophet ever dear,

His equal now cannot be found,—
By searching the wide world around.

With Gods he soared in the realms of day;
And men he taught the heavenly way.
'Mid the foaming billows of angry strife—
He stood at the helm of the ship of life.
The earthly Seer; the heavenly Seer,
I love to dwell on his mem'ry dear;—
The chosen of God, and the friend of men,
He brought the priesthood back again,
He gazed on the past, on the present too;—
And ope'd the heavenly world to view.

Of noble seed—of heavenly birth,
He came to bless the sons of earth;
With keys by the Almighty given,
He opened the full rich stores of heaven,
O'er the world that was wrapt in sable night
Like the sun he spread his golden light.
He strove,—O, how he strove to stay,
The stream of crime in its reckless way—
He urged the wayward to reclaim;
With a mighty mind, and a noble aim.

The saints;—the saints; his only pride,
For them he lived, for them he died!
Their joys were his;—their sorrows too;—
He lov'd the saints;—he lov'd Nauvoo.
Unchanged in death, with a Savior's love
He pleads their cause, in the courts above.
The Seer;—the Seer—Joseph the Seer!
O, how I love his memory dear,
The just and wise, the pure and free,
A father he was, and is to me.
Let fiends now rage in their dark hour;
No matter, he is beyond their power.

He's free;—he's free;—the Prophet's free!
He is where he will ever be.
Beyond the reach of mobs and strife,
He rests unharm'd in endless life.
His home's in the sky;—he dwells with the Gods
Far from the furious rage of mobs.
He died; he died—for those he lov'd
He reigns;—he reigns in the realms above,

He waits with the just who have gone before,
To welcome the saints to Zion's shore;
Shout, shout ye saints—this boon is given,
We'll meet our martyr'd Seer in heaven.

Hymn composed by John Taylor for the dedication of the Seventies Hall,
at Nauvoo, Illinois, on Thursday, Dec. 26, 1844.

CHAPTER 3

Persecutions Endured by the Prophet and the Saints

(The following Memorial will only partly reveal the trials and persecutions the Prophet Joseph Smith and the Saints had to endure. The full history of these persecutions will never be known by mortals, neither can they be described by the pen of man.)

AMERICAN EXILES' MEMORIAL TO CONGRESS

To the Honorable Senators and Representatives of the United States of America, in Congress Assembled.

We, the undersigned members of the city council of the city of Nauvoo, citizens of Hancock County, Illinois, and exiles from the State of Missouri, being in council assembled, unanimously and respectfully, for ourselves and in behalf of many thousands of other exiles, memorialize the honorable Senators and Representatives of our nation upon the subject of the unparalleled persecution and cruelties inflicted upon us and upon our constituents, by the constituted authorities of the State of Missouri, and likewise upon the subject of the present unfortunate circumstances in which we are placed in the land of our exile. As a history of the Missouri outrages has been extensively published, both in this country and in Europe, it is deemed unnecessary to particularize all of the wrongs and grievances inflicted upon us in this memorial; as there is an abundance of well-attested documents to which your honorable body can at any time refer; hence we only embody the following important items for your consideration:

FIRST. Your memorialists, as free-born citizens of this great Republic, relying with the utmost confidence upon the sacred "Articles of the Constitution" by which the several States are bound together, and considering ourselves entitled to all the privileges and immunities of free citizens in what State soever we desired to locate ourselves, commenced a settlement in the county of Jackson, on the western frontiers of the State of Missouri in the summer of 1831. There we purchased lands from the government; erected several hundred houses, made extensive improvements, and shortly the wild and lonely prairies and stately forests were converted into well cultivated and fruitful fields. There we expected to spend our days in the enjoyment of all the rights and liberties bequeathed to us by the sufferings and blood of our noble ancestors. But alas! our expectations were vain. Two years had scarcely elapsed before we were unlawfully and unconstitutionally assailed by an organized mob, consisting of the highest officers in the county, both civil and military, who boldly and openly avowed their determination, in a written circular, to drive us from said county.

As a specimen of their treasonable and cruel designs, your honorable body are referred to said circular, of which the following is but a short extract, namely: "We, the undersigned citizens of Jackson county, believing that an important crisis is at hand as regards our civil society, in consequence of a pretended religious sect of people that have settled and are still settling in our county, styling themselves Mormons, and intending, as we do, to rid our society, 'peaceably' if we can—'forcibly', if we must; and believing, as we do, that the arm of the civil law does not afford us a guarantee, or at least a sufficient one, against the evils which are now inflicted upon us and seem to be increasing by the said religious sect, deem it expedient and of the highest importance to form ourselves into a company for the better and easier accomplishment of our purpose." This document was closed in the following words: "We therefore agree after timely warning and receiving adequate compensation for what little property they cannot take with them, they refuse to leave us in peace as they found us, we agree to use such means as may be sufficient to remove them, and to that end we each pledge to each other our bodily power, our lives, fortunes, and sacred honors."

To this unconstitutional document were attached the names of nearly every officer in the county, together with the names of hundreds of others. It was by this band of murderers that your memorialists, in the year 1833, were plundered of their property, and robbed of their peaceable homes. It was by them their fields were laid waste, their houses burned, and their men, women, and children, to the number of about twelve hundred persons, banished as exiles from the county, while others were cruelly murdered by their hands.

SECOND. After our expulsion from Jackson county we settled in Clay county, on the opposite side of the Missouri river, where we purchased lands both from the old settlers and from the land office; but soon we were again violently threatened by mobs, and obliged to leave our homes and seek out a new location.

THIRD. Our next settlement was in Caldwell county, where we purchased the most of the lands in said county, besides a part of the lands in Daviess and Carroll counties. These counties were almost entirely in a wild and uncultivated state, but by the persevering industry of our citizens, large and extensive farms were opened in every direction, well stocked with numerous flocks and herds. We also commenced settlements in several other counties of the State, and once more confidently hoped to enjoy the hard earned fruits of our labor unmolested; but our hopes were soon blasted. The cruel and murderous spirit which first began to manifest itself in the constituted authorities and inhabitants of Jackson county, and afterwards in Clay and the surrounding counties, receiving no check either from the civil or military power of the State, had in the meantime, taken courage, and boldly and fearlessly spread its contaminating and treasonable influence into every department of the government of said State. Lieutenant Governor Boggs, a resident of Jackson county, who acted a conspicuous part in our ex-

pulsion from said county, instead of being tried for treason and
rebellion against the constitution, and suffering the just penalty
of his crimes, was actually elected Governor and placed in the executive chair. Thus the inhabitants of the State were greatly encouraged to renew and with redoubled fury their unlawful attack
upon our defenseless settlements. Men, women, and children were
driven in every direction before their merciless persecutors. Robbed
of their possessions, their property, their provisions, and their all;
cast forth upon the bleak snowy prairies, houseless and unprotected,
many sank down and expired under their accumulated sufferings,
while others, after enduring hunger and the severities of the season, suffering all but death, arrived in Caldwell county, to which
place they were driven from all the surrounding counties only to
witness a still more heart-rending scene. In vain had we appealed
to the constituted authorities of Missouri for protection and redress of our former grievances; in vain we now stretched out our
hands, and appealed, as the citizens of this great Republic, to the
sympathies—to the justice and magnanimity of those in power; in
vain we implored, again and again, at the feet of Governor Boggs,
our former persecutor, aid and protection against the ravages and
murders now inflicted upon our defenseless and unoffending citizens. The cry of American citizens, already twice driven and deprived of liberty, could not penetrate their adamantine hearts. The
Governor, instead of sending us aid, issued a proclamation for our
EXTERMINATION AND BANISHMENT; ordered out the forces
of the State, placed them under the command of General Clarke,
who to execute these exterminating orders, marched several thousand troops into our settlements in Caldwell county, where, un-
restrained by fear of law or justice, and urged on by the highest
authority of the State, they laid waste our fields of corn, shot down
our cattle and hogs for sport, burned our dwellings, inhumanly
butchered some eighteen or twenty defenseless citizens, dragged
from their hiding places little children, and placed the muzzles of
their guns to their heads, shot them with the most horrid oaths
and imprecations. An aged hero and patriot of the revolution, who
served under General Washington, while in the act of pleading
for quarter, was cruelly murdered and hewed in pieces with an
old corn-cutter; and in addition to all these savage acts of barbarity,
they forcibly dragged virtuous and inoffensive females from their
dwellings, bound them upon benches used for public worship, where
they, in great numbers ravished them in a most brutal manner.
Some fifty or sixty of the citizens were thrust into prisons and
dungeons, where, bound in chains, they were fed on human flesh,
while their families and some fifteen thousand others, were, at the
point of the bayonet, forcibly expelled from the State. In the meantime, to pay the expenses of these horrid outrages, they confiscated
our property and robbed us of all our possessions. Before our final
expulsion, with a faint and lingering hope, we petitioned the State
Legislature, then in session; unwilling to believe that American
citizens could appeal in vain for a restoration of liberty, cruelly
wrested from them by cruel tyrants. But in the language of our
noble ancestors "our repeated petitions were only answered by

repeated injuries." The Legislature, instead of hearing the cries of 15,000 suffering, bleeding, unoffending citizens, sanctioned and sealed the unconstitutional acts of the Governor and his troops, by appropriating 200,000 dollars to defray the expenses of exterminating us from the State.

No friendly arm was stretched out to protect us. The last ray of hope for redress in that State was now entirely extinguished. We saw no other alternative but to bow down our necks, and wear the cruel yoke of oppression, and quietly and submissively suffer ourselves to be banished as exiles from our possessions, our property, our sacred homes; or otherwise see our wives and children coldly murdered and butchered by tyrants in power.

FOURTH. Our next permanent settlement was in the land of our exile, the State of Illinois, in the spring of 1839. But even here we are not secure from our relentless persecutor, the State of Missouri. Not satisfied in having drenched her soil in the blood of innocence, and expelling us from her borders, she pursues her unfortunate victims into banishment, seizing upon and kidnapping them in their defenseless moments, dragging them across the Mississippi river upon their inhospitable shores, where they are tortured, whipped, immured in dungeons, and hung by the neck without any legal process whatever. We have memorialized the former executive of this state, Governor Carlin, upon these lawless outrages committed upon our citizens, but he rendered us no protection. Missouri, receiving no check in her murderous career, continues her depredations, again and again kidnapping our citizens, and robbing us of our property; while others who fortunately survived the execution of her bloody edicts, are again and again demanded by the executive of that state, on pretense of some crime, said to have been committed by them during the exterminating expedition against our people. As an instance, General Joseph Smith, one of your memorialists, has been three times demanded, tried, and acquitted by the courts of this state, upon investigation under writs of habeas corpus, once by the United States court for the district of Illinois, again by the Circuit Court of the State of Illinois, and lastly, by the municipal court of the City of Nauvoo, when at the same time a *nulle prosequi* had been entered by the courts of Missouri, upon all cases of that state against Joseph Smith and others. Thus the said Joseph Smith has been several times tried for the same alleged offense, put in jeopardy of life and limb, contrary to the fifth article of the amendments to the Constitution of these United States; and thus we have been continually harassed and robbed of our money to defray the expense of those vexatious prosecutions. And what at the present time seems to be still more alarming, is the hostility manifested by some of the authorities and citizens of this State. Conventions have been called; inflammatory speeches made; and many unlawful and unconstitutional resolutions adopted, to deprive us of our rights, our liberties, and the peaceable enjoyment of our possessions. From the present hostile aspect, and from bitter experience in the State of Missouri, it is greatly feared that the barbarous scenes acted in that state will be reacted in this. If Missouri goes unpunished, others will be greatly encouraged to follow her murderous examples. The afflictions of your memorialists have already been overwhelming, too much for humanity, too much for American citizens to endure without complaint. We have groaned under the iron hand of tyranny and oppression these many years. We have been robbed of our property to the amount of two millions of dollars. We have been hunted as the wild beasts of the forest. We have seen our aged fathers who fought in the Revolution, and our innocent children, alike slaughtered by our persecutors. We have seen the fair daughters of American citizens insulted and abused in the most inhuman manner, and finally we have seen fifteen thousand souls, men, women, and children, driven by force of arms, during the severities of winter, from their sacred homes and firesides, to a land of strangers, penniless and unprotected. Under all these afflicting circumstances, we imploringly stretch forth our hands towards the highest councils of our nation, and humbly appeal to the illustrious Senators and Representatives of a great and free people for redress and protection.

Hear, O hear the petitioning voice of many thousands of American citizens who now groan in exile on Columbia's free soil. Hear, O hear the weeping and bitter lamentations of widows and orphans, whose husbands and fathers have been cruelly martyred in the land where the proud eagle exultingly floats. Let it not be recorded in the archives of the nations, that Columbia's exiles sought protection and redress at your hands, but sought it in vain. It is your power to save us, our wives, and our children, from a repetition of the blood-thirsty scenes of Missouri, and thus greatly relieve the fears of a persecuted and injured people, and your petitioners will ever pray.

> The names of the members of the city council, as petitioners, are omitted for want of space. The foregoing memorial was presented to congress in the spring of 1844, making the third time that those horrid scenes of murder have been laid before them since the beginning of our exile, but all to no purpose. Our petitions are unheeded or treated with contempt. And thousands of American citizens must linger out a life of wretched exile, deprived of the use of their own lands, and of the sacred rights of American Liberty.

Millennial Star, Vol. 11 :260-275.

APPEAL FOR AID AGAINST MOBS AND PERSECUTION
(LETTER TO THE PRESIDENT OF THE UNITED STATES AND THE GOVERNORS OF THE RESPECTIVE STATES.)

Nauvoo, Illinois, April 24, 1845.

His Excellency James K. Polk,
President of the United States

Hon. Sir:

Suffer us, Sir, in behalf of a disfranchised and long afflicted people to prefer a few suggestions for your serious consideration in hope of a friendly and unequivocal response, at as early a period as may suit your convenience, and the extreme urgency of the case seem to demand.

It is not our present design to detail the multiplied and aggravated wrongs that we have received in the midst of a nation that gave us birth. Most of us have long been loyal citizens of some one of these United States over which you have the honor to preside, while a few only claim the privileges of peaceable and lawful emigrants designing to make the Union our permanent residence.

We say we are a disfranchised people. We are privately told by the highest authorities of this state that it is neither prudent nor safe for us to vote at the polls, still we have continued to maintain our right to vote, until the blood of our best men has been shed, both in Missouri and Illinois, with impunity.

You are doubtless somewhat familiar with the history of our extermination from the state of Missouri, wherein scores of our brethren were massacred, hundreds died through want and sickness occasioned by their unparalleled sufferings; some millions of our property were confiscated or destroyed, and some fifteen thousand souls fled for their lives to the then hospitable and peaceful shores of Illinois; and that the state of Illinois granted to us a liberal charter (for the term of perpetual succession) under whose provision private rights have become invested, and the largest city in the state has grown up, numbering about twenty thousand inhabitants.

But Sir, the startling attitude recently assumed by the State of Illinois forbids us to think that her designs are any less vindictive than those of Missouri. She has already used the military of the state with the executive at their head to coerce and surrender up our best men to unparalleled murder, and that too under the most sacred pledges of protection and safety. As a salvo for such unearthly perfidy and guilt she told us through her highest executive officer, that the laws should be magnified and the murderers brought to justice; but the blood of her innocent victims had not been wholly wiped from the floor of the awful arena, where the citizens of a sovereign state pounced upon two defenseless servants of God our Prophet and our Patriarch, before the senate of that state rescued one of the indicted actors in that mournful tragedy from the sheriff of Hancock county and gave him an honorable seat in her hall of legislation, and all who were indicted by the grand jury of Hancock county for the murder of Generals Joseph and Hyrum Smith are suffered to roam at large watching for further prey.

To crown the climax of those bloody deeds the state has repealed all those chartered rights, by which we might have lawfully defended ourselves against aggressors. If we defend ourselves hereafter against violence whether it comes under the shadow of law or otherwise (for we have reason to expect it both ways) we shall then be charged with treason and suffer the penalty; and if we continue passive and non-resistant we must certainly expect to perish, for our enemies have sworn it.

And here, Sir, permit us to state that General Joseph Smith, during his short life, was arraigned at the bar of his country about fifty times charged with criminal offenses, but was acquitted every time by his country, his enemies, or rather his religious opponents, almost invariably being his judges. And we further testify that as a people, we are law abiding, peaceable, and without crime and we challenge the world to prove the contrary; and while other less cities in Illinois have had special courts instituted to try their criminals, we have been stripped of every source of arraigning marauders and murderers who are prowling around to destroy us except the common magistracy.

With these facts before you, Sir, will you write to us without delay as a father and friend and advise us what to do. We are members of the same great confederacy. Our fathers, nay some of us, have fought and bled for our country, and we love her Constitution dearly.

In the name of Israel's God and by virtue of multiplied ties of country and kindred, we ask your friendly interposition in our favor. Will it be too much for us to ask you to convene a special session of congress and furnish us an asylum, where we can enjoy our rights of conscience and religion unmolested? Or, will you in a special message to that body, when convened recommend a remonstrance against such unhallowed acts of oppression and expatriation as this people have continued to receive from the states of Missouri and Illinois? Or, will you favor us by your personal influence and by your official rank? Or will you express our views concerning what is called the 'Great Western Measure' of colonizing the Latter-day Saints in Oregon, the northwestern territory, or some location remote from the states, where the hand of oppression shall not crush every noble principle and extinguish every patriotic feeling?

And now, Honored Sir, having reached out our imploring hands to you, with deep solemnity, we would importune with you as a father, a friend, a patriot and the head of a mighty nation, by the Constitution of American Liberty, by the blood of our fathers who have fought for the independence of this Republic, by the blood of the martyrs which has been shed in our midst, by the wailings of the widows and orphans, by their murdered fathers and mothers, brothers and sisters, wives and children, by the dread of immediate destruction from secret combinations now forming for our overthrow, and by every endearing tie that binds man to man and renders life bearable, and that too, for aught we know for the last time, that you will lend your immediate aid to quell the violence of mobocracy, and exert your influence to establish us as a people in our civil and religious rights where we now are, or in some part of the United States, or at some place remote therefrom, where we may colonize in peace and safety as soon as circumstances will permit.

We sincerely hope that your future prompt measure towards us will be dictated by the best feelings that dwell in the bosom of humanity, and the blessing of a grateful people and of many ready to perish shall come upon you

We are Sir
with great respect,
Your Obt. Servts.

[Signed] BRIGHAM YOUNG,
WILLARD RICHARDS,
ORSON SPENCER,
ORSON PRATT,
W. W. PHELPS,
A. W. BABBITT,
J. M. BERNHISEL,

Committee in behalf of the Church of Jesus Christ of Latter-day Saints at Nauvoo, Illinois.

P.S. As many of our communications, postmarked at Nauvoo have failed of their destination and the mails around us have been intercepted by our enemies, we shall send this to some distant office by the hand of a special messenger. *D.H.C.* 7:402-404

MISSOURI MOBOCRACY

A pitiable yielding to murderous hate was exhibited in June, 1843, by Reynolds and Ford, the governors respectively of the great states of Missouri and Illinois. The adviser of Reynolds was John C. Bennett, the corrupt traitor; the adviser of Ford was Sam C. Owens, one of the leaders of the Jackson mob.

On the 13th day of June, Thomas Reynolds, governor of the state of Missouri, made a requisition upon the state of Illinois for the person of Joseph Smith, Jun., charged with treason, on the ground that he was a fugitive from justice. To show the close communion of the quartette, Reynolds, Bennett, Ford and Owens, it is well to note that Bennett and Owens, before any papers were issued, made their boasts that the governors of the two states would comply with their demands, and that Joseph Smith would be delivered to death at the hands of his old enemies in Missouri. And on the 10th of June, three days before the requisition was issued, Sam Owens and John C. Bennett had informed Governor Ford by letter that Joseph Reynolds, sheriff of Jackson County, (although the alleged offense of treason had been committed in Daviess County) would be appointed by Governor Reynolds of Missouri to receive the person of Joseph Smith from the officials of Illinois; and they, in the same letter, instructed Governor Ford to appoint Harmon T. Wilson of Hancock County, to serve the writ which they demanded Ford to issue. Their reason for wanting Reynolds of Jackson County is clear; he was known to be in sympathy with the mob there, while the officers of Daviess County might have an abhorrence of murder and might refuse to be so pliant as the assassins desired. While their reason for demanding the appointment of Harmon T. Wilson was stated in a letter to Ford by Sam C. Owens in the following words:

"Dr. Bennett further writes me that he has *made an arrange-*

ment with Harmon T. Wilson, of Hancock County, (Carthage, seat of justice,) in whose hands he wishes the writ that shall be issued by you to be put."

The plan as dictated to the governors by these villians was executed.

On the same day that the governor of Missouri appointed Reynolds to go to Illinois after the person of the Prophet, Joseph started with Emma and their children to see her sister Mrs. Wasson who lived near Dixon, Lee County, Illinois. Five days later, on the 18th of June, a message was received at Nauvoo from Judge James Adams, of Springfield, from which it was learned that Ford had issued the writ for Joseph and that it was on the way. Hyrum Smith immediately sent Stephen Markham and William Clayton on horseback, William riding Joe Duncan, to find and warn the Prophet. These devoted men traveled two hundred and twelve miles in sixty-six hours, and found Joseph between the town of Dixon and Wasson's place. When they told him of the danger he said:

"Do not be alarmed, I have no fear, and shall not flee. I will find friends and the Missourians cannot slay me, I tell you in the name of Israel's God."

Wilson and Reynolds had disguised themselves and proposed to be "Mormon" Elders, following Joseph to Wasson's. On the 23rd of June they reached that place while the family were at dinner and said: "We want to see Brother Joseph."

They seized him the instant they found him and presented cocked pistols to his breast, without showing any writ or serving any process. Joseph enquired: "What is the meaning of this?"

And Reynolds replied: "God damn you, be still, or I'll shoot you, by God."

Wilson joined in this awful profanity and threat, and they both struck the Prophet with their pistols. He only said:

"Kill me if you will, I am not afraid to die; and I have endured so much oppression that I am weary of life. But I am a strong man, and I could cast both of you down, if I would. If you have any legal process to serve, present it, for I am at all times subject to law and shall not offer resistance."

At this time, Stephen Markham walked toward them and the kidnappers swore they would kill him; but he paid no attention to their threats. Still bruising the Prophet with their pistols and threatening every instant to kill him if he spoke, they dragged him to a wagon without, and would have driven away not permitting him to say one word to his family or to obtain his hat and coat, but Stephen Markham interposed. He boldly seized the horses by the bits, and would not let them go until Emma could run from the house with the Prophet's clothing.

Stephen mounted a horse and started to Dixon where the kidnappers also proceeded at full speed without even allowing Joseph to speak to his wife or little children. The wretches had not shown any writ, nor had they told the Prophet what was the charge against him. During the whole journey of eight miles to Dixon they continued to strike his sides with their pistols and to swear that they would have his life. So brutal were their blows that he almost fainted, and each side was turned black and blue for a circumference of eighteen inches.

At Dixon they thrust him into a room at the tavern and guarded him there, while ordering fresh horses to be ready in five minutes. As Stephen Markham had raised an alarm at Dixon and proposed to get a lawyer, Reynolds once more declared his intention to shoot the Prophet. Joseph said: "Why do you make this threat so often. If you want to shoot me, do so. I am not afraid."

The continued calmness and the undaunted heroism of the Prophet had their effect upon his captors; and at last they desisted from their threats, although they continued their abuse. No doubt they would have killed him but they were too cowardly. They wanted to get him into Missouri where the murder could be consummated without any danger to them. The lawyers whom Stephen secured for the Prophet were not permitted by Reynolds and Wilson to consult their client; but the effect of this high-handed proceeding was to arouse the indignation of the landlord and his friends. They gathered around the hotel and told Reynolds that this might be the Missouri way, but it would not do for Dixon, where the people were law-abiding and would not permit any man to be kidnapped and dragged away without knowing the charge against him and without an opportunity for judicial examination. As a large crowd had gathered by this time and as they threatened to take summary action against the brigands, Reynolds and Wilson concluded to permit a consultation with the lawyers. As soon as he could get speech with the attorneys, Joseph told them that he had been taken prisoner without process, had been insulted, bruised and threatened; and that he wanted to sue out a writ of *habeas corpus*. At this Reynolds swore that he would only wait half an hour. A Mr. Dixon who had opposed Reynolds and Wilson in their outrageous doings, immediately sent messengers to the master in chancery and to Lawyer Walker to have them come to Dixon to get out a writ of *habeas corpus*.

The next morning the writ was issued, returnable before Judge Caton of the ninth judicial circuit at Ottawa, and duly served upon Reynolds and Wilson.

Writs were also obtained against them for threatening the life of Stephen Markham, for assaults upon Joseph and for false imprisonment; and these villains were soon placed in the custody of the sheriff of Lee County, whereupon their demeanor became as craven as it had before been bold and threatening.

In the meantime Joseph had sent William Clayton to Nauvoo to inform Hyrum of what was being done.

The Prophet still in captivity to Reynolds and Wilson, who in turn were in custody of Sheriff Campbell, proceeded that night to Pawpaw grove, thirty-two miles on the road to Ottawa. Here Reynolds and Wilson again began to abuse their captive; but Campbell came to his assistance and slept by his side that night to protect him from further assault.

Early the next morning the hotel was filled with citizens who wanted to see the Prophet and hear him preach. Fearing the effect of an address from Joseph, Sheriff Reynolds yelled: "I want you to understand that this man is my legal prisoner, and you must disperse."

This was false. No writ or other process had been served upon Joseph, and he was nobody's legal prisoner. But without waiting to discuss the legal question, an old man named David Town, who was lame and carried a large hickory walking stick, advanced upon Reynolds and said:

"You damned infernal puke, we'll learn you to come here and interrupt gentlemen. Sit down there, [pointing to a very low chair] and sit still. Don't you open your head till General Smith gets through talking. If you never learned manners in Missouri, we'll teach you that gentlemen are not to be imposed upon by a nigger-driver. You cannot kidnap men here. There's a committee in this grove that will sit on your case; and, sir, it is the highest tribunal in the United States, as from its decision there is no appeal."

Reynolds was made aware that Mr. Town was the head of a committee, just then assembled to deal with some land speculators who had attempted to impose upon honest settlers, and he obeyed with great meekness.

The Prophet talked an hour and a half on the subject of marriage, which was the topic selected for him by his congregation. From that hour on his freedom commenced.

Learning at Pawpaw grove that Judge Caton was absent in New York the party turned back to Dixon, arriving there about 4 o'clock in the afternoon of June 25th. A return of the writ of *habeas corpus* was made to the master in chancery, with the endorsement that the judge was absent; whereupon a new writ was issued, returnable before the nearest tribunal in the fifth judicial district authorized to hear and determine writs of *habeas corpus,* and Mr. Campbell, the sheriff of Lee County, at once served it upon Wilson and Reynolds. Arrangements were then made to go before Judge Stephen A. Douglas at Quincy, a distance of two hundred and sixty miles; and in the meantime, anticipating treachery, Stephen Markham started with a letter to the Prophet's friends informing them further of his movements. This action was deemed necessary; for the whole country seemed to be swarming with men anxious to carry Joseph into Missouri, where, according to the free boasts of Reynolds, Wilson and others his death was certain.

The party in charge of the Prophet proceeded toward Quincy. On Tuesday, the 27th of June, shortly after crossing Fox River, they met seven of the Prophet's friends. The brethren burst into tears at sight of Joseph; and as they embraced him he spoke to his captors who, it must be remembered, had not yet shown any writ or other process and were therefore kidnappers:

"I think I will not go to Missouri this time, gentlemen. These are my boys."

Then he mounted his favorite horse Joe Duncan;* and the en-

---

*The horse "Joe Duncan" owned by the Prophet is here identified. In a letter written by C. Bartholomew to the Compiler of this book is the following: "Brother Lundwall: Sister Huldah Thomas asked me to tell you that

tire company proceeded to a farm house and made a halt. This party of the Prophet's friends was under the leadership of Thomas Grover, and from them it was learned that Elders Charles C. Rich and Wilson Law with other and larger parties were seeking the Prophet to prevent his murder and abduction.

Reynolds and Wilson shook with fear. Peter W. Cownover, one of the Prophet's friends, said to Wilson: "What is the matter with you? Have you got the ague?"

Wilson managed to stammer, "No."

Reynolds asked: "Is Jem Flack in the crowd?"

Some one answered: "He is not now, but you will see him tomorrow about this time."

"Then," said Reynolds, "I am a dead man; for I know him of old."

Cownover told the foolish fellow not to be frightened, for no one intended to injure him.

Stephen Markham had turned back when he met this party and was with them. He walked up to Reynolds and offered his hand, when the bandit cried out: "Do you meet me as a friend? I expected to be a dead man when I met you again."

Markham replied: "We are friends, except in law; that must have its course."

At Andover that night Reynolds and Wilson gathered a party and held a consultation. They intended to raise a company, take the Prophet by force, escape from their own arrest, and run with him to the mouth of Rock River, on the Mississippi, where they said they had a company of men all ready to drag him into Missouri and wreak vengeance upon him. But for Stephen Markham's vigilance they would have executed this plan, but he foiled them by putting the sheriff of Lee County on his guard.

On Wednesday, the 28th of June, they encamped in a little grove at the head of Elleston Creek. While the animals were feeding, Reynolds said: "No, we will go from here to the mouth of Rock River and take steamboat to Quincy."

Markham replied: "No, for we are prepared to travel and will go by land."

Wilson and Reynolds both yelled out: "No, by God, we won't; we will never go by Nauvoo alive."

Both drew their pistols upon Markham, who turned to Sheriff Campbell saying: "When these men took Joseph a prisoner, they took even his pocket knife. They are now prisoners of yours and I demand that their arms be seized."

Reynolds and Wilson refused to yield their weapons; but when the sheriff threatened to call for assistance, they submitted.

While on this journey and resting in a little grove of timber where the ground was well sodded, one of the lawyers for Reynolds

the horse she told you about which her grandfather, James Duncan, gave to the Prophet Joseph Smith, was raised by her grandfather from a colt, and her mother, Matilda A. Duncan, helped take care of it when very small. When they came west her mother asked her father (James Duncan) what had become of the horse. He said: "I gave it to the Prophet." The Prophet named it Joe Duncan, after Joseph Smith and James Duncan."

and Wilson began to boast of his prowess as a wrestler. He offered to wager any sum that he could throw any man in the state of Illinois at side-hold. Stephen Markham, a side-hold wrestler, told the lawyer that he would not contest for money but would try a bout for fun. They grappled, and the man threw Markham, when a great shout arose from Joseph's enemies, and they began to taunt the Prophet and his friends.

Joseph turned to Brother Philemon C. Merrill, a young man from Nauvoo, subsequently adjutant in the Mormon Battalion, and now a resident of St. David, Arizona, and said: "Get up and throw that man."

Merrill was about to say that side-hold was not his game, but before he could speak the Prophet commanded him in such a way that his tongue was silenced. He arose to his feet filled with the strength of a Samson. Merrill lifted his arms and said to the lawyer: "Take your choice of sides."

The man took the left side with his right arm under; when the company all declared that this was not fair as he had a double advantage. Merrill felt such confidence in the word of the Prophet that it made no difference to him how much advantage his opponent took, and he allowed the hold. As they grappled Joseph said: "Philemon, when I count three, *throw him!*"

On the instant after the word dropped from Joseph's lips, Merrill, with the strength of a giant, threw the lawyer over his left shoulder, and he fell striking his head upon the earth.

Awe fell upon the opponents of the Prophet when they saw this, and there were no more challenges to wrestle during the journey.

While they were lodged at a farm house near Monmouth one night Reynolds and Wilson again plotted to raise a mob and seize Joseph; but Peter Cownover detected them, and Sheriff Campbell put them under restraint, feeling that they were no longer to be trusted. On Thursday, the 29th of June, another party of the Prophet's friends joined him: He called James Flack to his side and told him he must not injure Reynolds whatever the provocation might have been; for the Prophet had pledged himself to protect the Missouri sheriff.

The lawyers and Sheriff Campbell, with other civil officers, decided that the hearing upon the writ of *habeas corpus* might lawfully be held in Nauvoo, and they desired to go there rather than to Quincy; so the party turned in that direction. This occasioned great joy to Joseph. His bruises were forgotten, and that night when they reached the house of Michael Crane, on Honey Creek, he sprang from the buggy, walked up to the fence, and and leaped over without touching it.

A messenger had carried the news of the home-coming to Nauvoo, and on Friday, June the 30th, a joyous cavalcade went out to meet the Prophet. The meeting between Joseph and Hyrum was most touching. Joseph had just passed through one of the many perils of his life, but one of the few which Hyrum did not share; and his return caused Hyrum to weep for joy as he took the Prophet in his arms. The spectacle of the entry into Nauvoo was most imposing, for the delighted people sang for joy and made such demonstration of love and gladness in Joseph's behalf, that the lawyers and officers from Dixon were charmed and deeply impressed.

After they were within the city the multitude seemed unwilling to disperse; but Joseph said to them:

"I am out of the power of the Missourians again, thank God; and thank you all for your kindness and love. I bless you in the name of Jesus Christ. I shall address you in the grove, near the temple at 4 o'clock this afternoon."

A feast had been prepared at Joseph's house, and there he went—still in the hands of his captors, Reynolds and Wilson, who were the prisoners of Sheriff Campbell of Lee County; and all of these with about fifty of the Prophet's friends sat at his table. The place of honor was given to Reynolds and Wilson who were waited upon by Emma with as much courtesy as could have been bestowed upon a beloved guest. This kindness heaped coals of fire on their heads, for they remembered the time when they had dragged the Prophet from the side of his wife and little ones and had refused to permit him to say farewell.

Under the advice of the lawyers, Joseph with his captors was brought before the municipal court of Nauvoo, and all the writs and other papers were filed there. The case was heard upon its merits, and the Prophet was discharged. The lawyers concurred that in all the transactions since the day of his arrest Joseph held himself amenable to the law and its officers; and that the decision of the municipal court of Nauvoo was not only legal and just but was within the power of this tribunal under the city charter.

But before the actual hearing began in the municipal court, Reynolds and Wilson in company with Lawyer Davis, of Carthage, started for that place threatening to raise a mob with which to drag Joseph from Nauvoo. Desiring a larger force than they could readily command at Carthage, they applied to Governor Ford for the state militia. But the governor sent a trusted messenger to Nauvoo to obtain evidence concerning the seizure of the Prophet and his discharge on the writ of *habeas corpus;* and this gentleman secured a copy of all the papers and evidence in the case. Prominent citizens of Lee County added their affidavits; and several gentlemen went up to Springfield to represent the matter fairly to his Excellency. Whatever Ford's motive may have been—whether a desire to make political capital for his party with influential men who took the side of the Saints in this question, or whether he had fear that he would lose his personal prestige by precipitating the unlawful strife—he took the only proper course; and after long consideration, and upon the representation of his trusted messenger, he refused to order out the militia, and so reported to Sheriff Reynolds and Governor Reynolds of Missouri. The position which Ford assumed was that no resistance had been made to any writ issued by the state of Illinois, and therefore that Illinois had neither right nor interest in the matter.

On the 2nd and 3rd days of July parties returned who had been out from Nauvoo searching for the Prophet. One party had gone up the river on the little steamer *Maid of Iowa,* under command of Dan Jones, and had passed through a very adventurous voyage. This company was accompanied by Apostle John Taylor. Another party, under the leadership of General Charles C. Rich, had traveled five hundred miles on horse-back in seven days. They were all delighted to find the Prophet safe at home; and he blessed them for their love and devotion to him.

Life of Joseph the Prophet, by George Q. Cannon, pp. 415-424.

A PROMISE TO LIVE FIVE YEARS

BY JOSEPH THE PROPHET

Soon after the apostasy that took place in Kirtland our enemies began again to trouble us. Having seen our prosperity in everything to which we had set our hands previous to this, they became discouraged, and ceased their operations; but, suddenly discovering that there was a division in our midst, their fruitful imaginations were aroused to the utmost, to invent new schemes to accomplish our destruction.

Their first movement was to sue Joseph for debt, and, with this pretense, seize upon every piece of property belonging to any of the family. Joseph then had in his possession four Egyptian mummies, with some ancient records that accompanied them. These the mob swore they would take, and then burn every one of them. Accordingly, they obtained an execution upon them for an unjust debt of fifty dollars; but, by various stratagems, we succeeded in keeping them out of their hands.

The persecution finally became so violent that Joseph regarded it as unsafe to remain any longer in Kirtland, and began to make arrangements to move to Missouri. One evening, before finishing his preparations for the contemplated journey, he sat in council with the brethren at our house. After giving them directions as to what he desired them to do, while he was absent from them, and, as he was about leaving the room he said: "Well, brethren, I do not recollect anything more, but one thing, brethren, is certain, I shall see you again, let what will happen, for I have a promise of life five years, and they cannot kill me until that time is expired."

That night he was warned by the Spirit to make his escape, with his family, as speedily as possible; he therefore arose from his bed, and took his family, with barely beds and clothing sufficient for them, and left Kirtland in the dead hour of the night. The day following, the constable, Luke Johnson, an apostate, served a summons upon my husband, telling him that no harm was intended, and desired him to go immediately to the office.

History of the Prophet, by his Mother, Lucy Smith, pp. 217-18.

JOSEPH NOT TO SEE FORTY YEARS

The brethren of the Twelve took the propeller *Hercules* for Chicago at 10 a.m. Fare in the cabin $7. We had comfortable staterooms. We spent the day in writing and in social conversation with each other concerning the death of Joseph and Hyrum and the welfare of the church and our families. A variety of subjects were called up, each one expressing his feelings freely. President Brigham Young said he wished me to keep an account of things as they were passing, as he should look to me for his journal at a future day. Elder Wight said that Joseph told him, while in Liberty jail, Missouri, in 1839, he would not live to see forty years, but he was not to reveal it till he was dead.

From Elder Wilford Woodruff's Journal — *D. H. C.* 7:212.

WAS PERSECUTED FROM BOYHOOD TO END OF LIFE

Joseph Smith did more for the salvation of the human family in the short time he lived than any other man that ever lived in the world, Jesus Christ excepted. He lived to be 39 years old and endured a continued scene of persecution and oppression from the time that the angel of the Lord appeared to him, until the time of his death. He bore testimony to the work of the Lord through life and sealed his testimony with his own blood. I have been with the Prophet Joseph and heard his instructions weekly and sometimes daily. The last time I heard him speak in public he spoke to the Legion (Nauvoo Legion). After telling what he had passed through and what he had suffered from men because he preached the Gospel of Jesus Christ, he said: *From my boyhood up to the present time I have been hunted like a roe upon the mountains. I have never been allowed to live like other men. I have been driven, chased, stoned, whipped, robbed, mobbed, imprisoned, persecuted, accused falsely of everything bad. I have suffered till the Lord knows I have suffered enough."* *Diary of John Pulsipher.*

WHY LATTER-DAY SAINTS WERE PERSECUTED

BY JOSEPH THE PROPHET

Must we, because we believe in the fullness of the gospel of Jesus Christ, the administration of angels and the communion of the Holy Ghost, like the prophets and apostles of old,—must we be mobbed with impunity, be exiled from our habitations and property without remedy, murdered without mercy, and government find the weapons and pay the vagabonds for doing the jobs, and give them the plunder into the bargain? Must we, because we believe in enjoying the constitutional privilege and right of worshipping Almighty God according to the dictates of our own consciences, and because we believe in repentance, and baptism for the remission of sins, the gift of the Holy Ghost by the laying on of the hands, the resurrection of the dead, the millennium, the day of judgment and the Book of Mormon as the history of the aborigines of this continent,—must we be expelled from the institutions of our country, the rights of citizenship, and the graves of our friends and brethren, and the government lock the gate of humanity and shut the door of redress against us? If so, farewell freedom! adieu to personal safety! and let the red hot wrath of an offended God purify the nation of such sinks of corruption;

for that realm is hurrying to ruin where vice has the power to expel virtue.   *Life of Joseph the Prophet,* by George Q. Cannon, p. 433.

A CHARMED LIFE

By Jane H. Martineau

The recent death of Patriarch Benjamin F. Johnson in Mesa, Arizona, recalls to the writer an episode of the persecutions of the Latter-day Saints in Missouri in 1838, in which the deceased was a prominent actor; also, of a lady greatly beloved by all who knew her who has also passed to that better clime.

Mr. Johnson, then a young man of twenty years, had been taken prisoner by the ruffian horde styled an army, commanded by General Clark, and for eight days kept under guard at a camp fire in weather intensely cold with no shelter from the piercing winds by day or night; no bed except a few boughs between his body and the snow, which was more than a foot in depth; no covering of any kind, and his only resource against freezing at night a constant replenishing of the camp fire, making sleep almost impossible. In addition to all this, he was denied any food, and was only kept from starvation by the pity of the negro cook, who stealthily gave him scraps left from meals when he could do so unobserved.

The wretch who at Haun's Mill slew an old revolutionary soldier was in the camp carrying the corn cutter with which he had murdered the old man and which was still dyed with his blood. Day after day he threatened Johnson's life with it, saying he would get more "Mormon" blood upon it when he got ready, and others of the mob frequently told him, "We'll kill you tomorrow, sure, and in a way to make you yell right smart."

While sitting upon a log one day a brute came to him with rifle in hand, saying, "You give up Mormonism right now, or I'll shoot you." Receiving a decisive refusal, he exclaimed with fearful oaths, "I'll send you to hell right now," took deliberate aim not ten feet distant and pulled the trigger. No explosion occurred, and he cursed fearfully, saying he had used the gun for twenty years and it had never before misfired. He examined the lock, put in fresh priming and again essayed to shoot Johnson, but without effect, and a third time with the same result. A bystander told him to fix up his gun a little, and then, said he, "You can kill the cuss all right. "Yes," said the would-be murderer, "I'll put in a fresh load." He did so and again tried to kill Johnson. This time the gun burst and killed the wretch upon the spot, and a by-stander was heard to say, "You'd better not try to kill that man." And thus, day after day, Johnson was continually threatened with death.

But help was coming, and that by the compassion of a young girl, who visited every family in the "Mormon" settlement not many miles away and persuaded men and women to meet at the log school-house and pray for his release. They did so, and that night, next day, and the following night they kept unceasing in prayer. As one ceased praying another began, and then her and another. Some went home to breakfast, dinner or supper, and returned again to pray for the release of their brother.

At length this unceasing prayer was answered. About midnight of the second night the general in command caused Johnson to be brought to his tent, and said to him: "Johnson, I have had all I could do to save your life until now, but I can't save you from death any longer. The men swear they will kill you tomorrow. Give up your Mormonism and I will adopt you as my son—I have none—I am wealthy, and you shall inherit all I have, and your life will be saved."

Johnson said his religion was more to him than his life, and he would sooner die. Finding argument could not alter the young man's decision, the general said, "Well, all I can do is to turn you loose in the woods, and for you to escape if you can." He ordered a soldier to conduct Johnson to a deserted "Mormon" log house about half a mile from camp, leave him there and return, which he did, and the young man was free. But what a freedom—in snow two feet deep, no blanket, no arms to kill game or for self-defense and no food except about two quarts of parched corn. And he must make his way for miles—for days. He could not go to the "Mormon" village nearest at hand, as he would be sought for there, be retaken and murdered. And so he plodded through the woods, half starved and frozen, having to wade sloughs and brooks filled with snow or ice, and no chance to dry his frozen garments and limbs. He finally reached a house, but could not remain, as he found his foes were hunting the whole country for him. But here he obtained an old quilt, two or three "pones" of corn bread, a flint and steel to make a fire with, and with another man started on his weary journey that night to reach Fort Leavenworth, about two hundred miles distant. And this refuge, after days of fearful privation, they at last gained, being hospitably received and cared for.

And who was the Angel of Mercy in human form—a young girl in her teens, who gained his release and saved his life through the prayer of the Saints? It was Sister Eliza R. Snow, his intimate friend.

In closing this sketch I will say I have read the foregoing in father Johnson's journal, and have also heard it from his own lips, and have thought it well, for the rising generation, born and living in peace and comfort, to know something of what their fathers and mothers have had to endure for the Gospel's sake.

Millennial Star, Vol. 68:43-44.

IN 1843 JOSEPH THE PROPHET HAD BEEN ARRESTED 42 TIMES

I landed in the city of Nauvoo on the 9th of May, 1843, having then ended the 19-day journey by water and land which was a joyful home to me, and I longed to see the Prophet. I then had the opportunity of striking glad hands with him and my heart leaped in me for joy, for I had greater affection towards him than for any person on the earth. I viewed the Temple; then I remembered my night vision I had when yet in the eastern counties seeing the Temple in the same form as it really was and the city the same. After having been in the city over forty days till Brother Joseph and his wife was going to visit her relatives about seventy miles up the Mississippi river, all being peace at home save for a few false brethren who sought to overthrow or destroy his happiness, who gave notice to his enemies of Missouri, for the plan was then devised to take him to Missouri and kill him. There was a man named Harmon Wilson who followed him under the pretense of an old writ to take him, but the Lord was with him that night and told him what to do so he escaped the hands of his enemies and brought them to shame and confounded them that they was in fear and great trouble of themselves. *He then told us that was the 42nd suit brought against him falsely and he always was cleared by the laws of the land.*

Diary of George W. Laub.

LAWSUITS TO WHICH JOSEPH SMITH WAS SUBJECTED

By GEORGE A. SMITH

Joseph Smith, the Prophet, was subjected, during his short ministerial career of fifteen years, to about fifty vexatious lawsuits. The principal expense was incurred in liquidating lawyers' bills, and the brethren's time and expenditure in attending courts to defend the Prophet from mob violence. Magistrates' court expenses were generally one hundred dollars. The Prophet paid Generals Doniphan and Atchison for legal services at Richmond, Mo., in 1838-39, sixteen thousand dollars; but this amount was fruitlessly expended, as the benefits of the law were not accorded to him, because of the predominance and over-ruling power of a mob.

At the Prophet's trial at Monmouth, Ill., in 1841, before Judge Douglas, the lawyers' fees and expenses amounted to three thousand dollars. His next trial was before Judge Pope, U. S. District Court, in 1842-43, the expenses of which may be reasonably estimated at twelve thousand dollars.

Cyrus Walker charged ten thousand dollars for defending Joseph in his political arrest, or the attempt at kidnapping him at Dixon, Ill., in 1843. There were four other lawyers employed for the defense besides Walker. The expenses of the defense in this trial were enormous, involving the amounts incurred by the horse companies who went in pursuit to aid Joseph, and the trip of the steamer *Maid of Iowa*, from Nauvoo to Ottawa, and may be fairly estimated at one hundred thousand dollars.

J. D., Vol. 13:109-110.

THE BATTLE OF NAUVOO AS WITNESSED
BY A "JACK-MORMON"

By L. C. BIDAMON

I am a Virginian by birth, removed to Ohio with my parents when a boy, and there married, but lost my wife by death, and subsequently removed to Canton, Ohio. When I first arrived in Nauvoo in April, 1846, I found the city menaced by a wicked mob, who, notwithstanding the majority of the Mormons had already gone into the wilderness, were relentless in their persecutions of the few who remained behind. I was soon convinced that the Mormons were a much abused people, and as I have always felt inclined to stand up for justice and right at all times and under all circumstances, it was not long before my sympathies were with the Saints. I watched the doings of the mob with a keen eye, and felt indignant when I witnessed how illegal and vexatious lawsuits were gotten up, based upon trumped up charges, for the purpose of dragging defendants twenty or thirty miles into out-of-the-way places in order to waylay them, and often for the purpose of whipping and murdering them. And when they, in some instances, refused to go, knowing the object was to kill them, the mobbers set up a great hue and cry that the Mormons disobeyed the law.

I was finally appointed a trustee on the part of the "New citizens" to negotiate with the mobbers for peace, and was also sent to Governor Ford to lay our grievances before that official. At first he refused to listen to me and swore that he would not spend another dollar in the interest of Hancock county, having already had so much trouble with the people there. I knew, however, that our cause was just, and becoming indignant at the governor's action, I threatened that if he would not do his duty in the matter, I would appeal to the President of the United States. Seeing that I was in earnest, he at last listened to what I had to say, and agreed to send Major Parker with me back to Nauvoo with a posse of twelve men, which were to serve as a guard to protect those upon whom writs might be served in the future. The mob, however, would not recognize Parker's authority, and swore by all the devils and saints they could think of, that they would do as they d-d pleased and did not care for the governor nor anybody else; not even Jesus Christ, if He would dare to say a good word for the Mormons.

Some time afterwards I was sent to Springfield a second time to see the governor. I started down the river in a small rowboat, and the mobbers learning of my departure started in pursuit, crossed the river from Warsaw, and surrounded the house in which I had intended to stop for the night, at Churchville (now Alexandria, Mo.) There were twelve or fifteen of them. They came in and asked me how I would like to go with them to Mr. Brockman's camp. I answered that I should not like it at all, as I was fully aware that his men were not favorably disposed toward me. "But, by G-d," said they, "you will go," and they made a move as if they wanted to take me by force. Quick as thought I had my hand on my pistol, which in the next instant I held cocked in their faces, while I hallowed out: "Stand back there, or I will blow daylight thru you." The way these mobbers made for the door and scattered in all directions was a caution. Ordering my two men, whom I had engaged to row me down the river, to get the boat ready, I retreated with pistol in hand, got in the boat, pulled to the middle of the stream where the balls of the mobbers could not reach us, and arrived at Quincy in safety. From the latter place I continued the journey by stage to Springfield. While stopping at Mount Sterling a few hours, I was surrounded by the inhabitants who were very curious to know all about the situation at Nauvoo. I made such explanations as I thought proper, and after I was through, a hard-looking individual with dark features, came up to me and said he was a captain in Singleton's militia, and was going to Nauvoo the next day. All at once it came upon me that I should play the mobbers a trick, in order to avert the immediate danger which threatened Nauvoo, and keep the mob off until I had seen the governor. I asked the fellow if he would carry a letter for me to my brother in Nauvoo. He said he would on condition that I would let him know the contents of it. This I agreed to do. I then wrote a few lines, in which I pretended to advise the citizens of Nauvoo to refrain from shedding blood, if possible; "for," wrote I, "it would be an easy matter for you with your hell acres and hell half acres to destroy the whole mob force at once."

"What do you mean by hell acres and hell half acres?" demanded my man.

"Oh, I don't like to tell you that," said I.

"Then by G-d," ejaculated he, "I will not carry your letter."

"Very well," said I, "provided you can keep a secret, I will explain to you." He thought he could, and I then proceeded to tell him that every approach to Nauvoo was undermined and large quantities of powder deposited in such a manner that by the pulling of certain wires, mechanically arranged, it could be exploded at will. Of course there was not a word of truth in that, but he drank it all in and went immediately to the mob camp, where the letter was read. It had the desired effect. The mob, although quite strong enough to have taken Nauvoo at once, concluded to wait for reinforcements, which gave me time to return from my visit to the governor, before the final attack was made.

The governor returned me with orders to Major Flood, of Quincy, for him to proceed to Nauvoo and assist in adjusting the difficulties between the Mormons and the mob. That gentleman was at first unwilling to go, but finally concluded to do so, taking with him a number of other leading men of Quincy. When we arrived at Montrose, we could distinctly hear the cannonading on the prairie east of Nauvoo, and having crossed the river, I sent the Quincy delegation in my carriage out to the mob camp. These gentlemen tried their best to establish peace between the fighting parties, but all in vain; all they succeeded in doing was that they induced the mob to promise to cease hostilities until the next day. As the delegation was returning to Nauvoo several shots were fired after them. I happened to pick up a spent ball, which I presented to Mr. Wood, saying that here was a compliment from the belligerents. At seeing this, Mr. Wood became so indignant that he jumped to his feet, exclaiming, "Give me a gun, and I will stand by you and see it all through. In all my intercourse with people—and I have dealt even with heathens—I have never, in all my life, seen such infamy among mankind." I advised Mr. Wood to keep at a safe distance and witness what was going on, that he might live to testify of our doings, for we all expected to fight till the last. Mr. Wood, who was a wealthy man, subsequently showed great kindness in a substantial manner toward the afflicted Saints, by sending up large quantities of provisions, partly of his own stock, and partly such as he had influenced others to give.

Previous to this I, together with a few other men, was sent to the mob camp at Green Plains with a view to bringing about a compromise. On that occasion it became my lot to deliver a speech in defense of the Mormons. Now, I am not a very religious man, and not at all superstitious; in fact, I am inclined to be rather skeptic, but I believe I was inspired on that occasion to portray the condition of the people in Nauvoo, and to plead in behalf of suffering innocence, for even the feelings of the hardened mobocrat Williams seemed to be touched as he listened to me; for I plainly saw tears coursing their way down his guilty cheeks. I told them that the remnant of the Mormons were making preparations to get away as fast as possible, and all they asked for was a little more time in which to dispose of their property and raise means for their journey. And furthermore that some of the heads of families were in the service of the United States, marching toward Mexico, and their families could not conveniently be moved until these soldiers had drawn their pay. I was apparently making a good impression upon the mobbers, when Thomas C. Sharp, the notorious editor of the *Warsaw Signal*, interrupted me and told me that the war was between the Mormons and the old citizens, and that I had no right to interfere, and further that if we, whom they designated Jack Mormons, did not stand aloof, we should share the same fate as the Mormons. When I alluded to the sufferings of the women and children, he burst out in terrible rage, saying, after uttering a fearful oath: "Drive the women into the river and throw their d-d young ones in after them."

It was finally agreed that we should meet at Warsaw the following day and make another attempt at compromising. Here I was asked by Mr. Williams to sign a document to the effect that we would see all the Mormons out of Nauvoo within a reasonable time. This I emphatically refused to do, and said that I would see him in hell a thousand fathoms deep before I would put my signature to such a paper. At last I became so disgusted with him that I invited him to come out into the street for five minutes, and we would then and there settle the matter at once so far as we two were concerned. But he refused to engage in that kind of experience.

When I think of the doings of these fellows, even at this late day (October 7, 1888), it makes my blood boil within; it was a shame, gentlemen, a burning shame, the way your people were treated at that time.

I returned from Warsaw without effecting any compromise, and our next move was to defend ourselves the best we could.

We turned the steamboat shafts into cannon, repaired our small arms, manufactured ammunition, and were determined to sell our lives as dear as possible. The famous battle of Nauvoo is a matter of history. I fought by the side of the gallant Captain Anderson, who fell as one of the noble defenders of human rights, but at last we were forced to capitulate, and so incensed were the mobbers at the active part I had taken in the defense, that they put me and two others on the death list, threatening to kill us at sight. To avert their murderous intent, I absented myself from Nauvoo for a few months, and did not return until February, 1847. During my absence the robbers plundered my house, the one I had bought of President Young, carrying away and destroying everything they could get a hold of, including my stock of wagons and house furniture, which were never returned to me, save some of the carpets which I had purchased of the Temple committee. When Governor Ford, in his history of Illinois, says that he was not posted in regard to the crimes enacted by the mob at Nauvoo at that time, he tells a wicked lie, for I visited him twice myself, and told him all about it; and I also know that he was duly informed by others.

In regard to Joseph Smith, candor compels me to say that he was a noble man, yes, a noble man, indeed. I never met his equal in all my life, and I only saw him once, but that occasion I shall never forget. A certain phrenologist had invited me to accompany him to Nauvoo to pay Joseph a visit, the professor desiring to make an examination of his head. We found Joseph walking in the garden; he received us kindly and soon invited us into the house, where I had a two hours' conversation with him. His manners, movements and whole deportment made a deep and lasting impression upon me, and convinced me that he was not the impostor and wicked man he had been represented by his enemies to be; to me he appeared to be a good, honest and noble-hearted man, and from all I have ever learned about him since, I have not had occasion to change my opinion about him.

In answer to further inquiry, the major described the Prophet as a very good looking man, with light complexion and light brown hair. He was strongly built and well proportioned, was about six feet high, and weighed 200 pounds.

Infancy of the Church, by Andrew Jenson and Edward Stevenson, pp. 49-51.

JOSEPH SMITH BEFORE THE COURT AT MONMOUTH, ILL.

On Saturday, June 5th, 1841, the Prophet Joseph Smith, on his return from Quincy, Ill., to which place he had accompanied his brother Hyrum and William Law on their mission to the East, he was arrested at the Bear Creek hotel by two officers on a warrant from Governor Carlin, of Illinois, to deliver him up to the authorities of Missouri. The Prophet Joseph succeeded in getting a writ of *habeas corpus*, and was taken to Monmouth on the Tuesday following. At the hearing, which resulted in the Prophet's discharge, one O. H. Browning, Esq., appeared in behalf of the defendant, and ably defended him. One of the brethren who was with the Prophet at the hearing sent the following report of the case to the *Times and Seasons,* which it published under date of June 15th (1841).

American Hotel,
Monmouth, Warren County, Illinois.
June 9th, 1841. Wednesday Evening.

We have just returned from the Court House, where we have listened to one of the most eloquent speeches ever uttered by mortal man, in favor of justice and liberty, by O. H. Browning, Esq., who has done himself immortal honor in the sight of all patriotic citizens who listened to the same. He occupied the attention of the court for more than two hours, and showed the falsity of the arguments of the opposed counsel, and laid down principles in a lucid and able manner, which ought to guide the court in admitting testimony for the defendant—Joseph Smith. We have heard Mr. Browning on former occasions when he has frequently delighted his audience by his eloquence; but on this occasion he exceeded our most sanguine expectations. The sentiments he advanced were just, generous and exalted; he soared above the petty quibbles which the opposite counsel urged, and triumphantly, in a manner and eloquence peculiar to himself, avowed himself the friend of humanity, and boldly, nobly and independently stood up for the rights of those who had waded through seas of oppression and floods of injustice and had sought a shelter in the state of Illinois. It was an effort worthy of a high-minded and honorable gentleman, such as we have ever considered him to be since we have had the pleasure of his acquaintance. Soon after we came out of Missouri he sympathized with us in our afflictions, and we were indeed rejoiced to know that he yet maintains the same principles of benevolence. His was not an effort of a lawyer anxious to earn his fee, but the pure and patriotic feeling of Christian benevolence and a sense of justice and of right.

While he was answering the monstrous and ridiculous arguments urged by the opposing counsel, that Joseph Smith might go to Missouri and have his trial, he stated the circumstances of our being driven from that state, and feeling by and emphatically pointed out the impossibility of our obtaining justice there. There we were forbidden to enter in consequence of the order of the Executive, and that injustice and cruelties of the most barbarous and atrocious character had been practiced upon us, until the streams of Missouri had run with blood, and that he had seen women and children barefoot and houseless, crossing the Mississippi to seek refuge from ruthless mobs. He concluded his remarks by saying that to tell us to go to Missouri for trial was adding insult to injury, and then said:

"Great God! have I not seen it? Yes, my eyes have beheld the blood-stained traces of innocent women and children, in the drear winter, who have traveled hundreds of miles barefoot, through frost and snow, to seek a refuge from their savage pursuers. 'Twas a scene of horror sufficient to enlist sympathy from an adamantine heart. And shall this unfortunate man, whom their fury has seen proper to select for sacrifice, be driven into such a savage band, and none dare to enlist in the cause of justice? If there was no other voice under heaven ever to be heard in this cause, gladly would I stand alone and proudly spend my latest breath in defense of an oppressed American citizen."   *The Elders Journal, pp. 267-68.*

EARLY CHURCH HISTORY FOREVER UNTOLD

BY BENJ. F. JOHNSON

Your invitation through a late issue to the "Old veterans of the Nauvoo exodus," to give items from their experience relating to that period, almost prompts a smile. For to those whose broader experience takes in from before the settlement at Kirtland and succeeding vicissitudes of the Church, the Nauvoo experience appears but modern. Who has yet written in detail the circumstances of poverty and persecution in which the Temple at Kirtland was

built? that attended the gathering up of Zion's camp, with all of
its experience in going and returning from Missouri? that grew
out of the Kirtland bank? the great property boom and financial
crisis of 1837? the apostasy at Kirtland and the persecution of the
Prophet by his friends? his flight to Missouri and the struggles of
the poor left behind? Who has written the history of the "poor
camp"?

The first large emigration company of the Saints, consisting
of some seventy wagons, was organized and led by Joseph Young,
E. Smith, Henry Herriman, Jonathan Dunham, Jonathan Hale and
others. In great poverty it started from Kirtland on July 4, 1837,
and arrived at Far West on October 20, just in time to get every
experience of mob violence and exposure through the ensuing
winter. While Joseph Young and others were stopping at Haun's
Mill they barely escaped the massacre there. Where is published
the appalling condition of the Saints at Adam-ondi-Ahman, driven
in from the surrounding country and in the midst of deep snows,
without shelter for the aged, the feeble or the sick, when infants
were born to a manger of snow and starvation was near to all;
followed by the expulsion and gathering again at the "Old Commerce grave yard," afterwards Nauvoo? In 1839 every house was
a hospital, but without nurse or attendant for the sick, for at this
time there were hardly well ones enough to bury the dead. This
experience with the arrival of the Prophet and others from Missouri
prisons, with the building of another Temple under persecution
and poverty, the martyrdom, etc., was all prior to our exodus from
Nauvoo, and much of this still remains unpublished, if written.

Having since 1831 been near the front in each evolution of the
Church, you will pardon that "smile"; for to me the butt end of our
experience appears prior to our expulsion from Nauvoo, in which,
as in the others, I was near to the front. After the martyrdom of
the Prophet, having been for years associated with him in business,
I was called by President Young to occupy and keep open the
Nauvoo mansion, vacated by his death, and, having Sheriff Backenstos as boarder and all outside officers and strangers to entertain,
I had excellent opportunity to learn much from the outside that
interested us as a people. When it was decided or agreed that as a
people we should leave Nauvoo, with others I was appointed to
organize a company of fifty and to take measures preparatory to
emigration. To this end we started the making of wagons, occupy-
ing as we had need the divisions in the basement story of a large
brick barn belonging to the mansion. After the killing of Frank
Worill by Sheriff Backenstos and posse, the hatred and fury of our
enemies generally increased. A report became current abroad that
many anti-Mormons were being murdered in Nauvoo, and the
Nauvoo mansion was cited as the probable place for great crimes.
To allay the excitement a troop of soldiers was by order of the
governor sent to investigate and to examine the premises for
bodies said to be secreted about the barn. They came and made a
formal examination after which they appeared satisfied and quietly
left. But the end was not yet, for the rumor continued as a number
of our mechanics were seen about the basement of the barn, creating

renewed suspicion. Such was the condition when President Young called for those ready to commence crossing the river, for which I was doing all possible to prepare. I am not certain of the date, but I think it was the sixth of February that private word was brought me in the evening that a squad of soldiers would be in the city before morning with an order for my arrest. There was no time to prepare. I must go at once. So with two of my family, leaving my wife and children in a skiff at midnight, in a fearful storm, we crossed the river which the day following was closed up with ice. A waiting vehicle took us to camp on Sugar Creek, where on arrival we were without shelter from the storm or supplies for our comfort. But we were at least among friends.

Millennial Star, 56:150-151.

THE PROPHET JOSEPH WITH COMPANIONS IN A MISSOURI DUNGEON

In one of those tedious nights we had lain as if in sleep till the hour of midnight had passed, and our ears and hearts had been pained, while we had listened for hours to the obscene jests, the horrid oaths, the dreadful blasphemies and filthy language of our guards, Colonel Price at their head, as they recounted to each other their deeds of rapine, murder, robbery, etc., which they had committed among the "Mormons" while at Far West and vicinity. They even boasted of defiling by force wives, daughters and virgins, and of shooting or dashing out the brains of men, women and children.

I had listened till I became so disgusted, shocked, horrified, and so filled with the spirit of indignant justice that I could scarcely refrain from rising upon my feet and rebuking the guards; but had said nothing to Joseph, or any one else, although I lay next to him and knew he was awake. On a sudden he arose to his feet, and spoke in a voice of thunder, or as the roaring lion, uttering, as near as I can recollect, the following words:

"Silence, ye fiends of the infernal pit. In the name of Jesus Christ I rebuke you, and command you to be still; I will not live another minute and hear such language. Cease such talk, or you or I die this instant!"

He ceased to speak. He stood erect in terrible majesty. Chained and without a weapon; calm, unruffled and dignified as an angel, he looked upon the quailing guards, whose weapons were lowered or dropped to the ground; whose knees smote together, and who, shrinking into a corner, or crouching at his feet, begged his pardon, and remained quiet till a change of guards.

I have seen the ministers of justice, clothed in magisterial robes, and criminals arraigned before them, while life was suspended on a breath, in the Courts of England; I have witnessed a Congress in solemn session to give laws to nations; I have tried to conceive of kings, of royal courts, of thrones and crowns; and of emperors assembled to decide the fate of kingdoms; but dignity and majesty have I seen but once, as it stood in chains, at midnight, in a dungeon in an obscure village of Missouri.

Autobiography of Parley P. Pratt, pp. 228-230.

CHRISTIAN MOBOCRACY AS DESCRIBED BY
ONE WHO EXPERIENCED IT

BY CORDELIA SMITH REEDER ELLINGFORD

Through the violent persecutions of the Saints, Willard G. Smith's parents were obliged to sell their home and all other possessions, saving a meager outfit with which they started for Missouri in the spring of 1838. Willard, though a boy, was old enough to sense and fully realize these persecutions, and the dangers with which they were menaced all the way, on that terrible journey, every mile full of horror and uncertain dread. Often they were warned by complete strangers to travel other roads as mobs were congregated to kill them. They would thus be forced to travel unbeaten trails at night with the stars as guides. They were obliged to camp occasionally and get a few days work to replenish their scant provisions.

They left Ohio in April and reached Missouri in October. On the 23rd of October they were stopped by an armed mob. All firearms and ammunition were taken from them; they were taken back five miles, placed under guard, and detained for three days with no consideration and little to eat, constantly threatened with complete annihilation.

On the morning of October 30th they arrived at a little place called Haun's Mill, a small settlement on Shoal Creek, composed of Latter-day Saints. They received a cordial, hearty welcome. Father said the people had bees and had just taken out their honey, which was in pans and buckets. They were told, "Help yourselves; eat all you want."

They passed a few hours in this friendly atmosphere before they noticed a sort of suppressed anxiety among the people. The men all gathered in groups and seemed to be discussing some vital problem. Grandfather with his three little boys, Willard, Alma and Sardis, were standing at a brush fire heating a wagon tire to re-set. Grandmother was busy with the usual work of a Pioneer mother and traveler. I will try to give you the story of the subsequent events in fathers' own graphic words:

"Myself and two little brothers were with father when, without warning a large body of mounted men, blackened and painted like Indians, rode up yelling, and commenced shooting at the crowd. The men at the shop called for quarter; to this the mob paid no attention. The men then called for the women and children to run for their lives.

"We were surrounded on three sides by the mob; the old mill and mill pond were on the other. The men ran for the shop, taking the little boys with them. My two little brothers ran in with father. I followed but when I started to enter the shop my arms flew up and braced themselves against each side of the door, preventing my entrance. In my frenzy of fear I again tried to enter the shop, and again my arms were braced to prevent going in. After the third futile attempt, I ran around the corner of the shop and crawled into a pile of lumber, hiding as best I could. I had been there but a few seconds when the mob began shooting at me and splinters flew all about me. I crawled out and ran into an empty house on the slope near the pond. I had only been there a few minutes when I heard a suppressed groan. I listened again and then I saw a board over a potato cellar move very slightly. I raised the boards and there saw an old Revolutionary soldier by the name of Thomas McBride, who had been wounded before the women had fled and they had hidden him in this pit. Father McBride asked to be helped out and begged for water. I went with a cup to the pond, or mill race, for the water. As I stooped to fill the cup I was deliberately fired upon, the bullets spattering like hail in the water. I escaped without a scratch. I gave the suffering patriot a drink and pleaded with him to remain in the pit, telling him the mob would kill him if they found him. He replied, 'Help me out; I am dying in here.' This I did. The mob found him and as he raised his aged hands in supplication, they were cut and hacked, the fingers split down with an old dull corn cutter. By the time the old gentleman was made as comfortable as possible, the bullets were flying thick around us. I decided I must seek safety elsewhere. I ran out of this house into another one close by. Here I heard sobs and whispered comfortings which seemed to come from the corner where the bedstead stood. I went and lifted up the bed valence and crouched way back were six little girls. The mob saw me go in there and soon the splinters and bullets were flying around us. I said, 'Come, we must get out of here or we will all be killed.' So we left and ran toward the mill dam, finally reaching the mill race which we crossed on a board. The mob fired at us as we went up the creek bank on the other side. The bullets spattered again in the water and cut down the brush on all sides of us; but not one of us was grazed by a bullet, although several passed through the clothing of the children.

"Two of these little girls I afterwards knew. They were the daughters of Brother Champlain, the man who was knocked down in the shop, and was thought to be dead, thus hearing all the controversies of the mob when they entered the shop to finish their fiendish work.

"After our race for life, the little girls scurried off like prairie chickens into the brush and tall corn. I, knowing father and my little brothers were in the shop and the mob were still firing at them, took shelter behind a large tree, where I could be pretty safe and still watch the mob. This I did until they ceased firing, when they dismounted and went into the shop where they finished their fiendish work by killing all who were not dead. From here they went into all the cabins and tents and destroyed all their groceries and furnishings. After taking the horses and belongings of their victims, they rode off, howling like Indians.

"As soon as I was sure they had gone, I started for the shop. I was the first person to enter this holocaust (wholesale destruction by fire and sword), stepping over the dead body of my father in doing so. I looked around and found my brother, Sardis, dead, with the top of his head shot away; and my little brother, Alma, almost lifeless, lying among a pile of dead where he had been

thrown by the mob, who evidently thought him dead. I picked
Alma up from the dirt and was carrying him from the shop when
I met my mother, who screamed and said, 'Oh! They have killed my
little Alma!' I said, 'Alma is alive but they have killed father and
Sardis.' I begged mother not to go in but to help me with Alma.
Our tent had been devastated by the mob, even the straw tick cut
open and straw scattered about, taking the tick with them. Mother
leveled the straw, laid some clothes over it and on this awful bed
we placed Alma, and cut his pants off. We could then see the extent of his injury. The entire ball and socket joint of the left hip
was entirely shot away, leaving the bones three or four inches
apart. It was a sickening sight, one I shall never forget. Mother
was full of divine, trusting faith, a most marvelous, wonderful
woman. As soon as Alma could talk, mother asked him if he knew
who made him. He said, 'Yes, mother, God did.' She then told
him that the wicked mob had shot his hip away and asked, 'Do
you think God can make a new one?' Alma replied, 'Yes, I know He
can.' Mother then said, 'All right, let's pray to the Lord and ask
Him to do so.' So we all gathered around him on his bed of straw
and mother prayed, dedicating him to the Lord, asking God to
spare his life if He could make him strong and well but to take him
to Himself if this were impossible. In her terrible excitement and
sorrow, her only help seemed her Heavenly Father. So she prayed
for guidance, pleading for help in this dire extremity. By inspiration her prayers were answered and she knew what to do. She
placed little Alma in a comfortable position on his stomach, telling
him, 'The Lord has made it known to me that He will make you
well, but you must lie on your stomach for a few weeks.'

"Mother was inspired to take the white ashes from the campfire, place them in water to make a weak lye, with which she washed
the wound; all the crushed bone, mangled flesh and blood were
thus washed away, leaving the wound clean and almost white like
chicken breast. Then she was prompted how to make a poultice
for the wound. Mother asked me if I knew where I could get some
Slippery Elm tree roots. I said I knew where there was such a tree.
She gave me a lighted torch of shag bark hickory with which to
find my way."

I remember asking my father, "Weren't you afraid when you
went off alone in the dark?" "Of course I was but mother told me
the Lord would protect me and I believed her. I took the torch and
ax and soon got the roots from which mother made a poultice,
with which she filled the wound. As often as the poultice turned
dark it was removed and the wound washed and refilled."

"This is not intended as a history of those terrible days. I will
just say the Lord fulfilled His promise to the faithful in this case.
The prayers of implicit, trusting faith were answered. A new hip
gradually replaced the one that was shot away. Alma was fully
restored to health, walked without a limp, and was a dancing master
in his young days. He devoted years of his life to missionary work,
was a man of faith, full of integrity, beloved by all who knew him."

When a girl of 18 years, I visited with my father at the home
of my grandmother. On our last evening with her, she gathered

her children and grandchildren about her and again related incidents connected with her wonderful life. Once more we heard the story of their combined sufferings at Haun's Mill, and of the Divine help and support received during their awful experience. As a fitting climax, grandmother said, "Alma, for the benefit of these children, that it may be a living, burning testimony of God's power, will you let them see your hip?" I shall never forget the electrical thrill of conviction that ran like fire through my entire system as I gazed upon the handiwork of God. A broad, thick, strong ligament or muscle had united the trunk of the body with the limb, constituting a joint or the necessary equivalent for perfect free use of the body.

The day after the massacre at Haun's Mill, father helped his mother and others bury the dead from the shop. An old dry well was found and into this the dead were lowered, covered with straw, filled with dirt and debris, and covered with rock and brush. Their harassments were pitiful; their suffering beyond description. My father was the only help during these terrible weeks, every day finding renewed persecution. After Alma improved so they could think of trying to leave the state, great difficulties presented themselves. They were alone, their team, wagon, and all equipment stolen. Grandmother visited Captain Cumstock, leader of the mob, and here she found one horse but Captain Cumstock told her she could have it by paying five dollars for its keep. She walked out, took off her apron, tied it around her horse and led him off with the men looking at her. They never objected. She gathered a meager outfit and was soon on the way to Quincy, Illinois. They were ill prepared for this trip. Grandmother, in her journal, said, "I started the 1st of February for the state of Illinois, without friends or money. Mobbed all the way. I drove my own team and slept out of doors. I had four small children. We suffered much with hunger, cold and fatigue. For what? For our religion. Where, in a boasted land of liberty, 'Deny your faith or die' was the cry."

Grandmother, with her little family, finally reached Quincy, Illinois, where they suffered all the trials, persecutions, and wanderings of the Saints. Here grandmother married again, a man having the same name, Warren Smith, and also following the same business as my grandfather. From here they went with the Latter-day Saints to Nauvoo, where father seemed to enjoy life. He joined the martial band, played the kettledrum in Nauvoo Legion, and entered fully into the activities of the growing community. His associations were always dear to him. If ever a man loved another, my father loved the Prophet Joseph Smith. He loved to talk of him, would relate little incidents of kindness and consideration shown him by the Prophet, which meant so much to a boy.

Father's school was situated near the Nauvoo Mansion and was taught by one of the Prophet's sisters. Here he used to play with young Joseph, Jr., and his brother, David. His home was quite a distance from school and father used to bring his lunch. One time the Prophet, passing at noon and seeing father eating, stopped and said: "Willard, I don't want you to bring your lunch from home any more. You come to my home every day and eat with my boys." Father told of occasions when the Prophet would place his arms affectionately about him and drawing him close would give him loving advice and counsel. Father told our family of the Prophet's love for boys, his interest in their sports and activities, how he would take off his coat and join the boys in a game of ball, or other sports—all of which made him become almost revered by the boys. Father worked on the Nauvoo Temple as stone cutter and glazier, assisted in making the oxen on which rested the baptismal font, and when it was completed was one of the first to receive his blessings therein. Of the awful martyrdom of the Prophet and his brother, Hyrum, father couldn't talk without tears filling his eyes and choking his speech. Father was employed at the livery stable where the team of horses was stabled which carried visitors to and from Carthage jail. The regular driver being ill, father was asked to drive the very group to the jail which killed the Prophet and his brother, Hyrum. He heard their vile blasphemous boastings of their intended deed and was utterly helpless. After the murder, father marched with muffled drum at the head of those who brought their bodies back to Nauvoo.

His grief at having to leave beautiful Nauvoo and all earthly possessions was keen, since love of home and family was strong with him. He left Nauvoo, driving a team for Beeson Lewis, later transferred to President Young's Company of Advance Pioneers. He was in this company when the call came for five hundred men to form a company of infantry for the Mexican War. After a decision had been reached by those directly concerned, President Young stepped upon a wagon tongue, calling out: "Is there a drummer boy present?" My father stepped forward, saying, "Yes, sir, I am one." President Young replied, "All right, Willard, you drum for recruits." Which father did, thus becoming virtually the first volunteer in this memorable body of valiant men, who made one of the most hazardous, heroic marches recorded in modern history.

The trials of the Mormon Battalion have been graphically recorded and described in a general way by different historians, but no one can describe their acute sufferings on this uncharted, perilous march over hot, burning sand, under scorching sun, with short rations and little water. Father told of one particular instance, after a two days' march, with very little water to start with, the last twenty-four hours entirely without. With their tongues swollen out of their mouths, they were forced to march along or be left by the wayside. With many loitering on the way, unable to keep up, the Battalion came to a "buffalo wallow," a deep depression or sort of springy place where water had drained and here the buffalo had wallowed and their deep tracks were full of dirty, stagnant water, full of animal life and all kinds of filth, but it was wet, and hailed by the boys with delight. They spread their soiled handkerchiefs over these depressions and sucked the moisture through them. Father said the condition of their tongues was such that the sense of taste was gone. He also said he considered it providential that relief came to them in small quantities for had they come to a running stream or spring, they would have injured, if not killed themselves by drinking too much. They suffered for food on long forced marches. One day father and his companion saw a dead bird under a desert bush. After they camped at night, they quietly left camp, retraced their route, found the bird, which proved to be a crow. In their starving condition this, though not considered a choice morsel, was cooked and thoroughly enjoyed.

The Battalion finally reached San Diego, where they had an opportunity to rest, with plenty of food. From here they made a forced march to Santa Ana, where they fully expected to have an engagement with the enemy. Again, those seeking promotion and notoriety were disappointed. When the Battalion arrived, the enemy had all fled to the mountains. From here they went to Los Angeles. While the Company were standing at ease in the street, there came a ragged, dejected man, in clothes much too small for him. He was dirty, a regular derelict vagabond. He accosted Captain Hancock, saying, "Gentlemen, I am glad to see you. I have been waiting here days for you, for I heard there was a company of Mormons coming." "Well," said Brother Hancock, "what can we do for you?" The man replied, "I hoped there would be some one in the company who had friends killed in the Haun's Mill massacre, who would kill me, because I was there. I was the man who shot that little boy's brains out in the blacksmith shop. His cries and pitiful pleadings have never been from before my eyes and I want to die." Brother Hancock took him to father, where he repeated his story. He said, "I shot that boy with a double-barreled shotgun. His pleadings still ring in my ears. I hope you will grant my request." He wore an old army shirt, buttoned over shoulder and down the right side. Tearing this open, he threw himself down on his knees, saying, "I want to die; I want you to kill me." My father stepped back from him, saying, "There is a just God in heaven who will avenge that crime. I will not stain my hands with your blood." This man loitered around camp for days until the officers had time taken away.*

---

*In this connection the notes made by Elder Seymour B. Young are very informative: "On Saturday afternoon in company with Elder Winegar we boarded the Burlington train for the town of Breckenridge, 85 miles east of Kansas City, and arrived at this old town about 8 p.m. Their county fair had been running for three days and would close this evening. About the center of the small park in which the fair was located was a mill stone, said to have been taken from Mr. Haun's mill. This mill was owned and in running order on Shoal Creek at the time of the massacre of the Saints on September 6, 1838, where eighteen of the brethren were shot down and killed and three others escaped who had been dangerously wounded. About 6 o'clock in the evening, on the date above registered, 200 armed men on horseback made their appearance and at once opened fire, without warning, upon the little company of Mormon families encamped near Mr. Haun's mill and on his premises. This band of miscreants shot down every man that they could see moving in the vicinity of the camp of Latter-day Saints. The brethren ran in every direction to keep from being murdered, and some twelve or thirteen of them, with two little boys, took shelter in the blacksmith shop, a small log building which Warren Smith, one of the brethren, had rented of Mr. Haun and in which he had engaged in shoeing the horses and fixing the wagons of the immigrating saints. When these twelve brethren and two little boys took shelter in the blacksmith shop, the mob coolly and deliberately surrounded the same and, placing the muzzles of their guns through the openings between the logs, shot every one of the occupants and then

TYPICAL MISSOURI JUSTICE

(A short account of an affray that took place between the Latter-day
Saints and a portion of the people of Daviess County, Mo., at an election
held in Gallatin Aug. 6, 1838.)

BY JOHN L. BUTLER

Polls opened with the usual ceremonies. There were present
about forty or fifty Missourians and eight or ten of the saints (viz.)
Hyrum Nelson and Brother Riley Stewart, Jackson Stewart, Moses
Daly, Washington Voris, Father Harvey Olmstead, Samuel Brown
and Perry Durphy. There was a rush to the polls on the part of the
Missourians until they were principally through with the voting
when William Peniston, one of the candidates stood upon the head
of a whiskey barrel and made a very inflammatory speech against
the saints, stating that he had headed a company to order the
Mormons off their farms and possessions, stating at the same
time that he did not consider the Mormons had any more right to
vote than the niggers. When he was through he called on all hands
to drink, which they did, for whiskey passed free and they drank
as freely. I, at the time retired a little back from the crowd
rather behind the little grocery near by where they were voting.
I heard the word G— damn 'em; kill 'em G— Damn 'em. From the
noise and bustle I knew there was fighting. I felt at first not to go
in amongst them, for I did not want to have any trouble, but wished
to vote and thought after voting I would start home immediately.
I did not like the spirit manifested. It then came to my mind that
they might be fighting the brethren. As I went over I saw they had
attacked the brethren with sticks, clapboards (or shakes) and
anything they could use to fight with. They were all in a muss
together, everyone of the Missourians trying to get a lick at a
Mormon. It made me feel indignant to see from four to a dozen
mobbers on a man and all damning 'em and G— damning the
"Mormons." I saw they were all well armed with clubs or some
other weapon to fight with. I turned around and ran a few steps
to get a stick. I soon found one suitable though rather large. It

---

entered the shop and proceeded to examine the bodies by punching them with
their guns to see if life remained in any of them.

The two little boys, after their father fell near the bellows of the shop,
crawled over behind his body to hide from the butchers. The mob also poked
these two little fellows with their guns and when they cried out, they proceeded to finish them as they thought. The one, the younger of the two,
Sardis Smith, was heard to say: "Please, mister, don't shoot me, I am only
a little boy." But the villain replied, "Nits make lice," and placing his gun
against the little boy's ear fired and blew the top of his head off. His older
brother, Alma Smith, thirteen years of age, also received a very dangerous
wound in the region of the right hip, from which he almost bled to death
before he was rescued by his angel mother, whose husband had been murdered
and also her little son, Sardis—this fearful and horrible assassination perpetrated on an innocent and defenseless band of immigrants because they
claimed to be Latter-day Saints.

Over the mill stone at the fairgrounds in Breckenridge was a placard
reading as follows: "This stone was taken from the battleground where
eighteen Mormons were killed and buried in a well near Haun's Mill on Shoal
Creek, September 6, 1838."

was a piece of the heart of an oak which I thought I could handle with ease and convenience. Returning to the crowd many thoughts ran through my mind. First, I remembered that I never in my life struck a man in anger. I had always lived in peace with all men. The stick I had to fight with was so large and heavy that I could sink it into every man's head that I might chance to strike. I did not want to kill anyone, but merely to protect my brethren. I went in with the determination to rescue my brethren from such miserable curs at all hazards. Thinking when hefting my stick that I must temper my lick just so as not to kill. Furthermore, a power rested upon me such as I never felt before. When I got in reach of them I commenced to call out loud for peace and at the same time making my stick move to my own utter astonishment tapping them as I thought lightly, but they fell as dead men, their heads often striking the ground first. I took great care to strike none except those who were fighting the brethren. When I first commenced there were some six or eight men on old Mr. Durphy and a few steps further ten or a dozen men on Brother Olmstead and Brother Nelson. But they were so thick around them that they could not do execution to advantage. I continued to knock down every man I could reach that was lifting a stick against the brethren. After getting through and seeing the brethren on their feet I looked and saw some of the men lying on the ground as though they were dead. Some of them were being held up by their friends; some were standing leaning against the little grocery. While gazing on the scene Brother Riley Stewart had in his hand (what the backwoodsman calls a *knee*) to place between weight poles on log cabins—a piece of timber about two and a half feet long, small at one end, and struck Dick Welding an overhand blow on the head cutting the side of his head three or four inches in length. It looked like he was certainly killed. I told Stewart he had better leave for he had killed that man. He started to run and got off about twenty or twenty-five paces when about ten or a dozen men took after him throwing sticks and stones at him and anything they could get, swearing they would kill him. I saw they would overpower him and I called for him to come back for we could do better business when together. He took a circuitous route to keep from meeting those pursuing him. At the crisis one of the mob drew a glittering dirk with blade about six inches long, waving it in the air and at the same time swearing it should drink Stewart's heart's blood. He started to meet Stewart as he was returning back to the crowd. As he was several steps ahead of me I sprang with all the power that was in me to overtake him before he met Stewart. Just as he and Stewart met he made a blow at his neck or breast, but as Stewart was passing in a run the dirk passed over his left shoulder close by his neck and struck in his right shoulder blade which bent the point of it around as much as an inch. Just as he made his lick I reached forward as far as I could and hit him on the side of the head and fetched him helpless to the ground. At the same instant I received a blow from one behind me with the butt end of a loaded horsewhip which took me right between the shoulders. I felt the jar only in my breast and had I not been stooping forward as I was at the time I made my blow, he would have taken me on the head no doubt and perhaps fetched me down.

While Stewart was running off, James Welding, Dick's brother came along and saw his brother lying in his gore. He bawled and swore that they had killed Dick. He picked up a stone swearing he would kill every Mormon in Daviess County before Saturday night. Just as the word came out of his mouth, Washington Voris, standing near him, hit him square in the mouth with a stone that would weigh about two pounds I think and straightened him out on the ground. As he arose with his mouth badly cut and bleeding he put his hand on his face and began to cry saying that he never saw people hit as hard as the Mormons. They had killed Dick and mashed his mouth, and off he ran bellowing in the brush.

I will mention another occurrance which took place. Brother Olmstead previous to the affray had purchased half a dozen earthen bowls and as many teacups and saucers which he had tied up in a new cotton handkerchief and swung to his wrist. One of the mob struck at him when he raised his arm and the blow struck the dishes and broke them. He then commenced using them over their heads and when the fight was over I saw him empty out his broken earthenware on the ground in pieces not larger than a dollar. His handkerchief looked like it had been chewed by a cow. I have thought ever since that time that they had fun picking the pieces of earthenware from their heads, for they certainly were pretty well filled.

The whole scene was soon over. I think it lasted about two or three minutes from the first to the last blow. I have seen as many as two hundred men at an election in old Kentucky fighting each other for six or eight minutes with clubs, knives, brick bats, etc., with about one tenth the execution. I believe there were as many as thirty men with bloody heads and some of them badly hurt. I knocked down about six or eight men myself. I never struck a man the second time and while knocking them down I really felt that they would sometime embrace the gospel.

I felt the spirit as above stated to rest upon me with power. I felt like I was seven or eight feet high and my arms three or four feet long, for certainly I ran faster than I ever did before and could reach farther and hit a man and they could not reach me to harm me. Col. Peniston who was the author of the scrape ran up to the grocery on the hill. I looked out for him to get a clip at him.

After the fight was over we gathered our men on some hewn house logs and told the mob that we would fight them as long as blood ran warm in our veins if they still persisted. But they begged for peace after they saw their men lying around. They came to me and wanted me to go and vote. I told them I would if they would clear the road to the polls which they did immediately. But I could see that if I went in the poll box they would be all around me and thus take me prisoner for some of their men who would die. I told them I was a law-abiding man and that I did not intend to be tried by a mob. I then mounted a good horse and left.

Before the fighting began John L. Butler called the brethren together and made a speech, saying: "We are American citizens; our fathers fought for their liberty in the American Revolution and we will maintain the same principles."

MASONS ALSO PERSECUTED

Elder Heber C. Kimball, who had been a Mason since 1823, has said of the martyrdom:

Joseph and Hyrum Smith were Master Masons, yet they were massacred through the instrumentality of some of the leading men of that fraternity, and not one soul of them has ever stepped forth to administer help to me or my brethren belonging to the Masonic Institution, or to render us assistance, although bound under the strongest obligations to be true and faithful to each other in every case and under every circumstance, the commission of crime excepted.

Yes, Masons, it is said, were even among the mob that murdered Joseph and Hyrum in Carthage Jail. Joseph, leaping the fatal window, gave the masonic signal of distress. The answer was the roar of his murderers' muskets and the deadly balls that pierced his heart.

In 1878, Zina D. Huntington Young said of this theme, "I am the daughter of a Master Mason; I am the widow of the Master Mason who, when leaping from the window of Carthage jail, pierced with bullets, made the Masonic sign of distress, but those signs were not heeded except by the God of Heaven."

"They gave us a city charter," said Heber C. Kimball, "and then took it from us again, and that too without any just cause. They gave us a charter for a Masonic lodge, and then went to work and killed some of the men to whom the charter was given."

When the enemy surrounded the jail, rushed up the stairway, and killed Hyrum Smith, Joseph stood at the open window, his martyr-cry being these words, "O Lord My God!" This was not the beginning of a prayer, because Joseph Smith did not pray in that manner. This brave, young man who knew that death was near, started to repeat the distress signal of the Masons, expecting thereby to gain the protection its members are pledged to give a brother in distress.

Mormonism and Masonry, pp. 16-17, by E. Cecil McGavin.

EARLY PERSECUTIONS OF THE PROPHET

BY JOHN REID

I will return to the persecutions which followed General Smith, when his cheeks blossomed with the beauty of youth, and his eyes sparkled with innocence. Those bigots soon made up a false accusation against him and had him arraigned before Joseph Chamberlain, a justice of the peace, a man that was always ready to deal justice to all, and a man of great discernment of mind. The case came on about 10 o'clock a.m. I was called upon to defend the prisoner. The prosecutors employed the best counsel they could get, and ransacked the town of Bainbridge and county of Chenango for witnesses that would swear hard enough to convict the prisoner; but they entirely failed. *Yes, sir, let me say to you that not one blemish nor spot was found against his character, he came from that trial, notwithstanding the mighty efforts that were made to convict him of crime by his vigilant persecutors, with his character unstained by even the appearance of guilt.* The trial closed about 12 o'clock at night. After a few moments' deliberation, the court pronounced the words "not guilty," and the prisoner was discharged. But alas! the devil, not satisfied with his defeat, stirred up a man not unlike himself, who was more fit to dwell among the fiends of hell than to belong to the human family, to go to Colesville and get another writ, and take him to Broome county for another trial. They were sure they could send that boy to hell, or to Texas, they did not care which; and in half an hour after he was discharged by the court, he was arrested again, and on the way to Colesville for another trial. I was again called upon by his friends to defend him against his malignant persecutors, and clear him from the false charges they had preferred against him. I made every reasonable excuse I could, as I was nearly worn down through fatigue and want of sleep; as I had been engaged in lawsuits for two days, and nearly the whole of two nights. But I saw the persecution was great against him; and here let me say, Mr. Chairman, singular as it may seem, while Mr. Knight was pleading with me to go, a peculiar impression or thought struck my mind, that I must go and defend him, for he was the Lord's anointed. I did not know what it meant, but thought I must go and clear the Lord's anointed. I said I would go, and started with as much faith as the Apostles had when they could remove mountains, accompanied by Father Knight, who was like the old patriarchs that followed the ark of God to the city of David. * * * * * The next morning about 10 o'clock the court was organized. The prisoner was to be tried by three justices of the peace, that his departure out of the county might be made sure. Neither talents nor money were wanting to insure them success. They employed the ablest lawyer in that county, and introduced twenty or thirty witnesses before dark, but proved nothing. They then sent out runners and ransacked the hills and vales, grog shops and ditches, and gathered together a company that looked as if they had come from hell and had been whipped by the soot boy thereof; which they brought forward to testify one after another, but with no better success than before, although they wrung and twisted into every shape, in trying to tell something that would criminate the prisoner. Nothing was proven against him whatever. Having got through with the examination of their witnesses about 2 o'clock in the morning, the case was argued about two hours. There was not one particle of testimony against the prisoner. No, sir, he came out like the three children from the fiery furnace, without the smell of fire upon his garments. The court deliberated upon the case for half an hour with closed doors, and then we were called in. The court arraigned the prisoner and said: "Mr. Smith, we have had your case under consideration, examined the testimony and find nothing to condemn you, and therefore you are discharged." They then proceeded to reprimand him severely; not because anything derogatory to his character in any shape had been proven against him by the host of witnesses that had testified during the trial, but merely to please those fiends in human shape who were engaged in the unhallowed persecution of an innocent man, sheerly on account of his religious opinions.

After they had got through, I arose and said: "This court puts me in mind of a certain trial held before Felix of old, when the enemies of Paul arraigned him before the venerable judge for some alleged crime, and nothing was found in him worthy of death or of bonds. Yet, to please the Jews, who were his accusers, he was left bound contrary to law; and this court has served Mr. Smith in the same way, by their unlawful and uncalled for reprimand after his discharge, to please his accusers." We got him away that night from the midst of three hundred people without his receiving any injury; but I am well aware that we were assisted by some higher power than man; for to look back on the scene, I cannot tell how we succeeded in getting him away. I take no glory to myself; it was the Lord's work and marvelous in our eyes.—*Times and Seasons*, vol. v, pp. 549-552.

D.H.C. 1:93-96.

CHAPTER 4

Persecution Led by Modern Preachers

MODERN MINISTERS A PERSECUTING CLASS

Whenever God has authorized his servants to deliver His messages, the counterfeit have also existed, as in the days of Moses, Elijah, the Apostles of old, and in our day. Christ said to the Scribes and Pharisees, the very men who put him to death, "Ye generation of vipers, how can ye escape the damnation of hell." The Redeemer said to the Prophet Joseph Smith in our day, of these modern Scribes and Pharisees, these modern priests of Baal: "Their creeds were an abomination in His sight; their professors were all corrupt; they draw near to me with their lips but their hearts are far from me; they teach for doctrine the commandments of men; they have a form of godliness but they deny the power thereof."

To summarize the part these modern priests have played in this generation, the following is quoted from Elder B. H. Roberts' reply to the Salt Lake City Ministerial Association:

"I have been meeting your class, gentlemen, for now thirty years; and have had controversies of various kinds with it during that time, and I know you as a class quite thoroughly. I speak from experience, not malice, and comparing you as a class with other classes of men whom I have known, it is just a plain, solemn truth that you are, as a class, narrow, bigoted, intolerant, petty; and I say that in the very best of feeling." * * * *

"These gentlemen reviewers express two fears. One is that they will be charged, because of issuing this review, with misrepresentation. Well, I don't wonder at that, and I think we have proven that you have misrepresented. But they also fear that we will charge them with persecution. Gentlemen, we acquit you of the intention of persecution. When the Revs. Phineas Ewing, Dixon, Cavanaugh, Hunter, Bogart, Isaac McCoy, Riley, Pixley, Woods and others carried on an agitation in Missouri against "Mormonism" and the "Mormons" that resulted in burning hundreds of our homes and driving our people—including women and children, remember—to bivouac out in the wilderness at an inclement season of the year; when the mob incited by these reverends, your prototypes, gentlemen, laid waste our fields and gardens, stripped our people of their *earthly* possessions, keeping up that agitation until twelve thousand or fifteen thousand people were driven from the state of Missouri, dispossessed of several hundred thousand acres of land—two hundred and fifty thousand acres, to be exact—which they had entered, and rendered them homeless—we might call, we do call, that persecution. When the Rev. Mr. Levi Williams led the mob that shot to death Joseph Smith and his brother Hyrum Smith in Carthage prison, and when the Rev. Mr. Thomas S. Brockman led the forces against Nauvoo, after the great body of the people had withdrawn from that city, and expelled the aged, the widow and the fatherless, and laid waste the property of the people—we think we are justified in calling that persecution, of which, right reverend gentlemen were the chief instigators. And when in this territory some years ago one wave of agitation followed another, until a reign of terror was produced, and a regime was established under which men guilty at most of a misdemeanor, could neverthe-less be imprisoned for a term of years covering a lifetime, and fined to the exhaustion of all they possessed, under the beautiful scheme of segregating the offense into numerous counts in each indict-ment; and when in that reign of terror women were compelled to clasp their little ones to their breasts and go out among strangers, exiled from their homes—we might be inclined to call that per-secution."

THE CAUSE OF PERSECUTION OF THE SAINTS

BY BENJAMIN F. JOHNSON

And now your question as to the cause of the early persecu-tions of the Saints. To answer this question, we should go back to its inception to find the cause for the hate that is ever behind to incite persecution. Between the present and former dispensations there is a striking analogy. Jesus appeared to the learned, haughty, dignified and opulent Jews as the "poor illiterate carpenter's son of Nazareth," a despised "Galilean," who claimed to be the son of the Highest, the Great Jehovah, that "without" him there was nothing made that was made, that he held "all power both in Heaven and on Earth," that he could "destroy the temple and rear it up in three days," etc., while the multitude turned from them to follow the "lowly Nazarene," hence their envy and jealousy which ripened into hate and in their nailing Him as a malefactor to the cross; and just so has it been in our day.

Joseph Smith, of lowly birth, was a farm boy of common class, poor, illiterate and without distinction other than being religiously inclined; he attended revivals, was in the anxious circles honestly seeking religion and to learn which was the right church; and calling upon the Lord in simple faith that he might know. Both the Father and the Son in a pillar of light descended, and in teach-ing him commanded that "he join no religious sect, as their *creeds* were all an abomination in His sight."

This blow, by an ignorant son of poverty at fourteen years of age, in the face of all Christendom, was an insult to the dignity of all priestly learning, greatness and wealth; but with their millions in Bible, missionary and other societies for converting the world, all their greatness defied and denounced by an ignorant boy, their con-tempt led to hatred and persecution. And when that boy became a man, he claimed to have revelations, and that an angel had delivered to him golden plates containing a history of a fallen people, and that God, through him, was about to restore the ancient gospel in its purity, which, if true, would blot out all their greatness. Inspired by hate, they made lies their weapons with which to fight the truth; both of which are attributes of the devil.

THE JOHNSON RESIDENCE

The old "Father Johnson Homestead" at Hiram, unaltered, but just as it stood in 1830-31, when it was the home of the Johnson family, and some of its rooms were occupied by the Prophet and his family. It was the right hand upper room (east end) that was used by the Prophet Joseph as a translation room, and where he, with Sidney Rigdon as scribe, revised the English translation of the Bible.

REAR OF JOHNSON RESIDENCE

The room shown in the rear of the Johnson residence (the one where the door stands open) is that occupied by the Prophet and his family in the winter of 1832, and from which he was dragged at midnight March 25, 1832, by a mob, cruelly beaten, tarred and feathered, and only saved from a still more horrible violence by the mercy of God. The door immediately facing the reader is the one from which the Prophet was dragged. The day following (Sunday) he preached, scarified as he was, from the front steps of Father Johnson's residence to an immense congregation.

whose servants they were, as "blind leaders of the blind." The multitudes were blinded by the popular prejudice and cry of "away with them"; and all going together to the pit; just as the Master saw, and upon the cross "prayed His Father to forgive them as they knew not what they did." Our Prophet Joseph, like the Master, was held in contempt by learned priests, bigots and hypocrites, and like Him, was scorned, despised, and derided by the rich; and by all Christendom was derided without cause, and persecuted unto death by those who would not know him.

Excerpt from letter of Benjamin F. Johnson to George S. Gibbs.

JOSEPH SMITH IS TARRED AND FEATHERED

By John D. Barber

While on a mission in the Northern States, and laboring in the city of Grand Rapids, Michigan, on March 24, 1902, I, in company with Lorenzo Sorenson of Smithfield, Utah, were tracting from house to house and called at the home of a Mr. Silas Raymond who was in possession of two relics in the shape of a tar bucket and a dark lantern used the night of the horrible mobbing of the Prophet Joseph which occurred on March 25, 1832. Mr. Raymond answered the door and when we introduced ourselves as Mormon missionaries, he uttered an oath "G— D— you Mormons, come in. I want to show you something." He excused himself and returned in a few minutes with a tar bucket which was made from a block of wood 8 inches in diameter and 10 or 12 inches in height, chiseled out to make a bucket, a hole bored through each side at the top and a piece of rope knotted at each end to make the handle. It was a very crude affair. It was covered with hard tar both inside and out and had never been used for anything after the mobbing. The lantern was called a dark lantern; and was about the size of a one gallon can. It had a pointed top on it to shed rain and a wire handle attached, with a little door cut in the side, through which a candle was put into the can and lighted. There were perforations— diamondshape, heart shape and crescent shape, also decorations were used to let the light flicker out.

Upon returning with these relics he uttered another oath: ("There they are, G—d—you.") and placed them before us saying:—"Pick 'em up; handle 'em; look 'em over," and stated that they were used on the night of the mobbing of the Prophet Joseph Smith at Hiram, Ohio, while at the home of Brother Johnson.

He stated that this bucket filled with liquid tar was poured over the head of Joe Smith and he was rolled onto a feather tick which had been ripped open and was rolled into the feathers.

Mr. Raymond stated that his father was one of the leaders of the mob and that from the time of this mobbing something seemed to have come upon his father that he was never well again; was finally confined to his bed where slow death came upon him, mortification setting in at his toes and he died by inches as mortification worked its way upward. Before dying he called his family together and talked with them regarding the mobbing and their future course in life, stating that his days were numbered, but he wanted to tell them that so far as he was concerned they could please themselves which religious denomination they affiliated themselves with, but for his part he was convinced that Joe Smith was all that he ever claimed to be—a prophet of God.

After viewing these relics, and returning to our rooms, we thought a great deal about them and wrote to President Joseph F. Smith, President of the Church, asking if he thought such relics would be genuine. We received an answer to our letter stating that there was no question but what they were genuine and instructed us to buy the relics from Mr. Raymond if a reasonable price could be agreed on, so that they could be put in the Church museum. Mr. Raymond refused to sell them stating that they had been handed down from his father's death to the oldest member of the family and they were to be kept in the family as long as they desired to have them. He said they were of no use to him, the Church should have them but it was his father's request that they should be kept in the family.

Two of this Mr. Raymond's aunts joined the Church and moved West with the Saints.

Signed: John D. Barber

STATE OF UTAH   }
COUNTY OF SUMMIT } ss.

John D. Barber being duly sworn, deposes and says that the foregoing statement is a true recital of events as they occurred and happened according to his knowledge.

In witness whereof, he has set his hand and signature this 28th day of September, 1948.   CHAS. L. FROST
County Clerk in and for the
County of Summit, State of
Utah.

THE FATE OF OTHERS IN THIS AFFAIR

In connection with the above persecution, the following is quoted from E. Cecil McGavin's book: *Historical Background of the Doctrine and Covenants*, (p. 196). "Within a few years all the men who took part in that raid had suffered a painful death. Miles Norton who poisoned the Johnson watch dog was killed by a ram in the barnyard, its spiral horn being thrust through Norton's body. Warren Waste and Carnot Mason boasted of having bent the Prophet's legs over his back, holding them in that position as he lay on the ground face downward. Waste was later killed by a falling log while he was building a house. Mason died from a spinal affliction that was more painful than a Boston Crab. The man who tried to pour the poison into his mouth was buried alive while digging a well."

DEVILS INCARNATE LED BY SECTARIAN MINISTERS

(An account of the mobbing which took place [March 25th, 1832] at Hiram, where Joseph lived, at the time, with "Father Johnson," is thus related by Joseph):

"On the 25th of March, the twins before mentioned, which had been sick of the measels for some time, caused us to be broken of our rest in taking care of them, especially my wife. In the evening I told her she had better retire to rest with one of the children, and I would watch with the sickest child. In the night she told me I had better lay down on the trundle bed, and I did so, and was soon after awoke by her screaming *murder!* when I found myself going out of the door, in the hands of about a dozen men; some of whose hands were in my hair, and some hold of my shirt, drawers and limbs. The foot of the trundle bed was towards the door, leaving only room enough for the door to swing. My wife heard a gentle tapping on the windows, which she then took no particular notice of, (but which was unquestionably designed for ascertaining whether we were all asleep,) and soon after the mob burst open the door and surrounded the bed in an instant, and, as I said, the first I knew I was going out of the door in the hands of an infuriated mob. I made a desperate struggle, as I was forced out, to extricate myself, but only cleared one leg, with which I made a pass at one man, and he fell on the door steps. I was immediately confined again; and they swore by God, they would kill me if I did not be still, which quieted me. As they passed around the house with me, the fellow that I kicked came to me and thrust his hand into my face, all covered with blood, (for I hit him on the nose,) and with an exulting horse laugh, muttering 'he, hee, G——d damn ye, I'll fix ye.'

"Then they seized me by the throat and held on until I lost my breath. After I came to, as they passed along with me, about thirty rods from the house, I saw Elder Rigdon stretched out on the ground, whither they had dragged him by the heels. I supposed he was dead.

"I began to plead with them, saying, 'you will have mercy, and spare my life, I hope.' To which they replied, 'G——d damn ye, call on yer God fer help, we'll show ye no mercy'; and the people began to show themselves in every direction; one coming from the orchard had a plank, and I expected they would kill me, and carry me off on the plank. They then turned to the right, and went on about thirty rods farther, about sixty rods from the house, and thirty from where I saw Elder Rigdon, into the meadow, where they stopped, and one said, 'Simonds, Simonds' (meaning, I suppose, Simonds Rider,) 'pull up his drawers, pull up his drawers, he will take cold. Another replied: 'aint ye going to kill 'im? aint ye going to kill 'im?' when a group of mobbers collected a little way off, and said: 'Simonds, Simonds, come here'; and Simonds charged those who had hold of me to keep me from touching the ground, (as they had done all the time) lest I should get a spring upon them. They went and held a council, and as I could occasionally overhear a word, I supposed it was to know whether it was best to kill me. They returned after a while, when I learned that they had concluded not to kill me, but pound and scratch me well, tear off my shirt and drawers, and leave me naked. One cried, 'Simonds, Simonds, *where's the tar bucket?*' 'I don't know,' answered one, 'where 'tis; Eli's left it.' They ran back and fetched the bucket of tar, when one exclaimed, 'G——d damn it, let us tar up his mouth;' and they tried to force the tar-paddle in my mouth.

I twisted my head around, so that they could not; and they cried out, 'G—d damn ye, hold up yer head, and let us give ye some tar.' They then tried to force a vial into my mouth, and I broke it in my teeth. All my clothes were torn off me except my shirt collar; and one man fell on me and scratched my body with his nails like a mad cat, and then muttered out: 'G—d damn ye, that's the way the Holy Ghost falls on folks.'

"They then left me, and I attempted to arise, but fell again; I pulled the tar away from my lips, etc., so that I could breathe more freely, and after awhile I began to recover, and raised myself up, when I saw two lights. I made my way towards one of them, and found it was Father Johnson's. When I had come to the door, I was naked, and the tar made me look as though I had been covered with blood, and when my wife saw me she thought I was all mashed to pieces, and fainted. During the affray abroad, the sisters of the neighborhood had collected at my room. I called for a blanket; they threw me one and shut the door: I wrapped it around me and went in."

In this inhuman onslaught, Sidney Rigdon was dragged by his heels over the frozen ground until his head was badly lacerated, which rendered him delirious for several days. "Father Johnson" was also roughly handled. Joseph's friends spent the remainder of the night in removing the tar and washing and cleansing his body, so that he could be clothed again. The next day was Sunday, and true to his mission, and agreeably with his determined purpose to do the will of heaven, he went to meeting, with his "flesh all scarified and defaced," and preached to a congregation, among whom were the identical mobbers who had thus invaded his home, dragged him from his imploring wife and sick children, and abused him in a manner disgraceful even to the character of savages, and in the afternoon baptized three individuals.

Owing to the exposure to which the sick children were subjected through this sudden and cruel demonstration, one of them received a severe cold and died soon afterwards.

The mobbers were mostly, if not entirely, professors of religion. Simonds Rider, the leader of the mob, was a Campbellite preacher. Not satisfied with the cruelties inflicted, they kept up their aggressive demonstrations around "Father Johnson's" for some time afterwards.   *The Martyrs*, pp. 22-24.

THE FIRST APOSTATES OF THE CHURCH

By B. H. Roberts

Beautiful for situation is Hiram, one of the many incorporated hamlets of northern Ohio.

A mile and a half westward from what Hiramites call the "center," meaning by that the college campus and the neat modern cottage homes that face it as a public square, is the old "Johnson homestead," where the Prophet Joseph Smith lived for some months during the eventful years of 1831 and 1832. Here in the east upper room he, with Sidney Rigdon as scribe, "translated" or what would be more appropriate to say "revised" the King James' translation of the Bible. Here, on the front steps of the Johnson residence, the Prophet frequently preached to the multitudes that came from the surrounding country to hear him. Here several revelations were received, including what will doubtless be regarded as the grandest revelation of all, that God has given in this dispensation of the fullness of times—namely, the vision of the future glories to which men may attain. That revelation which upsets the theology of modern Christendom, and makes it clear that God is indeed just, and that men can be, and will be judged according to the deeds done in the body whether they be good or evil.

Here, too, the Prophet suffered one of the most painful and brutal persecutions that overtook him in his eventful career. On the night of the 25th of March, 1832, the Johnson residence was quietly surrounded by a mob of the Prophet's enemies, determined to kill him, or do him great bodily injury. Worn out with watching over the sick children of John Murdock, whom the prophet's wife Emma, had taken to rear as her own, Joseph did not hear the tapping on the windowpane, which was doubtless made by the mob to ascertain if all were asleep in the household. The first thing the Prophet was conscious of was the screams of his wife and the fact that he was being carried bodily from the house into the field. (See preceding article: "Devil's Incarnate Led by Sectarian Ministers.")

The treatment of Sidney Rigdon on the same occasion was more severe. He was dragged by the heels over the hard frozen ground for a distance of some 30 rods, beaten into insensibility, covered with tar and feathers, and left for dead. He was living just across the road from Father Johnson's, in a log house, at the time of the outrage, and for several days was delirious. The villagers point out to this day the oak tree under which he was tarred and feathered. "Why did the mob abuse these men," I asked Hartwell Rider, to whom I had been recommended as the "wise man" of the village, well versed in the history and folklore of the neighborhood. "Well, the people did not want Hiram to be a Mormon center; and there was a man down at Shallersville whose wife had joined the Mormon Church and was agoing with the Mormons to Missouri—that was their Zion then, you know." By the way, this Hartwell Rider, with whom I talked for the better part of half a day, is the son of Simonds Rider, a noted Campbellite preacher, who joined the Church at Hiram in 1831. From remarks made by the different members of the mob who assaulted the Prophet on that night of the 25th of March, 1832, Simonds Rider was the leader of the mob; but his son Hartwell denies it, and asks that it be erased from the "Mormon" books. "Well," I replied, "that may be somewhat difficult, but I am happy to know that you denounce the mobbing, and are anxious to sever the association of your father's name with such an infamy."

It may be of interest to remark also that Simonds Rider and Ezra Booth were among the first apostates of the Church. The thing which took Rider out of the Church is rather humorous.

It is claimed by his son, Hartwell, who seems a little ashamed that his father ever was a "Mormon," that a revelation was received by Joseph to the effect that Rider was to be an Elder in the Church, and preach the Gospel, "but unfortunately," says the son, "both in the revelation and in the Elder's certificate the name Rider was spelled R-y-d-e-r instead of R-i-d-e-r." This led the former Campbellite preacher to "suspect" the inspiration that could make a mistake in orthography, and so he left the Church! Ezra Booth generally, though erroneously supposed to be the first apostate from the Church, also lived at Hiram for a time, and here wrote the anti-"Mormon" letters which will be his chief claim to fame. "What became of Booth after he left the Mormon Church?" I asked Hartwell Rider, "Did he prosper, was he a successful man?" The old man shook his head. "No; if you mean in a business way. Nor in any other way, for matter of that. You see, he was not a strong man. He tried to please everybody to whom he preached. He was not a man to take a stand and draw people to him. He preached for the Methodists for a while, after he left the Mormons, and then he went to spiritualism, then became an infidel and died here a few years ago at Garretsville without any faith in God or man." "Alas!" I mentally exclaimed, "how alike is the fate of those who turn from the faith in the restored Gospel of Jesus Christ! What a sad repetition it is—this wrecking of faith in 'God and man' when men who have received the light turn from it to darkness! It was promised in the very inception of the work that it should be a saver of life unto life or of death unto death, and truly the experience of the Church proves the declaration true. Anti-Mormon writers cite the fact here alluded to as an evidence of the soul-destroying power of Mormonism, saying that it leaves a trail of infidelity wherever it has been received. That is true, however, only in so far as men having once given to it their allegiance, then turn away from it. The beggarly elements from which it called them could never seem quite the same to them after they had once tasted the good word of God and the powers of the world to come." But those who have remained true to "Mormonism" and the obligations it enjoins, have not lost faith either in God or man; but have died happy in the hope and may I not say, knowledge, of the reality of that eternal life which God, who cannot lie, promised before the world began.

Thoughtful men will look deeper for the meaning of what all admit is a singular fact, viz.: that those who accept "Mormonism" and then turn from it end in believing in nothing: and they will see in that fact the evidence that these men have touched in their lives some very vital truth, and proving recreant to it has left them truth-stranded, by which I mean stripped of the truth or the power to comprehend it or hold to it. In them the word of God is verified: "For it is impossible for those who were once enlightened, and have tasted of the heavenly gift and were made partakers of the Holy Ghost . . . if they shall fall away to renew them again to repentance; seeing they crucify to themselves the Son of God afresh and put Him to an open shame."

Deseret Semi-Weekly News, Oct. 13, 18—.

THE MOTHER OF HARLOTS WILL PERSECUTE THE SAINTS

BY ORSON PRATT

Although the great "mother of abominations" has not gathered together in multitudes upon the face of the earth against the Lamb of God and his Saints, yet there has been enough fulfilled to show that the balance will be accomplished. Has this great and abominable power, under the name of the "mother of harlots," popularly called Christendom, fought against the Saints in this country? Let the history of this Church answer that question; let the scenes we have passed through in the land of Missouri testify; let the tribulation this people had to endure in the State of Illinois bear witness. We will not refer to persecutions in Utah, for here we have had but little compared with scenes we have passed through in former years. Suffice it to say, multitudes have been gathered together, under the influence of what? Under the influence of that great and abominable church or system called "the mother of harlots."

When we come to search to the bottom of this matter, we find that it has been the great influence which has produced all the persecutions that have come upon the Latter-day Saints since the organization of this Church. How many preachers were gathered together in the western part of Missouri, at the time we were driven from the State, to give their advice in a pretended court-martial to have some fifteen or twenty of the leaders of this people taken out and shot on the public square the next morning? There were not less than seventeen priests who advised the measure.

When we come to hunt for the great influence that has existed on the multitudes that gathered to persecute the Saints of the Lamb of God, we find it proceeding from the pulpit. Through the false-hoods of priests and the publishing of false principles, they have endeavored to set on the frenzied multitude to put to death the Latter-day Saints and deprive them of citizenship.***

Let us now go to Canada, and there a religious influence existed, mobs arose, multitudes were gathered together, and the Saints were stoned, hunted, and driven to and fro, and had to flee from place to place. This persecution was raised by the "mother of harlots," the "mother of abominations," because of what? Because we told them the Lord had revealed the same kind of religion in our day that he had eighteen hundred years ago. Go to England, and the same has happened there. Multitudes and multitudes started up against us. The Elders have had forty to fifty police to guard them from their meetings to their homes, to keep them from being destroyed by the tens of thousands of people that *blockaded* the streets for miles in length.

I know these things to be facts from actual experience. I have passed through them. I have had tens of thousands rush upon me with the fury of tigers, and they were only restrained by the power of God.*** Go to Denmark and we find the same opposing power; and whenever this Church has been organized, or a branch established, the "mother of abominations" has marshalled her host.

Masterful Writings of Orson Pratt, by N. B. Lundwall, pp. 138-140.

CHAPTER 5

Conspiracies Against the Life of
the Prophet Joseph

JUDASES OF THE PROPHET JOSEPH

At a meeting of the city council in December, 1843, the subject of the menace to the city and the mayor was under consideration, and Joseph said among other things:

> I am exposed to far greater danger from traitors among ourselves than from enemies without, although my life has been sought for many years by the civil and military authorities, priests and people of Missouri; and if I can escape from the ungrateful treachery of assassins, I can live *as Caesar might have lived, were it not for a right-hand Brutus.* I have had pretended friends betray me. All the enemies upon the face of the earth may roar and exert all their power to bring about my death, but they can accomplish nothing, unless some who are among us, who have enjoyed our society, have been with us in our councils, participated in our confidence, taken us by the hand, called us brother, saluted us with a kiss, join with our enemies, turn our virtues into faults, and, by falsehood and deceit, stir up their wrath and indignation against us, and bring their united vengeance upon our heads. All the hue and cry of the chief priests and elders against the Savior could not bring down the wrath of the Jewish nation upon his head, and thereby cause the crucifixion of the Son of God, until Judas said unto them. 'Whomsoever I shall kiss he is the man; hold him fast.' Judas was one of the Twelve Apostles, even their treasurer, and dipped with their Master in the dish, and through his treachery, the crucifixion was brought about; and WE HAVE A JUDAS IN OUR MIDST.

The Judas spirit manifested itself in Nauvoo in the spring of 1844. Alarmed by the Prophet's declaration that there was a right hand Brutus near him, some of the men who were willing to betray him feared that their machinations were discovered and that vengeance might be wreaked upon them. William Law and William Marks both feared or affected to fear for their lives. They made complaint which reached the ears of the Prophet, and he ordered an investigation in which they were allowed the fullest license to examine witnesses. The result was to show to them how utterly groundless was their fear; but further it showed to all the Saints that these men were not faithful. The people said:

"Is it possible that Brother Law or Brother Marks is a traitor and would deliver Joseph into the hands of his enemies in Missouri? If not, what can be the meaning of this? The righteous are bold as a lion."

Joseph merely quoted:

"The wicked flee when no man pursueth."

But from this time on he knew from what quarter to expect the kiss of Judas. Jealousy of the Prophet and their personal impurity led several leading men to apostasy and to a thirst for

Joseph's blood. Among them were William Law, Wilson Law, Chauncey L. Higbee, Francis M. Higbee and Robert D. Foster. They became his avowed enemies; but in secret sympathy with them were Sidney Rigdon, William Marks and Austin A. Cowles.

William Law was the leader of the movement. He declared that Joseph was a fallen Prophet, and he attempted to set up a church of his own. These apostates sought by every means in their power to precipitate bloodshed in Nauvoo. They flagrantly violated the law; insulted, abused and threatened the officers; usurped official prerogatives; attempted to shoot Joseph; and spread throughout the country, and even beyond its confines, the most wicked misrepresentations and complaints concerning Joseph and the municipal administration of Nauvoo.

The Prophet had long known of their treachery and had warned the Saints that Judases were in their midst, without naming the individuals. He knew that in a little time the traitors would betray themselves. When this expectation of the Prophet's was realized and the Saints were enabled to see the perfidy of these men, they were excommunicated.

After this it seemed as if Satan was turned loose in their souls. Having no longer any profit in concealment they blazoned forth their hatred for the Prophet and their own iniquities. Some of them confessed that they knew that their sins were finding them out and that they would soon have no reputation to lose anyhow, and therefore they would persecute the Prophet and try to drag him down with them. At this time anonymous letters threatening the lives of Joseph and Hyrum were received and every conceivable annoyance was perpetrated upon them.

On Saturday, the 25th day of May, 1844, the Prophet was informed that he had been indicted at Carthage for the alleged offenses of polygamy and perjury on the testimony of William Law and others. Two days later learning that warrants were out for him from the circuit court upon these indictments, he determined to proceed to Carthage and give himself up. He had a double purpose to serve in this action: He desired as usual to show his respect for law and legal process; and he wanted to avoid having a Carthage mob come into Nauvoo to serve the writs. At Carthage he was informed by Charles Foster and other apostates, who repented their purpose for the moment, that a plot had been laid for his death and that it was determined that he should not leave that place alive. He secured lawyers and endeavored to have his case brought forward for trial; but the prosecution insisted upon delay and secured a postponement until the next term. In the meantime Joseph was to be released on bail satisfactory to the sheriff; and that officer told him to go his way without bonds until called upon.

His friends gathered around him when he prepared to depart for home, and by this means his life was saved, for armed men threatened him and tried by force and stratagem to detain him in Carthage until after dark that they might the better accomplish the assassination. But he knew their plot and departed, riding Joe Duncan and accompanied by Hyrum and others, and reached home at 9 o'clock that evening.

Life of Joseph the Prophet, by Geo. Q. Cannon, pp. 430, 449-51.

CHARACTER OF CONSPIRATORS

By George Q. Cannon

William and Wilson Law, Chauncey L. and Francis M. Higbee, Dr. Robert D. Foster, and others, were rank, bloodthirsty apostates. They were leagued together, and had for their associates men who were resolved to kill the prophet if they could. "Anti-Mormon" organizations and mobs could have had but little influence if all who had made profession of being Latter-day Saints had been true to their brethren and their religion. But these men had transgressed the laws of God, they had indulged in adultery, whoredom and lust, and had, therefore, lost the Spirit of the Lord.

Besides these open and avowed apostates, there were men still remaining in the Church who sympathized with them, and who, at heart, were traitors to Joseph, and the work of God. Prominent among these were Sidney Rigdon, William Marks and Austin A. Cowles. There were many others, also, of lesser note. One of these was a man by the name of James Blakeslee. We recollect very distinctly hearing him, one Sunday, during this Spring (1844,) speak from the public stand, and in the course of his remarks he bore testimony to the truth of the work of God, and that Joseph was a prophet of God. It was the afternoon of that same day, or if not that day it was directly afterwards, he went and united himself with William Law's party and became an open apostate. Law at that time was declaring that Joseph was a fallen prophet, and was trying to form a church of his own.   *Instructor*, Vol. 14.

AFFIDAVIT OF HANNAH R. LARSON AND ADESSA LARSON CHRISTENSEN

Hannah R. Larson whose maiden name was Hannah R. Stoddard, and Adessa Larson Christensen who is the daughter of Hannah R. Stoddard Larson, depose and say:

Charles Henry Stoddard was born on the 21st of April, 1827, in Newark, New Jersey, his parents being Israel Stoddard and Sarah Woodward. As a boy he was employed by the Prophet Joseph Smith, in Nauvoo, Illinois. While the Prophet was in hiding, he carried food to the Prophet and delivered messages to and from the Prophet. The Prophet trusted him implicitly. Upon one occasion, when in the street fixing a kite, with other boys, a man came up and inquired where the Prophet was, to which Charles replied: "He went to heaven on Hyrum's white horse and we are fixing this kite to send his dinner to him." No one suspected his important duties because of his youth.

While employed by the Prophet Joseph, William Law requested Charles to come and work for him. He did not want to. After consulting the Prophet, he decided to do so. During his employment with William Law, many private matters were talked of by Law and his associates in the presence of the boy, without any hesitation, perhaps thinking that the boy would not pay any attention to what was said. The boy was nevertheless on the alert and took full cognizance of what was going on.

Upon retiring one evening, in a lean-to attached to a building which was partly vacant and partly used for storage purposes, the lad was awakened by conversation being held in the vacant portion of the building. This building was a rendezvous of the bitter apostates and enemies of the Prophet among whom was William Law, who seemed to be a ringleader. The lad listened through a hole in the log structure through which light was also emerging, and learned that these men were plotting against the Prophet's life. He heard Law tell this group of apostates that he would have Charles clean, oil and load his gun which was one of his regular duties. After the group had disbanded and had all left the building, the lad dressed and hurried to the home of the Prophet and told him all that he had seen and heard and asked the Prophet what he should do. The Prophet told him to return and act as though nothing had happened, and to do as his employer requested, and admonished him to load the gun well. He told the boy that they could not hurt him until his time had arrived. The boy did as requested. The next morning, Mr. Law requested him to clean, oil and load his six shooter, which was faithfully done as the Prophet advised. When the opportune time arrived, Law aimed the revolver at the Prophet with the intention of killing him. He pulled the trigger but the gun mis-fired as did all of the other five loads in the six shooter. He cursed because the gun did not discharge, and blamed the boy for not loading the weapon properly. The boy replied that he had done it to the best of his ability. Law then aimed at a post and all six loads were discharged.

Years afterwards when Charles Henry Stoddard had emigrated to Utah, and living in Richmond, Utah, Joseph Smith, the son of the Prophet Joseph and also the president of the Reorganized Church, visited Stoddard and stayed over night in his home. This statement Hannah R. Stoddard also affirms as she saw him in Richmond.

The foregoing data was had from information told to Hannah R. Stoddard by her grandfather Charles Henry Stoddard, and by oft repeated stories recited to Adessa Larson Christensen by her grandfather George Henry Stoddard, the eldest son of Charles Henry Stoddard and Anna Telford, and is related to the best of their knowledge and memory.

In Witness to the truthfulness of the foregoing statement, the parties first before mentioned have hereunto signed their names.

Signed: Hannah R. Larson

Signed: Adessa Larson Christensen

TOWN OF ASHTON } ss.
STATE OF IDAHO }

Before me, a Notary Public in and for the State of Idaho, appeared Hannah R. Larson and Adessa Larson Christensen and affixed their signatures to the foregoing statement.

In witness whereof, I have hereunto affixed my Notarial Seal, this 15th day of October, 1949.

HIRAM G. FULLER
(SEAL)   Notary Public

JUDASES FIRST SIN AND NEXT BETRAY

By George Q. Cannon

Do you doubt the existence of a devil and of evil spirits? Need I ask the Latter-day Saints this? Have you not seen his spirit manifested? You have seen men and women in this Church who once were faithful and devoted to the work of God; but they fell into sin, and another spirit took possession of them. Men as high as members of the First Presidency have done this. *I remember very well William Law, counselor to the Prophet Joseph, a friend of the Prophet, a friend of God apparently, a staunch man in the Church; but he committed sin, and that man, who had occupied that high and exalted station, compassed the death of the Prophet. He was one of the chief conspirators in arranging plans for his destruction, and took an active part in urging on his martyrdom. Members of the council of the Twelve Apostles also partook of the same spirit.* It is the spirit that Satan possesses; for Jesus said of him that he was a liar and a murderer from the beginning. He is seeking constantly to destroy the work of God, filling men with his spirit, and urging them forward to acts of deadly hate, even to kill and to destroy. That is the spirit of Satan, and we see it manifested in men. *Millennial Star, 60:214.*

MURDEROUS INTENTIONS OF WILLIAM LAW

Affidavit of Jesse Price Before Aaron Johnson

"State of Illinois, County of Hancock, ss.

On the 5th day of August, 1844, personally appeared before me, Aaron Johnson, justice of the peace in and for said county, Jesse Price; and after being duly sworn according to law, deposeth and saith, that on or about the 18th of April, 1844, in the city of Nauvoo, county aforesaid, William Law said, 'I put pistols in my pockets one night, and went to Joseph Smith's house, determined to blow his infernal brains out, but I could not get the opportunity to shoot him then, but I am determined I will shoot him the first opportunity, and you will see blood and thunder and devastation in this place, but I shall not be here;' and deponent saith not further." *D.H.C. 7:227*

ANOTHER WITNESS TESTIFIES

By Sarah H. Thomas

Charles Henry Stoddard was born April 21, 1827, at New Jersey. His parents and family joined the church and moved to Nauvoo in 1842, he being 15 years old and the eldest of the family of six. They suffered the persecutions with the rest of the saints.

He lived with the Prophet Joseph for a while. *He also worked for William Law, one of the outlaws and leaders of the gang that was continually plotting and planning against the Prophet. Mr. Law, not knowing that Mr. Stoddard was a friend of the Prophet or interested in him in any way, was not as careful when talking of him as he otherwise would have been. Father (Mr. Stoddard) slept upstairs directly over the room where Mr. Law and his associates held their secret meetings and could hear distinctly all their plans, and as there happened to be a hole in the floor, he could look down and see who was there. He would then go and tell the Prophet of their plans and in this way he was kept posted to the traps that they set for him.*

In April 1846, two years after the death of the Prophet, they were ordered out of Nauvoo. They crossed the Mississippi river in an old wooden boat they had fixed. They took with them two feather beds, a little clothing and some provisions. When they were crossing the river, they looked back and saw their homes being burned. Through the exposure and hardships their parents and one brother (an infant) died; the mother died first and the babe five weeks later. Six weeks from the time the mother died, the father passed away, leaving five children homeless and almost penniless, but not friendless, as the saints were very kind to them and helped them all they could.

Dictated to the compiler of this book on Sunday, July 9, 1939.

CONSPIRACY OF NAUVOO

By Horace H. Cummings

The following note was dictated to the Compiler of this book on Aug. 8, 1932, by Horace H. Cummings, the author of the article: The Nauvoo Conspiracy.

"The article called **THE NAUVOO CONSPIRACY**, printed in Volume 5, beginning about page 250, of the **CONTRIBUTOR**, which was the Y.M.M.I.A. organ at that time; the incidents related in that article were related to my parents by Dennison L. Harris, who was Bishop of Monroe, Sevier County, at that time, at our home during the spring conference of 1883, Brother Harris stopping at our home as our guest. The incidents seemed so important and so intensely interesting that I wrote them in my journal in detail. As the CONTRIBUTOR was offering a prize for a Christmas Story, I extended my journal account somewhat and wrote that article in competition for the prize. Before submitting the article to the press, however, at the request of President John Taylor, I read it to him line by line as he was in Nauvoo at the time the narration deals with and the incidents happened and of course was with the Prophet at the time he was killed. He was familiar with many of the things to which the article refers and added certain elements to the story. When completed, President Taylor gave it his hearty approval for publication as a valuable document concerning Church history which had never been previously published. The secret was held between the Prophet and his body guard, John Scott who was the brother of Robert Scott, the companion of Dennison L. Harris.

"The Prophet Joseph placed the two young men above mentioned under covenant that they would not reveal what took place as related in this CONSPIRACY for twenty years. The first time that it was revealed was at the dedication of the St. George Temple, when Brother Harris revealed it to President Brigham Young,

whereupon President Young called in Brother Gibbs who took the
narration in shorthand for church record purposes."
Signed: Horace H. Cummings

Those who have read the life of Joseph Smith, the Prophet,
must be familiar with the fact that from his earliest boyhood he
was ever the object of bitter persecution.   Notwithstanding the
numerous published accounts of mobbings, drivings, bodily injuries, aggravating accusations, mock trials, and murderous attempts upon his life which he endured, and with which the people are familiar, there are, no doubt, many events and trials yet
hidden from the world in the bosoms of his most familiar friends
which may have caused him far greater agony than many of those
with which the public are acquainted.   Among these the following
narrative may be classed, as it has never before been published,
and the facts it contains may have had an important influence in
hastening, if not really accomplishing, the death of the Prophet.

Early in the spring of 1844 a very strong and bitter feeling
was aroused against Joseph, among many of his brethren in and
around Nauvoo; and some who held high positions in the Church
and were supposed to be his best friends, turned against him and
sought by various means in their power to do him injury.   Many
murmured and complained, and some of the more wicked even
watched their opportunity to take his life, and were continually
plotting to accomplish that end.   At length this wicked feeling became so strong and general among a certain class, that it was resolved to form an organization, or secret combination, that would
better enable them to accomplish their wicked purposes.

Accordingly a secret meeting was appointed to take place in
the new brick house of William Law, Joseph's first counselor, on
a certain Sabbath, and invitations to attend it were carefully extended to members of the Church whom it was thought were dis-
affected, or in sympathy with these wicked views and desires.
Among those who received invitations to attend this meeting was
Brother Dennison L. Harris, now the Bishop of Monroe, Sevier
County, Utah, then but a young man of seventeen years of age.
Austin A. Cowles, at that time a member of the High Council, was
one of the leaders in this wicked movement, and being a near
neighbor and on intimate terms with Brother Harris, he had given
young Dennison an invitation to the secret meeting, and told him
also to invite his father, but to be sure and not breathe a word
about it to anyone else, as it was to be kept a profound secret.
Dennison was much perplexed over the invitation he had received,
and certain things that Brother Cowles had told him; and while sitting on his father's woodpile, thinking them over and wondering
what he had better do, another young man, named Robert Scott,
who lived but a short distance away, came over, sat down on the
log, and the two began to converse upon various subjects such as
generally engage the conversation of young men of their age.   It
seems they had been intimate companions for several years; and
they had not conversed long before each discovered that the other
had something on his mind which troubled him, but which he
did not like to reveal.   Finally, one proposed that, as they had

always been confidants, they now exchange secrets, on condition that neither should reveal what the other told him.

Both readily agreed to this, and when each had told the cause of his anxiety, it proved to be the same—both had received an invitation to the same secret meeting. Robert Scott, having been reared by William Law, seemed to be almost a member of his family, and on this account had been invited by him to attend the meeting.

"Well, Den," said Robert, after a short pause, "are you going to attend the meeting?"

"I don't know," replied Dennison, "are you?"

"I don't know whether to go or not," said Robert; "suppose we go in the house and tell your father of his invitation, and see what he says about it."

They entered the house and consulted for some time with Dennison's father, Emer Harris, who was a brother of Martin Harris, one of the three witnesses of the Book of Mormon. They informed him of his invitation to the same meeting, and told him many other things that Brother Cowles had told Dennison. He decided to go at once and lay the whole matter before the Prophet Joseph Smith, who was then in Nauvoo, and ask his advice. He immediately went to Joseph's house, a distance of about two and a half miles, and informed him of the whole affair. Joseph listened with interest until he had finished, when he said: "Brother Harris, I would advise you not to attend those meetings, nor pay any attention to them. You may tell the boys, however, that I would like to have them go, but I want them to be sure to come and see me before the meeting takes place. I wish to give them some counsel."

Subsequent events showed the wisdom of Joseph in advising Brother Emer Harris not to attend the meeting, and selecting young men to do the work he wished to have accomplished. Brother Harris returned and told the boys what Joseph desired them to do, and they readily agreed to comply with his request. Accordingly, on the next Sunday before the secret meeting took place, Robert and Dennison called at the house of Joseph to learn what he wished them to do. He told them he desired that they should attend the meeting, pay strict attention, and report to him all their proceedings at the first favorable opportunity. He moreover cautioned them to have as little to say as possible, and to avoid giving any offense.

They attended the meeting as desired. There were quite a number present, and the time was mostly occupied in planning how to get at things the best, and effect an organization. Strong speeches were also made against the Prophet, and many lies were told to prejudice the minds of those present against him. This portion of the proceedings was not a difficult task, for the element of which the audience was composed was only too susceptible to such evil impressions, and those who spoke were eminently successful in producing the desired impressions, and arousing the feelings of enmity toward the Prophet, that they might wish to use in accomplishing his overthrow. It seems that the immediate cause of these wicked proceedings was the fact that Joseph had recently presented the revelation on Celestial Marriage to the High Council for their approval, and certain members were most bitterly opposed to it, and denounced Joseph as a fallen Prophet, and were determined to destroy him.

The meeting adjourned to convene again on the following Sabbath, and the two young men were invited to attend the next one also, but were cautioned not to tell a soul of what had transpired at the first one. At the first suitable opportunity they called upon Joseph, related to him what had taken place, and gave him the names of those who had taken part in the proceedings. The leading members among the conspirators, for such they really were, were William and Wilson Law, Austin A. Cowles, Francis and Chauncey Higbee, Robert Foster and his brother, two Hicks brothers, and two merchants, Finche and Rollinson, who were enemies to the Church. After hearing their report and asking several questions, which they answered to the best of their knowledge, Joseph said: "Boys, I would like you to accept their invitation and attend the second meeting. But come to me again next Sunday, before their meeting convenes, as I may have something more to say to you before you go."

At the expiration of a week they again went to see Joseph, who gave them the necessary advice, after which they went to the meeting. This time the conspirators were still more vehement in their abusive remarks about Joseph. New crimes that he had committed had been discovered, and the old ones were much magnified. Their accusations were not only against him, but against his brother Hyrum and other prominent men in Nauvoo. There seemed to be no end to the wickedness of which these good men were accused, as most of the time, until a late hour, was occupied by different ones in denouncing and accusing Joseph and his friends of the most heinous crimes. Before the meeting adjourned, however, it was agreed that they should all endeavor to work the matter up as much as possible during the week, that something definite might be accomplished towards effecting a more complete organization without further delay. The meeting was to convene again on the following Sunday. As the boys had kept quiet and said nothing against any of their proceedings, it was supposed, of course, that they were in sympathy with the movement, and an invitation was accordingly extended for them to attend the next meeting.

As on the previous occasion, the young men watched a fitting opportunity of reporting to Joseph without arousing the suspicions of any that attended the meeting. He listened attentively to the recital of all that had taken place at the second meeting, after which he said: "Boys, come to me again next Sunday. I wish you to attend the next meeting also." The boys promised to do so, and left the room. They kept the meetings and their connection with them, however, a profound secret from the rest of their friends, and at the appointed time again went to the house of Joseph to receive their usual instructions. This time he said to them, with a very serious countenance: "This will be your last meeting; this will be the last time that they will admit you into their councils. They will come to some determination. But be sure," he continued, "that you make no covenants, nor enter into any obligations whatever with them. Be strictly reserved, and make no promise either to conspire against me or any portion of the community. Be silent, and do not take any part in their deliberations." After a pause of some moments, he added: "Boys, this will be their last meeting, and they may shed your blood, but I hardly think they will, as you are so young. If they do, I will be a lion in their path! Don't flinch. If you have to die; die like men; you will be martyrs to the cause, and your crowns can be no greater. But," said he again, "I hardly think they will shed your blood."

This interview was a long one. Joseph's sensitive feelings were touched by the faith, generosity and love manifested by these young men in their willingness to undertake such a hazardous enterprise at his bidding. He blessed them and made them precious promises for their sacrifice, and told them if their lives were taken their reward would be all the greater. After leaving Joseph's house with his sincere wishes for their safety, the boys waited anxiously for the time of meeting to arrive. They fully realized the dangers into which they were about to plunge themselves, yet they did not shrink. They knew it was their duty, and they determined to attempt it at all hazards. They were now familiar with the names of the persons conspiring against Joseph, the object they had in view, and many of their plans for accomplishing that object. Moreover, they were supposed by the would-be murderers to be in perfect sympathy with all their hellish designs; and if, by any circumstance, they should arouse the suspicion that they were present at Joseph's request. or even with his knowledge, their lives in such a crowd would, indeed, be of little value. They determined to trust in the Lord and die rather than betray the Priesthood. Their feelings may perhaps be imagined as the time of meeting drew near, and they started off in the direction of William Law's house, where it was to be held. They certainly displayed faith that every young man in Israel should cultivate.

On arriving at the rendezvous they found, to their surprise and discomfiture, that the entrance to the house was guarded by men armed with muskets and bayonets. After being scrutinized from head to foot, and carefully cross-questioned, they succeeded in passing the guards and gaining admittance. From this it will be seen that great care was taken to prevent any person from entering, except those whom they knew to be of their party, and ready to adopt any measures that might be suggested against the Prophet Joseph. On entering they found considerable confusion and much counseling among the members of the conspiracy. All seemed determined that Joseph should die, yet objections were raised by some to each of the plans proposed.

The Prophet was accused of the most wicked acts, and all manner of evil was spoken of him. Some declared that he had sought to get their wives away from them, and had many times committed adultery. They said he was a fallen Prophet, and was leading the people to destruction. Joseph was not the only one against whom they lied. His brother Hyrum and many of the leading men in Nauvoo were accused of being in league with him and sharing his crimes. In these councilings and plannings, consider-able time was spent before the meeting was called to order, and anything definite commenced. The boys, however, followed Jo-seph's instructions, and remained quiet and reserved. This seemed to arouse the suspicions of some that they were not earnestly in favor of their wicked purposes, and some of the conspirators began to take especial pains to explain to the young men the great crimes that Joseph had committed, and the results that would follow if his wicked career were not checked, with a view to convincing them that their severe measures against Joseph were for the best good of the Church, and persuading them to take an active part with them in accomplishing this great good. The two boys, however, sat together quietly, and would simply answer their arguments by saying that they were only young boys, and did not understand such things, and would rather not take part in their proceedings.

As before stated, Brother Scott had been reared in the family of William Law, and the latter pretended great friendship for him on that account, and was very anxious to explain to him the object of the proposed organization, and induce him to join. He would come around and sit beside Robert, put his arm around his neck, and persuade, argue, and implore him to join in their effort to rid the Church of such a dangerous impostor. At the same time Broth-er Cowles would sit beside Brother Harris in the same attitude, and labor with him with equal earnestness. The boys, however, were not easily convinced. Still, in their replies and remarks, they carefully tried to avoid giving the least offense or arousing any suspicions regarding the true cause of their presence. They said they were too young to understand the "spiritual wife doctrine," of which Joseph was accused, and many of the other things that they condemned in the Prophet. Joseph had never done them any harm, and they did not like to join in a conspiracy against his life.

"But," they would urge, "Joseph is a fallen Prophet; he receives revelations from the devil, and is deceiving the people, and if some-thing decisive is not done at once to get rid of him, the whole Church will be led by him to destruction." These and many other arguments were vainly brought forth to induce the boys to join them, but they still pretended not to understand nor take much in-terest in such things. At length they ceased their persuasions, and, things having developed sufficiently, they concluded to proceed with the intended organization.

An oath had been prepared which each member of the organ-ization was now required to take. Francis Higbee, a justice of the peace, sat at a table in one end of the room, and administered the oath to each individual separately, in the following manner: The candidate would step forward to the table, take up a Bible, which had been provided for the purpose, and raise it in his right hand, whereupon the justice would ask him in a solemn tone, "Are you ready?" And, receiving answer in the affirmative, would continue in a tone and manner that struck awe to the minds of the boys as they listened: *"You solemnly swear, before God and all holy angels, and these your brethren by whom you are surrounded, that you will give your life, your liberty, your influence, your all, for the destruc-*

tion of Joseph Smith and his party, so help you God!" The person being sworn would then say, "I do," after which he would lay down the Bible and sign his name to a written copy of the oath in a book that was lying on the table, and it would be legally acknowledged by the justice of the peace.

The boys sat gazing upon this scene, wondering how intelligent beings who had once enjoyed the light of truth could have fallen into such depths of wickedness as to be anxious to take such an oath against the Prophet of God and his faithful followers. They also felt no little uneasiness concerning their own fate, and almost dreaded the moment when the last one should have taken the oath. *At length that portion of the business was accomplished, and about two hundred persons had taken the oath.* Among that number were three women, who were ushered in, closely veiled to prevent being recognized, and required to take the same oath. Besides doing this, they also testified that Joseph and Hyrum Smith had endeavored to seduce them; had made the most indecent and wicked proposals to them, and wished them to become their wives. After making affidavit to a series of lies of this kind, they made their exit through a back door. One of the women, whom the boys suspected as being William Law's wife, was crying, and seemed to dislike taking the oath, but did so as one who feared that the greatest bodily injury would surely follow a refusal.

After the oath had been administered to all but the two boys, Law, Cowles and others again commenced their labors to get them to take it, but met the same success as before. Arguments, persuasions and threats were in turn used to accomplish their desire, but in vain. They exhausted their ingenuity in inventing arguments, lies and inducements to get the boys to unite with their band. "Have you not heard," they said, "the strong testimony of all present against Joseph Smith? *Can a man be a true Prophet who would commit adultery? He is a fallen Prophet, and is teaching the people doctrines that his own imagination or lustful desires have invented, or else he received that revelation from the devil.* He will surely lead the whole Church to destruction if his career is not stopped. *We can do nothing with him by the law, and for the sake of the Church we deem it our solemn duty to accomplish his destruction and rescue the people from this peril.* We are simply combining and conspiring to save the Church, and we wish you to join us in our efforts, and share the honors that will be ours. Come, take the oath, and all will be well."

"Oh, we are too young," they replied, "to understand or meddle with such things, and would rather let others who are older and know more do such work. We came to your meetings because we thought you were our friends and gave us a kind invitation. We did not think there was any harm in it; but if you will allow us to go now, we will not trouble any more of your meetings. Joseph Smith has never done us any harm, and we do not feel like injuring him."

"Come, boys," said another of the crowd, "do as we have done. You are young and will not have anything to do in the affair, but we want you should keep it a secret, and act with us; that's all."

"No," replied the boys in a firm but cool tone, as they rose to leave, "we cannot take an oath like that against any man who has never done us the least injury." They would gladly have passed out and escaped the trouble they saw brewing for them; but, as they feared, they were not allowed to depart so easily. One of the band exclaimed in a very determined voice: "No, not by a d——d sight! You know all our plans and arrangements, and we don't propose that you should leave in that style. You've got to take that oath, or you'll never leave here alive."

The attention of all was now directed to the two boys, and considerable confusion prevailed. A voice shouted, "Dead men tell no tales!" whereupon a general clamor arose for the boys to take the oath or be killed. Even their pretended friends, Cowles and Law, turned against them. "If you do not take that oath," said one of the leading members, in a blood curdling tone, "we will cut your throats." The looks and conduct of the rest showed plainly that he had spoken only what they were ready to execute. It was evident the mob was eager for blood. That moment certainly must have been a trying one, but it seemed that fear had suddenly vanished from the bosoms of the two boys, and they coolly but positively again declared that they would not take that oath, nor enter into any other movement against the Prophet Joseph.

The mob was now enraged, as they thought they were betrayed, and it was with the greatest difficulty that the leaders succeeded in keeping them from falling upon the boys and cutting them to pieces. The leaders, however, were no less determined that the boys should die; but as the house in which the meeting was held stood but a short distance back from the street, they thought it better to be more quiet about it, lest some one might be passing and discover what was going on. Order was at last restored, when it was decided to take the boys down the cellar, where the deed could be more safely accomplished. Accordingly, a guard, with drawn swords and bowie knives, was placed on either side of the boys, while two others, armed with cocked muskets and bayonets. at their backs, brought up the rear as they were marched off in the direction of the cellar. William and Wilson Law, Austin Cowles, and others, accompanied them to the cellar. Before committing the murderous deed, however, they gave the boys one more chance for their lives. One of them said: "Boys, if you will take that oath your lives shall be spared; but you know too much for us to allow you to go free, and if you are still determined to refuse, we will have to shed your blood." But the boys, with most commendable courage, in the very jaws of death, once more rejected the only means that would save their lives.

At this juncture, when it seemed that each moment would end the earthly existence of these two noble young men, a voice from some one in the crowd, as if by Divine interposition, called out just in time to save their lives: "Hold on! Hold on there! Let's talk this matter over before their blood is shed!" and with great difficulty some of the more cautious ones succeeded in quieting those whose anger and excitement prevented them from weighing well what they were on the verge of committing, and considering the consequences that would inevitably follow. Thus the instantaneous death of the boys was prevented, while the crowd retired to the farther end of the room and consulted earnestly together, in so low a tone, however, that the boys could not hear what they said. It was evident, however, that they were nearly equally divided in their views of the feasibility of putting the boys to death. Some appeared to be enraged and fully determined to shed their blood, while others were equally resolved to prevent the cruel deed. During the discussion the boys distinctly heard one of them say: "The boys' parents very likely know where they are, and if they do not return home, strong suspicions will be aroused, and they may institute a search that would be very dangerous to us. It is already late, and time that the boys were home."

This was a very important consideration, as well as a very unexpected circumstance in favor of the boys. Hope rose high in their breasts as the discussion continued, and one by one of the more excited conspirators was silenced, if not convinced, until at length the tide turned in favor of the boys, and it was decided that they should be released. Some openly, and many in their feelings, opposed this resolution, as they considered it as unsafe to liberate the boys to reveal all their plans, as to kill them and get them out of the way.

A strong guard was provided to escort them to a proper distance, lest some of the gang might kill them before they made their escape. They placed a strict injunction upon the boys not to reveal anything they had seen or heard in these meetings, and declared if they did, any member of the conspiracy would kill them at first sight. This caution and threat were repeated several times in a way that gave the boys to understand that they meant all they said, and would just as leave slay them as not if they suspected anything had been revealed by them.

Everything being ready, the boys started off in charge of the guard. Right glad were they to once more gain the open air with so good a prospect for their lives, and they breathed a sigh of relief and satisfaction when they were out of sight of the house in which they had endured such great peril. They took an unfrequented road down toward the Mississippi River, which runs around one side of Nauvoo. Some of the guard were very much dissatisfied with the way the tables had turned, and, when they had got a safe distance from the house, they halted to consider if it would not be best to slay the boys on their own responsibility. They would gladly have murdered them if they could have done so with any hopes of having the deed remain undiscovered; but, after some discussion, they contented themselves by reiterating the cautions and threats that had been given to the boys before starting. They continued their march until within a few rods of the river, when they halted, and one of the guards said:

"Well, I guess we have gone about far enough, and had better turn back." Then turning to the boys, he continued, "Boys, if you ever open your mouths concerning anything you have seen or heard in any of our meetings, we will kill you by night or by day, wherever we find you, and consider it our duty."

"Oh, don't fear on that account," replied the boys, anxious to allay their uneasiness, lest they still might take a notion to slay them and cast their bodies into the river, "we can see that it is greatly to our advantage and necessary to our peace and safety to keep silent concerning these things."

"I'm glad you've got sense enough to see it in that light," was the rejoinder, in a tone that indicated his mind was somewhat relieved.

During this conversation, one of the boys looking towards the river, to his great surprise, saw a hand rise into view from behind the bank and beckon for them to come that way. The guards, after admonishing them once more to be silent, and telling them their lives depended upon their keeping the secret, turned to retrace their steps just as one of the boys, anxious to put them at ease as much as possible, said to his companion: "Let's go down to the river."

"Yes," returned the guard, evidently pleased with the arrangement; "you had better go down to the river."

The reader will readily understand that the meeting had lasted until a late hour in the afternoon, and the conspirators had already detained the boys so long, that they were afraid their parents and friends, some of whom perhaps knew where the boys had gone, would become anxious and begin to suspect foul play, and possibly might institute a search which would prove exceedingly disadvantageous to the conspiracy. The boys, therefore, very adroitly proposed to go to the river, so if they were found there it would be sufficient explanation for their long absence. The guards perceived the idea instantly, and it pleased them, for it indicated to them that the boys wished to keep the secret, and avoid being questioned too closely.

The boys started off on a run toward the river, but, lest the guards should watch them, and discover the presence of Joseph, whose hand it was they had seen above the bank, they directed their course to a point about a quarter of a mile beyond where Joseph was, knowing that he would follow them. On reaching the river, they stepped down the bank, and there awaited the arrival of the Prophet, while the guards returned to the meeting.

It seems that Joseph, knowing the danger into which the boys had gone, had become so uneasy at their long absence, that he could no longer remain at home, so he and one of his body guard, John Scott, who was the brother to Robert, started out to see if they could discover what had become of them. Perhaps they suspected the boys had been murdered, and that their bodies would be thrown into the stream, as William Law's house, where the meeting was held, was but a short distance from the river. At all events, they were there under the bank when the boys were liberated, and now glided around close to the water's edge to the point where the boys were awaiting them.

It was a joyful meeting; Joseph seemed delighted to see that the boys had escaped with their lives. The party walked on to a point nearly opposite Joseph's store, where a board fence came down to the edge of the river, forming, together with the orchard trees and shrubbery, a suitable retreat where they could converse without any danger of being seen or heard.

"Let us sit down here," said Joseph. All four of them entered the secluded retreat, and, when they were seated, he continued: "Boys, we saw your danger and were afraid you would not get out alive, but we are thankful that you got off safely. Now relate to me all that you have witnessed."

The boys then gave him a complete account of all they had witnessed and passed through; repeated to him the oath they had seen and heard administered to some two hundred individuals separately; gave him the names of all they knew that had taken the oath; in short, they gave him a most accurate recital of all they had seen and heard.

Joseph and his companion listened very attentively, and, as the boys proceeded, a very grave expression crept over the countenance of the former, showing that a deep anxiety was preying upon his mind. When the recital was finished, a pause of some length ensued. Joseph was very much moved, and at length burst out: "O, brethren, you do not know what this will terminate in!" But proceeded no further, for his feelings were so strong that he burst into tears.

In great agitation, Brother John Scott, who was an intimate and trusted friend of Joseph, sprang forward, and throwing his arms around the Prophet's neck, exclaimed: "O, Brother Joseph! do you think they are going to kill you?" and they fell on each others' necks and wept bitterly. The scene is difficult to describe. The thought of losing their friend and Prophet by the hands of such a bloodthirsty mob was sufficient to wring their hearts; and those brave men who, but a few moments before, had fearlessly faced death, and scorned the proffered conditions on which their lives might be spared, now wept like children, and mingled their tears with those of their leader.

Joseph was the first to master his feelings, and, raising Brother Scott's arms from off his neck, he said, in a deep and sorrowful tone: "I fully comprehend it!" He then relaxed into a solemn study, while his brethren anxiously watched the changes of his countenance as if they would read the thoughts and feelings that were preying upon his heart. The scene was painful and impressive. Each moment they expected to hear him say that his work on earth was done, and that he would have to be slain to seal his testimony.

After a long silence he finally continued: "Brethren, I am going to leave you. I shall not be with you long; it will not be many months until I shall have to go."

This remark still left them in doubt as to his future fate, but had such significance that Brother Scott again anxiously inquired: "Brother Joseph, are you going to be slain?"

Joseph, for some reason, evaded a direct reply, but continued in a tone that told too plainly of the sorrow he felt: "I am going away, and will not be known among this people for twenty years or more. I shall go to rest for a season."

This reply did not clear away their doubts any more than the former one, but it was evident he intended to leave the people and keep hid more closely than he ever had done, or else, with prophetic vision, he discerned the final outcome of his enemies' efforts, and, through compassion, forebore to crush the spirits of his brethren by telling them plainly the whole truth.

Subsequent events leave us still in doubt as to the real purport of his words. The dark clouds of persecution from enemies without, fearfully augmented by traitors from within, grew so threatening toward the close of the Prophet's life, that he saw something must be done for the safety of himself and the people. He therefore conceived the idea of moving the Saints once more, and this time far beyond the cruel blasts of persecution, and seek shelter behind the barriers of the Rocky Mountains. He called for a company of volunteers to explore the great West, and find the most suitable place for the Saints to settle. Quite a number volunteered and began to make preparations for the journey.

It is a well known fact that just previous to surrendering himself to be taken to Carthage, Joseph got into a boat and started across the river, evidently to evade his enemies. He intended to keep out of their hands until this company had procured a suitable outfit for such an undertaking, when he would have accompanied them. Some of his brethren, however, begged him not to desert the people in such a time of trouble and danger, and at their importunity he returned to Nauvoo, and we all know the result. He was induced to surrender himself to the officers of the law, was cast into prison, and there cruelly murdered by a bloodthirsty mob.

Perhaps, in reply to Brother Scott's question, Joseph was revolving these plans in his mind, and looking forward to the time when he and the Saints would be beyond the reach of persecution; it is now impossible to tell, but the events which followed rather indicate that he foresaw his death. However, he continued in great earnestness:

"They accuse me of polygamy, and of being a false Prophet, and many other things which I do not now remember; but I am no false Prophet; I am no impostor; I have had no dark revelations; I have had no revelations from the devil; I made no revelations; I have got nothing up myself. The same God that has thus far dictated me and directed me and strengthened me in this work, gave me this revelation and commandment on celestial and plural marriage, and the same God commanded me to obey it. He said to me that unless I accepted it and introduced it, and practiced it, I, together with my people, would be damned and cut off from this time henceforth. And they say if I do so, they will kill me. O, what shall I do? If I do not practice it I shall be damned with my people. If I do teach it, and practice it, and urge it, they say they will kill me, and I know they will. But," said he, "we have got to observe it. It is an eternal principle, and was given by way of commandment and not by way of instruction."

It will be seen from these outbursts of his soul what a conflict was going on in his mind, and the agony that he endured can only be imagined by those who knew his sensitive and generous spirit. Persecution and imprisonment from the hand of an enemy would be passed by almost unnoticed when compared with these murderous thrusts from the daggers of alienated friends. Death, to a man who was so familiar with the unseen world and the happiness to be enjoyed there, was stripped of its terrors. His fear of simply losing his life caused him little anxiety. But his whole soul was in the work which the Lord had given him to do, and such bloodthirsty opposition to a commandment of God among his brethren caused the greatest anxiety and grief. His greatest trials are, no doubt, hid deepest from our view.

The consultation lasted for a long time before they separated to their homes, and impressions were made on the minds of our two young heroes that will last forever. They got an insight into the life of the Prophet and the nature of the work he had to perform, that had never before entered their imaginations. Their love for him and the cause in which he was laboring was increased, and gladly would they have laid down their lives to have saved his.

Before separating, however, Joseph placed a seal upon the boys' lips, and made them promise that they would not reveal what had transpired that day to a living soul—not even to their own fathers, for at least twenty years. The object of placing this injunction upon them no doubt was for their own safety, as their lives would probably have been taken if any of the conspirators should ever find out that any of their proceedings had been revealed. The boys kept their promise, and now, after a lapse of so many years, these important facts, which throw light upon many of the acts and sayings of Joseph Smith, which his brethren could never before fully understand, are revealed and placed with other important records in the archives of the Church.

The muse of history, too often blind to true glory, has handed down to posterity many a warrior, the destroyer of thousands of his fellowmen, and left us ignorant of the valorous deeds of real heroes, whose lot chanced to be more humbly cast; but in that day, when all men's actions will be revealed upon the housetops, we shall, no doubt, see the names of Dennison L. Harris and Robert Scott among the world's heroes as stars of no small magnitude.

"Fact is stranger than fiction," and in value they cannot be compared. I respectfully submit the above narrative, which is a true recital of events that actually transpired. The manuscript has been carefully scrutinized by proper authorities who are satisfied of its authenticity and have approved its publication, as an important and accurate item of history connected with the Church.

GOVERNOR THOMAS FORD, A CONSPIRATOR

(D. H. C. 6:586-590)

TERRITORY OF UTAH, }
GREAT SALT LAKE CITY } ss

Personally appeared before me, Thomas Bullock, Recorder of

Great Salt Lake County, Alfred Randall, who deposes and says, that about ten o'clock on the morning of the (26th) twenty-sixth day of June, one thousand eight hundred and forty-four, he was in Carthage, Hancock county, Illinois, and as the troops, under Governor Thomas Ford, were in squads around the square, he went up to several of them, and heard one of the soldiers say: "When I left home I calculated to see old Joe dead before I returned." when several others said, "So did I," "So did I," and "I'll be damned if I don't," was the general reply.

One fellow then spoke up and said "I shouldn't wonder if there is some damned Mormon hearing all we have to say." Another who stood next to Randall, replied, "If I knew there was, I would run him through with my bayonet."

In a few minutes Randall went to another crowd of soldiers, and heard one say, "I guess this will be the last of old Joe." From there Randall went to Hamilton's Hotel, where Governor Thomas Ford was standing by the fence side, and heard another soldier tell Governor Thomas Ford, "The soldiers are determined to see Joe Smith dead before they leave here." Ford replied, "If you know of any such thing keep it to yourself."

In a short time Randall started for his own home, stayed all night, and arrived in Nauvoo on the twenty-seventh of June, when Governor Ford was making his notorious speech to the citizens. And further this deponent saith not.   ALFRED RANDALL.

Subscribed and sworn to before me this twelfth day of February, one thousand eight hundred and fifty-five.

THOMAS BULLOCK,
Recorder, Great Salt Lake County.

*   *   *   *   *

On the 26th day of June, A. D. 1844, near the mansion in the city of Nauvoo, I fell in company with Col. Enoch C. March and Geo. T. M. Davis, Esq., from Alton, Illinois, editor of the *Telegraph*, who had just arrived from Carthage, where they said they had been for some days, in company with Governor Ford and others, in council upon the subject of the arrest and trial of Joseph and Hyrum Smith, who were then prisoners in the county jail in Carthage.

After considerable conversation between myself and them on the subject of the Mormon religion, and the reasons why I had embraced that faith, and renounced my former religious discipline —viz. that of the Methodists, Mr. March asked me what I thought of Joe Smith, and if I had any hopes of his return to Nauvoo in safety.

I answered that I knew Joseph Smith was a true Prophet of the living God, as good and virtuous a man as ever lived upon the earth; that the Book of Mormon was true as holy writ, and was brought forth precisely in the way and manner it purported to be, by the gift and power of the Lord Almighty, and from no other source; and that the revelations he had received and published were eternal truth, and heaven and earth would pass away before one jot or tittle of the same should fail, and all that he pretended and testified to concerning the ministration of holy angels from the heavens to him, the Urim and Thummim, the voice of God, his correspondence with the heavens, was the truth and nothing but the truth; and that in relation to his return I had no doubt but that he would be honorably discharged upon his trial by the court, and would be preserved in safety from the power of his enemies; that he was in the hands of his God, whom he loved and faithfully served; and He, who held the destinies of nations in His own hands, would deliver him from his enemies, as He had done hundreds of times before.

Col. March replied, "Mr. Wright, you are mistaken, and I know it; you do not know what I know; I tell you they will kill Joe Smith before he leaves Carthage, and I know it, and you never will see him alive again." Said I, "Enoch, I do not believe it, he is in the hands of God, and God will deliver him." Says he, "I know better; when you hear of him again, you will hear he is dead, and I know it. The people at Carthage wanted permission from the Governor to kill you all and burn up your city, and Ford (the Governor) asked me if I thought it was best to suffer it. I replied, 'No, no, for God's sake, Ford, don't suffer it, that will never do, no never. Just see for a moment, Ford, what that would do; it would be the means of murdering thousands of innocent men, women and children, and destroying thousands of dollars' worth of property, and that would never do, it would not be sanctioned, it would disgrace the nation. You have now got the principal men here under your own control, they are all you want, what more do you want? When they are out of the way the thing is settled, and the people will be satisfied, and that is the easiest way you can dispose of it'; and Governor Ford concluded upon the whole that was the best policy, and I know it will be done."

MAYOR'S OFFICE, GREAT SALT LAKE CITY, UTAH TERRITORY,
Jan. 13th, A. D. 1855.

Personally appeared before me, Jedediah M. Grant, Mayor of said City, Jonathan Calkins Wright, who being duly sworn, deposeth and saith that the foregoing statements contained in his report of the conversation between himself and Enoch C. March, in presence of Geo. T. M. Davis, Esq., on the 26th day of June, 1844, in the city of Nauvoo, is true to the best of his knowledge and belief; and further this deponent saith not.

JONATHAN CALKINS WRIGHT.

Sworn to and subscribed before me, this 13th day of January, 1855, in Great Salt Lake City, Utah Territory.

J. M. GRANT,
Mayor of Great Salt Lake City.

*   *   *   *   *

Personally appeared before me, Thomas Bullock, County Recorder in and for Great Salt Lake County, in the Territory of Utah, Orrin P. Rockwell, who being first duly sworn, deposeth and saith

that about the hour of 3 o'clock in the afternoon of the 27th day
of June, one thousand eight hundred forty-four, a short time only
before Governor Ford addressed the citizens of Nauvoo, he (Ford)
and his suit occupied an upper room in the mansion of Joseph Smith,
in the city of Nauvoo, when he, the said Rockwell, had of necessity
to enter said upper room for his hat, and as he entered the door,
all were sitting silent except one man, who was standing behind
a chair making a speech, and while in the act of dropping his right
hand from an uplifted position, said, "The deed is done before this
time," which were the only words I heard while in the room, for
on seeing me they all hushed in silence. At that time I could not
comprehend the meaning of the words, but in a few hours after I
understood them as referring to the murder of Joseph and Hyrum
Smith in Carthage jail.   ORRIN P. ROCKWELL,

Subscribed and sworn to before me, the fourteenth day of
April, 1856.   THOMAS BULLOCK.
Recorder of Great Salt Lake County.

* * * * *

STATE OF DESERET, GREAT SALT LAKE COUNTY.

Personally appeared before me, Thomas Bullock, Recorder in
and for Great Salt Lake County, this third day of October, one
thousand eight hundred and fifty, William G. Sterrett, who being
first duly sworn, deposeth and saith that on the twenty-seventh day
of June, one thousand eight hundred and forty-four, in the city of
Nauvoo, county of Hancock, and State of Illinois, I heard Thomas
Ford, Governor of Illinois, address an assembly of several thousand
citizens, gathered around the frame of a building situated at the
corner of Water and Main streets. He reproached the people in
severe terms for the course they had taken in resisting the *posse
comitatus*, and among other things, "The retribution thereof will
be terrible, and you must make up your minds for it. I hope you
will not make any more trouble, but be a law-abiding people, for
if I have to come again it will be worse for you."

And your deponent further saith, that about half-past five in
the afternoon the said Governor Thomas Ford and his guard visited
the Temple and the workshops on the Temple block.

Mr. Alpheus Cutler, one of the building committee of the
Temple, sent me to watch them in and about the Temple. I was
close to the Governor when one of his men called him to look at one
of the oxen of the font in the basement of the Temple, that had
part of one horn broken off. The Governor stepped up to it, and
laying his hand on it remarked, "This is the cow with the crumply
horn, that we read of." One of the staff continued, "That tossed
the maiden all forlorn," and they all had a laugh about it.

Several of the horns were broken off the oxen by the Governor's
attendants. A man who stood behind me said, "I'll be damned but
I should like to take one of those horns home with me, to show as a
curiosity, but it is a pity to break them off."

After they had passed round the font, one of them remarked,
"This temple is a curious piece of workmanship, and it was a

damned shame that they did not let Joe Smith finish it, so that we could have seen what sort of a finish he would have put on it, for it is altogether a different style of architecture from any building I have ever seen or read about." Another said, "But he is dead by this time, and he will never see this temple again."

I replied, "They cannot kill him until he has finished his work." The Governor thereupon gave a very significant grin, when one of his suit who stood next to me said, "Whether he has finished his work or not by God he will not see this place again, for he's finished before this time."

Another of his suit pulled out his watch and said, "Governor, it's time we were off, we have been here too long already. Whether you go or not, I'm going to leave, and that damned quick." The Governor said, "Yes, it's time for us to be going." They then all left the stone shop, mounted their horses, which were hitched near the temple, and went out of the city towards Carthage by way of Mulholland Street, taking with them one of the horns that the company had knocked off. Further this deponent saith not.

WM. G. STERRETT.

Sworn to and subscribed before me, this day and year first above written.   THOMAS BULLOCK,
Great Salt Lake County Recorder.

JUDASES TO THE PROPHET JOSEPH

BY BENJ. F. JOHNSON

The days of tribulation were now fast approaching, for just as the Prophet so often told us, so it came to pass; and those he had called around him as a cordon of safety and strength were worse than a rope of sand, and were now forging his fetters. William Law was his first counselor; Wilson Law, Major General of the Legion; Wm. Marks, President of the stake; the Higbees, his confidential attorneys, and Dr. Foster, his financial business agent. All of these and many others entered into secret covenant so much worse than Judas, that they would have the Prophet's life, just in fulfillment of what he had said so often, publicly. With all their power, they began to make a party strong enough to destroy the Prophet.   *My Life's Review*, p. 99.

A MODERN NERO SPEAKS

BY GEORGE Q. CANNON

While the events which we have been narrating were transpiring at Carthage, Governor Ford was at Nauvoo. He left Carthage that morning (the 27th) to go there, notwithstanding he had been told, both before leaving and while on the road, that it was the intention of the mob to attack the jail and kill the prisoners. After reaching Nauvoo, the people were called together, and he made an address to them. It was one of the most infamous and insulting speeches ever delivered by a man in his position to a free people, and created considerable feeling among those who listened to it.

Among other things he said:

"A great crime has been done by destroying the *Expositor* press and placing the city under martial law, and a *severe atonement must be made,* so prepare your minds for the emergency. Another cause of excitement is the fact of your having so many firearms; the public are afraid that you are going to use them against the Government. I know there is a great prejudice against you on account of your peculiar religion, but you ought to be praying Saints, not military Saints. Depend upon it, a little more misbehavior from the citizens, and the torch, which is now already lighted, will be applied, the city may be reduced to ashes, and extermination would inevitably follow; and it gives me great pain to think there is danger of so many innocent women and children being exterminated. If anything of a serious character should befall the lives or property of the persons who are prosecuting your leaders, you will be held responsible."

While speaking he stood upon the unfinished frame of a building on the corner below Joseph's Mansion—on the same spot from which Joseph, not long before, had delivered his last address to the Saints. There were a few of his men who stood beside him. While he was speaking there was a concussion heard, as though it might be the faint sound of thunder from afar, and one of those who stood beside him heard it, looked around with some anxiety and said something to Ford, who soon finished his remarks. After he descended to the ground, he ordered his troops to get ready to return to Carthage. He was in haste to get away from Nauvoo, and the anxiety which he displayed excited comment at the time, though none, probably, suspected the true cause of his hurry. The writer was then a boy, he plainly heard the sound of which mention has been made, and looked around the cloudless sky to see whence it proceeded. It was about the time that the dreadful tragedy was being enacted at Carthage, and as a cannon was fired by the mob, on the road between Carthage and Warsaw, as a signal that the bloody deed had been accomplished, it was thought that the sound was the faint report of that signal. After the meeting Governor Ford and one of his companions walked up Water Street in the direction of Joseph's store, behind which they went and held an animated conversation. Here they probably discussed the events which they had reason to believe had taken place at Carthage; for the writer is firmly of the opinion, from the impressions their conduct made upon him at the time, that they knew or fully believed that the massacre had been accomplished. Their conversation ended, they walked quickly back to the Mansion, mounted their horses and rode off.

A few miles outside of Nauvoo the Governor and his party met two messengers, Brothers Geo. D. Grant and David Bettisworth, hastening to Nauvoo with the sad news of the murder of Joseph and Hyrum and the shooting of Elder Taylor. The Governor would not let them proceed, but took them back with him to Bro. Grant's house, one and a half miles east of Carthage. This he did to prevent their carrying the news, that he and the people of Carthage might have time to get out of harm's way, and to remove the county records and public documents from that town. After he reached Carthage, and had had an interview with Dr. Richards, he went to the public square and advised all who were present to disperse. He expected, he said, the "Mormons" would be so exasperated, that they would come and burn the town. He set them the example himself, which they were not slow to follow, by riding on as hard as he could in the direction of Quincy. He left Nauvoo about half past six in the evening, having rode there from Carthage in the morning; but he did not consider himself far enough from Nauvoo to take any rest until nearly fifty miles lay between himself and that city! Then he thought he might refresh himself a little; but he lost no more time than absolutely necessary and pushed hastily on to his home.   *Instructor*, Vol. 15.

FEDERAL AND STATE OFFICIALS ALSO IN CONSPIRACY

9:40 A.M. June 27, 1844: Mr. Woods and Mr. Reid called. They said another consultation of the officers had taken place, and the former orders of the Governor for marching to Nauvoo with the whole army were countermanded.

Dr. Southwick was in the meeting, seeing what was going on. He afterward told Stephen Markham that the purport of the meeting was to take into consideration the best way to stop Joseph Smith's career, as his views on government were widely circulated and took like wildfire. They said if he did not get into the Presidential chair this election, he would be sure the next time; and if Illinois and Missouri would join together and kill him, they would not be brought to justice for it. There were delegates in said meeting from every state in the Union except three, Governor Ford and Captain Smith were also in the meeting.   *D. H. C.* 6:605-6.

From reliable statements federal officials were there. The mob, therefore, that killed the Prophet included federal officials, state officials, members of Masonry, apostates, as well as the rabble, all crying: "Away with him, his blood be upon us and our children," a prototype of the scene enacted nineteen hundred years ago.

CHAPTER 6

Imprisonment in Liberty Prison

"MORMONISM" SURVIVES LIBERTY JAIL

BY PRESIDENT B. H. ROBERTS

Liberty Jail! How paradoxical the title! Liberty and prison are antithetical, and are supposed to have nothing in common; but when it is known that this particular prison is associated with "liberty" simply because it stood in a little Missouri town of that name—the county seat of Clay county, and about fifteen miles directly north of Independence—the seeming paradox vanishes. As will be seen by reference to the cut of this "Mormon" historical monument, Liberty prison is fallen into ruins, and some years ago was entirely obliterated. The prison was built of rough-dressed limestone, the surface of which was of a yellowish color. It faced east and was about two hundred yards from the court house. Its dimensions were about twenty by twenty-two feet. It had a heavy door in the east made strong and of considerable thickness by spiking inch oak planks together. In the south side there was a small opening a foot and a half square with strong iron bars, two inches apart, firmly imbedded in the stones of the wall. The contract for erecting this building was let in April, 1833, and in the December following the jail was completed. It cost the county six hundred dollars, Solomon Fry being the contractor.

It was within these gloomy walls that the Prophet Joseph Smith endured some of the most cruel sufferings that were crowded into his eventful life. For several months during the winter of 1838-9 he was imprisoned within the rude walls of this old structure, awaiting a trial for offenses charged against himself and brethren during the troubles in upper Missouri in the fall of 1838. Those imprisoned with him were his brother Hyrum Smith, Lyman Wight, Caleb Baldwin, Alexander McRae and Sidney Rigdon; but the last named prisoner was admitted to bail after a short time of imprisonment, owing to the delicate state of his health.

The rise of persecution against the Latter-day Saints in Missouri, which culminated in the expulsion of more than twelve hundred of them from their homes in Jackson county, in the winter of 1838; as also their subsequent settlement in several counties north of the Missouri river in 1836, together with the final expulsion of some fifteen thousand of the Saints from the confines of Missouri, in 1838, under the exterminating order of the governor of the state, Lilburn W. Boggs, and executed by the state militia, are circumstances which belong rather to the domain of history than to this article. It will be sufficient here to say that the measures taken by the Saints for self-protection were construed into acts of aggressive warfare; and acts of self-defense were made

LIBERTY PRISON
as it was when the Prophet Joseph was incarcerated therein.

Construction of walls of Liberty Prison which were four feet thick.

criminal. It was for his connection with these measures of self-protection and self-defense that the Prophet and his associates were arraigned before courts where well known mobocrats sat as judges, and imprisoned these men to await the slow process of courts reluctant to bring them to trial lest the exposure of the proceedings in upper Missouri would bring reproach upon the state. We are concerned here, however, only with Liberty jail and the Prophet's life within its walls. His suffering was great and went far beyond the irritation which comes to active spirits when confined, unwholesome food, and the petty tyranny of unfriendly guards. The Prophet could not forget that while he himself was compelled to endure this enforced inactivity his own family and the entire Church, stripped of their earthly possessions, were being driven from the state at an inclement season of the year under circumstances of extreme cruelty. It was reflecting upon these conditions which wrung from him the soul-cry with which one of his revelations opens:

> O God! where art thou? And where is the pavilion that covereth thy hiding place? How long shall thy hand be stayed, and thine eye, yea thy pure eye, behold from the eternal heavens, the wrongs of thy people and of thy servants, and thine ear be penetrated with their cries? Yea, O Lord, how long shall thou suffer these wrongs and unlawful oppressions before thine heart shall be softened towards them, and thy bowels be moved with compassion towards them?'

To which the Lord made answer:

> My son, peace be unto thy soul; thine adversity and thine afflictions shall be but a small moment; and then, if thou endure it well, God shall exalt thee on high; thou shalt triumph over all thy foes; thy friends do stand by thee, and they shall hail thee again, with warm hearts and friendly hands; thou art not yet as Job; thy friends do not contend against thee, neither charge thee with transgression, as they did Job; and they who do charge thee with transgression, their hope shall be blasted, and their prospects shall melt away as the hoar frost melteth before the burning rays of the rising sun.
>
> The ends of the earth shall inquire after thy name, and fools shall have thee in derision, and hell shall rage against thee, while the pure in heart, and the wise, and the noble, and the virtuous, shall seek counsel, and authority, and blessings constantly from under thy hand, and thy people shall never be turned against thee by the testimony of traitors.

In the foregoing may be observed a prophecy which has met with remarkable fulfilment—the Prophet's people have never been turned against him by the testimony of traitors, however determined they may have been in such efforts.

It was not all gloom in Liberty prison, either, during the time the Prophet and his brethren occupied it. As in all cases where the servants of God are imprisoned, the sweet and peaceful influences of the Holy Spirit were enjoyed. Within those gloomy prison walls some important revelations were received; petitions and remonstrances drafted, and letters of counsel and direction written to the Saints by the Prophet and his associates. Friends visited them from time to time, to assure the Prophet of their esteem and confidence. The wives of some of the prisoners, including the Prophet's, visited them to inquire of their welfare and take their leave of them before departing from the state.

The Prophet and his brethren having no confidence in the integrity of the courts of Missouri, and conscious of their own innocence, made several efforts to escape from Liberty jail, but without success. In April the prisoners were taken to Daviess county for trial, but finding Judge Thomas C. Birch on the bench, a man who had been connected with the court-martial which had condemned the prisoners to be shot in the public square at Far West, but a few months before, they asked for a change of venue to Marion county. This was denied, but one was given them to Boone county. Judge Birch made out the *mittimus* without date, name or place and the prisoners en route for the next place of trial, with the connivance of their guards, made their escape, and ten days later arrived among their friends, who meantime had gathered to the city of Quincy and vicinity, in Illinois.

Improvement Era, July, 1928.

LIBERTY JAIL

By Thomas C. Romney

Liberty Jail received its name from the city in which it is located. This jail or prison was constructed in the early part of the last century, likely in the late twenties or early thirties. It stood facing the east, twenty feet back from the street and was not more than two hundred and fifty yards from the present court house. The cost of the building was approximately $600.00. The prison does not stand today but a dwelling house has been built over a part of the foundation, nothing of the original remaining except the stones on the floor of the dungeon and about three feet running full length of two of the original walls. It was purchased by Wilford Wood for the Church of Jesus Christ of Latter-day Saints on June 19, 1939.

The place has a special significance to the Latter-day Saints, for herein the Prophet Joseph Smith and five of his brethren were confined over a period of nearly six months, on the false charge of treason. The Elders incarcerated with him were Hyrum Smith, Sidney Rigdon, Caleb Baldwin, Lyman Wight and Alexander McRae. Sidney Rigdon did not serve the entire term of the other brethren due to a serious illness that enabled him to get out on bail.

The indignities suffered by the Prophet and his companions were indescribable. In a letter written by the Prophet, he said: "We are kept under a strong guard, night and day, in a prison of double walls and doors, prescribed in our liberty of conscience; our food is scant, uniform and coarse. We have been compelled to sleep on the floor with straw and not blankets sufficient to keep us warm; and when we have a fire we are obliged to have almost a constant smoke."

His brother Hyrum said that poison was administered to them three or four times, with the result that it vomited them almost to death, and they would be two or three days in a torpid, stupid state;

not caring if they should pass away in death. Hyrum also declared that they were offered food that appeared to be human flesh, and which was referred to by one of the guards as "Mormon beef." Only one of their number tasted it. Alexander McRae confirms the testimony of Hyrum Smith relative to the results of poison being in the food in his declaration that all that partook of it were afflicted, "some being blind two or three days, and it was only by much faith and prayer that the effect was overcome."

During these days of trial, the Prophet Joseph was always the one to whom the other brethren went for comfort and strength. Said Brother McRae: "We never suffered ourselves to go into any important measure without asking Brother Joseph to inquire of the Lord in relation to it. Such was our confidence in him as a prophet that when he said: "Thus saith the Lord" we were confident it would be as he said, "for we never found his word fail in a single instance."

The Prophet's courage was sublime. In the midst of the greatest afflictions imaginable, he expressed himself thus: "We are determined to endure tribulation as good soldiers unto the end; when you read this you will know that prison walls, iron doors, screeching hinges, guards and jailors, have not destroyed our confidence, but we say, and that from experience, that they are calculated in their very nature to make the soul of an honest man feel stronger than the power of hell."

Yet at times, like the Master before him, he cried out against the indignities heaped upon him and his people by the enemies of truth. Note the anguish of spirit in these words uttered by him: "And again the cries of orphans and widows would not have ascended up to God against them. Nor would innocent blood have stained the soil of Missouri. But oh, the relenting hand; the inhumanity and murderous disposition of the people. It shades all nature; it beggars and defies all description; it is a tale of woe, a lamentable tale; yes, a sorrowful tale. It cannot be found among heathens; it cannot be found among the nations where kings and tyrants are enthroned; it cannot be found among the savages of the wilderness; yea, and I think it cannot be found among wild and ferocious beasts of the forest, that a man should be mangled for sport; women robbed of all they have—their last morsel of subsistence and then be violated to gratify the hellish desires of the mob."

THE HISTORIC LIBERTY JAIL

BY ANDREW JENSON AND EDWARD STEVENSON

This morning, (September 18, 1888) early we took train for Cameron, a fine city in Clinton county, where we changed cars and continued our journey to Liberty, Clay county, arriving here at 11 A.M. Without any difficulty we found the old jail where Joseph and his brethren were incarcerated from November, 1838, to April, 1839. By the assistance of a colored neighbor we soon succeeded in gaining an entrance to the interior of the half-tumble-down building, which we found very filthy indeed, filled with cobwebs and insects of numerous kinds which had their abode in the rotten timbers. Mr. Theodore Shively, who has charge of the property for the present owner (Mortimer Dearing, a wealthy banker of Kansas City), told us that the jail had not been opened and entered until today for many years. The smell from the decaying timber and dead insects was something sickening, and a couple of minutes' stay there made us wish for the fresh air outside. How the Prophet and his fellow prisoners could endure life in such a hole for upwards of five months is more than we can comprehend. Of course it was not so filthy then, but the openings for ventilation and light seem to have been so small that it cannot possibly have been a healthy abode for human beings at any time. We found the space inside to measure about 14½ feet from east to west, and 14 feet from north to south. From the basement floor to the ceiling we should judge it to be about 14 feet, two feet of which is under ground. The middle floor, which, while Joseph and his fellow prisoners were there, divided the space into an upper and lower story, has been torn away, but we could see where it had been and should say that the cell or lower room at that time measured 6½ feet, and the upper about 7 feet from floor to ceiling.

Joseph and his fellow-prisoners were confined in the upper room. The only openings giving light and ventilation to the cell part are two very small grated windows, through the wall, one on the south and another on the north side. These openings, each of which has a heavy square iron bar running horizontally through the middle, are two feet wide and six inches high. Above them there are, near the roof, two larger openings, two feet in width and one foot in height, giving light and air to the upper story. In each of these two upper windows there are five square iron bars standing perpendicularly and fastened very securely in the timbers of the building. In fact the whole structure is a double building, the inner being built of hewn oak logs about a foot square and the outside of rock. The floor and ceiling are constructed of the same material, thus making a huge wooden box. The rock walls are two feet thick, and in building them a space of about one foot was left between the rock and timber, which space was filled up with loose rock. Thus it will be seen that the prison walls are virtually four feet thick. Several loads of rock were also placed on top of the log ceiling, in order to make escape through the roof impossible. The outside dimensions of the building are: 22½ feet long, 22 feet wide and 12 feet high to the square. The door is on the east end, facing the street, and is 5½ feet high and 2½ feet wide, and opens to what was the upper apartment. The west gable and most of the west wall have tumbled down and also part of the north wall, thus leaving the timber or inside structure partly exposed. The east wall and gable are in a good state of preservation, and only one corner of the south wall is torn down. The building stands on the west side of what is known as Main street, one-and-one-half blocks north of the northwest corner of the Liberty court house square. It stands back from the street about 20 feet, on an uncultivated acre lot, which the owner has offered to sell for $2,500, but no one seems to care for purchasing the property. To reach the building from the street, we had to make a path through the thick growth of grass and weeds. Some of the latter, being more than six feet high, partly hid the building from view.

We also learned from official sources that the old jail continued to be used as a prison until about the year 1856, when it was deemed unsafe, and for a couple of years and more Clay county criminals were sent to Platte City, in the neighboring county on the west, for safekeeping. In 1858 the present Liberty court house was erected, with apartments for prisoners. For years afterwards the old jail was utilized as an ice-house, but has not been used for any purpose whatever during the last decennium or more. The roof fell in years ago, and the rock wall is crumbling down more and more every season, so there is every reason to believe that in a few years, even if permitted to stand as it does now, there will be nothing but a heap of rocks and rotten timber left to designate the place where this historic building stood. We secured the aid of a photographer, who took a very good negative, showing the ruins as they stand at the present time.

Having made all the observations we wanted around the jail, we visited a number of the old settlers of the town, among whom were Col. Luke W. Burris, a county official, Ben H. Stean, a bright business man, James H. Ford, an ex-official, Dr. Marsh and others. Mr. Ford is 72 years old, served as deputy sheriff of Clay county in 1838-39, and had Joseph Smith and fellow prisoners under his charge during their incarceration, acting under the direction of Samuel Hadley, the county sheriff. On many occasions he had taken the prisoners out one at a time for walks around the town, in order to give them an opportunity to enjoy the fresh air and get better meals than the jail fare allowed. On these walks he had often had lengthy conversations with the Prophet, who to him appeared to be far above the average man in intelligence, and seemed to be very deep and thoughtful, although good natured and even jocular in his manners. He had never looked upon Joseph Smith and his friends in prison as real criminals, but ascribed their incarceration mainly to the excitement and bigotry of the times. Mr. Ford remembered the time when the prisoners tried to break jail, and said he discharged his pistol on that occasion, but hoped he did not hurt anybody. This is evidently the shot fired after Cyrus Daniels, one of the visiting brethren, who fell into a hole just as the report of a pistol was heard, and a ball came whistling by. Mr. Ford said that in stopping the prisoners from getting out he also struck a heavy blow at the head of a boyish-looking man, whose name he believed was Snow.

Mr. Ford also accompanied the prisoners to Gallatin, Daviess county, in April, 1839, and said when they arrived there, they were handed over to some half-a-dozen of the strongest and roughest men of Daviess county, who at first crowded the prisoners into a corner of a room, refusing to allow them any liberties at all, but after a little, when they began to converse with the prisoners, they became quite sociable with them, and a reputed champion wrestler of Daviess county wanted to try strength with the Mormon Prophet. Joseph excused himself, saying he was a prisoner and could not engage in exercises of that kind under the circumstances; but finally, through the solicitations of the guard and the man promising not to get angry if he was thrown, Joseph consented to wrestle with him. Consequently a ring was made and the two stepped forth. The Missourian took recourse to all the trickery known to him in the art of wrestling, but was unsuccessful in his attempts to throw Joseph. Finally the latter gathered up his strength, made a first real attempt and threw his opponent flat upon his back in a pool of water. This made the fellow mad, although he had agreed not to get offended if thrown, and he wished to fight, but the guard interfered and the Daviess county champion was much humiliated afterwards in being made the object of considerable ridicule on the part of his companions, he having previously boasted that he could easily throw Joseph Smith.

We asked Mr. Ford if he knew anything about human flesh having been offered the prisoners. He answered emphatically no. So far as his knowledge went, such a thing was not even thought of, much less done. We suggested that it might possibly have been done without his knowledge, but he thought not. Samuel Tillery, he said, was the man who boarded the prisoners, and he did not believe him guilty of such an act. Mr. Ford was satisfied that the prisoners were treated humanly throughout, and given all the attention and privileges the law and circumstances would allow.

Infancy of the Church, pp. 25-27.

JOSEPH AND COMPANIONS GIVEN HUMAN FLESH TO EAT

By JOSEPH A. McRae

In a letter written from Carthage Jail, Carthage, Illinois, by Joseph A. McRae, dated March 7, 1939, to the Compiler of this book, Brother McRae says:

Respecting the incident you mention, my paternal grandmother told me many times, for I asked her to repeat to me the experiences she had in the early period of the church, and this is what she said, speaking to me: "I visited my husband several times while he was in the Liberty Jail. I carried letters to and from the Prophet, that were sent by his family. Your father was born at Far West while your grandfather was in prison and I took him to the jail to have him blessed. The Prophet blessed him and gave him the name of Joseph.

"Several times when I visited, I sat at the table and ate with them. The food was brought in and we all sat down together. The Prophet always deferred to his brother Hyrum, and as he was the eldest he had Hyrum sit at the head of the table and serve. Any meat that was to be carved was carved by Hyrum. One day a piece of roast meat was brought in that looked very dark, as though it had been burned. Brother Hyrum took the carving knife and fork, put the fork into the meat and they fell from his hands. He picked up the tools again and attempted to carve the meat and they fell from his hands again. After the second attempt, the Prophet said: 'Do not touch it, for it is human flesh.' It was afterwards told that the guards boasted they had cut a piece of the flesh from the thigh of an old negro and had fed it to the Mormons."

THE LOYAL AND DISLOYAL EXEMPLIFIED

About December, father Smith (the Prophet Joseph's Father) gave out that there would be a prayer and fast meeting for Brother Joseph and Hyrum while they were in prison, for the Lord to bless them and enable them to bear the cruelties that they had to suffer and pass through. My mother and my wife went to go to meeting; it was to open about sunrise in a place that was built by Joseph; but when they got to the door it was locked and they thought that they were at prayer, and father Smith and his folks and brother John Taylor came up and they said to them, "Why do you not go in?" They said that they were at prayer. "At prayer," said father Smith, "no, it cannot be." So he tried the door and found it locked on the inside. He said that some of the apostates had got there before them and they had done it to break up their meeting. He called to them to open the door but no one answered or took any notice whatever. By this time several had gathered together and some wanted to take an axe and cut the door down so that they could get in but father Smith said, "No, we must not do that," and Brother Taylor said that if they had deprived us of meeting in the house they could not deprive us of praying to God our Heavenly Father to look down in tender mercy upon His servants and enable them to bear their afflictions and the wrongs that they had to pass through. So father Smith said, "Let us hold meeting in this house, pointing to one of the houses belonging to one of the brethren and they that cannot get inside can hear outside, and we will have a good meeting, although the devil has tried to frustrate our design." They did hold the meeting and they that were there said that they never saw such a meeting. The Lord was with them to bless and answer their prayers. They broke up about four o'clock in the afternoon, and the apostates had not come out yet. There was the Whitneys and Thomas B. Marsh and a great many more in there. What their business was I never found out, but some plan to help and destroy Mormonism.

Some few days before that a man by the name of McLellin, one who had been high in the Church and Kingdom of God and had held the office of one of the Twelve, he and another man went into Brother Joseph's house and commenced searching over his things and Sister Emma asked him why he done so, and his answer was because he could. He took all the jewelry out of Joseph's box and took a lot of bed clothes and in fact plundered the house and took the things off. While Joseph was in prison he suffered with the cold, and he sent home to his wife, Emma, to send him some quilts or bed clothes for they had no fire there and he had to have something to keep him from the cold. It was in the dead of winter. My wife was up there when the word came and she said that Sister Emma cried and said they had taken all of her bed

clothes except one quilt and blanket and what could she do.   So
my wife, with some other sisters said, send him *them* and we will
see that you shall have something to cover you and your children.
My wife then went home and got some bed clothes and took them
over to her.   *Diary of John Lowe Butler*

IN A LOATHSOME DUNGEON IN MISSOURI

Prayer and Prophecies written by Joseph Smith, the Prophet,
while a prisoner in the jail at Liberty, Missouri, dated March 20,
1839. Their petitions and appeals directed to the executive officers
and the judiciary had failed to bring them relief. See *History of the
Church*, Vol. 3, p. 289.

*O God, where art thou?   And where is the pavilion that cov-
ereth thy hiding place?*

*How long shall thy hand be stayed, and thine eye, yea thy
pure eye, behold from the eternal heavens the wrongs of thy people
and of thy servants, and thine ear be penetrated with their cries?*

*Yea, O Lord, how long shall they suffer these wrongs and un-
lawful oppressions, before thine heart shall be softened toward
them, and thy bowels be moved with compassion toward them?*

*O Lord God Almighty, maker of heaven, earth and seas, and
of all things that in them are, and who controllest and subjectest
the devil, and the dark and benighted dominion of Sheol,—stretch
forth thy hand; let thine eye pierce; let thy pavilion be taken up;
let thy hiding place no longer be covered; let thine ear be inclined;
let thine heart be softened, and thy bowels moved with compassion
toward us.*

*Let thine anger be kindled against our enemies; and, in the
fury of thine heart, with thy sword avenge us of our wrongs.*

*Remember thy suffering saints, O our God; and thy servants
will rejoice in thy name forever.*

The Answer

*My son, peace be unto thy soul; thine adversity and thine af-
flictions shall be but a small moment;*

*And then, if thou endure it well, God shall exalt thee on high;
thou shalt triumph over all thy foes.*

*Thy friends do stand by thee, and they shall hail thee again,
with warm hearts and friendly hands.*

*Thou art not yet as Job; thy friends do not contend against
thee; neither charge thee with transgression, as they did Job.*

The Answer to Apostates

*And they who do charge thee with transgression, their hope
shall be blasted, and their prospects shall melt away as the hoar
frost melteth before the burning rays of the rising sun;*

*And also that God hath set his hand and seal to change the
times and seasons, and to blind their minds, that they may not
understand his marvelous workings; that he may prove them also
and take them in their own craftiness;*

Also because their hearts are corrupted, and the things which

Photographic copy of letter written by the Prophet Joseph to his wife Emma while in Liberty Prison.

they are willing to bring upon others, and love to have others suffer, may come upon themselves to the very uttermost;

That they may be disappointed also, and their hopes may be cut off;

And not many years hence, that they and their posterity shall be swept from under heaven, saith God, that not one of them is left to stand by the wall.

I want you to take the best care
of the family you can which I believe
you will do all you can I was sorry to learn
that Frederick was sick but I trust he is
well again and that you are all well I
want you to try to gain time and write to
me a long letter and tell me all you can
and even if old major is alive yet and what
those little prattlers say that cling around
your neck do you tell them I am in prison
that their lives might be saved
I want all the church to make out
a bill of damages and apply to the uni-
-ted States Court as soon as possible
however they will find out what can
be done themselves you expressed my
feelings concerning the order and I believe
that there is a way to get redress for
such things but God ruleth all things
after the council of his own will my
trust is in him the salvation of my
soul is of the most importants
to me for as much as I know
for a certainty of Eternal things
if the heavens linger it is nothing
to me I must steer my bark safe
which I intend to do I want you
to do the same yourself or even Joseph did
in Egypt

Letter concluded on next page.

Cursed are all those that shall lift up the heel against mine anointed, saith the Lord, and cry they have sinned when they have not sinned before me, saith the Lord, but have done that which was meet in mine eyes, and which I commanded them.

But those who cry transgression do it because they are the servants of sin, and are the children of disobedience themselves.

And those who swear falsely against my servants, that they

I want you to have the Epistle coppy
- ed immediately and let it go to the
Brethren first into the hands of Father
for I want the production for my
record if you lack for money or for
bread do let me know it as soon as
possible my nerve trembles from close
confinement but if you feel as I do
you dont care for the imperfections
of my writing for my part a word of
consolation from any source is
cordially received by me I feel like
Joseph in Egypt doth my friends
yet live if they live do they remem-
- ber me have they regard for me if so
let me know it in time of trouble
my Dear Emma do you think that my
being cast into prison by the mob
renders me less worthy of your friendship no I do not think so but
when I was in prison and ye visited
me inasmuch as you have don it to
the least of these you have don it to
me these shall enter into life
Eternal but no more
your Husband J Smith Jr

---

might bring them into bondage and death—

Wo unto them; because they have offended my little ones they shall be severed from the ordinances of mine house.

Their basket shall not be full, their houses and their barns shall perish, and they themselves shall be despised by those that flattered them.

They shall not have right to the priesthood, nor their posterity after them from generation to generation.

It had been better for them that a millstone had been hanged about their necks, and they drowned in the depth of the sea.

The Answer to Mobocrats

Wo unto all those that discomfort my people, and drive, and murder, and testify against them, saith the Lord of Hosts; a generation of vipers shall not escape the damnation of hell.

Behold, mine eyes see and know all their works, and I have in reserve a swift judgment in the season thereof, for them all;

For there is a time appointed for every man, according as his works shall be.

The Answer to the Saints

God shall give unto you (the saints) knowledge by his Holy Spirit, yea by the unspeakable gift of the Holy Ghost, that has not been revealed since the world was until now;

Which our forefathers have awaited with anxious expectation to be revealed in the last times, which their minds were pointed to, by the angels, as held in reserve for the fulness of their glory;

A time to come in the which nothing shall be withheld, whether there be one God or many Gods, they shall be manifest.

All thrones and dominions, principalities and powers, shall be revealed and set forth upon all who have endured valiantly for the gospel of Jesus Christ.

And also, if there be bounds set to the heavens, or to the seas; or to the dry land, or to the sun, moon, or stars—

All the times of their revolutions; all the appointed days, months, and years, and all the days of their days, months and years, and all their glories, laws, and set times, shall be revealed, in the days of the dispensation of the fulness of times—

According to that which was ordained in the midst of the Council of the Eternal God of all other gods before this world was, that should be reserved unto the finishing and the end thereof, when every man shall enter into his eternal presence, and into his immortal rest.

How long can rolling waters remain impure? What power shall stay the heavens? As well might man stretch forth his puny arm to stop the Missouri river in its decreed course, or to turn it up stream, as to hinder the Almighty from pouring down knowledge from heaven, upon the heads of the Latter-day Saints.

Behold, there are many called, but few are chosen. And why are they not chosen?

Because their hearts are set so much upon the things of this world, and aspire to the honors of men, that they do not learn this one lesson—

That the rights of the priesthood are inseparably connected with the powers of heaven, and that the powers of heaven cannot be controlled nor handled only upon the principles of righteousness.

That they may be conferred upon us, it is true; but when we undertake to cover our sins, or to gratify our pride, our vain ambition or to exercise control, or dominion, or compulsion, upon the souls of the children of men, in any degree of unrighteousness, be-

hold, the heavens withdraw themselves; the Spirit of the Lord is grieved; and when it is withdrawn, Amen to the priesthood, or the authority of that man.

Behold, ere he is aware, he is left unto himself, to kick against the pricks, to persecute the saints, and to fight against God.

We have learned, by sad experience, that it is the nature and disposition of almost all men, as soon as they get a little authority, as they suppose, they will immediately begin to exercise unrighteous dominion.

Hence many are called, but few are chosen.

No power or influence can or ought to be maintained by virtue of the priesthood, only by persuasion, by long-suffering, by gentleness, and meekness, and by love unfeigned;

By kindness, and pure knowledge, which shall greatly enlarge the soul without hypocrisy, and without guile—

Reproving betimes with sharpness, when moved upon by the Holy Ghost, and then showing forth afterwards an increase of love toward him whom thou hast reproved, lest he esteem thee to be his enemy;

That he may know that thy faithfulness is stronger than the cords of death.

Let thy bowels also be full of charity towards all men, and to the household of faith, and let virtue garnish thy thoughts unceasingly; then shall thy confidence wax strong in the presence of God, and the doctrine of the priesthood shall distil upon thy soul as the dews from heaven.

The Holy Ghost shall be thy constant companion, and thy scepter an unchanging scepter of righteousness and truth, and thy dominion shall be an everlasting dominion, and without compulsory means it shall flow unto thee forever and ever.   D. & C. Sec. 121.

* * * *

The ends of the earth shall inquire after thy name, and fools shall have thee in derision, and hell shall rage against thee,

While the pure in heart, and the wise, and the noble, and the virtuous, shall seek counsel and authority and blessings constantly from under thy hand,

And thy people shall never be turned against thee by the testimony of traitors;

And although their influence shall cast thee into trouble, and into bars and walls, thou shalt be had in honor; and but for a small moment and thy voice shall be more terrible in the midst of thine enemies, than the fierce lion, because of thy righteousness; and thy God shall stand by thee for ever and ever.

If thou art called to pass through tribulation; if thou art in perils among false brethren; if thou art in perils among robbers; if thou art in perils by land or by sea;

If thou art accused with all manner of false accusations; if thine enemies fall upon thee; if they tear thee from the society of thy father and mother and brethren and sisters; and if with a drawn sword thine enemies tear thee from the bosom of thy wife, and of thine offspring, and thine elder son, although but six years of age, shall cling to thy garments, and shall say, My father, my father, why can't you stay with us? O my father, what are the men going to do with you? and if then he shall be thrust from thee by the sword, and thou be dragged to prison, and thine enemies prowl around thee like wolves for the blood of the lamb;

And if thou shouldest be cast into the pit, or into the hands of murderers, and the sentence of death passed upon thee; if thou be cast into the deep; if the billowing surge conspire against thee; if fierce winds become thine enemy; if the heavens gather blackness, and all the elements combine to hedge up the way; and above all, if the very jaws of hell shall gape open the mouth wide after thee, know thou, my son, that all these things shall give thee experience, and shall be for thy good.

The Son of Man hath descended below them all. Art thou greater than he?

Therefore, hold on thy way, and the Priesthood shall remain with thee, for their bounds are set, they cannot pass. Thy days are known, and thy years shall not be numbered less; therefore, fear not what man can do, for God shall be with you forever and ever.

D. & C. Sec. 122.

A RECORD OF MOBOCRACY TO BE KEPT

And again, we would suggest for your consideration the propriety of all the saints gathering up a knowledge of all the facts and sufferings and abuses put upon them by the people of this State;

And also of all the property and amount of damages which they have sustained, both of character and personal injuries, as well as real property;

And also the names of all persons that have had a hand in their oppressions, as far as they can get hold of them, and find them out;

And perhaps a committee can be appointed to find out these things, and to take statements, and affidavits, and also to gather up the libelous publications that are afloat;

And all that are in the magazines, and in the encyclopedias, and all the libelous histories that are published, and are writing, and by whom, and present the whole concatenation of diabolical rascality, and nefarious and murderous impositions that have been practised upon this people—

That we may not only publish to all the world but present them to the heads of government in all their dark and hellish hue, as the last effort which is enjoined on us by our Heavenly Father, before we can fully and completely claim that promise which shall call him forth from his hiding place; and also that the whole nation may be left without excuse before he can send forth the power of his mighty arm.

It is an imperative duty that we owe to God, to angels, with whom we shall be brought to stand, and also to ourselves, to our wives and children, who have been made to bow down with grief, sorrow, and care, under the most damning hand of murder, tyranny and oppression, supported, and urged on and upheld by the influence of that spirit which hath so strongly riveted the creeds of the fathers, who have inherited lies, upon the hearts of the children, and filled the world with confusion, and has been growing stronger and stronger, and is now the very mainspring of all corruption, and the whole earth groans under the weight of its iniquity.

It is an iron yoke; it is a strong band; they are the very handcuffs, and chains, and shackles, and fetters of hell.

Therefore it is an imperative duty that we owe, not only to our own wives and children, but to the widows and fatherless, whose husbands and fathers have been murdered under its iron hand;

Which dark and blackening deeds are enough to make hell itself shudder, and to stand aghast and pale, and the hands of the very devil to tremble and palsy.

And also it is an imperative duty that we owe to all the rising generation, and to all the pure in heart—

For there are many yet on the earth among all sets, parties, and denominations, who are blinded by the subtle craftiness of men, whereby they lie in wait to deceive, and who are only kept from the truth because they know not where to find it—

Therefore, that we should waste and wear out our lives in bringing to light all the hidden things of darkness, wherein we know them; and they are truly manifest from heaven—

These should then be attended to with great earnestness.

Let no man count them as small things; for there is much which lieth in futurity, pertaining to the saints, which depends upon these things.

You know, brethren, that a very large ship is benefited very much by a very small helm in the time of a storm, by being kept workways with the wind and the waves.

Therefore, dearly beloved brethren, let us cheerfully do all things that lie in our power; and then may we stand still with the utmost assurance to see the salvation of God, and for his own arm to be revealed.   D. & C. Sec. 123.

CHAPTER 7

The Only Way to Escape Martyrdom

THE PROPHET JOSEPH WAS INSPIRED TO FLEE TO THE ROCKY MOUNTAINS

The Prophet Joseph did what the Lord required of him, viz: appeal the cause of the Saints to the judge, to the governor and lastly to the President of the nation: all to no avail. His only course now was to flee to the Rocky Mountains.

The same evening that they returned from Carthage with the letter from the governor, Joseph called Hyrum, Willard and some others together in his upper room and, after reading the governor's letter, he remarked: "There is no mercy—no mercy here." Hyrum said, "No, just as sure as we fall into their hands, we are dead men." Joseph replied, "Yes, what shall we do, Brother Hyrum?" He replied, "I don't know." All at once Joseph's countenance brightened up, and he said, "The way is open; it is clear to my mind what to do. All they want is Hyrum and myself. There is no doubt they will come here and search for us. Let them search, they will not harm you in person or in property, and not even a hair of your head. *We will cross the river tonight, and go away to the West.*"

At midnight, the same night, Joseph, Hyrum, and Dr. Richards called for O. P. Rockwell, and at 2 a.m. all four got into a boat and started to cross the Mississippi River. O. P. Rockwell rowed the boat. The boat was very leaky, and it kept Joseph, Hyrum and the Doctor very busy bailing out the water with their boots and shoes, to prevent it from sinking. At daybreak Joseph, Hyrum and Willard landed on the Iowa side of the river, and O. P. Rockwell returned to Nauvoo for horses, *that the start might be made at once to the Rocky Mountains.*

The same morning a posse arrived in Nauvoo to arrest Joseph but as he could not be found they returned to Carthage. They said that if Joseph and Hyrum were not given up that the governor would send his troops and guard the town until they were found.

Messengers were sent at once across the river by Emma, entreating Joseph to return and give himself up. Others also crossed the river to persuade them to return. *They found Joseph, Hyrum and Willard in a room by themselves with provisions ready for the start.* They begged Joseph to return, and some accused him of deserting the flock when the wolves came, like the shepherd in the fable. To which Joseph replied: "If my life is of no value to my friends, it is of none to myself." He then turned to Hyrum and said, "Brother Hyrum, you are the oldest, what shall we do?" Hyrum answered, "Let us go back and give ourselves up, and see the thing out." After studying a few minutes, Joseph replied, "If you go back, I shall go with you, but we will be butchered."

Improvement Era, Vol. 10:566-7.

PLANS OF THE PROPHET JOSEPH TO GO TO THE ROCKY MOUNTAINS

BY HISTORIAN EDWARD W. TULLIDGE

In 1880 the Reorganized Church of Jesus Christ of Latter-day Saints published *The Life of Joseph the Prophet*, at Plano, Illinois. A portion of the "Preface" to this history states:

In presenting this work to the reading public, it has been the aim of the publishers to place within the reach of those who cared to know, a more correct standard from which to determine the character and work of Joseph Smith, the founder, under divine direction, of the Church of Jesus Christ of Latter-day Saints. It is with the consciousness that the work is not so complete nor perfect as desirable, owing to the imperfect facilities for obtaining dates and facts that were at the disposal of the publishers, that it is offered; but the determination to place in the hands of friends of the Church, something from friendly authentic sources, has hastened its preparation and publication. * * * * *

The publishers ask that a patient reading be accorded the work, that the lack long felt may be at least partially supplied.

On pages 510 to 513 of this history, the following is recorded by Mr. Tullidge:

"June 22, 1844. About 9 p.m. Hyrum came out of the mansion and gave his hand to Reynolds Cahoon, at the same time saying: '*A company of men are seeking to kill my brother Joseph, and the Lord has warned him to flee to the Rocky Mountains to save his life.* Good-bye, Brother Cahoon, we shall see you again.' In a few moments afterwards Joseph came from his family. His tears were flowing fast. He held a handkerchief to his face, and followed after brother Hyrum without uttering a word.***

"At about midnight Joseph, Hyrum, and Dr. Richards called for O. P. Rockwell at his lodging and all went up the river bank until they found Aaron Johnson's boat, which they got into and started about 2 a.m. to cross the Mississippi River. O. P. Rockwell rowed the skiff, which was very leaky, so that it kept Joseph, Hyrum and the Doctor busy bailing out the water with their boots and shoes to prevent it from sinking.

"*Sunday, 23rd. At daybreak arrived on the Iowa side of the river. Sent O. P. Rockwell back to Nauvoo with instructions to return the next night with horses for Joseph and Hyrum, pass them over the river in the night secretly, and be ready to start for the Great Basin in the Rocky Mountains.****

"At 1 p.m. Emma sent over O. P. Rockwell, requesting him to entreat of Joseph to come back. Reynolds Cahoon accompanied him with a letter which Emma had written to the same effect, and she insisted that Cahoon should persuade Joseph to come back and give himself up. *When they went over they found Joseph, Hyrum and Willard in a room by themselves, having flour and other provisions on the floor ready for packing.*

THE NAUVOO MANSION AND NAUVOO HOUSE

The former is one block from the Mississippi River, the latter is but a few feet from the River.
The top of the Old Homestead is seen to the left diagonally from the Mansion and the Nauvoo House, hidden in the trees across the street.
"The graves of the Martyrs are located a few feet from the Old Homestead."

"Reynolds Cahoon informed Joseph what the troops intended to do, and urged upon him to give himself up, inasmuch as the Governor had pledged his faith and the faith of the State to protect him while he underwent a legal and fair trial. Reynolds Cahoon, L. D. Wasson and Hiram Kimball accused Joseph of cowardice for wishing to leave the people, adding that their property would be destroyed, and they left without house or home—like the fable, when the wolves came the shepherd ran from the flock, and left the sheep to be devoured. To which Joseph replied: 'If my life is of no value to my friends, it is of none to myself.'

"Joseph said to Rockwell, 'What shall I do?' Porter replied, 'You are the oldest and ought to know best; and as you make your bed I will lay with you.' Joseph then turned to Hyrum, who was talking with Cahoon, and said, 'Brother Hyrum, you are the oldest, what shall we do?' Hyrum said, 'Let us go back and give ourselves up, and see the thing out.' After studying a few moments Joseph said, 'If you go back, I shall go with you, but we shall be butchered.' Hyrum said, 'No, no; let us go back and put our trust in God, and we shall not be harmed. The Lord is in it. If we live or have to die, we will be reconciled to our fate.'

"About 4 p.m. Joseph, Hyrum, the Doctor and others started back. While walking towards the river Joseph fell behind with O. P. Rockwell. The others shouted to him to come on. Joseph replied, 'It is of no use to hurry, for we are going back to be slaughtered.' ***They recrossed the river at half past five. When they arrived in his mansion in Nauvoo Joseph's family surrounded him, and he tarried there all night."

"Monday, 24th. ***Governor Ford having sent word by the posse that those eighteen persons (Joseph, Hyrum and the others included in Morrison's original warrant) should be protected by the militia of the State; they, upon the assurance of that pledge, at half past six a.m. started for Carthage. Willard Richards, Daniel Jones, Henry G. Sherman, Alfred Randall, James Davis, Cyrus H. Wheelock, A. C. Hodge, and several other brethren, together with James W. Woods as counsel, accompanying them. * * *

"Joseph paused when they got to the temple, and looked with admiration first on that and then on the city, and remarked, 'This is the loveliest place and the best people under the heavens.' As he passed out of the city he called on Daniel H. Wells, Esq., who was unwell, and on parting he said, 'Squire Wells, I wish you to cherish my memory; and not think me the worst man in the world either.' "

ORIGIN OF THE PLAN FOR THE EXODUS

BY SAMUEL W. RICHARDS

The children and family of the Prophet, and others upon their testimony, have published extensively, both through the press and otherwise, that the movement of the Saints to the Rocky Mountains was not any plan or purpose of the Prophet Joseph, but that the plan or movement was entirely that of Brigham Young; but it is well known that he and his co-workers of the twelve were on missions abroad, and did not return to Nauvoo until sometime after the Prophet's martyrdom, and hence knew nothing of the movement planned, only as informed by others after their return. The refusal of the people at a general conference to accept Sidney Rigdon as their leader, and the appointment of Brigham Young as Joseph Smith's successor to lead the people, placed the latter where he was entitled to the inspiration of the Spirit to be his guide, and this led him to act in harmony with the Prophet Joseph's plans which were well known to those who had been with him, and who had become the counselors and advisers to Brigham Young, now chosen and standing in the Prophet Joseph's place before the people.

As is well known, after the people had expressed their choice in general conference that Brigham Young should be their leader and adviser, measures were at once adopted to carry out what was known to be the revealed will of God to Joseph concerning the removal of the Saints to the mountains, which was successfully accomplished, and which has placed them in the midst of prosperity; both temporal and spiritual, giving evidence of God's approval. I testify to the following facts which I know personally to be true.

In the winter of 1843-4, in the city of Nauvoo, Illinois, the then gathering place of the people known as Latter-day Saints, Joseph Smith, the Prophet and leader of that people, selected and organized a company of twenty-five, mostly young men, for a pioneer company to visit the Rocky Mountains and southern California, to find a suitable place for the Saints to remove and gather to, where they could be free from those who viewed them as enemies, and were constantly hunting him, as their leader, to take his life.

This, then, seemed to be a necessary movement, as the people had already been driven from their former homes in Missouri, with a considerable loss of life attending, and a like event now threatened those who were gathering in and about Nauvoo.

In view of such a condition and emergency, the Prophet deemed it advisable to have the western wilderness explored, before the exodus of the people from their present homes and gathering place be advised.

One of the apostles of the Church, viz., Willard Richards, who was with the Prophet at his martyrdom, was an almost constant companion of the Prophet, was sent to me to learn if I would be one of the number. Upon being assured that it was the wish of the Prophet Joseph Smith, I readily consented, and my name was placed upon the list. My former experience, under the influence of that man's personal, prophetic power, would have caused me to say yes to almost anything he could have asked.

Arrangements were made for the purpose, and weekly meetings were held, during the latter part of the winter, for the purpose of instructing the company in what would be expected of them, in filling the mission for which they were now being set apart. These meetings were held under the presidency of the Prophet's brother, Hyrum, Joseph being so closely hunted for his life that he was seldom with us. His brother Hyrum, Sidney Rigdon, and those of the twelve apostles then present in the city, were in attendance at these meetings, which were otherwise of a strictly private nature.

At these meetings, the spirit of prophecy was abundantly enjoyed by those giving instructions. Upon one occasion, after Sidney Rigdon had been speaking, the president of the meeting arose and said, "The spirit weighs down mightily, there has been enough said," and dismissed the meeting without further ceremony.

I had attended two or three of these meetings before I heard of what the Prophet Joseph had said while selecting the parties for the company, that he wanted young men of faith who could go upon the mountains of Israel, and talk with God face to face as Moses did upon Mount Sinai, and learn where he would have his people locate for their future welfare, and the kingdom's development.

Upon hearing this, the first response of my soul was, "I am not the one wanted, and I will decline at once;" but as I was about to offer my resignation, a voice whispered to me, "Wait! no hasty action!" I complied with the whisperings of the voice, went home and retired for the night, after first pleading most earnestly with the Lord to let me know what I should do in the matter, which seemed to me the most important of my life. I retired to my bed, and during the four hours of my sleep, my prayer was more than answered; and in the morning, I was ready to continue my relation with the company, and prepare the outfit required for the journey.

I performed the journey in my sleep, and had shown to me important events to transpire, and the condition of the earth itself to the complete restoration of its Eden beauty and grandeur as when man was first placed upon it, in a state of innocence and immortality, to which condition all must come in the restoration of all things spoken of by prophets and holy men, since the world began. It was no ordinary dream to be obscured, and to pass away from memory with the returning light of morning, but it was an impress upon the spirit which left the body and traversed the regions of space, while it surveyed the work of a thousand years in the restoration of the earth, and man upon it; an impress never to be obliterated from the mind.

Upon returning to my natural condition of wakefulness and human thought relating to my pioneer call, my whole soul responded: "Here am I, Lord," and I continued my attendance at the meetings, and my preparations for the journey. During these meetings, many things were spoken of concerning future development, perfectly in accord with what had been shown to me, and I felt more than ever assured of the divine approval of the Prophet Joseph's determination in the matter.

When all things seemed to have been satisfactorily arranged, and future movements of the company determined, Joseph took his departure from Nauvoo, crossed the river, and was making ready to visit awhile among the Indians, thinking it would be safer than to remain in Nauvoo; and, as I understood, that he might be ready to join the pioneer company when they should leave, and be their leader in search of a resting place for the Saints to be gathered to, as he well knew that where he should make a home, the Saints would cheerfully, under his direction, locate.

But this was not to be realized. As soon as it was known that the Prophet had left the city, with a view of a prolonged absence, a company of the brethren followed him, and insisted upon his return to the city. They felt that if he went away, and it was known, that not only would the work stop, but enemies who had been hunting his life would at once drive the people from their homes, and destroy and lay waste, as had been done in Missouri. This committee said things to him that grieved him very much, calling him a coward and other like reflections, so that he told them, "If my life is not worth anything to you, it is not to me; if I return, I go as a lamb to the slaughter." But this did not change their determination that he should return, which he did, and the result is well known.

This turn of affairs changed the entire program which had been arranged for the pioneer company, and the Church was to take their departure without the information desired, as to where it would be most desirable for them to make an abiding place for future growth and development.

While at Nauvoo, on his return, he addressed the people of the city, as he was about to be taken to Carthage for safe keeping, as promised him by the Governor of the state. Here he made a similar statement to the people, that he went as a lamb to the slaughter, which proved so verily true, as the world well knows.

At a meeting held February 21, 1844, in the Mayor's office, Nauvoo, the following names were accepted as pioneers to explore the Rocky Mountains and Lower California:

VOLUNTEERS	REQUESTED TO GO
Jonathan Dunham	Alphonzo Young
David D. Yearsley	Geo. D. Watt
Phineas H. Young	James Emmett
David P. Fullmer	Daniel Spencer

At a meeting on the 23rd of February, 1844, these names were accepted, Joseph Smith, Hyrum, and Sidney Rigdon being present:

VOLUNTEERS

Samuel Bent	Joseph A. Kelting
Samuel Rolfe	Daniel Avery
S. W. Richards	Seth Palmer
Amos Fielding	Charles Shumway
John S. Fullmer	Ira S. Miles
Almon L. Fullmer	Hosea Stout
Moses Smith	Rufus Beach

Thomas Edwards

Witness: A. Milton Musser.

Witness my signature:
Samuel W. Richards.

Improvement Era, 7:927-931.

THE PROPHET JOSEPH KNEW OF THE EXODUS IN THE DAYS OF KIRTLAND

BY WILFORD WOODRUFF

I arrived in Kirtland April 26, 1834, and there met Joseph and Hyrum Smith in the street. I was introduced to Joseph Smith. It was the first time that I had ever seen him in my life. He invited me to spend the Sabbath with him, and I did so. They had meeting on Sunday.

On Sunday night the Prophet called on all who held the Priesthood to gather into the little log schoolhouse they had there. It was a small house, perhaps fourteen feet square. But it held the whole of the Priesthood of the Church of Jesus Christ of Latter-day Saints who were then in the town of Kirtland, and who had gathered together to go off in Zion's Camp. That was the first time I ever saw Oliver Cowdery, or heard him speak; the first time I ever saw Brigham Young and Heber C. Kimball, and the two Pratts, and Orson Hyde and many others. There were no Apostles in the Church then except Joseph Smith and Oliver Cowdery. When we got together the Prophet called upon the Elders of Israel with him to bear testimony of this work. Those that I have named spoke and a good many I have not named bore their testimonies. When they got through the Prophet said: "Brethren, I have been very much edified and instructed in your testimonies here tonight, but I want to say to you before the Lord, that you know no more concerning the destinies of this Church and Kingdom than a babe upon its mother's lap. You don't comprehend it." I was rather surprised. He said: "It is only a little handful of Priesthood you see here tonight, but this Church will fill North and South America—it will fill the world." Among other things he said: *"It will fill the Rocky Mountains. There will be tens of thousands of Latter-day Saints who will be gathered in the Rocky Mountains and there they will open the door for the establishing of the Gospel among the Lamanites who will receive the Gospel and their endowments, and the blessings of God. This people will go into the Rocky Mountains; they will there build Temples to the Most High. They will raise up a posterity there, and the Latter-day Saints who dwell in these mountains will stand in the flesh until the coming of the Son of Man. The Son of Man will come to them while in the Rocky Mountains."* General Conference Report, April 8, 1898, p. 57.

THE PROPHET JOSEPH PROPHESIED THE EXODUS OF THE SAINTS WESTWARD

Saturday, August 6, 1842: Passed over the river to Montrose, Iowa, in company with General Adams, Colonel Brewer, and others, and witnessed the installation of the officers of the Rising Sun Lodge Ancient York Masons, at Montrose, by General James Adams, Deputy Grand-Master of Illinois. While the Deputy Grand-Master was engaged in giving the requisite instructions to the Master-elect, I had a conversation with a number of brethren in the shade of the building on the subject of our persecutions in Missouri and the constant annoyance which has followed us since we were driven from that state. *I prophesied that the Saints would continue to suffer much affliction and would be driven to the Rocky Mountains; many would apostatize, others would be put to death by our persecutors or lose their lives in consequence of exposure or disease, and some of you will live to go and assist in making settlements and build cities and see the Saints become a mighty people in the midst of the Rocky Mountains.* D. H. C. 5:85.

THE ROCKY MOUNTAINS — A PLACE OF REFUGE AND DESTINY FOR SAINTS

By Samuel W. Richards

My brethren, sisters and friends: Quite unexpected to me, prior to coming into this meeting, I have been requested to say a few words to you on some matters touching my history and experience with the Prophet Joseph Smith. I am thankful that I can say I was quite intimate with him while he was living upon the earth. There is a little experience I had with him that perhaps no other person living today could relate. In the winter of 1843-44, about six months prior to the death of the Prophet Joseph

Smith, a messenger was sent to me from Nauvoo to ask if I would be one of a company of pioneers to explore the Rocky Mountains and to find a place for the Church to go. That request came from the Prophet Joseph Smith. At the time I thought it a little strange that I should be called upon for a mission of this kind, as I was but a young man, in my teens; but my acquaintance up to that time with the Prophet Joseph was such that I could not say no. I replied, "Yes, I will do anything that the Prophet Joseph wants me to do, that is in my power to do." Consequently, I gave my name in to be one of a company of twenty-four young men who were selected to travel and explore the Rocky Mountains and find a place for the Church to go to, because the persecution was getting so strong then in Nauvoo that the Prophet Joseph foresaw that the Church would have to leave, retire from the civilized world, and go into the mountains. This was then a wild country.

I am reminded that when I was in Europe, in the early fifties, it was reported to the British Government that I was emigrating many people from Great Britain into a wild country, where they were liable to perish, and it was thought that this emigration ought to be stopped. Because of this I was ordered to appear in London and give an account of what I was doing. I was then presiding over the British Mission, and emigrated many people to this country. I responded to this call, and spent about five hours before a committee of sixteen members of Parliament telling them what I was doing. I had been to this valley myself and knew what it was. I told them that I was sending people to a country where they could own a farm and be as independent in their living as the lords and peers were there. I satisfied them, and they all shook hands with me at the end of our interview and wished me well, and I was invited by a number of them to come again to London and spend some time with them. I speak of this to show that the feeling of the people at that time was that this was a wild country, and we were coming here to perish.

It was the purpose of the Prophet Joseph to come here and locate with his people. He organized this company and held weekly meetings with them for several weeks in Nauvoo, and when he had them sufficiently instructed, as he thought, to properly understand what was to be the character of their mission and fit-out, he went across the river and made a start to go toward the mountains. It was his intention to go to the mountains with us, as a company of pioneers. But he was followed by those who did not like the idea of his leaving, and while they were pleading with him to return, he told them, "If I go back, I go as a lamb to the slaughter." Nevertheless, they determined he should return, and he went back to Nauvoo. From there he went to Carthage, and we all know the history of what followed.

Suffice it to say, I attended four meetings of this company and at one of them, which was in charge of Hyrum Smith, and three or four of the Twelve were also present, it was said that Joseph the Prophet had remarked that he wanted young men for that mission who could go upon the mountains and talk with God face to face, as Moses did upon Mount Sinai. When I heard that

NAUVOO IN 1950.

1. *Lot where Temple was erected.*

2. *Boat landing in days of Nauvoo.*

3. *Mississippi River.*

4. *Main St. (Now—1950—plotted as 7th St. The "Nauvoo Mansion" is hidden in the trees on Main and Water Streets, one block from the river. See air photo on page* 121.

5. *Young St.—Same now as in* 1846.

6. *Mulholland St.—Same now as in* 1846. *Is now the business street of Nauvoo.*

statement, I felt in my soul that I was not the one to go; and just before the meeting closed I got up out of my seat for the purpose of going to Brother Hyrum Smith and telling him I was not the one to go for I did not feel that I could meet these conditions, but as I got up there was a voice came to me and I heard it distinctly as from one standing by my side, saying, "Stop; rest awhile." I took my seat again, and instead of telling the Prophet Hyrum that I did not feel I could go, I went home, and before retiring I knelt by my bedside and prayed to my heavenly Father. If I ever prayed in earnest it was then, that I might know before morning whether I was a suitable one to go on that expedition, under the terms specified. The idea of going into the mountains and talking with God face to face, as Moses did on Mount Sinai, was more than I, as a boy, could think of encountering.

No one perhaps need wonder that I should shrink from such a consideration. I retired to my bed and remained there about four hours, and during that four hours I got the answer to my prayer, and when I awoke I was prepared to go upon that journey and do just as the Prophet wanted me to do. During that four hours I saw all that I expect to see if I should live a thousand years. Someone came to me and told me where to go, and I performed that journey that night while I lay upon my bed. I came to this valley first. I don't know how I got here, but I went down through these valleys and into Southern California. It had been stated that possibly we might have to go that far. When I came here I had to pass four sentinels, and in passing them I gave a countersign, which I got direct from heaven at the time it was needed. I passed them all, and went on down into Southern California. Then I was prompted to go farther, and I went into the northern part of Mexico. I returned from there to Jackson County, Missouri, and there I stayed and helped build the temple. I saw the temple thoroughly completed; in fact, I labored upon it until it was completed. When this was done, the vision continued, and I went and laid down my body in the ground, and my spirit left this tabernacle. Then I traversed this continent from end to end. I saw the Garden of Eden as it was in the beginning and as it will be restored again. It was a land filled with verdure and vegetation, and with all manner of fruits, on which man was living. I saw it filled with cities, towns and villages, and people happy, living under the administration of divine providence. It was a Garden of Eden in very deed.

Now, all this I saw while I was sleeping, and it was so impressed upon me that it can never be forgotten. I saw that this was the result of the Latter-day Saints coming to these valleys of the mountains and following the direction that the Prophet Joseph indicated. I could tell a long story about this matter, if I had the time to do it, but it is not best that I should. I wish, however, to make the statement distinctly, that this coming to the mountains of the Saints of God and establishing themselves here was under the special direction of the Prophet Joseph Smith. Although there are those who say to the contrary, this is my testimony. The Prophet Joseph Smith had all this planned, and

THE NAUVOO MANSION.

The home of the Prophet Joseph Smith at the time of the martyrdom.

THE OLD HOMESTEAD

in which the Prophet Joseph lived prior to moving into the Nauvoo Mansion.

if he had been allowed to have had his way, I believe he might have been with us even today. He would certainly have gone with that company to these mountains and have located the people. I was one of that company, and I think I have the names of the rest. However, the conditions became so severe at Nauvoo that the people had to pick up and leave in a body, before there was time for this company to make the proposed exploration. The Prophet Joseph and his brother, Hyrum, were martyred in Carthage, and the mob would not let the people remain in Nauvoo.

These are the facts in regard to this matter, and I am proud and thankful that I know of these things, and am glad that the Saints are building up these valleys of the mountains as I saw them built up in vision. If the people of God will only go on and keep His commandments, the time will come when the whole land will be filled with towns, cities, and villages, and the earth will bring forth all that is necessary for the support and sustenance of the people thereof.   Amen.

General Conference Report, April, 1905.

PROPHECY HELD IN ABEYANCE

By O. B. Huntington

My father was living in a good hewed log house in 1840 when one morning as the family all sat at breakfast old Father Joseph Smith, the first Patriarch of the Church and father of the Prophet Joseph, came in and sat down by the fireplace, after declining to take breakfast with us, and there he sat some little time in silence looking steadily in the fire. At length he observed that we had been driven from Missouri to this place; and with some passing comments, he then asked this question: "And how long, Brother Huntington, do you think we will stay here?" As he asked this question I noticed a strange, good-natured expression creep over his whole being—an air of mysterious joy. Father answered, after just a moment's hesitation, "Well, Father Smith, I can't begin to imagine." "We will just stay here seven years," he answered. "The Lord has told Joseph so—just seven years," he repeated. "Now this is not to be made public; I would not like to have this word go any further," said the Patriarch, who leaned and relied upon his son Joseph in all spiritual matters as much as boys generally do upon their parents for temporalities. There were then two or three minutes of perfect silence. Then the old gentleman with more apparent secret joy and caution in his countenance, said, "And where do you think we will go to when we leave here, Brother Huntington?" Father did not pretend to guess; unless we went back to Jackson county. "No," said the old Patriarch, his whole being seeming to be alive with animation. "The Lord has told Joseph that when we leave here we will go into the Rocky Mountains; right into the midst of the Lamanites."

This information filled our hearts with unspeakable joy, for we knew that the *Book of Mormon* and this gospel had been brought to light more for the remnants of Jacob upon this continent than for the Gentiles. Father Smith again enjoined upon us profound secrecy in this matter and I don't think it was ever uttered by one of Father Huntington's family. The history of Nauvoo shows that we located in Nauvoo in 1839, and left it in 1846.

The Church did move to the Rocky Mountains into the midst of the Indians or Lamanites — or more properly speaking the Jews—and here we expect to live until we move to the spirit land or the Lord moves us somewhere else.

Young Woman's Journal, Vol. 2:314-15.

ANSON CALL'S TESTIMONY AS RELATED BY HISTORIAN EDWARD W. TULLIDGE

It is thought important that the following statement from a biography of Anson Call, by Edward Tullidge, should be made part of the history of this prophetic incident, as doubtless the testimony of Brother Call relates to the same incident as that described in the Prophet's text of the History, notwithstanding some confusion of dates that exists in the Call testimony. It will be seen that the Prophet fixes the date of his prophecy on Saturday, the 6th of August, 1842. In Whitney's *History of Utah*, Vol. IV—(Biographical section of the history, p. 143), the date on which Call heard the prophecy, is given as the 8th of August, 1842. While in Tullidge's biography of Call the date is given as the 14th of July, 1843, evidently in error. There is no entry in the Prophet's journal for the 8th of August, 1842, and the entries for the 8th of August, 1843, and the 14th of July 1843, relate to matters of quite a different character. Tullidge, in relating Anson Call's recollection of the incident also says that J. C. Bennett was present on the occasion, which must also be an error, as the rupture between Bennett and the Church and its authorities occurred and he had left Nauvoo previous to the 6th of August, 1842. In the Call statement as published by Tullidge, the name of Mr. Adams, the Deputy Grand Master Mason in charge of the ceremonies, is given as George, it should be James.

On the 14th of July, 1843 (this date is in error. See footnote on page 85, vol. 5 of *Documentary History of the Church*), with quite a number of his brethren, he crossed the Mississippi River to the town of Montrose, to be present at the installment of the masonic lodge of the "Rising Sun." A block school house had been prepared with shade in front, under which was a barrel of ice water. Judge George Adams was the highest masonic authority in the state of Illinois and had been sent there to organize this lodge. He, Hyrum Smith and J. C. Bennett, being high Masons, went into the house to perform some ceremonies which the others were not entitled to witness. These, including Joseph Smith, remained under the bowery. Joseph, as he was tasting the cold water, warned the brethren not to be too free with it. *With the tumbler still in his hand, he prophesied that the Saints would yet go to the Rocky Mountains; and, said he, "this water tastes much like that of the crystal streams that are running from the snow capped mountains."* We will let Mr. Call describe this prophetic scene: "I had before seen him in a vision and now saw while he was talking, his countenance changed to white; not the deadly white of a bloodless face, but a living brilliant white. He seemed absorbed in gazing at something at a great distance and said, 'I am gazing upon the valleys of those mountains.' This was followed by a vivid description of the scenery of these mountains as I have since become acquainted with it. Pointing to Shadrach Roundy and others, he said: 'There are some men here who shall do a great work in that land.' Pointing to me, he said: 'There is Anson, he shall go and shall assist in building cities from one end of the country to the other, and you (rather extending the idea to all those he had spoken of) shall perform as great a work as has been done by man, so that the nations of the earth shall be astonished and many of them will be gathered in that land and assist in building cities and temples, and Israel shall be made to rejoice.'

"It is impossible to represent in words this scene which is still vivid in my mind, of the grandeur of Joseph's appearance, his beautiful descriptions of this land and his wonderful prophetic utterances as they emanated from the glorious inspirations that overshadowed him. There was a force and power in his exclamations of which the following is but a faint echo: 'Oh the beauty of those snow capped mountains. The cool refreshing streams that are running down through those mountains gorges.' Then gazing in another direction, as if there was a change in locality: 'Oh the scenes that this people will pass through! The dead that will lay between here and there.' Then turning in another direction as if the scene had again changed: 'Oh the apostasy that will take place before my brethren reach that land!' But he continued: 'The priesthood shall prevail over all its enemies, triumph over the devil and be established upon the earth never more to be thrown down.' He then charged us with great force and power, to be faithful in those things that had been and should be committed to our charge, with the promise of all the blessings that the priesthood could bestow. 'Remember these things and treasure them up. Amen.'

"Although I felt that Joseph was wrapt in vision, and that his voice was the voice of God, little did I then realize the vast significance of those prophetic declarations compared with what I do now, with the experiences of the forty-five years that have intervened since they were uttered. As he drew to a close the door of the house opened and we entered the building to transact the business for which we had gathered. It is impossible to express the feelings that came over me when Joseph prophesied upon my head. I queried in my head how it was possible for me to accomplish this great work with the persecution, the poverty and sickness that I had thus far to contend with. These prophecies were ever fresh in my mind until in the process of fulfillment I arrived in these mountains. When misfortune overtook me they buoyed me up, for I claimed the promises of the Lord and they strengthened me. After arriving here I still expected their fulfillment. The remainder of the narrative will witness that my expectations have not been in vain."

Tullidge's *Histories of Utah*, Vol. 2, Biographical Appendix pp. 271-2.

SPIRITUAL GIFT ENJOYED IN THE TEMPLE

In the January 5, 1946, issue of the *Deseret News,* Church Section, compiled by Preston Nibley, events that occurred in the Nauvoo Temple under date of December 27 and 30th, 1845, are recorded. In the *Journal History,* President Brigham Young, under date of the 27th, states:

"In the evening I went to the Temple and met with brothers Heber C. Kimball, Parley P. Pratt, Orson Pratt, Amasa Lyman and George A. Smith. We retired to my room for prayer at 6:45 p. m.

"After prayers, a general conversation ensued. The visit of the marshal and the emigration to California were the prominent topics. Elder Parley P. Pratt read from Hasting's account of California."

Under date of December 30th, President Young's account continues:

"The labors of the day having been brought to a close at so early an hour, viz., eight thirty, it was thought proper to have a little season of recreation. Accordingly, Brother Hanson was invited to produce his violin, which he did and played several lively airs, accompanied by Elisha Averett on his flute; among others some very good lively dancing tunes. This was too much for the gravity of Brother Joseph Young, who indulged in dancing a hornpipe, and was soon joined by several others, and before the dance was over, several French fours were indulged in. The first was opened by myself, with Sister Whitney, and Elder Kimball and partner. The spirit of dancing was increased until the whole floor was covered with dancers; and while we danced before the Lord, we shook the dust from our feet as a testimony against this nation.

"After the dancing had continued about an hour, several excellent songs were sung, in which the brethren and sisters joined. The "Upper California" was sung by Erastus Snow, after which I called upon Sister Whitney, who stood up, and invoking the gift of tongues, sang a beautiful song of Zion in tongues. The interpretation was given by her husband, Bishop Whitney, and me. It related to our efforts to build this house to the privilege we now have of meeting in it, our departure shortly to the country of the Lamanites, their rejoicing when they hear the Gospel, and of the gathering of Israel.

MODERN ISRAEL, DRIVEN FROM CIVILIZATION, LED OF GOD WESTWARD

By ERASTUS SNOW

When the pioneers left the confines of civilization, we were not seeking a country on the Pacific, neither a country to the north or south *we were seeking a country which had been pointed out by the Prophet Joseph Smith in the midst of the Rocky Mountains, in the interior of the great North American continent.* When the leader of that noble band of pioneers set out with his little company from the Missouri River, they went, as did Abraham, when he left his father's house—knowing not whither he went—only 'God had said, Go out from your father's house unto a land which I will show you. That band of pioneers went out, not knowing whither they went, only they knew that God had commanded them to go into a land which He would show them. And whenever the Prophet Brigham Young, the leader of that band of Pioneers, was asked the question: "Whither goes thou?" the only answer he could give was: *"I will show you when we come to it."*

The prayers of that band of pioneers, offered up day and night, continually unto God was to lead us, as He had promised, unto a land which, by the mouth of His servant Joseph, He had declared He would give us for an inheritance. *Said the Prophet Brigham: "I have seen it, I have seen it in vision, and when my natural eyes behold it, I shall know it."* They, therefore, like Abraham of old, journeying by faith, knowing not whither they went, only knew that God had called them to go out from among their brethren, who had hated, despised and persecuted them, and driven them from their possessions, and would not that they should dwell among them. *And when they reached this land the Prophet Brigham said: "This is the place where I, in vision, saw the ark of the Lord resting; this is the place whereon we will plant the soles of our feet, and where the Lord will place His name amongst His people."* And he said to that band of pioneers: "Organize your exploring parties, one to go south, another north, and another to go west, and search out the land, in the length and the breadth thereof, learn the facilities for settlement, for grazing, water, timber, soil and climate that we may be able to report to our brethren when we return;" and when the parties were organized, said he unto them: "You will find many excellent places for settlement. On every hand in these mountains, are locations where the people of God may dwell, but when you return from the south, west and north to this place, you will say with me, 'This is the place which the Lord has chosen for us to commence our settlements, and from this place we shall spread abroad and possess the land!'"

J. D. 16:207.

WHY THE CHURCH MOVED WEST

In reply to the assertion of the *Lamoni Herald* that Joseph Smith the Prophet knew nothing about the projected expedition to the Rocky Mountains, and did not predict the movement of the Saints to this region, we have already made some quotations from Church history and now proceed to give others. There are living witnesses in Utah to the truth of that which is found in the written records, and their testimony remains incontrovertible.

The following extracts from the history are all taken from the *Millennial Star* as they previously appeared in the *Deseret News,* in regular order according to their dates, and are integral parts of the complete record, the original manuscript being preserved in the office of the Church Historian in this city:

Under date of Tuesday, February 20, 1844, the following occurs in the history:

"At 10 a. m., went to my office, where the Twelve Apostles

and some others met in council with Brothers Mitchell Curtis and Stephen Curtis, who left the Pinery on Black river, the 1st of January. They were sent by Lyman Wight and Bishop Miller to know whether Lyman should preach to the Indians, the Menominees and Chippeways having requested it. . . . I instructed the Twelve Apostles to send out a delegation and investigate the locations of California and Oregon, and hunt out a good location where we can remove to after the Temple is completed and where we can build a city in a day, and have a government of our own, get up into the mountains where the devil cannot dig us out, and live in a healthy climate where we can live as old as we have a mind to."

Wednesday, February, 21st.—"Council of the Twelve met in my office. I insert the minutes:

"At a meeting of the Twelve at the mayor's office, Nauvoo, February 21, 1844, seven o'clock p. m., B. Young, Parley P. Pratt, O. Pratt, W. Woodruff, J. Taylor, Geo. A. Smith, W. Richards, and four others being present, called by previous notice, by instruction of President Joseph Smith, on the 20th inst., for the purpose of selecting a company to explore Oregon and California, and select a site for a new city for the Saints.

"Jonathan Dunham, Phinehas H. Young, David D. Yearsley and David Fulmer volunteered to go; and Alphonzo Young, James Emmett, George D. Watt and Daniel Spencer were requested to go. Voted, the above persons to be notified to meet with the Council on Friday evening next at the Assembly room."—Willard Richards, clerk.

Friday, February 23rd.—"Met with the Twelve in the Assembly room concerning the Oregon and California exploring expedition. Hyrum and Sidney present. I told them I wanted an exploration of all that mountain country. Perhaps it would be best to go direct to Sante Fe. Send twenty-five men; let them preach the Gospel wherever they go. Let that man go that can raise $500, a good horse and mule, a double barrel gun, one barrel rifle and other smooth-bore, a saddle and bridle, a pair of revolving pistols, bowie knife and a good sabre. Appoint a leader and let him beat up for volunteers. I want every man who goes to be a king and a priest. When he gets to the mountains he may want to talk with his God. When with the savage nations have power to govern, etc. If we don't get volunteers, wait till after the election."

"Geo. D. Watt said, 'Gentlemen, I shall go.' Samuel Bent volunteered; Jos. A. Kelting, ditto; David Fulmer, ditto; James Emmett, ditto; Daniel Spencer, ditto; Samuel Rolfe, ditto; Daniel Avery, ditto; Samuel W. Richards, ditto."

Saturday, February 24th. "At home. Had an interview with Brother Phelps at 9 o'clock. Seth Palmer, Amos Fielding, Charles Shumway and John S. Fullmer volunteered to go to Oregon and California."

Sunday, February 25th. "I preached at the Temple block. Hyrum also preached. Evening I attended prayer meeting in the assembly room. I gave some important instructions and

prophesied that within five years we should be out of the power
of our old enemies, whether they were apostates or of the world,
and told the brethren to record it, that when it comes to pass
they need not say they had forgotten the saying."

Monday, February 26th. "Ira S. Miles volunteered to join
the mountain exploring expedition."

Tuesday, February 27th. "Almon L. Fullmer and Hosea
Stout volunteered to go on the western exploring expedition."

Wednesday, February 28th. "Thomas S. Edwards volunteered
to join the exploring expedition to the Rocky Mountains."

Thursday, February 29th. "Moses Smith and Rufus Beach
volunteered to join the Oregon exploring expedition."

Under date of Monday, March 4th, Joseph Smith's journal
says: "I instructed a letter to be writtten to James Arlington
Bennett to consult him on the subject of nominating him for Vice
President. I here insert the letter:"

The letter, which appears in full in the journal of Joseph
Smith, contains this paragraph:

"All is right at Nauvoo. We are now fitting out a noble company to explore Oregon and California, and progressing rapidly
with the great Temple, which we expect to roof this season."

Under date of March 11th, 1844, we find the following:

"At home till 9. Then spent the day in council in the lodge
room over Henry Miller's house. Present: Joseph Smith, Hyrum
Smith, Brigham Young, Heber C. Kimball, Willard Richards, Parley P. Pratt, Orson Pratt, John Taylor, Geo. A. Smith, William
W. Phelps, John M. Bernhisel, Lucian Woodworth, Geo. Miller,
Alexander Badlam, Peter Haws, Erastus Snow, Reynolds Cahoon,
Amos Fielding, Alpheus Cutler, Levi Richards, Newell K. Whitney, Lorenzo D. Wasson, and William Clayton, who I organized
into a special council to take into consideration the subject matter
contained in the above letters, (received from a committee at
Black River Falls), and also the best policy for this people to
adopt to obtain their rights from the nation and insure protection for themselves and children, and to secure a resting place in
the mountains or some uninhabited region, where we can enjoy
the liberty of conscience guaranteed to us by the Constitution
of our country, rendered doubly sacred by the precious blood of
our fathers, and denied to us by the present authorities who have
smuggled themselves into power in the State and nation."

On March 26th the Prophet Joseph Smith addressed a memorial to the Congress of the United States, asking for authority
to raise a company of 100,000 men in the United States, to proceed to the West in the neighborhood of Oregon and California,
the purpose of which is thus described in the memorial:

"To open the vast region of the unpeopled West and South
to our enlightened and enterprising yeomanry; to protect them in
their researches; to secure them in their locations, and thus
strengthen the government and enlarge her borders; to extend
her influence; to inspire the nations with the spirit of freedom
and win them to her standard; to promote intelligence; to cultivate and establish peace among all with whom we may have inter-

course as neighbors; to settle all existing difficulties among those not organized into an acknowledged government bordering upon the United States and Territories; to save the national revenue in the nation's coffers; to supersede the necessity of a standing army on our western and southern frontiers; to create and maintain the principles of peace and suppress mobs, insurrections and oppression in Oregon and all lands bordering upon the United States and not incorporated into any acknowledged national government; to explore the unexplored regions of our continent; to open new fields of enterprise for our citizens and protect them therein; to search out the antiquities of the land, and thereby promote the arts and sciences, and general information; to amalgamate the feelings of all with whom we may have intercourse on the principles of equity, liberty, justice, humanity, and benevolence; to break down tyranny and oppression, and exalt the standard of universal peace."

On March 30th, Elder Orson Hyde was appointed by the city council of Nauvoo, to carry the memorial and an ordinance accompanying it to Washington, for the consideration of both houses of Congress. This appointment appeared of record on the City Council minutes, with the seal of the corporation, signed by Joseph Smith, Mayor, and Willard Richards, recorder.

Elder Orson Hyde made a lengthy report of his labors to the General Council dated Washington, D. C., April 26th. In speaking of the difficulties in the way because of the personal desires and ambitions of prominent men, he says:

"Now all these politicians rely upon the arm of our government to protect them there; and if government were to pass an act establishing a territorial government west of the Rocky Mountains there would be at once a tremendous rush of emigration. But if government pass no act in relation to it, these men have not stamina or sufficient confidence in themselves and their own resources to hazard the enterprise."

In the same communication, Orson Hyde states that Orson Pratt was with him, and they drafted a bill to present to Congress, and he goes on to say:

"In case of a removal to that country, Nauvoo is the place of general rendezvous. Our course from thence would be westward through Iowa, bearing a little to the north till we come to the Missouri river, leaving the State of Missouri on the left, thence up the north fork of the Platte into the mouth of Sweetwater river, in longitude 107 degrees 45 minutes w. and thence up Sweetwater river to the South pass of the Rocky Mountains. And from said South pass in latitude 42 degrees, 28 minutes north to the Umpqua and Klamet valleys in Oregon, bordering on California, is about 600 miles, making the distance from Nauvoo to the best portions of Oregon, 1,700 miles."

All this goes to prove, beyond a doubt that the Prophet Joseph Smith had in his mind the establishment of a gathering place for the Saints on the Western slope of the Rocky Mountains, and that the idea of the migration toward the West originated in his mind long before it was carried into practical effect by President Brigham Young.

It is recorded in the history of Joseph Smith that about 7 p. m. June 22, 1844, Joseph Smith called Hyrum Smith, Willard Richards, John Taylor, W. W. Phelps, Abraham E. Hodge, John L. Butler, Alpheus Cutler, William Marks and some other brethren into his upper room, where he conferred with them in regard to what he should do, there being warrants out for his arrest and a spirit of murder in the air. Joseph decided that all the enemy wanted was to get himself and Hyrum, and that if they went away no harm would come to the people or their property. He said, "We will cross the river to-night and go away to the west."

*   *   *   *   *

These evidences form an array of testimony sufficient to make the proof positive and beyond reasonable question that Joseph Smtih, the Prophet of the nineteenth century, was under God, the originator and projector of the plan to colonize the Rocky Mountain valleys with Latter-day Saints, and build up a great commonwealth, devoted to civil and religious liberty, where all persons of every shade of belief could worship their God according to the dictates of their own consciences, without hindrance and without molestation.   *Millennial Star*, 62:417-421.

BRIGHAM YOUNG VINDICATED AS SUCCESSOR TO THE PROPHET

BY SAMUEL P. ORTON

In 1856 I crossed the plains in Captain Edward Bunker's handcart company. We got along very well until we ran short of flour; our rations being a quarter of a pound of flour per day without trimmings. Being young and healthy, I became very weak, and I prayed to the Lord that I might die; but my prayers were not answered. One day, about this time, there came an old buffalo past our camp; we killed him and I being very hungry ate some of the meat while it was warm. This nearly killed me. I was so sick I had to leave my cart and walk behind the company.

All at once a voice spoke to me and said "Samuel are you here?" I said, "Yes, I am here," and turned to see who it was that spoke to me, but saw no one. This set me to thinking what I was here for, and what I was going to Utah for. I wanted to know if the Gospel was true, and if the Father and the Son did appear to Joseph Smith and reveal it to him, and if Brigham Young was his lawful successor. If so, I wanted to see when I got to Salt Lake City that halo of light around the head of President Young that we see in pictures around the head of the Savior. While this train of thought was passing through my mind I had caught up with the company, feeling quite well, as my sickness had left me. We soon after met a team from Salt Lake City with some flour for us; so we got along all right during the rest of the journey. We arrived in Salt Lake City on the 5th of October. The next morning, it being Conference, I went to meeting in the old Bowery, and took my seat about the middle of the building. The people were coming in "pretty lively." I was watching to see if there was any one that I knew, but saw no one. Then on looking toward the stand I saw President Young there with the rays of light around his head as I had asked to see while on the plains, and the same rays seemed to faintly encircle the brethren on each side of him. Then the same voice that spoke to me on the plains, said to me plainly: "Now Samuel if ever you apostatize, here is your condemnation." I looked around me to see if any of the people heard the voice, but I thought they did not. This has ever since been a very valuable testimony to me.

Instructor, May 15, 1906.

THE ALMIGHTY DIRECTED PIONEERS TO SALT LAKE VALLEY

BY BRIGHAM YOUNG

I do not wish men to understand that I had anything to do with our being moved here, that was the providence of the Almighty. It was the power of God that wrought out salvation for this people, I never could have devised such a plan. . . .

We have faith, we live by faith; we came to these mountains by faith. We came here, I often say, though to the ears of some the expression may sound rather rude, naked and barefoot, and comparatively this is true. . . .

We had to have faith to come here. When we met Mr. Bridger on the Big Sandy River, said he, "Mr. Young, I would give a thousand dollars if I knew an ear of corn could be ripened in the Great Basin." Said I, "Wait eighteen months and I will show you many of them." Did I say this from knowledge? No, it was my faith. . . .

I cannot help being here. We might have gone to Vancouver's Island; and if we had, we should probably have been driven away or used up before this time.

But here we are in the valleys of the mountains, where the Lord directed me to lead the people.

The brethren who are in foreign countries desire to gather to the gathering-place of the Saints, and they have for the present to come to Great Salt Lake City. They cannot help that.

Why did we not go to San Francisco? Because the Lord told me not: "For there are lions in the way, and they will devour the lambs, if you take them there. . . ."

Talk about these rich valleys, why there is not another people on the earth that could have come here and lived. We prayed over the land, and dedicated it and the water, air and everything pertaining to them unto the Lord, and the smiles of heaven rested on the land and it became productive, and today yields us the best of grain, fruit and vegetables. . . .

You inquire if we shall stay in these mountains. I answer yes, as long as we please to do the will of God, our Father in Heaven. If we are pleased to turn away from the holy commandments of

*the Lord Jesus Christ, as ancient Israel did, every man turning
to his own way, we shall be scattered and peeled, driven before our
enemies and persecuted, until we learn to remember the Lord our
God and are willing to walk in his ways.**

(See Chapter 42, *Discourses of Brigham Young.*)

JOSEPH SMITH DIRECTED BRIGHAM YOUNG
TO THE ROCKY MOUNTAINS

BY GEORGE A. SMITH

We look around today and behold our city clothed with verdure
and beautified with trees and flowers, with streams of water running
in almost every direction, and the question is frequently asked:
"How did you ever find this place?" I answer, we were led to it
by the inspiration of God. *After the death of Joseph Smith, when
it seemed as if every trouble and calamity had come upon the
Saints, Brigham Young, who was President of the Twelve, then
the presiding Quorum of the Church, sought the Lord to know
what they should do, and where they should lead the people for
safety, and while they were fasting and praying daily on this
subject, President Young had a vision of Joseph Smith, who showed
him the mountain that we now call Ensign Peak, immediately north
of Salt Lake City, and there was an ensign fell upon that peak, and*

---

*FUTURE JUDGMENTS PREDICTED: When we go back to Jackson County,
we are to go back with power. Do you suppose that God will reveal his
power among an unsanctified people, who have no regard nor respect for
his laws and institutions, but who are filled with covetousness? No. When
God shows forth his power among the Latter-day Saints, it will be because
there is a union of feeling in regard to doctrine, and in regard to everything
that God has placed in their hands; and not only a union, but a sanctification
on their part, that there shall not be a spot or wrinkle as it were, but everything shall be as fair as the sun that shines in the heavens.

In order to bring about this, who knows how many chastisements God
may yet have to pour out upon the people calling themselves Latter-day
Saints? I do not know. Sometimes I fear, when I read certain revelations
contained in this book. In one of them the Lord says, "If this people will be
obedient to all of my commandments, they shall begin to prevail against their
enemies from this very hour, and shall not cease to prevail until the kingdoms
of this world shall become the kingdoms of our God and his Christ." That
promise was given almost forty years ago. In the same paragraph it says:
"Inasmuch as this people will not be obedient to my commandments and live
by every word that I have spoken, I will visit them with sore afflictions,
with pestilence, with plague, with sword and with the flame of devouring
fire." Is it not enough to make a person fear when God has spoken this concerning the Latter-day Saints? I do not know all things which await us. One
thing I do know—that the righteous need not fear. The Book of Mormon is
very expressive upon this subject. In the last chapter of the first book of
Nephi, the Lord, through the Prophet, speaks concerning the building up of
Zion in the latter days on the earth. He says his people should be, as it
were, in great straits, at certain times, but said the Prophet, "The righteous
need not fear, for I will preserve them, if it must needs be that I send down
fire from heaven unto the destruction of their enemies." This will be fulfilled
if necessary. Let the righteous among this people abide in their righteousness,
and let them cleave unto the Lord their God; and if there are those among
them who will not keep his commandments, they will be cleansed out by the
judgments of which I have spoken. (Excerpt from Sermon of Orson Pratt)
J. of D. 15:360.

Joseph said, "Build under the point where the colors fall and you will prosper and have peace." The pioneers had no pilot or guide, none among them had ever been in the country or knew anything about it. *However, they travelled under the direction of President Young until they reached this valley. When they entered it President Young pointed to that peak, and, said he, "I want to go there." He went up to the point and said, "This is Ensign Peak.* Now, brethren, organize your exploring parties, so as to be safe from Indians; go and explore where you will, and you will come back every time and say this is the best place." They accordingly started out exploring companies and visited what we now call Cache, Malad, Tooele, and Utah valleys, and other parts of the country in various directions, but all came back and declared this was the best spot.   J. D. 13:85-86.

BRIGHAM YOUNG'S FEELINGS ON LEAVING NAUVOO

(Excerpts from letter written to his brother Joseph, dated "Richardson's Point, Camp of Israel, fifty-five miles from Nauvoo, March 9." (1846)

"I feel as though Nauvoo will be filled with all manner of abominations. It is no place for the Saints, and the Spirit whispers to me that the brethren had better get away as fast as they can. We pray for you continually. I hope the brethren will not have trouble there, but the dark clouds of sorrow are gathering fast over that place. It is a matter of doubt about any of the Twelve returning to Nauvoo very soon. *It is not the place for me any more, till this nation is scourged by the hand of the Almighty, who rules in the heavens. This nation shall feel the heavy hand of judgment. They have shed the blood of prophets and saints and have been the means of the death of many. Do not think, Brother Joseph, that I hate to leave my house and home. No, far from that, I am so free from bondage at this time, that Nauvoo looks like a prison to me. It looks pleasant ahead, but dark to look back."*

Life of Brigham Young, by Edw. W. Tullidge, p. 37.

BRIGHAM YOUNG WOULD HAVE PREVENTED
THE MASSACRE OF JOSEPH SMITH

"Events have since proved that had Joseph led a band of pioneers in the spring of 1844 to the Rocky Mountains, Brigham was quite equal to master an exodus and remove the entire Church. When the mob force threatened Nauvoo, and the Governor, with an army, prepared to march against the devoted city, under the excuse of forestalling civil war, making the demand on the person of the Prophet for high treason, Joseph essayed to flee to the mountains. He had even started, crossing the river to the Iowa side, where he waited the enrolment of a chosen band of pioneers; *but a messenger from his wife and certain of his disciples, reproaching him as a shepherd who had deserted his flock, recalled him to Nauvoo. Such a reproach was, beyond all others, the last that the lion heart of*

Joseph could bear and he returned and gave himself up to the authorities of Illinois. But had Brigham Young been home he never would have permitted that return. He would have thundered indignation upon the craven heads of those who thus devoted their Prophet to almost certain death. Rather would he have sent a thousand elders to guard him to the mountains, for none loved Joseph better than did Brigham Young."

Life of Brigham Young, by Edw. W. Tullidge, p. 104-5.

PLANS FOR REMOVAL TO THE ROCKY MOUNTAINS

By Helen Mar Whitney

The Saints of Nauvoo well remember how the Prophet was warned by the Lord to flee to the Rocky Mountains, and had it not been for his wife, Emma, and a few faithless and frightened brethren, he would have come west, but it was otherwise ordained.

We cite Joseph Smith to other items (which he must have forgotten if he ever knew them) that are contained in his father's life, which was written and published by E. W. Tullidge. It contains an address delivered by Lieutenant General Joseph Smith to the Nauvoo Legion, in the afternoon of June 18, 1844, which was listened to by hundreds who are still living here in Utah, and from it I take the following extracts:

"It is thought by some that our enemies would be satisfied, with my destruction; but I tell you that as soon as they have shed my blood, they will thirst for the blood of every man in whose heart dwells a single spark of the spirit of the fulness of the gospel.** It is not only to destroy me but every man and woman who dares believe the doctrines that God hath inspired me to teach to this generation.

"We have turned the barren bleak prairie swamps of this State into beautiful towns, farms and cities, by our industry; and the men who seek our destruction and cry thief, treason, riot, etc. are those who themselves violate the laws, steal and plunder from their neighbors, and seek to destroy the innocent; heralding forth lies to screen themselves from the just punishment of their crimes by bringing distress upon this innocent people.

"We are American citizens. We live upon a soil for the liberties of which our fathers periled their lives and spilt their blood upon the battle-field. Those rights, so dearly purchased shall not be disgracefully trodden under foot by lawless marauders without at least a noble effort on our part to sustain our liberties.

"Will you stand by me to the death, and sustain, at the peril of your lives, the laws of our country, and the liberties and privileges which our fathers have transmitted unto us, sealed with their sacred blood?" "Aye," shouted thousands. He then said: "It is well. If you had not done it, I would have gone out there," (pointing to the west), "and would have raised up a mightier people."

Drawing his sword and presenting it to heaven, the Prophet said: *"I call God and angels to witness that I have unsheathed my sword with a firm and unalterable determination that this people shall have their legal rights, and be protected from mob violence, or my blood shall be spilt upon the ground like water, and my body consigned to the silent tomb. While I live, I will not tamely submit to the dominion of a cursed mobocracy. I would welcome death rather than submit to this oppression; and it would be sweet, oh, sweet to rest in the grave, rather than submit to this oppression, agitation, annoyance, confusion, and alarm upon alarm, any longer.*

"I call upon all friends of truth and liberty to come to our assistance; and may the thunders of the Almighty, and the forked lightnings of heaven, and pestilence, and war, and bloodshed come down on those ungodly men who seek to destroy my life and the lives of this innocent people.

"I do not regard my own life. I am ready to be offered a sacrifice for this people; for what can our enemies do? Only kill the body, and their power is then at an end. Stand firm, my friends; never flinch; do not seek to save your lives, for he that is afraid to die for the truth will lose eternal life. Hold out to the end, and we shall be resurrected, and become like Gods, and reign in celestial kingdoms, principalities, and eternal dominions, while this cursed mob will sink to hell, the portion of all those who shed innocent blood.

"God has tried you. You are a good people; therefore I love you with all my heart. Greater love hath no man than that he should lay down his life for his friends. You have stood by me in the hour of trouble, and I am willing to sacrifice my life for your preservation. May the Lord God of Israel bless you forever and ever. I say it in the name of Jesus of Nazareth, and in the authority of the Holy Priesthood, which He hath conferred upon me."**

On the 22nd of June, 1844, Joseph Smith and his brother Hyrum bade their families farewell. When he came from the house, the record says, "His tears were flowing fast. He held a handkerchief to his face, and followed after his brother Hyrum without uttering a word."

They were accompanied by Willard Richards and O. P. Rockwell, and it was after midnight when they started to cross the Mississippi. Bishop N. K. Whitney and others of their wise and faithful friends also followed them shortly afterwards. Joseph sent O. P. Rockwell back for horses, and the brethren were packing their provisions, when messengers came with a letter from Emma Smith, asking them to return and deliver themselves up, but at the same time those who were with them begged them not to return. *Joseph sent a messenger to his wife to inquire if she would take her children and flee with him, but she said she "could not give up the mansion."*   Plural Marriages as Taught by Joseph Smith, p. 19-22.

GOV. THOMAS FORD SAID THE PROPHET JOSEPH PLANNED THE EXODUS

"Your religion is new and it surprises the people as any great novelty in religion generally does. They cannot rise above the prejudices excited by such novelty. However truly, and sincerely

your own people may believe in it, the impression on the public
mind everywhere is that your leading men are imposters and rogues
and that the others are dupes and fools. This impression in the
minds of the great mass is sufficient to warrant them in considering and treating you as enemies and outcasts; as men to be cherished and trusted in nothing, because in their estimation some of
you are deluded, and others designing in matters of religion. If you
can get off by yourselves you may enjoy peace; but surrounded by
such neighbors I confess that I do not foresee the time when you will
be permitted to enjoy quiet. *I was informed by General Joseph
Smith last summer that he contemplated a removal west; and from
what I learned from him and others at that time I think if he had
lived he would have begun to move in the matter before this time.
I would be willing to exert all my feeble abilities and influence to
further your views in this respect if it was the wish of your people."*

Excerpt from letter of Gov. Thomas Ford to Brigham Young,
dated Springfield, April 8, 1845. *D. H. C.* 6:398.

THE SAINTS WILL BE OUT OF THE POWER OF THEIR ENEMIES IN FIVE YEARS

On Sunday, the 25th day of February, 1844, in a meeting at
the assembly room of the Saints in Nauvoo, Joseph prophesied that
within five years the Saints would be out of the power of their old
enemies, whether apostates or of the world; and he asked the
brethren to record the prediction.

About this time he was inspired to direct the glance of the
Apostles to the western slope where he said the people of God
might establish themselves anew, worship after their own sincere
convictions, and work out the grand social problems of modern
life. This subject was present in his mind and often upon his lips
during the brief remainder of his earthly existence.

Frequent councils were held and he directed the organization
of an exploring expedition to venture beyond the Rocky Mountains to seek a home for a righteous people denied every right of
citizenship within the boundaries of the United States then existing. His purpose was not to sever the Saints from this sublime
republic by any emigration; he saw that this country's domain
must soon stretch from ocean to ocean. The entire land of North
and South America was the Zion of the Lord, and the people might
settle in any spot where peace could be enjoyed, always remembering that in the due time of the Almighty the center stake must
be built up.

Work was stopped on the Nauvoo house by the Prophet's
direction and every effort concentrated upon the temple. He determined that the structure should be fitted to receive the wor-
shiping Saints of the Most High before they should go into volun-
tary exile or submit to expatriation. And though he did not live
to see the consummation of this purpose, it was literally fulfilled.
And though he did not live to see the exodus of the Saints nor to
send out the first pioneer party of explorers, his inspired suggestion was carried out; and through it his prediction was fulfilled

that the Saints in five years should be beyond the power of their old enemies.

In March, the Prophet addressed a memorial to Congress, asking for the passage of an ordinance to protect citizens of the United States emigrating into the western region. His purpose was to advance, under national authority, beyond the western boundary of the United States and establish American citizens in this vast domain preparatory to the hour when it should become annexed to our country. The ordinance he himself drafted, and in its provisions he betrayed his usual grandeur of purpose.

Life of the Prophet Joseph, By George Q. Cannon, pp. 447-448.

SAINTS, IF WORTHY, SHALL BE PROTECTED

By Orson Hyde

The Latter-day Saints once had homes amongst other people; but other people and other powers would neither protect nor defend us in the possession and enjoyment of them. Consequently, we were forced away to the home which God provided for us; *and he has promised us here his own protection and defense, if we prove faithful to him,—that if any people, any power, or any force should stretch out an arm to molest or oppress us, that people, that power, or that force should be broken like a potter's vessel when smitten by an iron rod.* "Whosoever falleth upon this stone shall be broken." "I will fight your battles," saith the Almighty. All who prefer the protection of Jehovah to the protection of the crumbling powers of this world, and whose hearts are pure and honest enough to merit that protection, may come and share it. "Come out of Babylon, my people, that ye be not partakers of her sins and that ye receive not of her plagues." *Millennial Star, 24:275.*

JOSEPH LONGED TO BE IN THE ROCKY MOUNTAINS

By Brigham Young

"Remarks have been made as to our staying here. I will tell you how long we shall stay here. If we live our religion, we shall stay here in these mountains forever and forever, worlds without end, and a portion of the Priesthood will go and redeem and build up the centre Stake of Zion. If we leave here, where shall we go to? Has any one discovered where we can again pitch our tents, when we leave this country? *In the days of Joseph we have sat many hours at a time conversing about this very country. Joseph has often said, 'If I were only in the Rocky Mountains with a hundred faithful men, I would then be happy, and ask no odds of mobocrats.'* And neither do I.

"Who are going to pull up stakes and leave here? If we forsake our God and our religion, then woe to us, for then we shall be all apostates together, and under such circumstances we have no promise of God for our protection; but if we live in the faith of the Son of God, we have the heavens, the power of God and of

angels on our side. I can tell you, as truly as Elisha said to his
servant: 'Fear not; for they that be with us are more than they
that be with them.' For, 'the mountain was full of horses and
chariots of fire around about Elisha.' "   *J. D.* 11:16.

TRAITORS ADVISED THE PROPHET TO RETURN

BY BENJ. F. JOHNSON

It was now June 1844, and mobs were destroying property,
burning homes of the Saints outside of Nauvoo, and threatening
the city. Governor Ford ordered out troops to enforce the law, but
they were not reliable, and all was excitement. On the 15th an
order came for the able-bodied men at Macedonia to hasten to
Nauvoo. On the 16th we started, and to avoid attack travelled all
night, across the prairie through mud, rain and darkness, terrible
to those who were there. The Prophet came out to greet us. Here
I remained a few days on duty, when I was sent by General Dunham, then in command, back to Macedonia to look after and keep
up a home-guard.

It was now revealed to the Prophet that his only safety was
in flight to the Rocky Mountains, and he crossed the river with a
few faithful friends with a full purpose not to return. But through
the persuasion and reproaches of his wife, Emma, and others, he
was induced to return and give himself up to the slaughter. With
all the persons who induced him to return I was well acquainted,
and I know that fearful has been the hand of the Lord to follow
them from the day they sought to steady the Ark of God, which
resulted in the martyrdom of his servants.

My Life's Review, pp. 101-102.

CHAPTER 8

Personal Farewells of the Prophet to his Friends

PROPHET'S LAST WORDS IN MORTALITY

Joseph laid out his right arm, and said to John S. Fullmer, "Lay your head on my arm for a pillow, Brother John;" and when all were quiet they conversed in a low tone about the prospects of their deliverance. Joseph gave expression to several presentiments that he had to die, and said "I would like to see my family again," and "I would to God that I could preach to the Saints in Nauvoo once more." Fullmer tried to rally his spirits, saying he thought he would often have that privilege, when Joseph thanked him for the remarks and good feelings expressed to him.

Henry G. Sherwood went up to Joseph and said "Brother Joseph, shall I return to Nauvoo and regulate about getting the arms and get the receipts for them?" Joseph inquired if he was under arrest, or expected to be arrested. Sherwood answered "No," when Joseph directed him to return ahead of the company, gather the arms and do as well as he could in all things. Joseph then said to the company who were with him, *"I am going like a lamb to the slaughter, but I am calm as a summer's morning. I have a conscience void of offense toward God and toward all men. If they take my life I shall die an innocent man, and my blood shall cry from the ground for vengeance, and it shall be said of me 'He was murdered in cold blood!'"* He then said to Father Sherwood, "Go, and God bless you." Sherwood then rode as swiftly as he could to Nauvoo.

Joseph paused when they got to the Temple, and looked with admiration first on that, and then on the city, and remarked, "This is the loveliest place and the best people under the heavens; little do they know the trials that await them." As he passed out of the city, he called on Daniel H. Wells, Esq., who was unwell, and on parting he said, "Squire Wells, I wish you to cherish my memory, and not think me the worst man in the world either."

The company (about fifteen) then started again for Carthage, and when opposite to the Masonic Hall, Joseph said, "Boys, if I don't come back, take care of yourselves; I am going like a lamb to the slaughter." When they passed his farm he took a good look at it, and after they had passed it, he turned round several times to look again, at which some of the company made remarks, when Joseph said: "If some of you had got such a farm and knew you would not see it any more, you would want to take a good look at it for the last time."

Joseph rode down home twice to bid his family farewell. He appeared solemn and thoughtful, and expressed himself to several individuals that he expected to be murdered. There appeared no alternative but that he must either give himself up, or the inhabitants of the city would be massacred by a lawless mob under sanction of the Governor.

I told Stephen Markham that if I and Hyrum were ever taken again we should be massacred, or I was not a prophet of God. I want Hyrum to live to avenge my blood, but he is determined not to leave me.   D. H. C. 6:601, 554, 555, 558.

WILFORD WOODRUFF SEES THE PROPHET JOSEPH FOR THE LAST TIME

I left New York for Nauvoo, via the lakes, and was on the steamer Chesapeake, with my wife and child when she was wrecked on Lake Michigan, and all came near being lost; but through the mercy of God we were again preserved from the perils of the waters. I arrived at Nauvoo on the 6th of October, 1841, where I again had the happy privilege of meeting with the Prophet Joseph and Apostles and my friends. I spent the winter of 1841-2 in Nauvoo, attending meetings and councils, and laboring with my hands for the support of myself and family until the 3rd of February, 1842, at which time Joseph Smith called me to take charge of the business department of the printing office, which I attended to until the 20th of January, 1844, when I left the office well supplied with materials, in the hands of Elder John Taylor. I received my endowments with the Twelve under the direction of the Prophet Joseph Smith in the winter of 1843. In the spring of 1844, I was appointed a mission with most of the Twelve to go through the Eastern States. On the 9th of May, 1844, I took the last parting hand with President Joseph Smith in his own house, with Brother Jedediah M. Grant. He blessed me and bade me God speed, but seemed very sorrowful, as he did in parting with all the Twelve. I have since been satisfied that he had a presentiment that it was his last parting with his brethren of the Apostles. I attended a conference at Boston, and on the 27th of June, 1844, while at the railway depot in Boston with Elder Brigham Young, waiting for trains to take us to Lowell, there seemed to be a dark cloud and sorrowful gloom come over us, which we could not comprehend at the time. While I was at Portland, Maine, and ready to step on board a steamer for Fox Islands I saw an account of the martyrdom of the Prophet and his brother Hyrum, and the Spirit bore record to me that it was true; so I returned to Boston, where the Twelve soon met together, and we hastened to Nauvoo, when we found the city enveloped in mourning.   *Millennial Star*, Vol. 51:242.

ORDERS FOR MACEDONIA TROOPS OF THE NAUVOO LEGION

By John L. Smith

In 1844, during the increase of troubles and mobocracy in Hancock county, Illinois, orders were issued for the Macedonia troop of the Nauvoo Legion to march to Nauvoo. The troops being assembled and the dispatches read, Captain Babbitt made the following speech, as near as my memory serves: "My men, I love you, but I will not go, and will say that not one of you who start for Nauvoo will ever reach that place alive." My father, president of the branch, stepped in front of the company, and in a clear distinct voice said: "Every man of you that goes at the call of the Prophet shall go and return safely and not a hair of your heads shall be lost; and I bless you in the name of the Lord."

The troop, seventy-five in number, quickly voted for Lieut. Yager to take command, and in one hour we were on the march. For some days previous the rain had been falling in torrents; creeks and sloughs were overflowing and the roads were ankle-deep in mud. Some six or eight of our party were mounted on horses, the balance trailing behind the baggage wagons, holding our arms and ammunition above our heads, as we were often waist-deep in water.

About five miles on our way, we encountered a band of mounted men with red flags flying. They were twice our number, and had gathered around a log house, some fifty yards to the left of the road. They rode around the house several times and fired at us as they made the circle, the bullets whistling through the air and some of them ploughing up the ground before reaching our line. Captain Yager placed our men in file at three paces space, directing each man to load well, but hold fire until we could see them wink; just as we were nearly opposite them they took fright and broke into a run across the prairie toward Carthage.

We reached Nauvoo about daylight, and encamped in front of Foster's big brick house near the Temple. Our camp equipage was placed by the side of a log which reached halfway across the street. While I was guarding the baggage, Joseph the Prophet rode up to the log, reached his hand to me and inquired after uncle and aunt. He held me by the hand and pulled me forward until I was obliged to step upon the log. When turning his horse sideways he drew me step by step to near the end of the log, when seeing that each foot left marks upon the bark he asked me what was the matter with my feet. I replied the prairie grass had cut my shoes to pieces and wounded my feet, but they would soon be all right. I noticed the hand he raised to his face was wet, and looking up I saw his cheeks covered with tears. He placed his hand on my head and said, "God bless you, my dear boy," and asked if others of the company were in the same plight. I replied that a number of them were. Turning his face toward Mr. Lathrop as the latter came to the door of his store, the Prophet said: "Let these men have some shoes." Lathrop said: "I have no shoes." Joseph's quick reply was: "Let them have boots, then."

Joseph then turned to me and said: "Johnnie, the troops will be disbanded and return home. I shall go to Carthage for trial, under the protection of the governor." Then leaning towards me, with one hand on my head, he said: "Have no fears, for you shall yet see Israel triumph and in peace." This was the last time I saw and spoke with Joseph the Prophet while living, and the sensation and impression made upon me will never be forgotten. On June 20, 1844, the troops disbanded, and we marched home, numbers of my brethren as well as myself being very thankful for the protection our boots afforded to our wounded feet.

On June 27, 1844, while 'on picket duty on one of the main streets of Macedonia, word came that Joseph and Hyrum had been murdered at Carthage. This we could scarcely believe to be true, though at the hour specified we heard the firing of guns from that direction, it being only a few miles distant. The report was confirmed soon after.

On the 29th my father and family, with the Saints generally, visited Nauvoo and passed through the room in the Mansion house where the bodies of the Prophet and Patriarch lay, while thousands viewed them. My eyes were dry and it seemed to me they would burn out of my head, but no tears relieved me. After the burial ceremonies were over we returned to Macedonia. Many threats were made, and much talk of murdering all the Smith relatives. During the summer we removed to Nauvoo and with the assistance of many friends we built a room or two adjoining my brother George A. Smith's house. My father administered hundreds of patriarchal blessings, having been ordained a Patriarch by Joseph and Hyrum before they were murdered. *Millennial Star,* 56:539-541.

THE LAST TIME I SAW THE PROPHET

By Mary Ellen Kimball

The last time I saw the Prophet, he was on his way to Carthage jail. Himself and his brother Hyrum were on horseback, also Brothers John Taylor and Willard Richards. They stopped outside Sister Clawson's house, at the house of Brother Rosecrans. We were on the porch. The streets of Nauvoo were narrow, and we could hear every word he said. He asked for a drink of water. They all took a drink. Some few remarks passed between them which I do not remember; after bidding goodbye, he said to Brother Rosecrans: "If I never see you again, or if I never come back, remember that I love you." This went through me like electricity. I went in the house and threw myself on the bed and wept like a child. *Juvenile Instructor,* 27:490; *Nauvoo the Beautiful,* p. 157.

FOREBODINGS OF THOMAS COTTAM

Thomas Cottam, whose home is in St. George, Washington County, Utah, first met the Prophet Joseph Smith, in April 1842, in Nauvoo, having emigrated there from England, his native country, where he received the gospel February 2nd, 1840. Brother Cottam states that the Prophet's appearance when he first saw him was just what he had previously conceived it to be—that of a noble, fine-looking man.

"My testimony of him is that he was a true Prophet of God, raised up in this last dispensation of the fullness of times, and that his sayings and teachings are true and faithful, and that he sealed his testimony with his blood."

"There are some things that are, as it were, engraved on my memory. One is particularly so. In Nauvoo I lived near Brother Caspar's on the creek, about a mile and a half from the Temple. Accidentally going into the city on that fatal day, the 27th of June, I met Brothers Joseph and Hyrum with others of the brethren and a posse of men on their leaving Nauvoo for Carthage for the last time. His appearance and demeanor conveyed plainly to my mind that he realized he was going as a lamb to the slaughter. I should judge his feelings to be similar to that of the Savior when he uttered these memorable words: 'O Jerusalem, Jerusalem, thou that killest the prophets, and stonest them which are sent unto thee, how often would I have gathered thy children together, even as a hen gathereth her chickens under her wings, and ye would not!' "

"As I was on guard in and around Nauvoo I did not see the bodies of our honored dead after they were brought home, but I recollect the feeling that came upon me when I just heard of their death. 'Can it be possible! can it be possible!' I repeated in my mind; 'well, I shall have to go back to England.' But it was only temporary, for I soon realized that there would be a leader for the people. Even some of the disciples of Jesus thought momentarily that they would have to return again to their fishing."

Instructor, Vol. 15.

A PROPHECY BY JOSEPH THE SEER

On the 16th of June (1844) Brother Joseph preached to the assembled Saints in the grove east of the Temple (while the rain fell heavily), from the revelations of St. John the Divine. After the city had been declared under martial law, the Legion was drawn up in front of the Mansion House and the Prophet, standing upon the framework of a building opposite, addressed them. He asked us if we loved him? if we would stand by him and sustain the laws of our country? And we all answered "Yes, yes." Then he said he was content; he would die for us. "I love you, my brethren; greater love hath no man than that he lay down his life for his friends; you have stood by me in the hour of trouble, and I am willing to sacrifice my life for your preservation." Then drawing his sword: "I call God and Angels to witness that this people shall have their legal rights or my blood shall be spilt upon the ground **** and my body consigned to the tomb, but if there is one drop of blood shed on this occasion, the sword shall never again be sheathed until Christ comes to reign over the earth**** Peace shall be taken from the land which permits these crimes against the Saints to go unavenged***. May God bless you forever and ever." And we all answered, "Amen."

On the 20th day of June Brother Joseph sent word to all the apostles to return home immediately; and on the 24th he, with seventeen others, went to Carthage.

At this time I was living at Big Mound, an English settlement about eight miles from Nauvoo, and there, while engaged in putting in sod corn I heard of the Prophet's and Hyrum's death. The next morning I started to Carthage with those who went after the bodies. We met them on the road, Dr. Richards having dressed the wounds of John Taylor and started for Nauvoo with Joseph's and Hyrum's bodies.

The wailing of the Saints when they saw the martyrs was terrible. Ten thousand people were addressed by Apostle Richards, who admonished them to keep the peace and trust to the law for a remedy for the awful crimes which had been committed and if the law failed, to call upon God in heaven to avenge us of our wrongs. The bodies were placed in coffins, the funeral was held, while deep grief filled our hearts and sorrow rested heavily upon us—a stricken people. The woe of the Saints cannot be described. Our Prophet and Patriarch dead, only two of the apostles with us and one of them supposed to be dying, and all this time we were in constant expectation of an attack by the mob army.

Life of Christopher Layton, pp. 19-21.

LAST ADMONITION OF JOSEPH THE PROPHET

A few words of counsel given by the Prophet Joseph Smith on the 22nd day of June, 1844. On this day our General called us out in order and to my astonishment counselled us to give up our arms that had been supplied for our defense by the authority of the state of Illinois, saying: "We will give to them that asketh of us and trust in God for our future welfare. I wish to render you my thanks as soldiers and citizens under my command. I proclaim as your general, you have done your duty faithfully in guarding this city and in preserving the lives of all the people as well as mine in a special manner; for I have seen you on duty without shoes and comfortable clothing, and if I had the means to buy or if I could obtain these necessary things for you I would gladly do it. But I cannot mortgage any of my property to get one dollar but I will say this: You will be called the first Elders of the Church, and your missions will be to the nations of the earth. You will gather many people into the fastnesses of the Rocky Mountains as a center for the gathering of the people, and you will be faithful because you have been true; and many of those that come under your ministry, because of their much learning, will seek for high positions, and they will be set up and raise themselves in eminence above you, but you will walk in low places unnoticed and you will know all that transpires in their midst, and those that are my friends will be your friends. *This I will promise to you, that when I come again to lead you forth, for I will go to prepare a place for you, so that where I am you shall be with me.*"

With these comforting sayings, he thanked us for past duties done. "You are now dismissed to take care of your wives and children and homes."

On the 23rd day of June, 1844, we heard a call upon the Legion to muster in Main street near the Mansion house. I again saw our General in his uniform upon a small frame. He again spoke to the Legion. Laying his hand upon the head of Levi W. Hancock who was sitting at his feet, he said: "This day the Lord has shown to me that which was never shown to me before, that

THE PROPHET JOSEPH ADDRESSING THE NAUVOO LEGION.

Unsheathing his sword the Prophet said: "I call God and angels to witness that this people shall have their legal rights or my blood shall be spilt upon the ground and my body consigned to the tomb but if there is one drop of blood shed on this occasion, the sword shall never again be sheathed until Christ comes to reign on earth."

I have thousands of friends that never pretended friendship, while others have sought to crawl into my bosom because of my good feelings towards them, and now are the vipers and do seek my life; and if they shall take it they will pursue you; they will do it anyhow. When you are obliged to fight, be sure that you do not stain your hands with the blood of women and children, and when your enemies call for quarters, be sure that you grant them the same, and then you will gain power over the world." He then raised his hand from Levi W. Hancock's head and also raised his voice, saying: "You will forever be named the Nauvoo Legion, and as I have had the honor of being your General and leader, I feel to say a few words to your comfort and I wish to ascertain your interest and faith in your mission of life that you are engaged in, even in the same cause, with the power of the Priesthood sealed upon you. Your calling is to minister life and salvation to all nations on the earth. Although things appear at the present crisis, by the works of our enemies, that they hold an overruling power over us, but I will liken these things to a wheel of fortune. If we are at this time under the wheel, it is sure to be rolling on, and as sure will the Saints, sometime be on top of this wheel, if they hang on for their fortune in view. If it was not for the tender bonds of love that binds me to you, my friends and brethren, death would be sweet to me as honey. Our enemies are after me, to trust my life to them, by their voucher and honor of the state and that by the Governor and authority of the state of Illinois. I therefore will say to you Saints and Elders of Israel: *Be not troubled nor give yourselves uneasiness, so as to make any rash moves or to take any hasty steps in doing any wrong whereby you will be cut short in your calling in preaching the Gospel to this generation, for you will yet be called upon to go forth and call upon the free men from Maine to gather themselves together to the Rocky Mountains; and the Redmen from the West and all people from the North and from the South and from the East, and go to the West, to establish themselves in the strongholds of their gathering places, and there you will gather the Redmen to their center from their scattered and dispersed situation, to become the strong arm of Jehovah, who will be a strong bulwark of protection from your foes.* These things I feel to tell you beforehand, that you may always be ready for your duty, for at this time I need the best of friends to stand by me, and on this occasion I would like to know of you all, by your own answer, Yes or No, Are you willing to lay down your lives for me?"

The answer was then heard with one unanimous voice, "Yes."

"I am your Father. Shall I not be your Father?" Then all, with a loud exclamation said, "Yes." He again said to us: "Now I am willing to lay my life down for you, and if innocent blood is spilt on this occasion" (he then drew his sword out of the scabbard, raising it above his head, saying) "I will call upon the mighty Gods to bear witness of this; I have drawn my sword and it shall never be sheathed again until vengeance is taken on all of our enemies. I will call upon the elements in our defense, the winds with the whirlwinds, the thunders and lightnings and the hail storms; the heavens shall tremble and with earthquakes shall the earth be shaken, with the seas heaving themselves beyond their bounds. These things shall be brought to bear against our enemies for our preservation as a people of the Lord. We have given up our arms and they have taken away our right of protection, by our City Charter, and now they desire that I shall surrender myself into their hands, which I have consented to do. I only go to return to you again."

With his blessing upon us, we were dismissed to go to our homes. Excerpts from *Diary of John E. Forsgren.*

THE SISTER OF THE PROPHET TESTIFIES

The following is from the Carthage, Ill., *Republican* of May 16 (1894), and will be of more than passing interest to the Latter-day Saints, as it relates to the only surviving sister of the Prophet Joseph Smith and to incidents which are deeply impressed in the history of the Mormon people:

A representative of the *Republican* recently paid a visit to the home of Fred Salisbury, residing some four miles northeast of Fountain Green, and was cordially received by that gentleman and his family, as well as by his venerable and noted mother, *Mrs. Catherine Salisbury*, who is a sister of the Prophet Joseph Smith. On the 27th day of June next will be the fiftieth anniversary of the massacre of Hyrum and Joseph Smith in the old stone jail at Carthage. The silver-crowned matriarch who will be 88 years old in July, bears a striking resemblance to her nephew, the present Joseph Smith, son of the Prophet, and president of the Reorganized Church of Jesus Christ of Latter-day Saints, at Lamoni, Iowa. Some resemblance to the martyred Prophet, as shown in some of the photographs of him, may be noted in the features of this venerable lady, but very little. Mrs. Salisbury, as well as her son, was ready to answer any questions relating to their noted relatives or the early reminiscences of Mormonism in Hancock County. "We have been interviewed by authors and newspaper writers," said Mrs. Salisbury, "but we have not always received justice in histories or published stories. All we ask is a fair representation."

Mrs. Salisbury also stated that her brother's life and acts had been most cruelly misrepresented. She loaned the writer a book written a number of years ago by Mrs. Lucy Smith, mother of Joseph, which she says is the most authentic account of the Smith family ever published. Mrs. Salisbury resided with her husband at Plymouth, in this county, during the Mormon ascendancy. She with her parents and brothers and sisters, save Joseph and Hyrum, first located near the present site of Bardolph, McDonough County, at the time the Mormons were driven out of Missouri. The major portion of the Mormons remained in Quincy two or three weeks after leaving Missouri until Joseph and Hyrum were liberated from jail. They then followed their leaders to Nauvoo, where the "New Zion" was built upon these beautiful hills.

"I heard brother Joseph's last sermon, delivered to a great audience in Nauvoo," said Mrs. Salisbury, and a look of tender sadness lighted up those dimming eyes as she spoke. *"In that sermon,"* continued the venerable lady, *"Brother Joseph said that there was seated on the speaker's stand beside him those who were conspiring to take his life, and who would be responsible for his death."*

Among the valuable relics exhibited to the visitor was a portrait of Joseph and Hyrum Smith, standing facing each other, dressed in the peculiar costumes worn by them as Prophets of the Church. "That is the position they assumed the last time I ever saw my brothers," said Mrs. Salisbury. "I left them on the Saturday (June 22, 1844) before the Thursday that they were murdered at Carthage. Brother Joseph shook my hand saying, "Sister Catherine as soon as this trouble blows over I will come down to Plymouth and make you a visit." Brother Hyrum simply said,

"Good-bye" in an impressive manner. I never saw them again in life. They were both very kind to me and whenever there was a church celebration or any big doings at Nauvoo they would always send for me."   *Millennial Star,* 56:549-551.

FOREBODINGS OF THE MARTYRDOM

By WILFORD WOODRUFF

While delivering an interesting address before the Female Relief Society of Nauvoo, he said, As he had this opportunity he was going to instruct the society, and point out the way for them to conduct themselves, that they might act according to the will of God; that he did not know that he should have many opportunities of teaching them, as they were going to be left to themselves; they would not have him to instruct them; that the church would not have his instructions long, and the world would not be troubled with him a great while, nor have his teachings; he spoke of delivering the keys to others, and that, according to his prayers, God had appointed him elsewhere.

The Prophet called the quorum of the twelve together several months before his death, and informed them that the Lord had commanded him to hasten their endowments; that he did not expect to remain himself to see the temple completed, but wished to confer the keys of the kingdom of God upon other men, that they might build up the church and kingdom according to the pattern given. And the Prophet stood before the twelve from day to day, clothed with the spirit and power of God, and instructed them in the oracles of God, in the pattern of heavenly things, in the keys of the kingdom, the power of the priesthood, and in the knowledge of the last dispensation in the fullness of times.

Millennial Star, 5:136.

TESTIMONY OF WILFORD WOODRUFF

DELIVERED ON FEBRUARY 23, 1892, IN THE ASSEMBLY HALL, SALT LAKE CITY, UTAH

Joseph Smith lived some fourteen years, if I mistake not, after he organized this Church. He also was slain. But before he died he organized the Church with Apostles, Patriarchs, Pastors, Teachers, and the whole government of the Church of God; and that Priesthood he organized or laid the foundation of which remained with the people after his death. The Twelve Apostles stood next to the First Presidency of the Church; and I am a living witness myself to this work. I am a living witness to the testimony that he gave to the Twelve Apostles when all of us received our endowments under his hands. I remember the last speech that he ever gave us before his death. It was before we started upon our mission to the East. He stood upon his feet some two or three hours. The room was filled as with consuming fire, his face was as clear as amber, and he was clothed upon by the power of God. He laid before us our duty. He laid before us the fullness of this great work of God; and in his remarks to us he said: "I have sealed upon my head every key, every power, every principle of life and salvation that God has ever given to any man who ever lived upon the face of the earth. And these principles and this priesthood and power belong to this great and last dispensation which the God of Heaven has set His hand to establish in the earth." "Now," said he, addressing the Twelve, "I have sealed upon your heads every key, every power, and every principle which the Lord has sealed upon my head." Continuing, he said, "I have lived so long—up to the present time—I have been in the midst of this people, and in the great work of labor and redemption. I have desired to live to see this Temple (at Nauvoo) built. But I shall never live to see it completed; but you will." Now, we did not suppose but what he would live. We did not comprehend what he meant. Neither did the Twelve in the days of the Savior comprehend what He meant when He said, "I am going away from you; if I go not the Comforter will not come unto you." So we did not understand Joseph when he said that he would not live to see that Temple completed; it was not given to us to realize it at that time.

After addressing us in this manner he said: "I tell you the burden of this kingdom now rests upon your shoulders; you have got to bear it off in all the world, and if you don't do it you will be damned." That was pretty strong language, but it was full of meaning, it was full of significance. Joseph was trained in the Priesthood before he came to this planet. He understood the Priesthood perfectly before he came here. He understood its work and its lineage, so far as lineage applies to offices in the Priesthood. He also understood that he was going away from this earth; but we did not know it until after he was put to death. I was in Boston with President Young the very hour that he and his brother Hyrum were slain. And at that moment there was a power of darkness surrounded us, a feeling of heaviness that I never felt before. I had never seen President Young feel so bad in my life as he did that hour. *Liahona, the Elders Journal*, April 16, 1910.

MERCY R. THOMPSON DESCRIBES THE PARTING PRIOR TO THE MARTYRDOM

I was present at a prayer meeting held in the upper room of the brick-stone building, at a time when his enemies were seeking his life.

At another time—a time never to be forgotten—I was present at a meeting when Joseph knelt down with the small congregation surrounding him, when every sentence he uttered seemed to convey to my mind, and to the minds of others present, the impression that this was our last meeting together—and so it was.

It seemed to me that there was nothing forgotten or omitted by him, at that time, which pertained either to himself or the Church generally. A few days after this he called at his brother Hyrum's to take leave of the family previous to their crossing the Mississippi River, intending to go west to the Rocky Mountains to seek out, if possible, a place of peace and safety for the Saints. His parting words to my sister Mary, as she wept at their going, were these:

"Sister Mary, don't feel bad, the Lord will take care of you, and He will deliver us, but I do not know how." The two brothers then started to cross the river, not knowing whether they would ever see their homes again or not. But on account of the feelings expressed by some of the brethren, who should have been their truest friends, and by their urgent request, sent after them, the brothers returned to Nauvoo the following day. Watching from a chamber window I saw them being rowed in a skiff across the river, until they landed, and walked up the river bank to Hyrum's house, where they both entered, Joseph seating himself, while Hyrum made some changes in his clothing, when they both went on to the Mansion.

Although I did not know that the brothers had returned home to be taken as "lambs to the slaughter," my feelings were indescribable, and the very air seemed burdened with sorrowful forebodings.

The awful scene at Carthage followed in a few days, and here all men must draw the veil, for until all the truth concerning these good men, and this black deed of their murderous foes, can be told and understood the history of this time will not be written. But the day will come when God will speak, and the Martyrs and their history shall be known.   *Instructor*, 27:400.

THE PROPHET'S LAST ADDRESS TO THE PEOPLE

After the city had been declared under martial law, the Legion was drawn up in front of the mansion to be addressed by the Prophet. He stood upon the frame of a building opposite his house, dressed in his full uniform as Lieutenant-General.

William W. Phelps read from an extra issue of the *Warsaw Signal** of the day before, calling upon all the old citizens to assist

---

*The *Warsaw Signal*, edited by an infamous man by the name of Thomas Sharp, took a prominent and diabolical part in arousing the spirit of murder. It published the minutes of mob meetings and resolutions adopted there, in which the most fiendish threats were made. Some of them are as follows:

"We therefore declare that we will sustain our press and the editor at all hazards; that we will take full vengeance, terrible vengeance, should the lives of any of our citizens be lost in the effort; that we hold ourselves at all times in readiness to co-operate with our fellow-citizens in this state, Missouri and Iowa, *to exterminate, utterly exterminate the wicked and abominable Mormon leaders*, the authors of our troubles.

"*Resolved*, That a committee of five be appointed forthwith to notify all persons in our township *suspected* of being the tools of the Prophet to leave immediately on pain of *instant vengeance. And we do recommend the inhabitants of the adjacent townships to do the same, hereby pledging ourselves to render all the assistance they may require.*

"*Resolved*, That the time, in our opinion has arrived, when the adherents of Smith, as a body, should be driven from the surrounding settlements into Nauvoo. That the Prophet and his miscreant adherents should then be demanded at their hands; and, if not surrendered, *a war of extermination should be waged, to the entire destruction*, if necessary for our protection, *of his adherents*. And we do hereby recommend this resolution to the consideration of the several townships, to the mass convention to be held at Carthage, hereby pledging ourselves to aid to the utmost the complete consummation of the

the mob in exterminating the leaders of the Saints and driving the people into exile.

Joseph then recounted the doings of the time at Nauvoo, and demonstrated that he and his brethren had been willing and were still as willing as ever to submit to the authority of law; that they had not transgressed the statutes; and that the effort making against them was the device of Satan. He told them that a pretext had been sought by their enemies in order that a band of infuriated mob-men might be congregated to fall upon Nauvoo, to murder, plunder and ravish the innocent.

The vast assemblage had listened to his words with breathless attention, for he spoke with a power transcending anything that the Saints had ever before heard, even from him whose speech was always soul-touching. Had he expressed a wish to fight, his people would have followed him with joy to the contest. It is no wonder that his words sank deep into their hearts; it is no wonder that to their sight he appeared grander than mortal. It was the last time for many of them in the flesh that they were to listen to the music of his voice or to feel the spell of his mighty inspiration. It was his last public address! In a few short days that god-like form, so perfect in its manly beauty, was to be locked in the embrace of the tomb; and that voice, whose angelic sweetness had comforted them in the hour of darkest woe, was to be hushed in death.

On the 20th of June he wrote to all the Apostles who were absent on missions to come home immediately. Only two of the Twelve were with him, Apostle John Taylor and Willard Richards. He had often stated to the Twelve that upon them would devolve the work when he was gone, and he knew that their presence would soon be needed. His consciousness of his impending fate and his fortitude were divine. His last deeds and his last thoughts were for the cause and the people whom he loved.

Life of the Prophet Joseph, By George Q. Cannon, pp. 467-8.

JOSEPH DESIRED HYRUM TO AVENGE HIS BLOOD

By George Q. Cannon

About this time, Joseph wrote also to those of the Twelve Apostles who were absent on missions, to come home immediately, as he was anxious to have them with him; for he felt that trouble was thickening around him; and no doubt he desired to have his friends—the men he could rely upon near to him in the hour of difficulty.

He was anxious to get Hyrum, his brother, out of the way. He advised him to take his family on the next steamboat to Cincinnati. If anything happened to himself, he was anxious that Hyrum should live. Said he: "I wish I could get Hyrum out of the way, so that he may live to avenge my blood; and I will stay with you and

object in view, that we may thereby be utterly relieved of the alarm, anxiety and trouble to which we are now subjected.

"*Resolved*, That every citizen arm himself to be prepared to sustain the resolutions herein contained."

History of Joseph the Prophet, By George Q. Cannon, pp. 461-2.

see it out." But Hyrum could not be moved. If Joseph suffered and
died, he was determined to suffer and die with him. Said he to the
prophet: "Joseph, I cannot leave you." *Instructor*, Vol. 15.

The Prophet Joseph Instructs the Twelve to Return to Nauvoo

Dear Brother B. Young: Nauvoo, June 17, 1844.

There has been for several days a great excitement among the
inhabitants in the adjoining counties. Mass meetings are held upon
mass meetings, drawing up resolutions to utterly exterminate the
saints. The excitement has been gotten up by the Laws, Fosters and
the Higbees, and they themselves have left the city, and are engaged
in the mob. They have sent their runners into the State of Missouri
to excite them to murder and bloodshed, and the report is that a
great many hundreds of them will come over to take an active part
in murdering the saints. The excitement is very great indeed.

It is thought by myself and others for you to return without
delay, and the rest of the Twelve and all the Elders that have gone
out from this place, and as many more good, faithful men as feel
disposed to come up with them. Let wisdom be exercised; and whatever they do, do it without a noise. You know we are not frightened,
but think it best to be well prepared and be ready for the onset; and
if it is extermination, extermination it is of course. Communicate
to the others of the Twelve with as much speed as possible, with
perfect stillness and calmness. A word to the wise is sufficient,
and a little powder, lead and a good rifle, can be packed in your
luggage very easy without creating any suspicion.

In haste, I remain yours in the firm bonds of the new and
everlasting covenant.   Hyrum Smith.

Large bodies of armed men, cannon and munitions of war are
coming on from Missouri in steamboats. These facts are communicated to the Governor and President of the United States, and you
will readily see that you will have to prepare for the onset.

In the bonds of the new and everlasting covenant, I remain
yours,   Joseph Smith.

The reader should bear in mind that not only the entire quorum of the Twelve, excepting John Taylor and Willard Richards,
were scattered on missions in the States east, but that about five
hundred of the ablest, strong-willed Elders were also from home
on the same campaign. To this fact, indeed, is largely to be ascribed
the opportunity of the martyrdom. It was Brigham Young's repeated affirmation ever after the death of his chief, that, had he,
with the Twelve, been home, Joseph should not have been given up.

Life of Joseph the Prophet, By Edw. W. Tullidge, pp. 480-82.

THE PROPHET JOSEPH HAD COMPLETED HIS WORK

By Parley P. Pratt

This great and good man was led, before his death, to call
the Twelve together from time to time and to instruct them in all

things pertaining to the kingdom, ordinances and government of God. He often observed that he was laying the foundation, but it would remain for the Twelve to complete the building. Said he: *"I know not why; but for some reason I am constrained to hasten my preparations, and to confer upon the Twelve all the ordinances, keys, covenants, endowments, and sealing ordinances of the priesthood, and so set before them a pattern in all things pertaining to the sanctuary and the endowment therein."*

Having done this, he rejoiced exceedingly; "for," said he, *"the Lord is about to lay the burden on your shoulders and let me rest awhile; and if they kill me,"* continued he, *"the kingdom of God will roll on, as I have now finished the work which was laid upon me, by committing to you all things for the building up of the kingdom according to the heavenly vision, and the pattern shown me from heaven."* With many conversations like this he comforted the minds of the Twelve, and prepared them for what was soon to follow.   *Millennial Star, 5:151.*

THE PROPHET'S TESTIMONY IN CARTHAGE JAIL

Joseph bore a powerful testimony to the guards of the divine authenticity of the Book of Mormon, the restoration of the Gospel, the administration of angels, and that the kingdom of God was again established upon the earth, for the sake of which he was then incarcerated in that prison, and not because he had violated any law of God or man.

* * * * *

Said Joseph, "Our lives have already become jeopardized by revealing the wicked and bloodthirsty purposes of our enemies; and for the future we must cease to do so. All we have said about them is truth, but it is not always wise to relate all the truth. Even Jesus, the Son of God had to refrain from doing so, and had to restrain His feelings many times for the safety of Himself and His followers, and had to conceal the righteous purposes of His heart in relation to many things pertaining to His Father's kingdom. When still a boy He had all the intelligence necessary to enable Him to rule and govern the kingdom of the Jews, and could reason with the wisest and most profound doctors of law and divinity, and make their theories and practice to appear like folly compared with the wisdom He possessed; but He was a boy only, and lacked physical strength even to defend His own person, and was subject to cold, to hunger and to death. So it is with the Church of Jesus Christ of Latter-day Saints; we have the revelation of Jesus, and the knowledge within us is sufficient to organize a righteous government upon the earth, and to give universal peace to all mankind, if they would receive it, but we lack the physical strength, as did our Savior when a child, to defend our principles, and we have of necessity to be afflicted, persecuted and smitten, and to bear it patiently until Jacob is of age, then he will take care of himself."   *D. H. C. 6:600, 608.*

CHAPTER 9

The Martyrdom

TWO MINUTES IN JAIL

BY WILLARD RICHARDS

Possibly the following events occupied near three minutes, but I think only about two, and have penned them for the gratification of many friends:

Carthage, June 27, 1844.

A shower of musket balls were thrown up the stairway against the door of the prison in the second story, followed by many rapid footsteps.

While Generals Joseph and Hyrum Smith, Mr. Taylor and myself, who were in the front chamber, closed the door of our room against the entry at the head of the stairs, and placed ourselves against it, there being no lock on the door, and no catch that was useable.

The door is a common panel, and as soon as we heard the feet at the stairs head, a ball was sent through the door, which passed between us, and showed that our enemies were desperadoes, and we must change our position.

General Joseph Smith, Mr. Taylor, and myself sprang back to the front part of the room and General Hyrum Smith retreated -thirds across the chamber directly in front of and facing the door.

A ball was sent through the door which hit Hyrum on the side of his nose, when he fell backwards, extended at length, without moving his feet.

From the holes in his vest (the day was warm, and no one had their coats on but myself), pantaloons, drawers, and shirt, it appeared evident that a ball must have been thrown from without, through the window, which entered his back on the right side, and passing through lodged against his watch, which was in his right vest pocket, completely pulverizing the crystal and face, tearing off the hands and mashing the whole body of the watch. At the same instant the ball from the door entered his nose.

As he struck the floor he exclaimed emphatically, *"I'm a dead man."* Joseph looked towards him and responded, "Oh dear! Brother Hyrum," and opening the door two or three inches with his left hand, discharged one barrel of a six-shooter (pistol) at random in the entry, from whence a ball grazed Hyrum's breast, and entering his throat passed into his head, while other muskets were aimed at him and some balls hit him.

Joseph continued snapping his revolver round the casing of the door into the space as before, three barrels of which missed fire, while Mr. Taylor with a walking stick stood by his side and knocked down the bayonets and muskets which were constantly discharging through the doorway, while I stood by him, ready to lend any assistance, with another stick, but could not come within striking distance without going directly before the muzzles of the guns.

When the revolver failed, we had no more firearms, and expected an immediate rush of the mob, and the doorway full of muskets, half way in the room, and no hope but instant death from within.

Mr. Taylor rushed into the window, which is some fifteen or twenty feet from the ground. When his body was nearly on a balance, a ball from the door within entered his leg, and a ball from without struck his watch, a patent lever, in his vest pocket near the left breast, and smashed it into pi, leaving the hands standing at 5 o'clock, 16 minutes, and 26 seconds, the force of which ball threw him back on the floor, and he rolled under the bed which stood by his side, where he lay motionless, the mob from the door continuing to fire upon him, cutting away a piece of flesh from his left hip as large as a man's hand, and were hindered only by my knocking down their muzzles with a stick; while they continued to reach their guns into the room, probably left handed, and aimed their discharge so far round as almost to reach us in the corner of the room to where we retreated and dodged, and then I recommenced the attack with my stick.

Joseph attempted, as the last resort, to leap the same window from whence Mr. Taylor fell, when two balls pierced him from the door, and one entered his right breast from without, and he fell outward, exclaiming, *"O Lord, my God."* As his feet went out of the window my head went in, the balls whistling all around. He fell on his left side a dead man.

At this instant the cry was raised, *"He's leaped the window,"* and the mob on the stairs and in the entry ran out.

I withdrew from the window, thinking it of no use to leap out on a hundred bayonets, then around General Smith's body.

Not satisfied with this I again reached my head out of the window, and watched some seconds to see if there were any signs of life, regardless of my own, determined to see the end of him I loved. Being fully satisfied that he was dead, with a hundred men near the body and more coming round the corner of the jail, and expecting a return to our room, I rushed towards the prison door, at the head of the stairs, and through the entry from whence the firing had proceeded, to learn if the doors into the prison were open.

When near the entry, Mr. Taylor cried out, *"Take me."* I pressed my way until I found all doors unbarred, returning instantly, caught Mr. Taylor under my arm, and rushed by the stairs into the dungeon, or inner prison, stretched him on the floor and covered him with a bed in such a manner as not likely to be perceived, expecting an immediate return of the mob. I said to Mr. Taylor. "This is a hard case to lay you on the floor, but if your wounds are not fatal, I want you to live to tell the story." I expected to be shot the next moment, and stood before the door awaiting the onset.   *D. H. C.,* 7:619-21.

CARTHAGE JAIL IN 1855.

WELL AT CARTHAGE JAIL IN 1855.

AN ACCOUNT OF THE MARTYRDOM OF JOSEPH SMITH

By President John Taylor

Being requested by Elders George A. Smith and Wilford Woodruff, Church historians, to write an account of events that transpired before, and took place at, the time of the martyrdom of Joseph Smith, in Carthage jail, in Hancock County, State of Illinois, I write the following, principally from memory, not having

---

CARTHAGE JAIL

The two illustrations opposite were sketched by Frederick Piercy in 1855, and were reproduced in the book: "Route from Liverpool to Great Salt Lake Valley." It is very probable that the jail and well looked exactly in 1844 as in 1855. Special attention is directed to the well, it was against it that the Prophet was set when four of the mob shot him.

In the book above quoted, Mr. Piercey says: "The landlord of the tavern (Hamilton House) took me to the jail and obtained admittance for me. The keeper was away, and I was shown over it by a young girl. The holes made in the wall by the bullets still remain unstopped. The bullet hole in the door is that made by the ball which caused the death of Hyrum. I was told that the stains of blood were still in the floor, but I could not see them, as the room was covered by a carpet. *** Having seen the place and made my sketches, I was glad to leave. Two lives unatoned for, and 'blood crying from the ground,' made the spot hateful."

*   *   *   *

Carthage jail was erected in 1839-40 by Wm. Metcalf as contractor, at a cost of $4,105.00. It is constructed of yellow limestone, taken from a quarry four miles northeast of the building. In 1866 Hancock county sold the jail to Bryant F. Petersen for $1,100.00. He sold it to James M. Browning for $1500.00. The Church of Jesus Christ of Latter-day Saints through President Joseph F. Smith as trustee-in-trust, purchased it from Mrs. Eliza M. Browning, widow of James M. Browning, for $4,000, by deed dated November 4, (1903).

There are three rooms on the ground floor: a living room, dining room and the debtor's room, with an attached kitchen which is seen in both illustrations of the jail produced in this book. The upper story contained the jailor's bedroom in which the Prophet and his three companions were at the time of the martyrdom, and the cell room (12' x 24½') to the north of the stair landing which was partitioned by bars. It was in this cell room that Willard Richards carried John Taylor at the time of the tragedy.

(See booklet published by Joseph A. McRae, entitled: "The Historic Carthage Jail."

---

access at this time to any public documents relative thereto farther than a few desultory items contained in Ford's "History of Illinois." I must also acknowledge myself considerably indebted to George A. Smith who was with me when I wrote it, and who, although not there at the time of the bloody transaction, yet, from conversing with several persons who were in the capacity of Church historians, and aided by an excellent memory, has rendered me considerable service.

These and the few items contained in the note at the end of this account are all the aid I have had. I would further add that the items contained in the letter, in relation to dates especially, may be considered strictly correct.

After having written the whole, I read it over to the Hon. J. M. Bernhisel, who with one or two slight alterations, pronounced it strictly correct. Brother Bernhisel was present most of the time. I am afraid that, from the length of time that has transpired since the occurrence, and having to rely almost exclusively upon my memory, there may be some slight inaccuracies, but I believe that in the general it is strictly correct. As I figured in those transactions from the commencement to the end, they left no slight impression on my mind.

In the year 1844, a very great excitement prevailed in some parts of Hancock, Brown and other neighboring counties of Illinois, in relation to the Mormons, and a spirit of vindictive hatred and persecution was exhibited among the people, which was manifested in the most bitter and acrimonious language, as well as by acts of hostility and violence, frequently threatening the destruction of the citizens of Nauvoo and vicinity, and utter annihilation of the Mormons and Mormonism, and in some instances breaking out in the most violent acts of ruffianly barbarity. Persons were kidnapped, whipped, persecuted and falsely accused of various crimes; their cattle and houses injured, destroyed, or stolen; vexatious prosecutions were instituted to harass and annoy. In some remote neighborhoods they were expelled from their homes without redress, and in others violence was threatened to their persons and property, while in others every kind of insult and indignity were heaped upon them, to induce them to abandon their homes, the County or the State.

These annoyances, prosecutions and persecutions were instigated through different agencies and by various classes of men, actuated by different motives, but all uniting in the one object —prosecution, persecution and extermination of the Saints.

There were a number of wicked and corrupt men living in Nauvoo and its vicinity, who had belonged to the Church, but whose conduct was incompatible with the Gospel; they were accordingly dealt with by the Church and severed from its communion. Some of these had been prominent members, and held official stations either in the city or Church. Among these were John C. Bennett, formerly mayor; William Law, counselor to Joseph Smith; Wilson Law, his natural brother, and general in the Nauvoo Legion; Dr. R. D. Foster, a man of some property, but with a very bad reputation; Francis and Chauncey Higbee, the latter a young lawyer, and both sons of a respectable and honored man in the Church, known as Judge Elias Higbee, who died about twelve months before.

Besides these, there were a great many apostates, both in the city and county, of less notoriety, who for their delinquencies, had been expelled from the Church. John C. Bennett and Francis and Chauncey Higbee were cut off from the Church; the former was also cashiered from his generalship for the most flagrant acts of seduction and adultery; and the developments in the cases were so scandalous that the High Council, before which they were tried, had to sit with closed doors.

William Law, although counselor to Joseph, was found to be

his most bitter foe and maligner, and to hold intercourse, contrary to all law, in his own house, with a young lady resident with him; and it was afterwards proven that he had conspired with some Missourians to take Joseph Smith's life, and was only saved by Josiah Arnold and Daniel Garn, who, being on guard at his house, prevented the assassins from seeing him. Yet, although having murder in his heart, his manners were generally courteous and mild, and he was well calculated to deceive.

General Wilson Law was cut off from the Church for seduction, falsehood, and defamation; both the above were also court-martialed by the Nauvoo Legion, and expelled. Foster was also cut off I believe, for dishonesty, fraud and falsehood. I know he was eminently guilty of the whole, but whether these were the specific charges or not, I don't know, but I do know that he was a notoriously wicked and corrupt man.

Besides the above characters and Mormonic apostates, there were three other parties. The first of these may be called religionists, the second politicians, and the third counterfeiters, black-legs, horse-thieves and cut-throats.

The religious party were chagrined and maddened because Mormonism came in contact with their religion, and they could not oppose it from the scriptures. Thus like the ancient Jews, when enraged at the exhibition of their follies and hypocrisies by Jesus and His apostles, so these were infuriated against the Mormons because of their discomfiture by them; and instead of owning the truth and rejoicing in it, they were ready to gnash upon them with their teeth, and to persecute the believers in principles which they could not disprove.

The political party were those who were of opposite politics to us. There were always two parties, the Whigs and Democrats, and we could not vote for one without offending the other; and it not unfrequently happened that candidates for office would place the issue of their election upon opposition to the Mormons, in order to gain political influence from the religious prejudices, in which case the Mormons were compelled, in self-defense, to vote against them, which resulted almost invariably against our opponents. This made them angry; and although it was of their own making, and the Mormons could not be expected to do otherwise, yet they raged on account of their discomfiture, and sought to wreak their fury on the Mormons. As an instance of the above, when Joseph Duncan was candidate for the office of governor of Illinois, he pledged himself to his party that, if he could be elected, he would exterminate or drive the Mormons from the State.* The consequence was that Governor Ford was elected. The Whigs, seeing that they had been out-generaled by the Democrats in securing the Mormon vote, became seriously alarmed, and sought to repair their disaster by raising a crusade against the people. The Whig newspapers teemed with accounts of the wonders and enormities of Nauvoo, and of the awful wickedness of a party which could consent to receive the support of such mis-

*See his remarks as contained in his *History of Illinois*, p. 269.

creants. Governor Duncan, who was really a brave, honest man, and who had nothing to do with getting the Mormon charters passed through the Legislature, took the stump on this subject in good earnest, and expected to be elected governor almost on this question alone.

The third party, composed of counterfeiters, black-legs, horse-thieves and cut-throats, were a pack of scoundrels that infested the whole of the western country at that time. In some districts their influence was so great as to control important State and County offices. On this subject Governor Ford has the following:

"Then, again, the northern part of the State was not desti-tute of its organized bands of rogues, engaged in murders, rob-beries, horse-stealing and in making and passing counterfeit money. These rogues were scattered all over the north, but the most of them were located in the counties of Ogle, Winnebago, Lee and De Kalb.

"In the County of Ogle they were so numerous, strong, and well organized that they could not be convicted for their crimes. By getting some of their numbers on the juries, by producing a host of witnesses to sustain their defense, by perjured evidence, and by changing the venue of one County to another, by con-tinuances from term to term, and by the inability of witnesses to attend from time to time at distant and foreign Counties, they most generally managed to be acquitted."*

There was a combination of horse-thieves extending from Galena to Alton. There were counterfeiters engaged in merchan-dising, trading, and store-keeping in most of the cities and vil-lages, and in some districts, I have been credibly informed by men to whom they have disclosed their secrets, the judges, sheriffs, constables, and jailers, as well as professional men, were more or less associated with them. These had in their employ the most reckless, abandoned wretches, who stood ready to carry into ef-fect the most desperate enterprises, and were careless alike of human life and property. Their object in persecuting the Mor-mons was in part to cover their own rascality, and in part to pre-vent them from exposing and prosecuting them; but the principal reason was plunder, believing that if they could be removed or driven they would be made fat on Mormon spoils, besides having in the deserted city a good asylum for the prosecution of their diabolical pursuits.

This conglomeration of apostate Mormons, religious bigots, political fanatics and black-legs, all united their forces against the Mormons, and organized themselves into a party, denominated anti-Mormons. Some of them, we have reason to believe, joined the Church in order to cover their infamous practices, and when they were expelled for their unrighteousness only raged with greater violence. They circulated every kind of falsehood that they could collect or manufacture against the Mormons. They also had a paper to assist them in their nefarious designs, called the *Warsaw Signal*, edited by a Mr. Thomas Sharp, a violent and

*Ford's *History of Illinois*, p. 246.

unprincipled man, who shrunk not from any enormity. The anti-Mormons had public meetings, which were very numerously attended, where they passed resolutions of the most violent and inflammatory kind, threatening to drive, expel and exterminate the Mormons from the State, at the same time accusing them of every evil in the vocabulary of crime.

They appointed their meetings in various parts of Hancock, M'Donough, and other counties, which soon resulted in the organization of armed mobs, under the direction of officers who reported to their headquarters, and the reports of which were published in the anti-Mormon paper, and circulated through the adjoining counties. We also published in the *Times and Seasons* and the *Nauvoo Neighbor* (two papers published and edited by me at that time) an account, not only of their proceedings, but our own. But such was the hostile feeling, so well arranged their plans, and so desperate and lawless their measures, that it was with the greatest difficulty that we could get our papers circulated; they were destroyed by postmasters and others, and scarcely ever arrived at the place of their destination, so that a great many of the people, who would have been otherwise peaceable, were excited by their misrepresentations, and instigated to join their hostile or predatory bands.

Emboldened by the acts of those outside, the apostate Mormons, associated with others, commenced the publication of a libelous paper in Nauvoo, called the *Nauvoo Expositor*. This paper not only reprinted from the others, but put in circulation the most libelous, false, and infamous reports concerning the citizens of Nauvoo, and especially the ladies. It was, however, no sooner put in circulation than the indignation of the whole community was aroused; so much so, that they threatened its annihilation; and I do not believe that in any other city of the United States, if the same charges had been made against the citizens, it would have been permitted to remain one day. As it was among us, under these circumstances, it was thought best to convene the city council to take into consideration the adoption of some measures for its removal, as it was deemed better that this should be done legally than illegally. Joseph Smith, therefore, who was mayor, convened the city council for that purpose; the paper was introduced and read, and the subject examined. All, or nearly all present, expressed their indignation at the course taken by the *Expositor*, which was owned by some of the aforesaid apostates, associated with one or two others. Wilson Law, Dr. Foster, Charles Ivins and the Higbees before referred to, some lawyers, storekeepers, and others in Nauvoo who were not Mormons, together with the anti-Mormons outside of the city, sustained it. The calculation was, by false statements, to unsettle the minds of many in the city, and to form combinations there similar to the anti-Mormon associations outside of the city. Various attempts had heretofore been made by the party to annoy and irritate the citizens of Nauvoo; false accusations had been made, vexatious lawsuits instituted, threats made, and various devices resorted to, to influence the public mind, and, if possible, to provoke us to the commission of some overt act that might make us amenable to the law. With a perfect knowledge, therefore, of the designs of these infernal scoundrels who were in our midst, as well as those who surrounded us, the city ,council entered upon an investigation of the matter. They felt that they were in a critical position, and that any move made for the abating of that press would be looked upon, or at least represented, as a direct attack upon the liberty of speech, and that, so far from displeasing our enemies, it would be looked upon by them as one of the best circumstances that could transpire to assist them in their nefarious and bloody designs. Being a member of the city council, I well remember the feeling of responsibility that seemed to rest upon all present; nor shall I soon forget the bold, manly, independent expressions of Joseph Smith on that occasion in relation to this matter. He exhibited in glowing colors the meanness, corruption, and ultimate designs of the anti-Mormons; their despicable characters and ungodly influences, especially of those who were in our midst. He told of the responsibility that rested upon us, as guardians of the public interest, to stand up in the defense of the injured and oppressed, to stem the current of corruption, and, as men and Saints, to put a stop to this flagrant outrage upon this people's rights.

He stated that no man was a stronger advocate for the liberty of speech and of the press than himself: yet, when this noble gift is utterly prostituted and abused, as in the present instance, it loses all claim to our respect, and becomes as great an agent for evil as it can possibly be for good; and notwithstanding the apparent advantage we should give our enemies by this act, yet it behooved us, as men, to act independent of all secondary influences, to perform the part of men of enlarged minds, and boldly and fearlessly to discharge the duties devolving upon us by declaring as a nuisance, and removing this filthy, libelous, and seditious sheet from our midst.

The subject was discussed in various forms, and after the remarks made by the mayor, every one seemed to be waiting for some one else to speak.

After a considerable pause, I arose and expressed my feelings frankly, as Joseph had done, and numbers of others followed in the same strain; and I think, but am not certain, that I made a motion for the removal of that press as a nuisance. This motion was finally put, and carried by all but one; and he conceded that the measure was just, but abstained through fear.

Several members of the city council were not in the Church. The following is the bill referred to:

*Bill for Removing of the Press of the "Nauvoo Expositor."**

Resolved by the city council of the city of Nauvoo, that the printing-office from whence issues the *Nauvoo Expositor* is a public nuisance; and also of said *Nauvoo Expositors* which may be or exist in said establishment; and the mayor is instructed to cause said establishment and papers to be removed without delay, in such manner as he shall direct.

Passed June 10th, 1844. GEO. W. HARRIS, President *pro tem.*
W. RICHARDS, Recorder.

Deseret News, No. 29, Sept. 23, 1857, p. 226.

After the passage of the bill, the marshal, John P. Greene, was ordered to abate or remove, which he forthwith proceeded to do by summoning a posse of men for that purpose. The press was removed or broken, I don't remember which, by the marshal, and the types scattered in the street.

This seemed to be one of those extreme cases that require extreme measures, as the press was still proceeding in its inflammatory course. It was feared that, as it was almost universally execrated, should it continue longer, an indignant people might commit some overt act which might lead to serious consequences, and that it was better to use legal than illegal means.

This, as was foreseen, was the very course our enemies wished us to pursue, as it afforded them an opportunity of circulating a very plausible story about the Mormons being opposed to the liberty of the press and of free speech, which they were not slow to avail themselves of. Stories were fabricated, and facts perverted; false statements were made, and this act brought in as an example to sustain the whole of their fabrications; and, as if inspired by Satan, they labored with an energy and zeal worthy of a better cause. They had runners to circulate their reports, not only through Hancock County, but in all the surrounding counties. These reports were communicated to their anti-Mormon societies, and these societies circulated them in their several districts. The anti-Mormon paper, the *Warsaw Signal,* was filled with inflammatory articles and misrepresentations in relation to us, and especially to this act of destroying the press. We were represented as a horde of lawless ruffians and brigands, anti-American and anti-republican, steeped in crime and iniquity, opposed to freedom of speech and of the press, and all the rights and immunities of a free and enlightened people; that neither person nor property were secure: that we had designs upon the citizens of Illinois and of the United States, and the people were called upon to rise *en masse,* and put us down, drive us away, or exterminate us as a pest to society, and alike dangerous to our neighbors, the State, and commonwealth.

These statements were extensively copied and circulated throughout the United States. A true statement of the facts in question was published by us both in the *Times and Seasons* and the *Nauvoo Neighbor*; but it was found impossible to circulate them in the immediate counties, as they were destroyed in the post-offices or otherwise by the agents of the anti-Mormons, and in order to get the mail to go abroad, I had to send the papers a distance of thirty or forty miles from Nauvoo, and sometimes to St. Louis (upward of two hundred miles), in insure their proceeding on their route, and then one-half or two-thirds of the papers never reached the place of destination, being intercepted or destroyed by our enemies.

These false reports stirred up the community around, of whom many, on account of religious prejudice, were easily instigated to join the anti-Mormons and embark in any crusade that might be undertaken against us: hence their ranks swelled in numbers, and new organizations were formed, meetings were held, resolutions passed, and men and means volunteered for the extirpation of the Mormons.

On these points Governor Ford writes: "These also were the active men in blowing up the fury of the people, in hopes that a popular movement might be set on foot, which would result in the expulsion or extermination of the Mormon voters. For this purpose public meetings had been called, inflammatory speeches had been made, exaggerated reports had been extensivly circulated, committees had been appointed, who rode night and day to spread the reports and solicit the aid of neighboring counties, and at a public meeting at Warsaw resolutions were passed to expel or exterminate the Mormon population. This was not, however, a movement which was unanimously concurred in. The county contained a goodly number of inhabitants in favor of peace, or who at least desired to be neutral in such a contest. These were stigmatized by the name of Jack-Mormons, and there were not a few of the more furious exciters of the people who openly expressed their intention to involve them in the common expulsion or extermination.

"A system of excitement and agitation was artfully planned and executed with tact. It consisted in spreading reports and rumors of the most fearful character. As examples: On the morning before my arrival at Carthage, I was awakened at any early hour by the frightful report, which was asserted with confidence and apparent consternation, that the Mormons had already commenced the work of burning, destruction, and murder, and that every man capable of bearing arms was instantly wanted at Carthage for the protection of the county.

"We lost no time in starting; but when we arrived at Carthage we could hear no more concerning this story. Again, during the few days that the militia were encamped at Carthage, frequent applications were made to me to send a force here, and a force there, and a force all about the country, to prevent murders, robberies, and larcenies which, it was said, were threatened by the Mormons. No such forces were sent, nor were any such offenses committed at that time, except the stealing of some provisions, and there was never the least proof that this was done by a Mormon. Again, on my late visit to Hancock County, I was informed by some of their violent enemies that the larcenies of the Mormons had become unusually numerous and insufferable.

"They admitted that but little had been done in this way in their immediate vicinity, but they insisted that sixteen horses had been stolen by the Mormons in one night near Lima, and, upon inquiry, was told that no horses had been stolen in that neighborhood, but that sixteen horses had been stolen in one night in Hancock County. This last informant being told of the Hancock story, again changed the venue to another distant settlement in the northern edge of Adams."*

In the meantime legal proceedings were instituted against the members of the city council of Nauvoo. A writ, here subjoined,

*Ford's *History of Illinois*, pp. 330-31.

CARTHAGE JAIL AS IT IS TODAY (1952).

Hyrum A. Knight and wife are seen in front of custodian's home, which is maintained by the Church.

was issued upon the affidavit of the Laws, Fosters, Higbees, and Ivins, by Mr. Morrison, a justice of the peace in Carthage, the county seat of Hancock, and put into the hands of one David Bettesworth, a constable of the same place.

Writ issued upon affidavit by Thomas Morrison, J. P., State of Illinois, Hancock County, ss.

"The people of the State of Illinois, to all constables, sheriffs, and coroners of said State, greeting:

"Whereas complaint hath been made before me, one of the justices of the peace in and for the county of Hancock aforesaid, upon the oath of Francis M. Higbee, of the said county, that Joseph Smith, Samuel Bennett, John Taylor, William W. Phelps, Hyrum Smith, John P. Greene, Stephen Perry, Dimick B. Huntington, Jonathan Dunham, Stephen Markham, William Edwards, Jonathan Holmes, Jesse P. Harmon, John Lytle, Joseph W. Coolidge, Harvey D. Redfield, Porter Rockwell, and Levi Richards, of said county, did, on the tenth day of June instant, commit a riot at and within the county aforesaid, wherein they with force and violence broke into the printing office of the *Nauvoo Expositor*, and unlawfully and with force burned and destroyed the printing press, type and fixtures of the same, being the property of William Law, Wilson Law, Charles Ivins, Francis M. Higbee, Chauncey L. Higbee, Robert D. Foster and Charles A. Foster.

"These are therefore to command you forthwith to apprehend the said Joseph Smith, Samuel Bennett, John Taylor, William W. Phelps, Hyrum Smith, John P. Greene, Stephen Perry, Dimick B. Huntington, Jonathan Dunham, Stephen Markham, William Edwards, Jonathan Holmes, Jesse P. Harmon, John Lytle, Joseph W. Coolidge, Harvey D. Redfield, Porter Rockwell, and Levi Richards, and bring them before me, or some other justice of the peace, to answer the premises, and farther to be dealt with according to law.

"Given under my hand and seal at Carthage, in the county aforesaid, this 11th day of June, A. D. 1844.

"Thomas Morrison, J. P."   (Seal.)*

The council did not refuse to attend to the legal proceedings in the case, but as the law of Illinois made it the privilege of the persons accused to go "or appear before the issuer of the writ, or any other justice of the peace," they requested to be taken before another magistrate, either in the city of Nauvoo or at any reasonable distance out of it.

This the constable, who was a mobocrat, refused to do; and as this was our legal privilege we refused to be dragged, contrary to law, a distance of eighteen miles, when at the same time we had reason to believe that an organized band of mobocrats were assembled for the purpose of extermination or murder, and among whom it would not be safe to go without a superior force of armed men. A writ of *habeas corpus* was called for, and issued by the

Deseret News, No. 30, Sept. 30, 1857, p. 233.

municipal court of Nauvoo, taking us out of the hands of Bettesworth, and placing us in the charge of the city marshal. We went
before the municipal court and were dismissed. Our refusal to obey
this illegal proceeding was by them construed into a refusal to
submit to law, and circulated as such, and the people either did
believe, or professed to believe, that we were in open rebellion
against the laws and the authorities of the State. Hence mobs began to assemble, among which all through the country inflammatory speeches were made, exciting them to mobocracy and violence.
Soon they commenced their depredations in our outside settlements, kidnapping some, and whipping and otherwise abusing
others.

The persons thus abused fled to Nauvoo as soon as practicable,
and related their injuries to Joseph Smith, then mayor of the city,
and lieutenant general of the Nauvoo Legion. They also went before magistrates, and made affidavits of what they had suffered,
seen and heard. These affidavits, in connection with a copy of all
our proceedings were forwarded by Joseph Smith to Mr. Ford, then
governor of Illinois, with an expression of our desire to abide law,
and a request that the governor would instruct him how to proceed
in the case of arrival of an armed mob against the city. The governor sent back instructions to Joseph Smith that, as he was
lieutenant general of the Nauvoo Legion, it was his duty to protect the city and surrounding country, and issued orders to that
effect. Upon the reception of these orders Joseph Smith assembled
the people of the city, and laid before them the governor's instructions; he also convened the officers of the Nauvoo Legion for the
purpose of conferring in relation to the best mode of defense. He
also issued orders to the men to hold themselves in readiness in
case of being called upon. On the following day General Joseph
Smith, with his staff, the leading officers of the Legion, and some
prominent strangers who were in our midst, made a survey of the
outside boundaries of the city, which was very extensive, being
about five miles up and down the river, and about two and a half
back in the center, for the purpose of ascertaining the position of
the ground, and the feasibility of defense, and to make all necessary arrangements in case of an attack.

It may be well here to remark that numbers of gentlemen,
strangers to us, either came on purpose or were passing through
Nauvoo, and upon learning the position of things, expressed their
indignation against our enemies, and avowed their readiness to
assist us by their counsel or otherwise. It was some of these who
assisted us in reconnoitering the city, and finding out its adapta-
bility for defense, and how to protect it best against an armed
force. The Legion was called together and drilled, and every means
made use of for defense. At the call of the officers, old and young
men came forward, both from the city and the country, and mustered to the number of about five thousand.

In the meantime our enemies were not idle in mustering their
forces and committing depredations, nor had they been; it was, in
fact, their gathering that called ours into existence; their forces
continued to accumulate; they assumed a threatening attitude, and

assembled in large bodies, armed and equipped for war, and threatened the destruction and extermination of the Mormons.

An account of their outrages and assemblages was forwarded to Governor Ford almost daily; accompanied by affidavits furnished by eye-witnesses of their proceedings. Persons were also sent out to the counties around with pacific intentions, to give them an account of the true state of affairs, and to notify them of the feelings and dispositions of the people of Nauvoo, and thus, if possible, quell the excitement. In some of the more distant counties these men were very successful, and produced the salutary influence upon the minds of many intelligent and well-disposed men. In neighboring counties, however, where anti-Mormon influence prevailed, they produced little effect. At the same time guards were stationed around Nauvoo, and picket-guards in the distance, At length opposing forces gathered so near that more active measures were taken; reconnoitering parties were sent out, and the city proclaimed under martial law. Things now assumed a beligerent attitude, and persons passing through the city were questioned as to what they knew of the enemy, while passes were in some instances given to avoid difficulty with the guards. Joseph Smith continued to send on messengers to the governor, (Philip B. Lewis and other messengers were sent). Samuel James, then residing at La Harpe, carried a message and dispatches to him, and in a day or two after Bishop Edward Hunter and others went again with fresh dispatches, representations, affidavits, and instructions; but as the weather was excessively wet, the rivers swollen, and the bridges washed away in many places, it was with great difficulty that they proceeded on their journeys. As the mobocracy had at last attracted the governor's attention, he started in company with some others from Springfield to the scene of trouble, and missed, I believe, both Brothers James and Hunter on the road, and, of course, did not see their documents. He came to Carthage, and made that place, which was a regular mobocratic den, his headquarters; as it was the county seat, however, of Hancock County, that circumstance might, in a measure, justify his staying there.

To avoid the appearance of all hostility on our part, and to fulfill the law in every particular, at the suggestion of Judge Thomas, judge of that judicial district, who had come to Nauvoo at the time, and who stated that we had fulfilled the law, but, in order to satisfy all he would counsel us to go before Esquire Wells, who was not in our Church, and have a hearing, we did so, and after a full hearing we were again dismissed.

The governor on the road collected forces, some of whom were respectable, but on his arrival in the neighborhood of the difficulties he received as militia all the companies of the mob forces who united with him. After his arrival at Carthage he sent two gentlemen from there to Nauvoo as a committee to wait upon General Joseph Smith, informing him of the arrival of his excellency, with a request that General Smith would send out a committee to wait upon the governor and represent to him the state of affairs in relation to the difficulties that then existed in the county. We met this committee while we were reconnoitering the city, to find out the best mode of defense as aforesaid. Dr. J. M. Bernhisel and myself were appointed as a committee by General Smith to wait upon the governor. Previous to going, however, we were furnished with affidavits and documents in relation both to our proceedings and those of the mob; in addition to the general history of the transaction, we took with us a duplicate of those documents which had been forwarded by Bishop Hunter, Brother James, and others. We started from Nauvoo in company with the aforesaid gentlemen at about 7 o'clock on the evening of the 21st of June, and arrived at Carthage about 11 p.m.

We put up at the same hotel with the governor, kept by a Mr. Hamilton. On our arrival we found the governor in bed, but not so with the other inhabitants. The town was filled with a perfect set of rabble and rowdies, who, under the influence of Bacchus, seemed to be holding a grand saturnalia, whooping, yelling and vociferating as if Bedlam had broken loose.

On our arrival at the hotel, and while supper was preparing, a man came to me, dressed as a soldier, and told me that a man named Daniel Garn had just been taken prisoner, and was about to be committed to jail, and wanted me to go bail for him. Believing this to be a ruse to get me out alone, and that some violence was intended, after consulting with Dr. Bernhisel, I told the man that I was well acquainted with Mr. Garn, that I knew him to be a gentleman, and did not believe that he had transgressed law, and, moreover, that I considered it a very singular time to be holding courts and calling for security, particularly as the town was full of rowdyism.

I informed him that Dr. Bernhisel and myself would, if necessary go bail for him in the morning, but that we did not feel ourselves safe among such a set at that late hour of the night.

After supper, on retiring to our room, we had to pass through another, which was separated from ours only by a board partition, the beds in each room being placed side by side, with the exception of this fragile partition. On the bed that was in the room which we passed through I discovered a man by the name of Jackson, a desperate character, and a reputed, notorious cut-throat and murderer. I hinted to the doctor that things looked rather suspicious, and looked to see that my arms were in order. The doctor and I occupied one bed. We had scarcely laid down when a knock at the door, accompanied by a voice announced the approach of Chauncey Higbee, the young lawyer and apostate before referred to.

He addressed himself to the doctor, and stated that the object of his visit was to obtain the release of Daniel Garn; that Garn he believed to be an honest man; that if he had done anything wrong, it was through improper counsel, and that it was a pity that he should be incarcerated, particularly when he could be so easily released; he urged the doctor, as a friend, not to leave so good a man in such an unpleasant situation; he finally prevailed upon the doctor to go and give bail, assuring him that on his giving bail Garn would be immediately dismissed.

During this conversation I did not say a word.

Higbee left the doctor to dress, with the intention of returning and taking him to the court. As soon as Higbee had left, I told
the doctor that he had better not go; that I believed this affair was
all a ruse to get us separated; that they knew we had documents
with us from General Smith to show to the governor; that I believed their object was to get possession of those papers, and, perhaps, when they had separated us, to murder one or both. The
doctor, who was actuated by the best of motives in yielding to the
assumed solicitude of Higbee, coincided with my views; he then
went to Higbee, and told him that he had concluded not to go that
night, but that he and I would both wait upon the justice and Mr.
Garn in the morning.

That night I lay awake with my pistols under my pillow, waiting for any emergency. Nothing more occurred during the night.
In the morning we arose early, and after breakfast sought an interview with the governor, and were told that we could have an audience, I think, at ten o'clock. In the meantime we called upon Mr.
Smith, a justice of the peace, who had Mr. Garn in charge. We represented that we had been called upon the night before by two
different parties to go bail for a Mr. Daniel Garn, whom we were
informed he had in custody, and that, believing Mr. Garn to be an
honest man, we had now come for that purpose, and were prepared
to enter into recognizances for his appearance, whereupon Mr.
Smith, the magistrate, remarked that, under the present excited
state of affairs, he did not think he would be justified in receiving
bail from Nauvoo, as it was a matter of doubt whether property
would not be rendered valueless there in a few days.

Knowing the party we had to deal with, we were not much
surprised at this singular proceeding; we then remarked that both
of us possessed property in farms out of Nauvoo in the country,
and referred him to the county records. He then stated that such
was the nature of the charge against Mr. Garn that he believed
he would not be justified in receiving any bail. We were thus confirmed in our opinion that the night's proceedings before, in relation
to their desire to have us give bail, was a mere ruse to separate us.
We were not permitted to speak with Garn, the real charge against
whom was that he was traveling in Carthage or its neighborhood:
what the fictitious one was, if I knew, I have since forgotten, as
things of this kind were of daily occurrence.

After waiting the governor's pleasure for some time we had
an audience; but such an audience!

He was surrounded by some of the vilest and most unprincipled men in creation; some of them had an appearance of respect-
ability, and many of them lacked even that. Wilson, and, I believe, William Law, were there, Foster, Frank and Chauncey Higbee, Mr. Mar, a lawyer from Nauvoo, a mobocratic merchant from
Warsaw, the aforesaid Jackson, a number of his associates, among
whom was the governor's secretary, in all, some fifteen or twenty
persons, most of whom were recreant to virtue, honor, integrity,
and everything that is considered honorable among men. I can well
remember the feelings of disgust that I had in seeing the governor
surrounded by such an infamous group, and on being introduced

to men of so questionable a character; and had I been on private business, I should have turned to depart, and told the governor that if he thought proper to associate with such questionable characters, I should beg leave to be excused; but coming as we did on public business, we could not, of course, consult our private feelings.

We then stated to the governor that, in accordance with his request, General Smith had, in response to his call, sent us to him as a committee of conference; that we were acquainted with most of the circumstances that had transpired in and about Nauvoo lately, and were prepared to give him all information; that, moreover, we had in our possession testimony and affidavits confirmatory of what we should say, which had been forwarded to him by General Joseph Smith; that communications had been forwarded to his excellency by Messrs. Hunter, James, and others, some of which had not reached their destination, but of which we had duplicates with us. We then, in brief, related an outline of the difficulties, and the course we had pursued from the commencement of the trouble up to the present, and handing him the documents, respectfully submitted the whole.

During our conversation and explanations with the governor we were frequently, rudely and impudently contradicted by the fellows he had around him, and of whom he seemed to take no notice.

He opened and read a number of the documents himself, and as he proceeded he was frequently interrupted by, "that's a lie!" "that's a God damned lie!" that's an infernal falsehood!" "that's a blasted lie!" etc.

These men evidently winced at the exposure of their acts, and thus vulgarly, impudently, and falsely repudiated them. One of their number, Mr. Marr, addressed himself several times to me while in conversation with the governor. I did not notice him until after a frequent repetition of his insolence, when I informed him that "my business at that time was with Governor Ford," whereupon I continued my conversation with his excellency. During the conversation, the governor expressed a desire that Joseph Smith, and all parties concerned in passing or executing the city law in relation to the press, had better come to Carthage; that, however repugnant it might be to our feelings, he thought it would have a tendency to allay public excitement, and prove to the people what we professed, that we wished to be governed by law. We represented to him the course we had taken in relation to this matter, and our willingness to go before another magistrate other than the municipal court; the illegal refusal of our request by the constable; our dismissal by the municipal court, a legally constituted tribunal; our subsequent trial before 'Squire Wells at the instance of Judge Thomas, the circuit judge, and our dismissal by him; that we had fulfilled the law in every particular; that it was our enemies who were breaking the law, and, having murderous designs, were only making use of this as a pretext to get us into their power. The governor stated that the people viewed it differently, and that, notwithstanding our opinions, he would recommend that the people should be satisfied. We then remarked to him that, should Joseph

Smith comply with his request, it would be extremely unsafe, in the present excited state of the country, to come without an armed force; that we had a sufficiency of men, and were competent to defend ourselves, but there might be danger of collision should our forces and those of our enemies be brought into such close proximity. He strenuously advised us not to bring our arms, and *pledged his faith as governor, and the faith of the State, that we should be protected, and that he would guarantee our perfect safety.*

We had at that time about five thousand men under arms, one thousand of whom would have been amply sufficient for our protection.

At the termination of our interview, and previous to our withdrawal, after a long conversation and the perusal of the documents which we had brought, the governor informed us that he would prepare a written communication for General Joseph Smith, which he desired us to wait for. We were kept waiting for this instrument some five or six hours.

About five o'clock in the afternoon we took our departure with not the most pleasant feelings. The associations of the governor, the spirit he manifested to compromise with these scoundrels, the length of time that he had kept us waiting, and his general deportment, together with the infernal spirit that we saw exhibited by those whom he had admitted to his councils made the prospect anything but promising.

We returned on horseback, and arrived at Nauvoo, I think, at about eight or nine o'clock at night, accompanied by Captain Yates in command of a company of mounted men who came for the purpose of escorting Joseph Smith and the accused in case of their complying with the governor's request, and going to Carthage. We went directly to Brother Joseph's, when Captain Yates delivered to him the governor's communication. A council was called, consisting of Joseph's brother, Hyrum, Dr. Richards, Dr. Bernhisel, myself, and one or two others.

We then gave a detail of our interview with the governor. Brother Joseph was very much dissatisfied with the governor's letter and with his general deportment, and so were the council, and it became a serious question as to the course we should pursue. Various projects were discussed, but nothing definitely decided upon for some time.

In the interim two gentlemen arrived; one of them, if not both, sons of John C. Calhoun. They had come to Nauvoo, and were very anxious for an interview with Brother Joseph.

These gentlemen detained him for some time; and, as our council was held in Dr. Bernhisel's room in the Mansion House, the doctor lay down; and as it was now between 2 and 3 o'clock in the morning, and I had had no rest on the previous night, I was fatigued, and thinking that Brother Joseph might not return, I left for home and rest.

Being very much fatigued, I slept soundly, and was somewhat surprised in the morning by Mrs. Thompson entering my room about 7 o'clock, and exclaiming in surprise, "What, you here! the brethren have crossed the river some time since."

"What brethren?" I asked.

"Brother Joseph, and Hyrum, and Brother Richards," she answered.

I immediately arose upon learning that they had crossed the river, and did not intend to go to Carthage. I called together a number of persons in whom I had confidence, and had the type, stereotype plates, and most of the valuable things removed from the printing office, believing that, should the governor and his force come to Nauvoo, the first thing they would do would be to burn the printing office, for I knew they would be exasperated if Brother Joseph went away. We had talked over these matters the night before, but nothing was decided upon. It was Brother Joseph's opinion that, should we leave for a time, public excitement, which was then so intense, would be allayed; that it would throw on the governor the responsibility of keeping the peace; that in the event of an outrage, the onus would rest upon the governor, who was amply prepared with troops, and could command all the forces of the State to preserve order; and that the act of his own men would be an overwhelming proof of their seditious designs, not only to the governor, but to the world. He moreover thought that, in the east, where he intended to go, public opinion would be set right in relation to these matters, and its expression would partially influence the west, and that, after the first ebullition, things would assume a shape that would justify his return.

I made arrangements for crossing the river, and Brother Elias Smith and Joseph Cain, who were both employed in the printing office with me, assisted all that lay in their power together with Brother Brower and several hands in the printing office. As we could not find out the exact whereabouts of Joseph and the brethren, I crossed the river in a boat furnished by Brother Cyrus H. Wheelock and Alfred Bell; and after the removal of the things out of the printing office, Joseph Cain brought the account books to me, that we might make arrangements for their adjustment; and Brother Elias Smith, cousin to Brother Joseph, went to obtain money for the journey, and also to find out and report to me the location of the brethren.

As Cyrus H. Wheelock was an active, enterprising man, and in the event of not finding Brother Joseph I calculated to go to Upper Canada for the time being, and should need a companion, I said to Brother Cyrus H. Wheelock, "Can you go with me ten or fifteen hundred miles?"

He answered, "Yes."

"Can you start in half an hour?"

"Yes."

However, I told him that he had better see his family, who lived over the river, and prepare a couple of horses and the necessary equippage for the journey, and that, if we did not find Brother Joseph before, we would start at nightfall.

A laughable incident occurred on the eve of my departure. After making all the preparations I could, previous to leaving Nauvoo, and having bid adieu to my family, I went to a house adjoining the river, owned by Brother Eddy. There I disguised myself so as not to be known, and so effectual was the transformation that those who had come after me with a boat did not know me. I went down to the boat and sat in it. Brother Bell, thinking it was a stranger, watched my moves for some time very impatiently, and then said to Brother Wheelock, "I wish that old gentleman would go away; he has been pottering around the boat for some time, and I am afraid Elder Taylor will be coming." When he discovered his mistake, he was not a little amused.

I was conducted by Brother Bell to a house that was surrounded by timber on the opposite side of the river. There I spent several hours in a chamber with Brother Joseph Cain, adjusting my accounts; and I made arrangements for the stereotype plates of the Book of Mormon and Doctrine and Covenants, to be forwarded east, thinking to supply the company with subsistence money through the sale of these books in the east.

My horses were reported ready by Brother Wheelock, and funds on hand by Brother Elias Smith. In about half an hour I should have started, when Brother Elias Smith came to me with word that he had found the brethren; that they had concluded to go to Carthage, and wished me to return to Nauvoo and accompany them. I must confess that I felt a good deal disappointed at this news, but I immediately made preparations to go. Escorted by Brother Elias Smith, I and my party went to the neighborhood of Montrose, where we met Brother Joseph, Hyrum, Brother Richards and others. Dr. Bernhisel thinks that W. W. Phelps was not with Joseph and Hyrum in the morning, but that he met him, myself, Joseph and Hyrum, W. Richards and Brother Cahoon, in the afternoon, near Montrose, returning to Nauvoo.

On meeting the brethren I learned that it was not Brother Joseph's desire to return, but that he came back by request of some of the brethren, and that it coincided more with Brother Hyrum's feelings than those of Brother Joseph. In fact, after his return, Brother Hyrum expressed himself as perfectly satisfied with the course taken, and said he felt much more at ease in his mind than he did before. On our return the calculation was to throw ourselves under the immediate protection of the governor, and to trust to his word and faith for our preservation.

A message was, I believe, sent to the governor that night, stating that we should come to Carthage in the morning, the party that came along with us to escort us back, in case we returned to Carthage, having returned.

It would seem from the following remarks of General Ford that there was a design on foot, which was, that if we refused to go to Carthage at the governor's request, there should be an increased force called for by the governor, and that we should be destroyed by them. In accordance with this project, Captain Yates returned with his *posse*, accompanied by the constable who held the writ.

The following is the governor's remark in relation to this affair:

"The constable and his escort returned. The constable made no effort to arrest any of them, nor would he or the guard delay their departure one minute beyond the time, to see whether an arrest could be made. Upon their return they reported that they had been informed that the accused had fled, and could not be found. I immediately proposed to a council of officers to march into Nauvoo with the small force then under my command, but the officers were of the opinion that it was too small, and many of them insisted upon a further call of the militia. Upon reflection I was of the opinion that the officers were right in the estimate of our force, and the project for immediate action was abandoned.

"I was soon informed, however, of the conduct of the constable and guard, and then I was perfectly satisfied that a most base fraud had been attempted, that, in fact, it was feared that the Mormons would submit, and thereby entitle themselves to the protection of the law. It was very apparent that many of the bustling, active spirits were afraid that there would be no occasion for calling out an overwhelming militia force, for marching into Nauvoo, for probable mutiny when there, and for the extermination of the Mormon race. It appeared that the constable and the escort were fully in the secret, and acted well their part to promote the conspiracy."*

In the morning Brother Joseph had an interview with the officers of the Legion, with the leading members of the city council, and with the principal men of the city. The officers were instructed to dismiss their men, but to have them in a state of readiness to be called upon in any emergency that might occur.

About half past six o'clock the members of the city council, the marshal, Brothers Joseph and Hyrum, and a number of others, started for Carthage, on horseback. We were instructed by Brother Joseph Smith not to take any arms, and we consequently left them behind. We called at the house of Brother Fellows on our way out. Brother Fellows lived about four miles from Carthage.

While at Brother Fellow's house, Captain Dunn, accompanied by Mr. Coolie, one of the governor's aides-de-camp, came up from Carthage *en route* for Nauvoo with a requisition from the governor for the State arms. We all returned to Nauvoo with them; the governor's request was complied with, and after taking some refreshments, we all returned to proceed to Carthage. We arrived there late in the night. A great deal of excitement prevailed on and after our arrival. The governor had received into his company all of the companies that had been in the mob; these fellows were riotous and disorderly, halloowing, yelling, and whooping about the streets like Indians, many of them intoxicated; the whole presented a scene of rowdyism and low-bred ruffianism only found among mobocrats and desperadoes, and entirely revolting to the best feelings of humanity. The governor made a speech to them to the effect that he would show Joseph and Hyrum Smith to them in the morning.

About here the companies with the governor were drawn up in line, and General Demming, I think, took Joseph by the arm and Hyrum (Arnold says that Joseph took the governor's arm), and as he passed through between the ranks, the governor leading in

---

*Ford's *History of Illinois*, p. 333.

front, very politely introduced them as General Joseph Smith and
General Hyrum Smith.*

All were orderly and courteous except one company of mobocrats—the Carthage Grays—who seemed to find fault on account
of too much honor being paid to the Mormons. There was afterwards a row between the companies, and they came pretty near
having a fight; the more orderly not feeling disposed to endorse or
submit to the rowdyism of the mobocrats. The result was that
General Demming, who was very much of a gentleman, ordered the
Carthage Grays, a company under the command of Captain Smith,
a magistrate in Carthage, and a most violent mobocrat, under
arrest. This matter, however, was shortly afterward adjusted, and
the difficulty settled between them.

The mayor, aldermen, councilors, as well as the marshal of
the city of Nauvoo, together with some persons who had assisted
the marshal in removing the press in Nauvoo, appeared before Justice Smith, the aforesaid captain and mobocrat, to again answer
the charge of destroying the press; but as there was so much excitement, and as the man was an unprincipled villain before whom
we were to have our hearing, we thought it most prudent to give
bail, and consequently became security for each other in $500 bonds
each, to appear before the County Court at its next session. We had
engaged as counsel a lawyer by the name of Wood, of Burlington,

---

*The *Deseret News* gives the following account of Joseph and Hyrum
Smith's passing through the troops in Carthage:

"Carthage, June 25, 1844.

"Quarter past nine. The governor came and invited Joseph to walk with
him through the troops. Joseph solicited a few moments' private conversation
with him, which the governor refused.

"While refusing, the governor looked down at his shoes, as though he
was ashamed. They then walked through the crowd, with Brigadier General
Miner R. Demming, and Dr. Richards, to General Demming's quarters. The
people appeared quiet until a company of Carthage Grays flocked round the
doors of General Demming in an uproarious manner, of which notice was
sent to the governor. In the meantime the governor had ordered the McDonough troops to be drawn up in line, for Joseph and Hyrum to pass in front of
them, they having requested that they might have a clear view of the General
Smiths. *Joseph had a conversation with the governor for about ten minutes,
when he again pledged the faith of the State that he and his friends should be
protected from violence.*

"Robinson, the postmaster, said, on report of martial law being proclaimed
in Nauvoo, he had stopped the mail, and notified the postmaster general of
the state of things in Hancock County.

"From the general's quarters Joseph and Hyrum went in front of the
lines, in a hollow square of a company of Carthage Grays. At seven minutes
before ten they arrived in front of the lines, and passed before the whole,
Joseph being on the right of General Demming and Hyrum on his left, Elders
Richards, Taylor and Phelps following. Joseph and Hyrum were introduced
by Governor Ford about twenty times along the line as General Joseph Smith
and General Hyrum Smith, the governor walking in front on the left. The
Carthage Grays refused to receive them by that introduction, and some of
the officers threw up their hats, drew their swords, and said they would introduce themselves to the damned Mormons in a different style. The governor
mildly entreated them not to act so rudely, but their excitement increased;
the governor, however, succeeded in pacifying them by making a speech, and
promising them that they should have 'full satisfaction.' General Smith and
party returned to their lodgings at five minutes past ten."

Deseret News, No. 35, Nov. 4, 1857, p. 274.

Iowa; and Reed, I think, of Madison, Iowa. After some little discussion the bonds were signed, and we were all dismissed.

Almost immediately after our dismissal, two men—Augustine Spencer and Norton—two worthless fellows, whose words would not have been taken for five cents, and the first of whom had a short time previously been before the mayor in Nauvoo for maltreating a lame brother, made affidavits that Joseph and Hyrum Smith were guilty of treason, and a writ was accordingly issued for their arrest, and the constable Bettesworth, a rough, unprincipled man, wished immediately to hurry them away to prison without any hearing. His rude, uncouth manner in the administration of what he considered the duties of his office made him exceedingly repulsive to us all. But, independent of these acts, the proceedings in this case were altogether illegal. Providing the court was sincere, which it was not, and providing these men's oaths were true, and that Joseph and Hyrum were guilty of treason, still the whole course was illegal.

The magistrate made out a mittimus, and committed them to prison without a hearing, which he had no right legally to do. The statute of Illinois expressly provides that "all men shall have a hearing before a magistrate before they shall be committed to prison;" and Mr. Robert H. Smith, the magistrate, had made out a mittimus committing them to prison contrary to law without such hearing. As I was informed of this illegal proceeding, I went immediately to the governor and informed him of it. Whether he was apprised of it before or not, I do not know; but my opinion is that he was.

I represented to him the characters of the parties who had made oath, the outrageous nature of the charge, the indignity offered to men in the position which they occupied, and declared to him that he knew very well it was a vexatious proceeding, and that the accused were not guilty of any such crime. The governor replied, he was very sorry that the thing had occurred; that he did not believe the charges, but that he thought the best thing to be done was to let the law take its course. I then reminded him that we had come out there at his instance, not to satisfy the law, which we had done before, but the prejudices of the people, in relation to the affairs of the press; that at his instance we had given bonds, which we could not by law be required to do to satisfy the people, and that it was asking too much to require gentlemen in their position in life to suffer the degradation of being immured in a jail at the instance of such worthless scoundrels as those who had made this affidavit. The governor replied that it was an unpleasant affair, and looked hard; but that it was a matter over which he had no control, as it belonged to the judiciary; that he, as the executive, could not interfere with their proceedings, and that he had no doubt but that they would immediately be dismissed. I told him that we had looked to him for protection from such insults, and that I thought we had a right to do so from the solemn promises which he had made to me and to Dr. Bernhisel in relation to our coming without guard or arms; that we had relied upon his faith, and had a right to expect him to fulfill his engagements after we had placed ourselves implicitly under his care, and complied with all his requests, although extrajudicial.

He replied that he would detail a guard, if we required it, and see us protected, but that he could not interfere with the judiciary. I expressed my dissatisfaction at the course taken, and told him, that, if we were to be subject to mob rule, and to be dragged, contrary to law, into prison at the instance of every infernal scoundrel whose oaths could be bought for a dram of whiskey, his protection availed very little, and we had miscalculated his promises.

Seeing there was no prospect of redress from the governor, I returned to the room, and found the constable Bettesworth very urgent to hurry Brothers Joseph and Hyrum to prison, while the brethren were remonstrating with him. At the same time a great rabble was gathered in the streets and around the door, and from the rowdyism manifested I was afraid there was a design to murder the prisoners on the way to jail.

Without conferring with any person, my next feelings were to procure a guard, and seeing a man habited as a soldier in the room, I went to him and said, "I am afraid there is a design against the lives of the Messrs. Smith; will you go immediately and bring your captain; and, if not convenient, any other captain of a company, and I will pay you well for your trouble?" He said he would, and departed forthwith, and soon returned with his captain, whose name I have forgotten, and introduced him to me. I told of my fears, and requested him immediately to fetch his company.

He departed forthwith, and arrived at the door with them just at the time when the constable was hurrying the brethren down stairs. A number of the brethren went along, together with one or two strangers; and all of us, safely lodged in prison, remained there during the night.

At the request of Joseph Smith for an interview with the governor, he came the next morning, Thursday, June 26th, at half past 9 o'clock, accompanied by Colonel Geddes, when a lengthy conversation was entered into in relation to the existing difficulties; and after some preliminary remarks, at the governor's request, Brother Joseph gave him a general outline of the state of affairs in relation to our difficulties, the excited state of the country, the tumultuous mobocratic movements of our enemies, the precautionary measures used by himself (Joseph Smith), the acts of the city council, the destruction of the press, and the moves of the mob and ourselves up to that time.

The following report is, I believe, substantially correct:

Governor—"General Smith, I believe you have given me a general outline of the difficulties that have existed in the country in the documents forwarded to me by Dr. Bernhisel and Mr. Taylor; but, unfortunately, there seems to be a great discrepancy between your statements and those of your enemies. It is true that you are substantiated by evidence and affidavit, but for such an extraordinary excitement as that which is now in the country there must be some cause, and I attribute the last outbreak to the destruction of the *Expositor*, and to your refusal to comply with the writ issued by Esquire Morrison. The press in the United States is looked upon as the great bulwark of American freedom, and its destruction in Nauvoo was represented and looked upon as a high-handed measure, and manifests to the people a disposition on your part to suppress the liberty of speech and of the press. This, with your refusal to comply with the requisition of a writ, I conceive to be the principal cause of this difficulty; and you are moreover represented to me as turbulent, and defiant of the laws and institutions of your country."

General Smith—"Governor Ford, you, sir, as governor of this State, are aware of the persecutions that I have endured. You know well that our course has been peaceable and law-abiding for I have furnished this State ever since our settlement here with sufficient evidence of my pacific intentions, and those of the people with whom I am associated, by the endurance of every conceivable indignity and lawless outrage perpetrated upon me and upon this people since our settlement here; and you know yourself that I have kept you well posted in relation to all matters associated with the late difficulties. If you have not got some of my communications, it has not been my fault.

"Agreeable to your orders, I assembled the Nauvoo Legion for the protection of Nauvoo and the surrounding country against an armed band of marauders; and ever since they have been mustered I have almost daily communicated with you in regard to all the leading events that have transpired; and whether in the capacity of mayor of the city, or lieutenant general of the Nauvoo Legion, I have striven, according to the best of my judgment, to preserve the peace and to administer even-handed justice; but my motives are impugned, my acts are misconstrued, and I am grossly and wickedly misrepresented. I suppose I am indebted for my incarceration to the oath of a worthless man, who was arraigned before me and fined for abusing and maltreating his lame, helpless brother. That I should be charged by you sir, who know better, of acting contrary to law, is to me a matter of surprise. Was it the Mormons or our enemies who first commenced these difficulties? You know well it was not us; and when this turbulent, outrageous people commenced their insurrectionary movements I made you acquainted with them officially, and asked your advice, and have followed strictly your counsel in every particular. Who ordered out the Nauvoo Legion? I did, under your direction. For what purpose? To suppress the insurrectionary movements. It was at your instance, sir, that I issued a proclamation calling upon the Nauvoo Legion to be in readiness at a moment's warning to guard against the incursions of mobs, and gave an order to Jonathan Dunham, acting major-general, to that effect.

"Am I, then, to be charged wtih the acts of others? and because lawlessness and mobocracy abound, am I, when carrying out your instructions, to be charged with not abiding law? Why is it that I must be made accountable for other men's acts? If there is trouble in the country, neither I nor my people made it; and all that we have ever done, after much endurance on our part, is to maintain and uphold the Constitution and institutions of our country, and to protect an injured, innocent, and persecuted people against misrule and mob violence.

"Concerning the destruction of the press to which you refer, men may differ somewhat in their opinions about it; but can it be supposed that after all the indignities to which they have been subjected outside, that people could suffer a set of worthless vagabonds to come into their city, and, right under their own eyes and protection, vilify and calumniate not only themselves, but the character of their wives and daughters, as was impudently and unblushingly done in that infamous and filthy sheet?

"There is not a city in the United States that would have suffered such an indignity for twenty-four hours. Our whole people were indignant, and loudly called upon our city authorities for a redress of their grievances, which, if not attended to, they themselves would have taken into their own hands, and have summarily punished the audacious wretches as they deserved. The principle of equal rights that has been instilled into our bosoms from our cradles as American citizens forbids us submitting to every foul indignity, and succumbing and pandering to wretches so infamous as these. But, independent of this, the course that we pursued we consider to be strictly legal; for, notwithstanding the result, we were anxious to be governed strictly by law, and therefore we convened the city council; and being desirous in our deliberations to abide by law, we summoned legal counsel to be present on the occasion. Upon investigating the matter, we found that our city charter gave us power to remove all nuisances. Furthermore, after consulting Blackstone upon what might be considered a nuisance, it appeared that that distinguished lawyer, who is considered authority, I believe, in all our courts, states among other things that 'a libelous and filthy press, may be considered a nuisance; and abated as such.' Here, then, one of the most eminent English barristers, whose works are considered standard with us, declares that a libelous and filthy press may be considered a nuisance; and our own charter, given us by the Legislature of this State, gives us power to remove nuisances; and by ordering that press to be abated as a nuisance, we conceived that we were acting strictly in accordance with law. We made that order in our corporate capacity, and the city marshal carried it out. It is possible there may have been some better way, but I must confess that I could not see it.

"In relation to the writ served upon us, we are willing to abide the consequences of our own acts, but are unwilling, in answering a writ of that kind, to submit to illegal exactions, sought to be imposed upon us under the pretense of law, when we knew they were in open violation of it. When that document was presented to me by Mr. Bettesworth, I offered, in the presence of more than twenty persons, to go to any other magistrate, either in our city, in Appanoose, or any other place where we should be safe, but we all refused to put ourselves into the power of a mob. What right had that constable to refuse our request? He had none according to law; for you know, Governor Ford, that the statute law in Illinois is, that the parties served with the writ 'shall go before him who issued it, or some other justice of the peace.' Why, then, should we be dragged to Carthage, where the law does not compel us to go? Does not this look like many others of our persecutions with which you are acquainted? and have we not a right to expect foul play? This very act was a breach of law on his part, an assumption of power that did not belong to him, and an attempt, at least, to deprive us of our legal and constitutional rights and privileges. What could we do, under the circumstances, different from what we did do? We sued for, and obtained a writ of *habeas corpus* from the municipal court, by which we were delivered from the hands of Constable Bettesworth, and brought before and acquitted by the municipal court. After our acquittal, in a conversation with Judge Thomas, although he considered the acts of the party illegal, he advised that, to satisfy the people, we had better go before another magistrate who was not in our Church. In accordance with his advice, we went before Esquire Wells, with whom you are well acquainted; both parties were present, witnesses were called on both sides, the case was fully investigated, and we were again dismissed. And what is this pretended desire to enforce law, and wherefore are these lying, base rumors put into circulation but to seek, through mob influence, under pretense of law, to make us submit to requisitions which are contrary to law and subversive of every principle of justice? And when you, sir, required us to come out here, we came, not because it was legal, but because you required it of us, and we were desirous of showing to you, and to all men, that we shrunk not from the most rigid investigation of our acts. We certainly did expect other treatment than to be immured in a jail at the instance of these men, and I think, from your plighted faith, we had a right so to expect, after disbanding our own forces, and putting ourselves entirely in your hands. And now, after having fulfilled my part, sir, as a man and an American citizen, I call upon you, Governor Ford, to deliver us from this place, and rescue us from this outrage that is sought to be practiced upon us by a set of infamous scoundrels."

Governor Ford.—"But you have placed men under arrest, detained men as prisoners, and given passes to others, some of which I have seen."

John P. Greene, City Marshal.—"Perhaps I can explain. Since these difficulties have commenced, you are aware that we have been placed under very peculiar circumstances; our city has been placed under a very rigid police guard; in addition to this, frequent guards have been placed outside the city to prevent any sudden surprise, and those guards have questioned suspected or suspicious persons as to their business. To strangers, in some instances, passes have been given to prevent difficulty in passing those guards; it is some of these passes that you have seen. No person, sir, has been imprisoned without a legal cause in our city."

Governor.—"Why did you not give a more speedy answer to the posse that I sent out?"

General Smith.—We had matters of importance to consult upon; your letter showed anything but an amiable spirit. We have suffered immensely in Missouri from mobs, in loss of property, imprisonment, and otherwise. It took some time for us to weigh duly these matters; we could not decide upon matters of such importance immediately, and your posse were too hasty in returning; we were consulting for a large people, and vast interests were at stake. We had been outrageously imposed upon, and knew not how far we could trust any one; besides, a question necessarily arose, How shall we come? Your request was that we should come unarmed. It became a matter of serious importance to decide how far promises could be trusted, and how far we were safe from mob violence."

Colonel Geddes.—"It certainly did look, from all I have heard, from the general spirit of violence and mobocracy that here prevails, that it was not safe for you to come unprotected."

Governor Ford.—"I think that sufficient time was not allowed by the posse for you to consult and get ready. They were too hasty; but I suppose they found themselves bound by their orders. I think, too, there is a great deal of truth in what you say, and your reasoning is plausible, but I must beg leave to differ from you in relation to the acts of the City Council. That Council, in my opinion, had no right to act in a legislative capacity, and in that of the judiciary. They should have passed a law in relation to the matter, and then the Municipal Court, upon complaint, could have removed it; but for the City Council to take upon themselves the law-making and the execution of the law, is, in my opinion, wrong; besides, these men ought to have had a hearing before their property was destroyed; to destroy it without was an infringement on their rights; besides, it is so contrary to the feelings of American people to interfere with the press. And, furthermore, I cannot but think that it would have been more judicious for you to have gone with Mr. Bettesworth to Carthage, notwithstanding the law did not require it. Concerning your being in jail, I am sorry for that; I wish it had been otherwise. I hope you will soon be released, but I can not interfere."

Joseph Smith.—"Governor Ford, allow me, sir, to bring one thing to your mind that you seem to have overlooked. You state that you think it would have been better for us to have submitted to the requisition of Constable Bettesworth, and to have gone to Carthage. Do you not know, sir, that that writ was served at the instance of an anti-Mormon mob, who had passed resolutions, and published them, to the effect that they would exterminate the Mormon leaders? And are you not informed that Captain Anderson was not only threatened but had a gun fired at his boat by this said mob in Warsaw when coming up to Nauvoo, and that this very thing was made use of as a means to get us into their hands; and we could not, without taking an armed force with us, go there without, according to their published declarations, going into the jaws of death? To have taken a force with us would only have fanned the excitement, and they would have stated that we wanted to use intimidation; therefore, we thought it the most judicious to avail ourselves of the protection of the law."

Governor Ford.—"I see, I see."

Joseph Smith.—"Furthermore, in relation to the press, you say that you differ from me in opinion. Be it so; the thing, after all, is only a legal difficulty, and the courts, I should judge, are competent to decide on that matter. If our act was illegal, we are willing to meet it; and although I cannot see the distinction that you draw about the acts of the City Council, and what difference it could have made in point of fact, law, or justice between the City Council's acting together or separate, or how much more legal it would have been for the Municipal Court, who were a part of the City Council, to act separately instead of with the councilors, yet, if it is deemed that we did a wrong in destroying that press, we refuse not to pay for it; we are desirous to fulfill the law in every particular, and are responsible for our acts. You say that the parties ought to have a hearing. Had it been a civil suit, this of course, would have been proper; but there was a flagrant violation of every principle of right—a nuisance; and it was abated on the same principle that any nuisance, stench, or putrefied carcass would have been removed. Our first step, therefore, was to stop the foul, noisome, filthy sheet, and then the next in our opinion would have been to have prosecuted the man for a breach of public decency. And, furthermore, again let me say, Governor Ford, I shall look to you for our protection. I believe you are talking of going to Nauvoo; if you go, sir, I wish to go along. I refuse not to answer any law, but I do not consider myself safe here."

Governor.—"I am in hopes that you will be acquitted, and if I go I will certainly take you along. I do not, however, apprehend danger. I think you are perfectly safe either here or anywhere else. I can not, however, interfere with the law. I am placed in peculiar circumstances and seem to be blamed by all parties."

Joseph Smith.—"Governor Ford, I ask for nothing but what is legal; I have a right to expect protection, at least from you; for, independent of law, you have pledged your faith and that of the State for my protection, and I wish to go to Nauvoo."

Governor.—"And you shall have protection, General Smith. I did not make this promise without consulting my officers, who all pledged their honor to its fulfillment. I do not know that I shall go tomorrow to Nauvoo, but if I do I will take you along."

At a quarter past ten o'clock the governor left.

At about half past twelve o'clock, Mr. Reed, one of Joseph's counsel, came in, apparently much elated; he stated that, upon an examination of the law, he found that the magistrate had transcended his jurisdiction, and that having committed them without an examination, his jurisdiction ended, that he had him upon a pinhook; that he ought to have examined them before he committed them, and that, having violated the law in this particular, he had no further power over them; for, once committed, they were out of his jurisdiction, as the power of the magistrate extended no farther than their committal, and that now they could not be brought out except at the regular session of the Circuit Court, or by a writ of *habeas corpus;* but that if Justice Smith would consent to go to Nauvoo for trial, he would compromise matters with him, and overlook this matter.

Mr. Reed further stated that the anti-Mormon or mob, had concocted a scheme to get out a writ from Missouri, with a demand upon Governor Ford for the arrest of Joseph Smith, and his conveyance to Missouri, and that a man by the name of Wilson had returned from Missouri the night before the burning of the press for this purpose.

At half past two o'clock Constable Bettesworth came to the jail with a man named Simpson, professing to have some order, but he would not send up his name, and the guard would not let him pass. Dr. Bernhisel and Brother Wasson went to inform the governor and council of this. At about twenty minutes to three Dr. Bernhisel returned, and stated that he thought the governor was doing all he could. At about ten minutes to three Hiram Kimball appeared with news from Nauvoo.

Soon after Constable Bettesworth came with an order from Esquire Smith to convey the prisoners to the court-house for trial. He was informed that the process was illegal, that they had been placed there contrary to law, and that they refused to come unless by legal process. I was informed that Justice Smith (who was also captain of the Carthage Grays) went to the governor and informed him of the matter, and that the governor replied, "You have your forces, and of course can use them." The constable certainly did return, accompanied by a guard of armed men, and by force, and under protest, hurried the prisoners to the court.

About four o'clock the case was called by Captain Robert F. Smith, J. P. The counsel for the prisoners called for subpoenas to bring witnesses. At twenty-five minutes past four he took a copy of the order to bring the prisoners from jail to trial, and afterwards he took names of witnesses.

Counsel present for the State: Higbee, Skinner, Sharp, Emmons, and Morrison. Twenty-five minutes to five the writ was returned as served, June 25th.

Many remarks were made at the court that I paid but little attention to, as I considered the whole thing illegal and a complete burlesque. Wood objected to the proceedings *in toto*, in consequence of its illegality, showing that the prisoners were not only illegally committed, but that, being once committed, the magistrate had no further power over them; but as it was the same magistrate before whom he was pleading who imprisoned them contrary to law, and the same who, as captain, forced them from jail, his arguments availed but little. He then urged that the prisoners be remanded until witnesses could be had, and applied for a continuance for that purpose. Skinner suggested until twelve o'clock next day. Wood again demanded until witnesses could be obtained; that the court meet at a specified time, and that, if. witnesses were not present, again adjourn, without calling the prisoners. After various remarks from Reed, Skinner, and others, the court stated that the writ was served yesterday, and that it will give until tomorrow at twelve m. to get witnesses.

We then returned to jail. Immediately after our return Dr.

Carthage Jail. June 27ᵗʰ 1844

Lawyer Browning
  Sir:

  Myself and brother Hyrum are in jail on charge of treason, to come up for examination on Saturday morning, 29ᵗʰ inst — and we request your professional services at that time, on our defense, without fail.

    Most Respectfully
      your serv't

      Joseph Smith

N. B. There is no cause of action, for we have not been guilty of any crime, neither is there any just cause of suspicion against us, but certain circumstances make your attendance very necessary. JS

Photographic copy of letter written by the Prophet Joseph to Lawyer Browning on the day of the martyrdom.

Bernhisel went to the governor, and obtained from him an order
for us to occupy a large open room containing a bedstead. I rather
think that the same room had been appropriated to the use of
debtors; at any rate, there was free access to the jailer's house, and
no bars or locks except such as might be on the outside door of the
jail. The jailer, Mr. George W. Steghall, and his wife, manifested a
disposition to make us as comfortable as they could; we ate at their
table, which was well provided, and, of course, paid for it.

I do not remember the names of all who were with us that night
and the next morning in jail, for several went and came; among
those that we considered stationary were Stephen Markham, John
S. Fullmer, Captain Dan Jones, Dr. Willard Richards, and myself.
Dr. Bernhisel says that he was there from Wednesday in the afternoon until eleven o'clock next day. We were, however, visited by
numerous friends, among whom were Uncle John Smith, Hiram
Kimball, Cyrus H. Wheelock, besides lawyers, as counsel. There
was also a great variety of conversation, which was rather desultory
than otherwise, and referred to circumstances that had transpired,
our former and present grievances, the spirit of the troops around
us, and the disposition of the governor; the devising for legal and
other plans for deliverance, the nature of testimony required; the
gathering of proper witnesses, and a variety of other topics, including our religious hopes, etc.

During one of these conversations Dr. Richards remarked:
"Brother Joseph, if it is necessary that you die in this matter, and
if they will take me in your stead, I will suffer for you." At
another time, when conversing about deliverance, I said, "Brother
Joseph, if you will permit it, and say the word, I will have you out
of this prison in five hours, if the jail has to come down to do it."
My idea was to go to Nauvoo, and collect a force sufficient, as I
considered the whole affair a legal farce, and a flagrant outrage
upon our liberty and rights. Brother Joseph refused.

Elder Cyrus H. Wheelock came in to see us, and when he was
about leaving drew a small pistol, a six-shooter, from his pocket,
remarking at the same time, "Would any of you like to have this?"
Brother Joseph immediately replied, "Yes, give it to me;" whereupon he took the pistol, and put it in his pantaloons pocket. The
pistol was a six-shooting revolver, of Allen's patent; it belonged to
me, and was one that I furnished to Brother Wheelock when he
talked of going with me to the east, previous to our coming to
Carthage. I have it now in my possession. Brother Wheelock went
out on some errand, and was not suffered to return. The report of
the governor having gone to Nauvoo without taking the prisoners
along with him caused very unpleasant feelings, as we were apprised that we were left to the tender mercies of the Carthage
Grays, a company strictly mobocratic, and whom we knew to be our
most deadly enemies; and their captain, Esquire Smith, was a most
unprincipled villain. Besides this, all the mob forces, comprising
the governor's troops, were dismissed, with the exception of one
or two companies, which the governor took with him to Nauvoo.
The great part of the mob was liberated, the remainder was our
guard.

We looked upon it not only as a breach of faith on the part of the governor, but also as an indication of a desire to insult us, if nothing more, by leaving us in the proximity of such men. The prevention of Wheelock's return was among the first of their hostile movements.

Colonel Markham then went out, and he was also prevented from returning. He was very angry at this, but the mob paid no attention to him; they drove him out of town at the point of the bayonet, and threatened to shoot him if he returned. He went, I am informed, to Nauvoo for the purpose of raising a company of men for our protection. Brother Fullmer went to Nauvoo after witnesses; it is my opinion that Brother Wheelock did also.

Some time after dinner we sent for some wine. It has been reported by some that this was taken as a sacrament. It was no such thing; our spirits were generally dull and heavy, and it was sent for to revive us. I think it was Captain Jones who went after it, but they would not suffer him to return. I believe we all drank of the wine, and gave some to one or two of the prison guards. We all of us felt unusually dull and languid, with a remarkable depression of spirits. In consonance with those feelings I sang a song, that had lately been introduced into Nauvoo, entitled, "A poor, wayfaring man of grief," etc.

THE POOR WAYFARING MAN OF GRIEF

A poor wayfaring man of grief
Had often crossed me on my way,
Who sued so humbly for relief
That I could never answer, Nay.

I had not power to ask his name;
Whither he went or whence he came;
Yet there was something in his eye
That won my love, I knew not why.

Once, when my scanty meal was spread,
He entered—not a word he spake!
Just perishing for want of bread;
I gave him all; he blessed it, brake.

And ate, but gave me part again;
Mine was an angel's portion then,
For while I fed with eager haste,
The crust was manna to my taste.

I spied him where a fountain burst,
Clear from the rock—his strength was gone,
The heedless water mock'd his thirst,
He heard it, saw it hurrying on.

I ran and raised the suff'rer up;
Thrice from the stream he drain'd my cup,
Dipp'd, and returned it running o'er;
I drank and never thirsted more.

'Twas night, the floods were out, it blew
A winter hurricane aloof;
I heard his voice, abroad, and flew
To bid him welcome to my roof.

I warmed, I clothed, I cheered my guest,
I laid him on my couch to rest;
Then made the earth my bed, and seem'd
In Eden's garden while I dream'd.

Stripp'd, wounded, beaten nigh to death,
I found him by the highway side;
I rous'd his pulse, brought back his breath,
Revived his spirit, and supplied

Wine, oil, refreshment—he was heal'd;
I had myself a wound conceal'd;
But from that hour forgot the smart.
And peace bound up my broken heart.

In pris'n I saw him next—condemned
To meet a traitor's doom at morn;
The tide of lying tongues I stemmed,
And honored him 'mid shame and scorn.

My friendship's utmost zeal to try,
He asked, if I for him would die;
The flesh was weak, my blood ran chill,
But the free spirit cried, "I will!"

Then in a moment to my view,
The stranger started from disguise:
The tokens in his hands I knew,
The Savior stood before mine eyes.

He spake—and my poor name he named—
"Of me thou hast not been asham'd;
These deeds shall thy memorial be;
Fear not thou didst them unto me."

The song is pathetic, and the tune quite plaintive, and was very much in accordance with our feelings at the time, for our spirits were all depressed, dull and gloomy, and surcharged with indefinite ominous forebodings. After a lapse of some time, Brother Hyrum requested me again to sing that song. I replied, "Brother Hyrum, I do not feel like singing," when he remarked, "Oh, never mind; commence singing, and you will get the spirit of it." At his request I did so. Soon afterwards I was sitting at one of the front windows of the jail, when I saw a number of men, with painted faces, coming around the corner of the jail, and aiming towards the stairs. The other brethren had seen the same, for, as I went to the door, I found Brother Hyrum Smith and Dr. Richards already leaning against it. They both pressed against the door with their shoulders to prevent its being opened, as the lock and latch were comparatively useless. While in this position, the mob, who had come up stairs, and tried to open the door, probably thought it was locked, and fired a ball through the keyhole; at this Dr. Richards and Brother Hyrum leaped back from the door, with their faces towards it; almost instantly another ball passed through the panel of the door, and struck Brother Hyrum on the left side of the nose, entering his face and head. At the same instant, another ball from the outside entered his back, passing through his body and striking his watch. The ball came from the back, through the jail window, opposite the door, and must, from its range, have been fired from the Carthage Grays, who were placed there ostensibly for our protection, as the balls from the fire-arms, shot close by the jail, would have entered the ceiling, we being in the second story, and there never was a time after that when Hyrum could have received the latter wound. Immediately, when the balls struck him, he fell flat on his back, crying as he fell, "I am a dead man." He never moved afterwards.

I shall never forget the deep feeling of sympathy and regard manifested in the countenance of Brother Joseph as he drew nigh to Hyrum, and, leaning over him, exclaimed, "Oh! my poor, dear brother Hyrum!" He, however, instantly arose, and with a firm, quick step, and a determined expression of countenance, approached the door, and pulling the six-shooter left by Brother Wheelock from his pocket, opened the door slightly, and snapped the pistol six successive times; only three of the barrels, however, were discharged. I afterwards understood that two or three were wounded by these discharges, two of whom, I am informed, died. I had in my hands a large, strong hickory stick, brought there by Brother Markham, and left by him, which I had seized as soon as I saw the mob approach; and while Brother Joseph was firing the pistol, I stood close behind him. As soon as he had discharged it he stepped back, and I immediately took his place next to the door, while he occupied the one I had done while he was shooting. Brother Richards, at this time, had a knotty walking-stick in his hands belonging to me, and stood next to Brother Joseph, a little farther from the door, in an oblique direction, apparently to avoid the rake of the fire from the door. The firing of Brother Joseph made our assailants pause for a moment; very soon after, however, they pushed the door some distance open, and protruded and discharged their guns into the room, when I parried them off with my stick, giving another direction to the balls.

It certainly was a terrible scene: streams of fire as thick as my arm passed by me as these men fired, and, unarmed as we were, it looked like certain death. I remember feeling as though my time had come, but I do not know when, in any critical position, I was more calm, unruffled, energetic, and acted with more promptness and decision. It certainly was far from pleasant to be so near the muzzles of those fire-arms as they belched forth their liquid flames and deadly balls. While I was engaged in parrying the guns, Brother Joseph said, "That's right, Brother Taylor, parry them off as well as you can." These were the last words I ever heard him speak on earth.

Every moment the crowd at the door became more dense, as they were unquestionably pressed on by those in the rear ascending the stairs, until the whole entrance at the door was literally crowded with muskets and rifles, which, with the swearing, shouting and demoniacal expressions of those outside the door and on the stairs, and the firing of the guns, mingled with their horrid oaths and execrations, made it look like pandemonium let loose, and was, indeed, a fit representation of the horrid deed in which they were engaged.

Stairway in Carthage Jail leading to the room to the right of the landing where Hyrum Smith was killed and where Joseph and Hyrum Smith, John Taylor, and Willard Richards were at the time of the martyrdom.

The landing showing the hole in the door made by the ball that killed Hyrum Smith.

After parrying the guns for some time, which now protruded thicker and farther into the room, and seeing no hope of escape or protection there, as we were now unarmed, it occurred to me that we might have some friends outside, and that there might be some chance of escape in that direction, but here there seemed to be none. As I expected them every moment to rush into the room—nothing but extreme cowardice having thus far kept them out—as the tumult and pressure increased, without any other hope, I made a spring for the window which was right in front of the jail door, where the mob was standing, and also exposed to the fire of the Carthage Grays, who were stationed some ten or twelve rods off. The weather was hot, we all of us had our coats off, and the window was raised to admit air. As I reached the window, and was on the point of leaping out, I was struck by a ball from the door about midway of my thigh, which struck the bone, and flattened out almost to the size of a quarter of a dollar, and then passed on through the fleshy part to within about half an inch of the outside. I think some prominent nerve must have been severed or injured, for, as soon as the ball struck me, I fell like a bird when shot, or an ox when struck by a butcher, and lost entirely and instantaneously all power of action or locomotion. I fell upon the window-sill, and cried out, "I am shot!" Not possessing any power to move, I felt myself falling outside of the window, but immediately I fell inside, from some, at that time, unknown cause. When I struck the floor my animation seemed restored, as I have seen it sometimes in squirrels and birds after being shot. As soon as I felt the power of motion I crawled under the bed which was in a corner of the room, not far from the window where I received my wound. While on my way and under the bed I was wounded in three other places; one ball entered a little below the left knee, and never was extracted; another entered the forepart of my left arm, a little above the wrist, and, passing down by the joint, lodged in the fleshy part of my hand, about midway, a little above the upper joint of my little finger; another struck me on the fleshy part of my left hip, and tore away the flesh as large as my hand, dashing the mangled fragments of flesh and blood against the wall.

My wounds were painful, and the sensation produced was as though a ball had passed through and down the whole length of my leg. I very well remember my reflections at the time. I had a very painful idea of becoming lame and decrepid, and being an object of pity, and I felt as though I would rather die than be placed in such circumstances.

It would seem that immediately after my attempt to leap out of the window, Joseph also did the same thing, of which circumstance I have no knowledge only from information. The first thing that I noticed was a cry that he had leaped out of the window. A cessation of firing followed, the mob rushed down stairs, and Dr. Richards went to the window. Immediately afterwards I saw the doctor going towards the jail door, and as there was an iron door at the head of the stairs adjoining our door which led into the cells for criminals, it struck me that the doctor was going in there, and

I said to him, "Stop, doctor, and take me along." He proceeded to the door and opened it, and then returned and dragged me along to a small cell prepared for criminals.

Brother Richards was very much troubled, and exclaimed, "Oh! Brother Taylor, is it possible that they have killed both Brother Hyrum and Joseph? it cannot surely be, and yet I saw them shoot them;" and, elevating his hands two or three times, he exclaimed, "Oh Lord, my God, spare thy servants!" He then said, "Brother Taylor, this is a terrible event;" and he dragged me farther into the cell, saying, "I am sorry I can do no better for you;" and, taking an old filthy mattress, he covered me with it, and said, "That may hide you, and you may yet live to tell the tale, but I expect they will kill me in a few moments." While lying in this position I suffered the most excruciating pain.

Soon afterwards Dr. Richards came to me, informed me that the mob had precipitately fled, and at the same time confirmed my worst fears that Joseph was assuredly dead. I felt a dull, lonely, sickening sensation at the news. When I reflected that our noble chieftain, the prophet of the living God, had fallen, and that I had seen his brother in the cold embrace of death, it seemed as though there was a void or vacuum in the great field of human existence to me, and a dark, gloomy chasm in the kingdom, and that we were left alone. Oh how lonely was that feeling! How cold, barren and desolate! In the midst of difficulties he was always the first in motion; in critical positions his counsel was always sought. As our prophet he approached our God, and obtained for us his will; but now our prophet, our counselor, our general, our leader was gone, and amid the fiery ordeal that we then had to pass through, we were left alone without his aid, and as our future guide for things spiritual or temporal, and for all things pertaining to this world or the next, he had spoken for the last time on earth!

These reflections and a thousand others flashed upon my mind. I thought, Why must the good perish, and the virtuous be destroyed? Why must God's nobility, the salt of the earth, the most exalted of the human family, and the most perfect types of all excellence, fall victims to the cruel, fiendish hate of incarnate devils?

The poignancy of my grief, I presume, however, was somewhat allayed by the extreme suffering that I endured from my wounds.

Soon afterwards I was taken to the head of the stairs and laid there, where I had a full view of our beloved and now murdered Brother Hyrum. There he lay as I had left him; he had not moved a limb; he lay placid and calm, a monument of greatness even in death; but his noble spirit had left its tenement, and was gone to dwell in regions more congenial to its exalted nature. Poor Hyrum! he was a great and good man, and my soul was cemented to his. If ever there was an exemplary, honest, and virtuous man, an embodiment of all that is noble in the human form, Hyrum Smith was its representative.

While I lay there a number of persons came around, among whom was a physician. The doctor, on seeing a ball lodged in my left hand, took a penknife from his pocket and made an incision in it for the purpose of extracting the ball therefrom, and having obtained a pair of carpenter's compasses, made use of them to draw or pry out the ball, alternately using the penknife and compasses. After sawing for some time with a dull penknife, and prying and pulling with the compasses, he ultimately succeeded in extracting the ball, which weighed about half an ounce. Some time afterwards he remarked to a friend of mine that I had "nerves like the devil," to stand what I did in its extraction. I really thought I had need of nerves to stand such surgical butchery, and that, whatever my nerves may be, his practice was devilish.

This company wished to remove me to Mr. Hamilton's hotel, the place where we had staid previous to our incarceration in jail. I told them, however, that I did not wish to go; I did not consider it safe. They protested that it was, and that I was safe with them; that it was a perfect outrage for men to be used as we had been; that they were my friends; that it was for my good they were counseling me, and that I could be better taken care of there than here.

I replied, "I don't know you. Who am I among? I am surrounded by assassins and murderers; witness your deeds! Don't talk to me of kindness or comfort; look at your murdered victims. Look at me! I want none of your counsel nor comfort. There may be some safety here; I can be assured of none anywhere," etc.

They G— d— their souls to hell, made the most solemn asseverations, and swore by God and the devil, and everything else that they could think of, that they would stand by me to death and protect me. In half an hour every one of them had fled from the town.

Soon after a coroner's jury were assembled in the room over the body of Hyrum. Among the jurors was Captain Smith, of the Carthage Grays, who had assisted in the murder, and the same justice before whom we had been tried. I learned of Francis Higbee as being in the neighborhood. On hearing his name mentioned, I immediately arose and said, "Captain Smith, you are a justice of the peace; I have heard his name mentioned; I want to swear my life against him." I was informed that word was immediately sent to him to leave the place, which he did.

Brother Richards was busy during this time attending to the coroner's inquest, and to the removal of the bodies, and making arrangements for their removal from Carthage to Nauvoo.

When he had a little leisure, he again came to me, and at his suggestion I was removed to Hamilton's tavern. I felt that he was the only friend, the only person, that I could rely upon in that town. It was with difficulty that sufficient persons could be found to carry me to the tavern; for immediately after the murder a great fear fell upon all the people, and men, women, and children fled with great precipitation, leaving nothing nor anybody in the town but two or three women and children and one or two sick persons.

It was with great difficulty that Brother Richards prevailed upon Mr. Hamilton, hotel-keeper, and his family, to stay; they would not until Brother Richards had given a solemn promise that he would see them protected, and hence I was looked upon as a hostage. Under these circumstances, notwithstanding, I believe they were hostile to the Mormons, and were glad that the murder had taken place, though they did not actually participate in it; and, feeling that I should be a protection to them, they staid.

The whole community knew that a dreadful outrage had been perpetrated by those villains, and fearing lest the citizens of Nauvoo, as they possessed the power, might have a disposition to visit them with a terrible vengeance, they fled in the wildest confusion. And, indeed, it was with very great difficulty that the citizens of Nauvoo could be restrained. A horrid, barbarous murder had been committed, the most solemn pledge violated, and that, too, while the victims were, contrary to the requirements of the law, putting themselves into the hands of the governor to pacify a popular excitement. This outrage was enhanced by the reflection that our people were able to protect themselves against not only all the mob, but against three times their number and that of the governor's troops put together. They were also exasperated by the speech of the governor in town.

The whole events were so faithless, so dastardly, so mean, cowardly, and contemptible, without one extenuating circumstance, that it would not have been surprising if the citizens of Nauvoo had arisen *en masse*, and blotted the wretches out of existence. The citizens of Carthage knew they would have done so under such circumstances, and, judging us by themselves, they were all panic-stricken, and fled. Colonel Markham, too, after his expulsion from Carthage, had gone home, related the circumstances of his ejectment, and was using his influence to get a company to go out. Fearing that when the people heard that their prophet and patriarch had been murdered under the above circumstances they might act rashly, and knowing that if they once got roused, like a mighty avalanche they would lay the country waste before them and take a terrible vengeance—as none of the Twelve were in Nauvoo, and no one, perhaps, with sufficient influence to control the people, Dr. Richards, after consulting me, wrote the following note, fearing that my family might be seriously affected by the news. I told him to insert that I was slightly wounded.

*Willard Richards' Note from Carthage Jail to Nauvoo.**

"Carthage jail, 8 o'clock 5 min. p. m., June 27th, 1844.

"Joseph and Hyrum are dead. Taylor wounded, not very badly. I am well. Our guard was forced, as we believe, by a band of Missourians from 100 to 200. The job was done in an instant, and the party fled towards Nauvoo instantly. This is as I believe it. The citizens here are afraid of the 'Mormons' attacking them; I promise them no. W. RICHARDS.

"N. B.—The citizens promise us protection; alarm guns have been fired. "JOHN TAYLOR."

Deseret News, No. 38, Nov. 25, 1857, p. 297.

I remember signing my name as quickly as possible, lest the tremor of my hand should be noticed, and the fears of my family excited.

A messenger was dispatched immediately with the note, but he was intercepted by the governor, who, on hearing a cannon fired at Carthage, which was to be the signal for the murder, immediately fled with his company, and fearing that the citizens of Nauvoo, when apprised of the horrible outrage, would immediately rise and pursue, he turned back the messenger, who was George D. Grant. A second one was sent, who was treated similarly; and not until a third attempt could news be got to Nauvoo.

Samuel H. Smith, brother to Joseph and Hyrum, was the first brother I saw after the outrage; I am not sure whether he took the news or not; he lived at the time in Plymouth, Hancock County, and was on his way to Carthage to see his brothers, when he was met by some of the troops, or rather mob, that had been dismissed by the governor, and who were on their way home. On learning that he was Joseph Smith's brother they sought to kill him, but he escaped, and fled into the woods, where he was chased for a length of time by them; but, after severe fatigue, and much danger and excitement, he succeeded in escaping, and came to Carthage. He was on horseback when he arrived, and was not only very much tired with the fatigue and excitement of the chase, but was also very much distressed in feelings on account of the death of his brothers. These things produced a fever, which laid the foundation for his death, which took place on the 30th of July. Thus another of the brothers fell a victim although not directly, but indirectly to this infernal mob.

I lay from about five o'clock until two next morning without having my wounds dressed, as there was scarcely any help of any kind in Carthage, and Brother Richards was busy with the dead bodies, preparing them for removal. My wife Leonora started early the next day, having had some little trouble in getting a company or a physician to come with her; after considerable difficulty she succeeded in getting an escort, and Dr. Samuel Bennett came along with her. Soon after my father and mother arrived from Oquakie, near which place they had a farm at that time, and hearing of the trouble hastened along.

General Demming, Brigadier General of the Hancock County Militia, was very much of a gentleman, and showed me every courtesy, and Colonel Jones also was very solicitous about my welfare.

I was called upon by several gentlemen of Quincy and other places, among whom was Judge Ralston, as well as by our own people, and a medical man extracted a ball from my left thigh that was giving me much pain; it lay about half an inch deep, and my thigh was considerably swollen. The doctor asked me if I would be tied during the operation; I told him no; that I could endure the cutting associated with the operation as well without, and I did so; indeed, so great was the pain I endured that the cutting was rather a relief than otherwise.

A very laughable incident occurred at the time; my wife Leonora went into an adjoining room to pray for me, that I might be sustained during the operation. While on her knees at prayer, a Mrs. Bedell, an old lady of the Methodist association, entered, and, patting Mrs. Taylor on her back with her hand, said, "There's a good lady, pray for God to forgive your sins, pray that you may be converted, and the Lord may have mercy on your soul."

The scene was so ludicrous that Mrs. Taylor knew not whether to laugh or be angry. Mrs. Taylor informed me that Mr. Hamilton, the father of the Hamilton who kept the house, rejoiced at the murder, and said in company that "it was done up in the best possible style, and showed good generalship;" and she further believed that the other branches of the family sanctioned it. These were the associates of the old lady referred to, and yet she could talk of conversion and saving souls in the midst of blood and murder: such is man and such consistency.

The ball being extracted was the one that first struck me, which I before referred to: it entered on the outside of my left thigh, about five inches from my knee, and, passing rather obliquely towards my body, had, it would seem, struck the bone, for it was flatted out nearly as thin and large as a quarter of a dollar.

The governor passed on, staying at Carthage only a few minutes, and he did not stop until he got fifty miles from Nauvoo. There had been various opinions about the complicity of the governor in the murder, some supposing that he knew all about it, and assisted or winked at its execution. It is somewhat difficult to form a correct opinion; from the facts presented it is very certain that things looked more than suspicious against him.

In the first place, he positively knew that we had broken no law.

Secondly. He knew that the mob had not only passed inflammatory resolutions, threatening extermination to the Mormons, but that they had actually assembled armed mobs and commenced hostilities against us.

Thirdly. He took those very mobs that had been arrayed against us, and enrolled them as his troops, thus legalizing their acts.

Fourthly. He disbanded the Nauvoo Legion, which had never violated law, and disarmed them, and had about his person in the shape of militia known mobocrats and violaters of the law.

Fifthly. He requested us to come to Carthage without arms, promising protection, and then refused to interfere in delivering us from prison, although Joseph and Hyrum were put there contrary to law.

Sixthly. Although he refused to interfere in our behalf, yet, when Captain Smith went to him and informed him that the persons refused to come out, he told him that he had a command and knew what to do, thus sanctioning the use of force in the violation of law when opposed to us, whereas he would not for us interpose his executive authority to free us from being incarcerated contrary to law, although he was fully informed of all the facts of the case, as we kept him posted in the affairs all the time.

Seventhly. He left the prisoners in Carthage jail contrary to his plighted faith.

Eighthly. Before he went he dismissed all the troops that could be relied upon, as well as many of the mob, and left us in charge of the "Carthage Grays," a company that he knew were mobocratic, our most bitter enemies, and who had passed resolutions to exterminate us, and who had been placed under guard by General Demming only the day before.

Ninthly. He was informed of the intended murder, both before he left and while on the road, by several different parties.

Tenthly. When the cannon was fired in Carthage, signifying that the deed was done, he immediately took up his line of march and fled. How did he know that this signal portrayed their death if he was not in the secret? It may be said some of the party told him. How could he believe what the party said about the gun signal if he could not believe the testimony of several individuals who told him in positive terms about the contemplated murder?

He has, I believe, stated that he left the "Carthage Grays" there because he considered that, as their town was contiguous to ours, and as the responsibility of our safety rested solely upon them, they would not dare suffer any indignity to befall us. This very admission shows that he did really expect danger; and then he knew that these people had published to the world that they would exterminate us, and his leaving us in their hands and taking of their responsibilities was like leaving a lamb in charge of a wolf, and trusting to its humanity and honor for its safe-keeping.

It is said, again that he would not have gone to Nauvoo, and thus placed himself in the hands of the Mormons, if he had anticipated any such event, as he would be exposed to their wrath. To this it may be answered that the Mormons did not know their signals, while he did; and they were also known in Warsaw, as well as in other places; and as soon as the gun was fired, a merchant of Warsaw jumped upon his horse and rode directly to Quincy, and reported "Joseph and Hyrum killed, and those who were with them in jail." He reported further that "they were attempting to break jail, and were all killed by the guard." This was their story; it was anticipated to kill all, and the gun was to be the signal that the deed was accomplished. This was known in Warsaw. The governor also knew it and fled; and he could really be in no danger in Nauvoo, for the Mormons did not know it, and he had plenty of time to escape, which he did.

It is said that he made all his officers promise solemnly that they would help him to protect the Smiths; this may or may not be. At any rate, some of these officers helped to murder them.

The strongest argument in the governor's favor, and one that would bear more weight with us than all the rest put together, would be that he could not believe them capable of such atrocity; and, thinking that their talk and threatenings were a mere ebullition of feeling, a kind of braggadocio, and that there was enough of good moral feeling to control the more violent passions, he trusted to their faith. There is, indeed, a degree of plausibility about this, but when we put it in juxtaposition to the amount of evidence that he was in possession of, it weighs very little. He had nothing to inspire confidence in them, and everything to make him mistrust them. Besides, why his broken faith? why his disregard of what was told him by several parties? Again, if he knew not the plan, how did he understand the signal? Why so oblivious to everything pertaining to the Mormon interest, and so alive and interested about the mobocrats? At any rate, be this as it may, he stands responsible for their blood, and it is dripping on his garments. If it had not been for his promise of protection, they would have protected themselves; it was plighted faith that led them to the slaughter; and to make the best of it, it was a breach of that faith and a nonfulfillment of that promise, after repeated warning, that led to their death.

Having said so much, I must leave the governor with my readers and with his God. Justice, I conceive, demanded this much, and truth could not be told with less; as I have said before, my opinion is that the governor would not have planned this murder, but he had not sufficient energy to resist popular opinion, even if that opinion led to blood and death.

It was rumored that a strong political party, numbering in its ranks many of the prominent men of the nation, were engaged in a plot for the overthrow of Joseph Smith, and that the governor was of this party, and Sharp, Williams, Captain Smith, and others were his accomplices, but whether this was the case or not I do not know. It is very certain that a strong political feeling existed against Joseph Smith, and I have reason to believe that his letters to Henry Clay, were made use of by political parties opposed to Mr. Clay, and were the means of that statesman's defeat. Yet, if such a combination as the one referred to existed, I am not apprised of it.

While I lay at Carthage, previous to Mrs. Taylor's arrival, a pretty good sort of a man, who was lame of a leg, waited upon me, and sat up at night with me; afterwards Mrs. Taylor, mother and others waited upon me.

Many friends called upon me, among whom were Richard Ballantyne, Elizabeth Taylor, several of the Perkins Family, and a number of the brethren from Macedonia and La Harpe. Besides these, many strangers from Quincy, some of whom expressed indignant feelings against the mob and sympathy for myself. Brother Alexander Williams called upon me, who suspected that they had some designs in keeping me there, and stated that he had, at a given point in some woods, fifty men, and if I would say the word he would raise another fifty, and fetch me out of there. I thanked him, but told him I thought there was no need. However, it would seem that I was in some danger; for Colonel Jones, before referred to, when absent from me, left two loaded pistols on the table in case of an attack, and some time afterward, when I had recovered and was publishing the affair, a lawyer, Mr. Backman, stated that he had prevented a man by the name of Jackson, before referred to, from ascending the stairs, who was coming with a design to murder me, and that now he was sorry he had not let him do the deed.

There were others also, of whom I heard, that said I ought to be killed, and they would do it, but that it was too damned cowardly to shoot a wounded man; and thus, by the chivalry of murderers, I was prevented from being a second time mutilated or killed. Many of the mob, came around and treated me with apparent respect, and the officers and people generally looked upon me as a hostage, and feared that my removal would be the signal for the rising of the Mormons.

I do not remember the time that I stayed at Carthage, but I think three or four days after the murder, when Brother Marks with a carriage, Brother James Allred with a wagon, Dr. Ells, and a number of others on horseback, came for the purpose of taking me to Nauvoo. I was very weak at the time, occasioned by the loss of blood and the great discharge of my wounds, so when my wife asked me if I could talk I could barely whisper, no. Quite a discussion arose as to the propriety of my removal, the physician and people of Carthage protesting that it would be my death, while my friends were anxious for my removal if possible.

I suppose the former were actuated by the above-named desire to keep me. Colonel Jones was, I believe, sincere; he had acted as a friend all the time, and he told Mrs. Taylor she ought to persuade me not to go, for he did not believe I had strength enough to reach Nauvoo. It was finally agreed, however, that I should go; but it was thought that I could not stand riding in a wagon or carriage, they prepared a litter for me; I was carried down stairs and put upon it. A number of men assisted to carry me, some of them had been engaged in the mob. As soon as I got down stairs, I felt much better and strengthened, so that I could talk; I suppose the effect of the fresh air.

When we got near the outside of the town I remembered some woods that we had to go through, and telling a person near to call for Dr. Ells, who was riding a very good horse, I said, "Doctor, I perceive that the people are getting fatigued with carrying me; a number of Mormons live about two or three miles from here, near our route, will you ride to their settlement as quick as possible, and have them come and meet us?" He started off on a gallop immediately. My object in this was to obtain protection in case of an attack, rather than to obtain help to carry me.

Very soon after the men from Carthage made one excuse after another until they had all left, and I felt glad to get rid of them. I found that the tramping of those carrying me produced violent pain, and a sleigh was produced and attached to the hind end of Brother James Allred's wagon, a bed placed upon it, and I propped up on the bed. Mrs. Taylor rode with me, applying ice and ice-water to my wounds. As the sleigh was dragged over the grass on the prairie, which was quite tall, it moved very easy and gave me very little pain.

When I got within five or six miles of Nauvoo the brethren commenced to meet me from the city, and they increased in number as we drew nearer, until there was a very large company of people of all ages and both sexes, principally, however, men.

For some time there had been almost incessant rain, so that in many low places on the prairie it was from one to three feet deep in water, and at such places the brethren whom we met took hold of the sleigh, lifted it, and carried it over the water; and when we arrived in the neighborhood of the city, where the roads were excessively muddy and bad, the brethren tore down the fences, and we passed through the fields.

Never shall I forget the difference of feeling that I experienced between the place that I had left and the one I had now arrived at. I had left a lot of reckless, bloodthirsty murderers, and had come to the City of the Saints, the people of the living God; friends of truth and righteousness, thousands of whom stood there with warm, true hearts to offer their friendship and services, and to welcome my return. It is true it was a painful scene, and brought sorrowful remembrance to mind, but to me it caused a thrill of joy to find myself once more in the bosom of my friends, and to meet with the cordial welcome of true, honest hearts. What was very remarkable, I found myself very much better after my arrival at Nauvoo than I was when I started on my journey, although I had traveled eighteen miles.

The next day as some change was wanting, I told Mrs. Taylor that if she could send to Dr. Richards, he had my purse and watch, and they would find money in my purse.

Previous to the doctor leaving Carthage, I told him that he had better take my purse and watch, for I was afraid the people would steal them. The doctor had taken my pantaloons' pocket, and put the watch in it with the purse, cut off the pocket, and tied a string around the top; it was in this position when brought home. My family, however, were not a little startled to find that my watch had been struck with a ball. I sent for my vest, and, upon examination, it was found that there was a cut as if with a knife, in the vest pocket which had contained my watch. In the pocket the fragments of the glass were found literally ground to powder. It then occurred to me that a ball had struck me at the time I felt myself falling out of the window, and that it was this force that threw me inside. I had often remarked to Mrs. Taylor the singular fact of finding myself inside the room, when I felt a moment before after being shot, that I was falling out, and I never could account for it until then; but here the thing was fully elucidated, and was rendered plain to my mind. I was indeed falling out, when some villain aimed at my heart. The ball struck my watch, and forced me back; If I had fallen out I should assuredly have been killed, if not by the fall, by those around, and this ball intended to dispatch me, was turned by an overruling Providence into a messenger of mercy, and saved my life. I shall never forget the feelings of gratitude that I then experienced towards my Heavenly Father; the whole scene was vividly portrayed before me, and my heart melted before the Lord. I felt that the Lord had preserved me by a special act of

mercy; that my time had not yet come, and that I had still a work
to perform upon the earth.

The Rise and Fall of Nauvoo, pp. 404-457.

From pages 547 to 624, Vol. 6, *Documentary History of the Church* is given
a more detailed account of events than what John Taylor has recorded, to
which the reader is referred.

AN EYE WITNESS TO JOSEPH SMITH'S DEATH

Col. M. B. Darnell of Sheldon, Iowa, has been visiting Salt Lake
City. He is an interesting figure to the people of Utah in that he is
probably the only living eye witness of the assassination of the
Prophet Joseph Smith at Carthage, Illinois, June 27, 1844.

"You know it is a long time since then," said Col. Darnell.
"It is fifty years ago, and my memory may be faulty in some particulars, but I will relate that only which I remember distinctly.
When the Mormons came to Commerce, they changed the name to
Nauvoo, and built the place up rapidly until there were about
15,000 people in the city. The inhabitants of that part of the state
were of the rougher element to a great extent. The county offices
were profitable positions, because there was big opportunity
for stealing, so there was considerable rivalry between Whigs
and Democrats as to who should get in. The Mormons were
not in it as a political party, but they held the balance of power,
and of course they voted for those they considered the best
men. This caused great hostility toward the Mormons on the
part of the 'antis.' They wanted to get rid of the Mormons for
political reasons, so they fed the feeling against them. There was
lots of stealing going on, and it was charged to the Mormons. The
women and children were taught to believe the Mormons guilty,
but I do not. I know that stealing was done by others, and that
the Mormons as a community were not chargeable with it. Of
course there may have been some Mormons who stole, but it was
mostly the rough element, and the fire-eating anti-Mormons accused the Mormons so as to get them driven out. The 'law and
order' men, as we called them, wanted the courts to settle all matters, and were called 'Jack-Mormons' by the 'antis.' I was a student under General M. R. Demming. He got me a commission as
lieutenant from Gov. Ford. He commanded the mob that arrested
the Smiths at Nauvoo, but he was there as a friend of order. I call
the *posse comitatus* that made the arrest a mob, because that was
what it really was. They went through the process of law merely
for form's sake. It was called a war at that time. When the posse
was called by the sheriff, John Carlin, I was in the crowd and considered myself summoned, as it were, to assist in making the arrest.
    "My recollection is we were there in Carthage a week. We
went just outside the town and pitched our tents. We camped there
and played soldiers as well as we knew how. Some way or other,
I do not know how, communication was had by which the Smiths
agreed to give themselves up, and the officers went out and met
them about half way in the prairie and brought them in. They
took them to the Hamilton house, a hotel, and held them there for

a couple of days, probably determining in their own mind what they were going to do. As an officer on Gen. Demming's staff it was my duty to take this company called the Carthage Greys, down to the hotel and form a hollow square, and they had a man with them by the name, I think, of Scribling. He was attorney or counselor for the prisoners, I understood. They put the prisoners in the center of the square and marched them down to the general headquarters while they had their conference. The posse had the Smiths in their power and seemed disposed to make terms of some kind to determine what course would be pursued. At the end of about a couple of days they were placed in jail, which was a two story stone structure and overhead were very nice rooms, in one of which there was a bed. They were called the debtors' rooms. Very soon after the prisoners were placed in jail, it might have been the same day, the troops as we called them, were all called together and Gov. Ford addressed them. In his speech he stated that the object of their assembling had been accomplished; that the writ had been executed and the parties were in jail. He commanded the troops to disband and go to their several places of abode, and most of them did so.

"On the afternoon of the day of the assassination, the mob who did the killing came up. They had their faces painted a sort of brown color. I saw this crowd of men coming up from the direction of the creek at the northwest corner of the pasture. I was standing within ten or twenty steps of the pasture gate east of the jail. The crowd was coming single file, and stooping down. They had on blue hunting shirts. I knew something terrible was going to happen. I was a youth at the time and became transfixed to the spot. As the crowd turned the southwest corner of the jail, about one-half of them went right up the stairway, the other half came right against me. I got out of their way, and a moment afterwards I heard the report of a gun in the house. That was supposed to be the shot which killed Hyrum Smith. Joseph started to jump through the window, and the mob fired at him. He came out on the east side of the building. There was a large well just underneath there and he fell just outside the curb. Joseph was killed while passing out of the window. The Carthage Greys, it is said— and I have no doubt with truth, for I look at this thing very different now from what I did then, because I know more about men, their motives and dispositions—I say there is no doubt that the Carthage Greys were cognizant of the fact that that mob was coming. I believe every man of them knew it, and I also believe that their guns were charged with blank cartridges. When they fired a few shots at the mob no one was hurt. The faces of the mob were painted a kind of Indian color. The Carthage Greys were a very nicely drilled company. It would seem to me that the mob were not any larger in number than the Carthage Greys. From my recollection I think the number was very nearly equal—about thirty or forty men in each. I do not believe that the estimate of one hundred men in the mob is at all correct. Probably there were fifty to eighty in the mob; I thought there were less. It was thought there at the time that Thomas C. Sharp was the ringleader—the

moving spirit of the mob. He commenced life as an attorney, but
did not succeed, and became a newspaper editor. When I last saw
him, several years ago, he was quite aged. I know there was such
a man as William M. Daniels, but do not know what became of
him. I knew Frank Worrell, commander of the guard at the jail. He
was afterwards killed outside of Nauvoo, during the Mormon war
in 1846. I also knew Alexander Sympson and his sons. They were
at the jail. They were fiery anti-Mormons.

"I remember to have seen Joseph Smith jump from the window. It was a terribly exciting time and it all happened in an
instant. I cannot describe it in any better way than by saying he
came out just as though some one big and powerful had thrown him
right through the window. Undoubtedly, however, he came by his
own effort. He certainly did not hang to the window. It seems
to me he came out head first, and he was shot while passing through
the window. I do not know that I really saw any one set him up
against the well. I know I partially saw it and got it from what
they said at the time. I could not hear distinctly what Joseph said
when he fell, but it seemed to me to be, "O Lord, My God." That
was all he said. I think he raised himself to a sitting position. A
young man went up and struck him either with the end of his gun
or a bayonet, after he was dead, you may say. I did not notice
whether they fired into him after he was set up by the well. I
have the idea, however, that the young man went up to him and
ran his bayonet through him, or rushed at him with his gun. I do
not believe there was a gun fired after he struck the ground, and
still I may be mistaken. I tell you those bullets came instantaneously. I did not notice any one raise a knife for the purpose of severing Joseph's head from his body, but I heard at the time that a
young man did so. Those things might have been true. I was not
one of the mob, but was one of the disbanded posse. I was going to
the pasture after my horse, and was so close at the time that if I
had been dressed like the mob I might have been considered one of
their number. The young man who struck Joseph claimed to be a
son of Gov. Boggs. He rushed from the mob after Joseph was set
up and struck him with the point of his gun or bayonet, and said,
"G— d— you ; you are the man that had my father shot." Of course
Joseph Smith might have been alive with the bullets in his body,
and have set himself up. I am satisfied he was alive then. If a
gun was fired at him after he fell from the window I don't remember
it. My memory is dim on some things, but I know there was great
excitement just at the time.

"The firing was all done in a moment. Then there was a sort
of recognition between the Carthage Greys and the mob, as they
mingled after Joseph was lying dead on the ground. I remember
now that there was some talk right on the ground there within
twenty minutes after the assassination about a man going up with
a knife to cut off Joseph's head or disembowel him. I did not hear
any reason given why he did not carry out his threat. I merely
heard the young man say what I have stated as he made a lunge
at him. I was away perhaps eleven or twelve feet. The guns were
rattling and the men were swearing.

"In a little while the mob went back the way they came, where I understood they had animals to help them away. I could not recognize the mobbers very well, because of their disguise, but I remember Sharp, Hendricks, Davis and some of the others, who were afterwards known as having been there. It was a terrible deed, and the law and order people there have no excuse for it. We were not civilized there then as we are now, but there was nothing to justify the assassination. It was the work of fiery anti-Mormons who wanted the Mormons driven out of the state."

Millennial Star, 56:252-55.

THE KILLING OF JOSEPH AND HYRUM

(Note: One day when visiting Mr. S. H. Goodwin, Secretary of the Masonic Lodge of Salt Lake City, he stated that when visiting the Chicago City Library, the Manuscript Department, he saw a letter written by Col. Williams, the leader of the mob who murdered the Prophet Joseph and his brother Hyrum, to a relative of his. I immediately wrote to President George S. Romney of the Northern States Mission, suggesting to him that he look into the matter and secure a copy of this letter. In a few weeks I received a note from Pres. Romney as follows:

"Brother Lundwall: This letter from Samuel Ottis Williams to Mr. Prickett is the only one I can find that in any way resembles the one you wrote to me about. Do you think it could be the one? I appreciate your letter very much. Many thanks.

Signed: Geo. S. Romney."

This letter follows verbatim:

My dear John: Carthage, July 10, 1844.

I have just this moment received your letter of the first and hasten to answer it. I proceed to give you a history of our difficulties with the Saints. About a month ago a paper was started in Nauvoo called the *Nauvoo Expositor* owned by several of the seceding saints which had for its purpose the exposure of the Smiths and all villainy practiced by them and in the City under their direction.

The first number of the paper was issued and the way it let out on Jo was a sin. Jo called the City Council together and after much deliberation and talk the new paper was declared a nuisance, and they passed an ordinance requiring the marshal of the city to destroy the press and pi the type and if any resistance was offered to destroy the house. The Mayor of the City (Jo) accordingly issued his writ to the Marshal commanding him to do the work which he did. He with his posse (the marshal) threw the press into the street and broke it up with a sledge hammer and burned the type. The Mormons also tried to catch the owners of the Press but they escaped. Several of them came here.

Complaint was made here before a Justice of the Peace, who issued his warrant and sent a constable to bring them. (Jo and all the others concerned, about 20 in number.) The Municipal Court of the City of Nauvoo discharged the balance on writs of Habeas Corpus. These potent words were entered on the record. "Honorably discharged. W." As soon as we heard of the press being destroyed a meeting of the old citizens was called and was in session at the time the officer returned from Nauvoo without the prisoners. Of course, such an excitement I never did see in my life.

There were about seven hundred of the old citizens assembled here and I tell you that we all felt that the time had come when either the Mormons or old citizens had to leave. The meeting determined to call for volunteers to rendezvous at four places in this county and when a sufficient number had assembled the constable that arrested Smith and the others was to call on us as a *posse comitatus* to help him arrest the accused. Our Brigadier General in the meantime called out the forces under his command. The meeting also appointed two persons to go to the Governor and get him to issue a call for the Militia.

They repaired to Springfield and returned with his Excellency—when the Gov. arrived here he found about 300 men armed and drilling four hours each day and standing guard at night. Our Company the Carthage Greys as soon as the meeting came to the conclusion it did, pitched our tents on the public square and went to work. The Gov. after his arrival made a speech to the troops and announced his determination to see the laws executed and immediately dispatched a messenger to Nauvoo to Smith telling him the consequences if he did not immediately surrender himself for trial, this was on Friday.

On Sunday a whole regiment marched into town from McDonough County and on the next Tuesday a Battalion from Schuyler County which made the forces here amount to about 1400 men. As the different forces marched into town they pledged themselves that no violence should be offered to the prisoners if they did come to Carthage.

On Tuesday the Gov. sent Capt. Dunn of the Union Dragoons of this county to Nauvoo with an order for the state arms with wagons and horses to bring them here. On the road between this place and Nauvoo they met Smith and the others accused coming to this place to give themselves up for trial. They returned to Nauvoo with Capt. Dunn and about two-thirds of the State Arms delivered to Capt. Dunn and the two Smiths, Jo and Hyrum came out here with Capt. Dunn with the arms.

On Wednesday morning the McDonough troops requested the Gov. to bring Smith, (Jo) along their lines, many of whom had never seen him. The two Smiths were after breakfast brought to the Headquarters of the Brigadier General and our company stationed at the door as a guard—your humble Servant had command of the Greys at this time. I brought the company up to the house and formed a square of three sides in front of the house with their muskets set at "Charge" and even then had some difficulty in keeping the crowd back so great was the anxiety to see the Smiths. We stood in this position about half an hour when I received orders from the Brig. Gen. to form the Grey's into a Hollow square and guard the Smiths and the Gov. and the Gen. to the right of the 57th Regt., which formed about 300 yards from the General's quarters, which was accordingly done, and when we arrived there I opened the square and let them out and marched the Greys back to their "quarters."

I was about to dismiss the company when the Smiths in company with the Brig. Gen. came past our quarters. The company in line at "order arms" when the Greys commenced hissing, groaning, and making all sorts of hellish sounds. I tried to stop it but could not. I was about to dismiss the company again when several of them requested me to march out and drill awhile. I accordingly marched out and started down a street on which the Tavern stands that Jo was stopping at. On the way we passed the Brig. Gen. and the Greys viped him the worst kind and arrived in a few minutes afterwards in front of the Tavern where Jo was when the same scene was enacted. Hissing, groaning, and all kinds of discordant sounds. I all the time tried my utmost to preserve silence, but had no more command than I would have had over a pack of wild Indians. At this demonstration of feeling on the part of the Greys, Jo actually fainted.

I will now tell you the reason of all the hissing and etc. The Greys thought we were ordered to escort Smith and that it was intended as an honor to be conferred on him, and the General always has been what we call a Jack Mormon. I believe I have told you what that is and therefore won't stop to explain now—A few days before at our Anti-Mormon meeting he attempted to make a speech and was hissed down.

Well to resume where we arrived at our quarters. I was informed that our company was ordered under "Arrest." A member of the company immediately mounted a wagon and made a speech to the troops and the remainder loaded their muskets with Ball Cartridges and swore that they would die sooner than give up their arms. A considerable number of the troops, say one half swore that the arms of the Greys should not be taken from them. If you had been here to see the excitement at this time you would have been astonished. I never saw anything to equal it. The Brig. Gen. had insulted the McDonough troops by introducing the Smiths in this way: "Gentlemen officers of the 57th Regt., I introduce to you Joseph and Hyrum Smith, Generals of the Nauvoo Legion." They at the same time, prisoners.

At this stage of the proceedings the Gov. came on the ground and stated that no honor was intended to be conferred on the Smiths: that it was done at the request of the 57th Regt., that they might see him. That he disapproved of the way of introducing the prisoners and rescinded the order of arrest. At this time the shout of the multitude ascended to the heavens. We cheered the Gov. for about two minutes and we made some noise. This settled all things for the present.

The same day an order was issued to all the troops to march on Friday into Nauvoo. The whole rendezvous on Thursday night at Golden Point about five miles below Nauvoo and the former order of march was revoked. The Gov. thinking that if, we once got into Nauvoo that he could not restrain the troops and that we would burn the place. On Friday morning all the troops except the

Union Dragoons—Carthage Greys and the Carthage Riflemen (the last a Militia Company) were disbanded and left for home. Jo and Hyrum all this time in jail. I forgot to say that 15 of these concerned in destroying the press came forward and gave bail for their appearance at the next term of the Circuit Court without an examination and immediately afterward Jo and Hyrum were arrested on a charge of Treason and the examination was postponed until Saturday the 29th which time they were destined never to see.

On Friday about 10 o'clock a.m. the Gov. under the escort of the Union Dragoons started for Nauvoo to address the people there. Leaving our company and the Militia Company to protect the prisoners. They being under a pledge to do so. All was quiet at this time. A guard of six men was placed at the jail with a sergeant to command it which was relieved about every three hours. When the Gov. had been gone about 2 hours he sent back a messenger to Capt. Smith stating that he was afraid some violence would be offered to the prisoners and that he expected him to do his duty. The same messenger was sent back to the Gov. that we would.

5 o'clock p.m. our look-out of the courthouse cried out, "there's about 400 Mormons coming down the fence to the jail." I cannot explain to you the situation of the jail and our encampment on paper. But when I see you (which I hope will be soon) I will show you. As soon as the alarm was given our company and the Militia Company was immediately formed and started for the jail which was about 700 yards from our quarters. At the time the alarm was given the mob were within about 200 yards of the jail. We marched double quick time and when we got to the jail both the Smiths were killed, and the mob running off. When the mob came up in front of the jail our guard challenged them. The mob demanded the prisoners. They were told that if they did not retire the guard would fire on them. The mob raised a shout and commenced jumping over the low fence in front of the jail when our guard fired on them. The guard were not hurt except some bruises. One of the guard who was the sergeant in command lost his sword and another his musket. The guard in return captured a musket and a rifle. The mob all had their faces blacked.

When we were marching to the jail about 150 yards from the jail, we saw Jo come to the window and turn back and in about a second or two afterwards he came to the window and tumbled out. He was shot several times and a bayonet run through him after he fell. From all the information I can get the mob were about 250 strong. The forces left to guard the prisoners about 60 to 65 strong. A messenger was immediately dispatched to the Gov. who returned here about 12 o'clock that night and advised us to evacuate the town. After the Smiths were killed all the women and children were removed from town and the men were determined to stay and protect their property, but when the Gov. came in and stated he believed our town would be in ashes before morning we all left and deserted the town.

Stop—there were six men in town at daylight Saturday morning. I was not one of them, I left Carthage about half past one and traveled all night through mud and water knee deep in some places. I arrived at Augusta about 7 o'clock Saturday morning having traveled 18 miles and considering the roads, was tolerably good walking. The Gov. was badly scared and stopped in this place but a few minutes and left for Augusta. Arrived there about day-light and left there directly after breakfast for Quincy where he now is.

What will be the result of the death of the Smiths I am entirely unable to say. The Mormons are very badly scared and I don't think they will do anything at present. The citizens of this place have nearly all returned.   Samuelson Ottis Williams

P. S. I think I will be in Edwardsville soon, anyhow as soon as I can leave. Our company is still under orders and I can't leave just yet. My family sent off to Rushville, 50 miles from here as soon as they could start after the Smiths were killed and I returned here with them yesterday. I suppose your letter has been lying here several days. This will account for its not being answered before. My family are all well, that is, my wife and boy and gal. I rather guess you will think I have inherited some of Old Henry T. Lusks principles in writing this letter, but I could not well make it shorter and besides I want to make you repent of taking such an unwarrantable privilege as to intrude upon the attention of

Your friend, S. Ottis Williams

WITNESSED THE PROPHET'S MARTYRDOM

By President E. H. Nye

"I and my companion spent an evening recently with a gentle-man who witnessed the killing of the Prophet Joseph Smith. He was then employed as a stage driver between Nauvoo and Keokuk, with Carthage as a half-way station, and came rattling into Carth-age with the stage. Driving past the old jail, he says, he saw the mob on one side and a large number of the regulars on the other. He drove past the jail on one side to the hotel, delivered his mail and passengers. Then, whirling around and passing on the other side of the jail to reach his stable, the shooting commenced as his passengers were getting out, and as he drove past the jail towards his stable, the Prophet Joseph jumped out of the window. He saw him fall and saw them set him up against the well. He says that as soon as the stableman took charge of the team, he jumped off and ran, frightened half out of his wits.

"This man speaks in the highest terms of commendation and praise of the Prophet Joseph and his family. He says that he arrived in Nauvoo at night, a stranger, about a year prior to the death of Joseph Smith, without money or friends, a boy about 14 years of age, having understood that his brother lived there. On inquiring for his brother, he learned that it was eight miles to his home, with snow on the ground and very cold. The gentleman of whom he inquired, took him over to a large house that he thought was a hotel, and told the man of the house the situation, who said, "Come in, son; we'll take care of you." He was taken in, warmed, fed and lodged. The next day was bitter cold, and the man of the house, who he learned was Joseph Smith, told him to content himself in peace; it was too cold for him to go out to his brother's place alone; some teams would be in from there, and then he could go out. The boy said he had no money, but he was told not to worry about that; they would take care of him. After this incident he became well acquainted with Joseph Smith, who always called him "sonny," and after the boy obtained the position of stage driver, Joseph Smith rode with him repeatedly.

"This man and wife, now in their old age, are investigating the doctrines of the gospel, with a strong probability that ere long they will enter the fold."   *Millennial Star*, 60:139-40.

LETTER WRITTEN BY THOMAS L. BARNES

(This Dr. Barnes is the identical person who is mentioned by John Taylor as the man who took the bullet from his hand, using a carpenter's compass and a dull pen knife. This letter* was written to Miranda Barnes Haskett, his eldest daughter, from Ukiah City, Mendocino County, California.)

Well, Miranda, I suppose you would like me to tell you something about the killing of the Smiths and what led to it. Some person made complaint under oath before a Justice of the Peace charging Jo Smith with some grave offence. I do not now remember what the offence was. A warrant was issued by the Justice of the Peace, and given to a Constable to serve. I met the Constable on his way to Nauvoo to serve the writ; I told (him) I would go with him, which I did. He served the writ on the accused without any trouble. As was usual in such cases, where a grave charge is made against a prominent person, almost every person in the vicinity would soon know it.

The City authorities was granted by their charter as they supposed unlimited authority. They issued a writ of habious corpus. (I believe that is what they called the writ.) and took the accused out of the Constable's hands and set him at liberty. While this proceeding was going on, in conversation with Mr. Smith, he said to me he was not guilty of that nor any other crime. Said he, let them charge me with any crime, I do not care what it is, I can prove that I was not there and did not do it. (I said to him if they will fix the time and place.) He answered as a matter of course or words to that effect.

Well the Constable returned to Carthage and made his return of his warrent. That fact that the Municipal authorities of Nauvoo had set the authorities of the state at defiance and taken a man charged with crime out of the hands of an officer of the law, caused great excitement all over that part of the state. Public

---

*Spelling exactly as in original letter.

meetings were held, inflamitory speeches were made in more than one place in the county. The Governor was petitioned to send the milita of the state to inforce obedience to the law. The governor sent some two or three companies of the state troops into the county. A part of the malitia rendisvoosed at Carthage and a part at Warsaw. It was arrainged that on a certain day they were to march to Nauvoo. They all professed to be ready and anxious to fight, if needs be kill, and drive the Mormons out of the county. In the meantim Smith had surrendered himsef to the officers of the law. The Governor disbanded the soldiers that was at Carthage, and sent word to them at Warsaw who was then on the march for Nauvoo. When they got the disbanding order many of them wer indignant at the Governor, resigned their offices and formed themselves into a mob determed to have satisfaction of the Smiths any way whether by authority of law or by violence. The men that was willing to set all laws aside and have the life of the Smiths at any .... formed a new company and started to Carthage where the Smiths Jo and Hyrum John Taylor the editor of the Mormon paper, and Willard Richards privet secretary to Jo Smith were. Joseph Smith was presumably in the hands of the Constable and the others his friends were with him to in charge of an officer.

The under sheriff and jailer lived in the jail. The jail was a two story stone house. The lower story and part of the upper story was occupied by the jailor and his family. The jail proper was in the north end of the building up stairs, divided off into cells. The front room up stairs was a kind of a family room. At the head of the stairs there was two doors, one entering into the family room and the other entering into the jail proper.

I have tried to be a little particular in discribing the house so as to give you an idea of the way the mob got to their victims. I said this new company or mob as they realy were had some understanding of some of the citizens of our town. I want you to know and believe, my daughter, that I had nothing (to) do with the murder of the Smiths, or any other person and during all the excitement I never did any thing to any one that I would not under like circumstances they should do to me.

I said I thought some of our citizens—citizens of Carthage I mean—was privy to the hole matter. One of them, a prominent man and a man of influence, came to me just befor the cowardly murder was committed and asked me to go out on the road toward Nauvoo and see what was going on out that way. I went and John Wilson an old citizen and Doctor Morrison a prominent Physician went with me. We went about three miles from Carthage, on the Nauvoo road, where we had a fine view of the country all around, the country being pararie all around, we could see very plain where the Carthage and Warsaw road was. We saw going on that road quite a company going hurriedly in the direction (of) Carthage. It was not long till we could see quite a number on the same road going toward Warsaw. We then went back to Carthage to report and what did we find. Such a sight as I hope never to see again.

When we saw that company going to and from Carthage my suspicions was arroused that all was not right. Afterwards my suspicions was strengthened from the fact that a guard of the "Carthage Greys" a part of a Millitary company had been left in charge of the accused to protect and kepe them safe, whose sworn duty it was to protect their prisoner as well as it was to keep him from running off. They were there I don't know just how many. I think from six to ten men on guard when the mob came rushing on them. they fired blank cartridges over the heads of the mob as I afterwards learned from some one of the guard. My impresion is that they were equal guilty as any one of the mob. Excuse me for calling the murders of the Smith a mob. I think that is the right name to call them, though I believe I do not know if that you had an uncle in the affair. Well after the brave guards had fired their blank carheridge on the mob as I was taken prisoners, the mob rushed up stairs to where the Smiths Taylor and Richards were enjoying themselves. Some said they were sipping their wine whether that is true or not I do not know. At any rate they were comfortably situated, and they had a right to suppose safely protected by the laws of the great state of Illinois.

When the false guard had made their hypocritical assault on the other part of the mob (I look upon them as being equally guilty as those that came from Warsaw.) They the attacking party rushed up stairs with murder in their hearts to where the accused were tryed to break open the door which it appears was held shut by all four of the men when the mob commenced firing their loaded arms through the door. It appears that one of the balls in the commencement of the attac pased through a panel of the door and hit Hyrum in his neck which probably broke his neck he fell back and died, as I was informed instantly. When I went into the room shortly afterwards his head was laying against the wall on the other sid from the door.

It is supposed when Hyrum fell the door was partially opened by the attacking party, so much so at any rate that I was informed that Jo Smith had what was common then what was and probable is now called one of Steves peper boxes. It is said and there is no dout but what it is true that he sliped his hand through the opening of the door and hit a young man from Warsaw about his neck or sholder which made it conveinent for the young man to remain for a while in Missouri. The attacing party forced the door open and commenced firing at Smith it is said they must have hit him an probably disabled him, as he stagered across the floor to the oposite side of the room where there was a window. It is said that there he gave the hailing sign of the distress of a Mason but that did him no good. In the room behind him was armed men, furious men, with murder in their hearts. Before him arround the well under the window there was a croud of desperate men, as he was receiving shots from behind which he could not stand, in despersation he leaped or rather fell out of the window near the well where he breathed his last. When I found him soon afterwards he was laying in the hall at the foot of the stairs where his blood had as I believe left indelible stain on the floor.

I suppose by this time you are anxious to know what became of Taylor and Richards; was they also killed, no they were not. Taylor was severely wounded Richards was not hurt. Shall I try to describe the wounds that Taylor received and got over them. Well let me tell you where we found him, I cannot impress your mind of his appearance as he appered to us when we wer called to him by the jailor. We found him in a pile of straw. It appeared that a straw bed had been emtied in the cell where he was when we found him. He was very much frightened as well as severly wounded. It took strong persuading of the jailor as well as our positive assuriance that we ment him no harm but was desirous of doing him some good. He finally consented to come out of his cell. When we examined him we found that he had been hit by four balls. One ball had hit him in his fore arm and pased down and lodged in the hand betwen the phalanges of his third and fourth fingers. Another hit on the left side of the pelvis cuttin through the skin and pasin .... leaving a superficial wound that you could lay your hand in. A third ball passed through his thigh lodging in his notus. A fourth ball hit his watch which he had in the fob in his pantaloons, which I suppose the Mormons have today, to show the precise time that their great leader was killed. The wounds had bled quite freely, the blood had had time to coagulate which it had done, and where the clothes and straw came in contact they all adhered together so that Mr. Taylor came out his self sought cell he was a pitable looking sight. We took the best care of him we could till he left us. He got well but never paid us for skill or good wishes.

You want to know what has become of Richards. He was not hurt. You will ask how did it happen that his comrads (were) so badly treated and he came off without receiving any damage whatever. It was in this way, as I suppose I think he told me so. The four braced themselves against the door to keep the mob out. He stood next to the hinges of the door so when the door opened it would turn back against the wall that divided the room that they were in from the prison room. So when they crowded the door open it shut him up against the wall and he stood there and did not move till the affair was all over, so they did not see him.

After we were through with Taylor I went to Richards and said to him Richards what does all this mean who done it. Said he, doctor I do not know, but I belive it was some Missourians that came over and have killed brothers Josef and Hyrum and wounded bro Taylor. Said I to him do you believe that, he said I do. Says I, will you write that down and send it to Nauvoo. He said he would if he could get any person to take it. I told him if he would write it I would send it. He wrote the note, I found the man that took it to Nauvoo.

Shall I tell you any more.

November 6, 1897

Your father Thomas L. Barnes.

THE ASSASSINATION OF
GENERALS JOSEPH SMITH AND HYRUM SMITH

BY ELIZA R. SNOW—1873

Ye heavens, attend! Let all the earth give ear!
Let Gods and seraphs, men and angels hear:
The worlds on high—the Universe, shall know
What awful scenes are acted here below!

Had nature's self a heart, her heart would bleed
At the recital of so foul a deed;
For never, since the Son of God was slain,
Has blood so noble flowed from human vein,
As that which now on God for vengeance calls
From Freedom's ground—from Carthage prison walls!

Oh, Illinois; thy soil has drunk the blood
Of prophets, martyr'd for the truth of God.
Once-lov'd America! what can atone
For the pure blood of innocence thou'st sown?
Where all the streams, in teary torrents shed
To mourn the fate of those illustrious dead,
How vain the tribute for the noblest worth
That graced thy surface, O degraded earth!
Oh, wretched murderers, fierce for human blood!
You've slain the Prophets of the living God,
Who've borne oppression from their early youth,
To plant on earth the principles of truth

Shades of our patriot fathers! can it be,
Beneath your blood-stained flag of Liberty,
The firm supporters of our country's cause,
Are butcher'd while submission to her laws?
Yes, blameless men, defamed by hellish lie,
Have thus been offer'd as a sacrifice
To appease the ragings of a brutish clan
That has defiled the laws of God and man!
'Twas not for crime or guilt of theirs they fell:
Against the laws they never did rebel.
True to their country, yet her plighted faith
Has prov'd an instrument of cruel death!

Great men have fallen, mighty men have died
Nations have mourn'd their fav'rites and their pride;
But two so wise, so virtuous, and so good,
Before, on earth, at once, have never stood
Since the creation—men whom God ordain'd
To publish truth when error long had reign'd;
Of whom the world itself unworthy prov'd;
It knew them not; but men with hatred mov'd
And with infernal spirits, have combin'd
Against the best, the noblest of mankind!

Oh, persecution! shall thy purple hand
Spread utter desolation through the land?
Shall Freedom's banner be no more unfurled?
Has peace indeed been taken from the world?
Then God of Jacob, in this trying hour
Help us to trust in thy Almighty power—
Support thy Saints beneath this awful stroke,
Make bare thine arm to break oppressions' yoke.

We mourn the Prophet, from whose lips have flow'd
The words of life thy Spirit has bestow'd—
A depth of thought no human art could reach,
From time to time roll'd in sublimest speech,
From thy celestial fountain, through his mind,
To purify and elevate mankind;
The rich intelligence by him brought forth
Is like the sunbeams spreading o'er the earth.

Now Zion mourns—she mourns an earthly head;
Her Prophet and her Patriarch are dead!
The blackest deed that men and devils know
Since Calv'ry's scene, has laid the brothers low!
One while in life, and *one* in death, they prov'd
How strong their friendship—how true they loved;
True to their mission until death they stood,
Then seal'd their testimony with their blood.

All hearts with sorrow bleed, and every eye
Is bath'd in tears, each bosom heaves a sigh,
Heart-broken widows' agonizing groans
Are mingled with the helpless orphans' moans!
Ye Saints! be still, and know that God is just
With steadfast purpose in His promise trust;
Girded with sackcloth, own His mighty hand,
And wait His Judgments on this guilty land!
The noble Martyrs now have gone to move
The cause of Zion in the Courts above.

CHAPTER 10

The Prophet's Body Not Permitted to be Mutilated

TESTIMONY OF WILLIAM M. DANIELS

He (Joseph the Prophet) seemed to fall easy. He struck partly on his right shoulder and back, his neck and head reaching the ground a little before his feet. He rolled instantly on his face. From this position he was taken by a young man, who sprang to him from the other side of the fence, who held a pewter fife in his hand, was barefoot and bare-headed, having on no coat, with his pants rolled above his knees and shirt-sleeves above his elbows. He set President Smith against the south side of the well-curb, that was situated a few feet from the jail. While doing this, the savage muttered aloud: "This is Old Jo; I know him. I know you, Old Jo. Damn you, you are the man that had my daddy shot." ****

When President Smith had been set against the curb, and began to recover from the effects of the fall, Col. Williams ordered four men to shoot him. Accordingly, four men took an eastern direction, about eight feet from the curb, Col. Williams standing partly at their rear, and made ready to execute the order. While they were making preparations, and the muskets were raised to their faces, President Smith's eyes rested upon them with a calm and quiet resignation. He betrayed no agitated feelings and the expression upon his countenance seemed to betoken his only prayer to be: "O᾽ Father, forgive them, for they know not what they do."

The fire was simultaneous. A slight cringe of the body was all the indication of pain that he betrayed when the balls struck him. He fell upon his face. One ball had entered the back part of his body. This is the ball that many people have supposed struck him about the time he was in the window. But this is a mistake. I was close by him, and I know he was not hit with a ball until after he was seated by the well-curb.****

The ruffian, of whom I have spoken, who set him against the well-curb, now secured a bowie knife for the purpose of severing his head from his body. He raised the knife and was in the attitude of striking, when a light, so sudden and powerful, burst from the heavens upon the bloody scene, (passing its vivid chain between Joseph and his murderers.) that they were struck with terrified awe and filled with consternation. This light, in its appearance and potency, baffles all powers of description. The arm of the ruffian, that held the knife, fell powerless; the muskets of the four, who fired, fell to the ground, and they all stood like marble statues, not having power to move a single limb of their bodies.

By this time most of the men had fled in great disorder. I never saw so frightened a set of men before. Col. Williams saw the light and was also badly frightened; but he did not entirely lose the use of his limbs or speech. Seeing the condition of these men he hallowed to some who had just commenced to retreat, for God's sake to come and carry off these men. They came back and carried them by main strength towards the baggage wagons. They seemed as helpless as if they were dead.   *The Martyrs*, pp. 79-81.

STATEMENT OF MRS. ELIZA MORGAN

My father Jacob Hofheins was born on December 4, 1812, in Baden, Germany. He emigrated to America in 1830 and joined the Mormon Church in 1835. He was a bodyguard of the Prophet Joseph Smith in the days of Nauvoo, and was present at the martyrdom of the Prophet at Carthage, Illinois. *I have heard him speak many times of the cruelty of the mobbers and have heard him state many times of the light that struck the fiend who raised his arm to cut off the head of the Prophet, the fiend's hand was paralyzed and fell to his side.* He saw the Prophet as he fell or leaped from the window of the Carthage jail and saw the mob set him against the well. My father stated emphatically and positively that he saw this. In 1846 he joined the Mormon Battalion. He witnessed the great mourning by the entire people, men, women and children, in Nauvoo, at the death of the Prophet Joseph Smith and Hyrum Smith his brother.

To all of the above statements, I solemnly testify I heard my father relate to me.

Signed: Mrs. Eliza Morgan

Signed in the presence of:
Mrs. Nina Garrett Morgan
N. B. Lundwall
at Levan, Utah, this 30th day of July, 1951.

HISTORY BY GEORGE Q. CANNON

Among the murderers outside was a man, barefoot and bareheaded, without a coat, his shirt-sleeves rolled up above his elbows and his pants above his knees; he lifted Joseph and propped him against the south side of the well curb which stood a few feet from the jail. Colonel Levi Williams then ordered four men to shoot him. They stood about eight feet from the curb, and fired simultaneously. A slight cringe of the body was noticed as the balls struck him, and he fell on his face. *The ruffian who set him against the well-curb, then took a bowie-knife, with the evident intention of cutting off his head. It was reported that a considerable sum of money had been offered, by the mob, for his head. As he raised the knife, and was in the attitude of striking, a light, so sudden and powerful, burst from the heavens upon the bloody scene, (passing its vivid chain between Joseph and his murderers) that they were struck with terror. The arm of the ruffian that held the knife, fell powerless; the muskets of the four who fired fell to the ground, and*

*they all stood like marble statues, not having the power to move a
single limb of their bodies.*

As Joseph fell from the window, the cry was raised, *"He has
leaped the window,"* and the mob on the stairs and in the entry ran
out as soon as they could. After shooting him, the murderers hurried off in a disorderly manner as fast as they could. Colonel Williams shouted to some who had just commenced their retreat, to
come back and help to carry off the four men who fired, who were
still paralyzed. They came and carried them away by main strength
to the baggage wagons, and they all fled toward Warsaw.

Life of Joseph the Prophet, by George Q. Cannon, Instructor, 15:110-11.

AN OFFICER OF ILLINOIS MILITIA TESTIFIES

"Wm. T. Head, an officer in Captain Lawn's company, and
tarrying in Carthage, *testified that he saw a certain man raise a
large knife to strike off the head of Joseph, when, all at once, and in
the midst of a clear day, with no cloud in sight, 'a terrible clap of
thunder rolled heavily, and forked lightning flashed in the face of
the murderers, and perfectly paralyzed a number of them.'*

"The ruffian, who had raised his knife and had sworn with a
dreadful oath to take the head off Joseph, stood perfectly paralyzed,
his arm uplifted with the knife suspended in air, and could not
move a limb. His comrades carried him off, and all fled in terror
from the scene."   *Autobiography of Parley P. Pratt, p. 477.*

HISTORIAN EDW. W. TULLIDGE'S DECLARATIONS

From the point where Joseph leaped the window, the record
continues: "He fell partly on his right shoulder and back, his neck
and head reaching the ground a little before his feet, and he rolled
instantly on his face.

*"From this position he was taken by a man who was barefoot
and bareheaded, and having on no coat, his pants rolled up above
his knees, and his shirt sleeves above his elbows. He set Joseph
against the south side of the well-curb, which was situated a few
feet from the jail, when Col. Levi Williams ordered four men to
shoot him. They stood about eight feet from the curb, and fired
simultaneously. A slight cringe of the body was all the indication
of pain visible when the balls struck him, and he fell on his face.
The ruffian who set him against the well-curb now gathered a bowie-
knife for the purpose of severing his head from his body. He
raised the knife, and was in the attitude of striking when a light,
so sudden and powerful, burst from the heavens upon the bloody
scene (passing its vivid chain between Joseph and his murderers),
that they were struck with terror. This light, in its appearance and
potency baffles all powers of description. The arm of the ruffian
that held the knife fell powerless, the muskets of the four who
fired fell to the ground, and they all stood like marble statues, not
having the power to move a single limb of their bodies.*

"The retreat of the mob was so hurried and disorderly as it
possibly could have been. Colonel Williams hallowed to some who

had just commenced their retreat to come back and help to carry off the four men who fired, and who were still paralyzed. They came and carried them away by main strength to the baggage wagons, when they fled towards Warsaw."

Upon the tide of grief that swept over Nauvoo, and the consternation that filled the hearts of the mob, when the awful deed became known, we will not dwell. Neither will we attempt to depict that scene of woe which occurred when the bodies of the slain were delivered into the hands of their families. A whole people had been cruelly, fiendishly betrayed and bereaved. Awful, beyond the power of words to picture, was the lament.

Today some of that very mob remain in peace near the scene of that atrocious crime, unwhipped of justice, and not one of that horde of assassins has ever felt the lash of the law.

Thus lived, and labored, and loved, and died the martyr prophet of the nineteenth century. Thus flashed athwart the black midnight of his age the light of the latter-days. But the darkness comprehended it not; and even as one of old was he betrayed and sacrificed.

Back to that scene on Calvary leaps the thought of man. Instinctively are associated the tragedy of that day and the tragedy of this. Across the ages stride the footsteps of the self-same genius. In the agony of death appears the self-same spirit. Nay, from out the agony of Calvary and of Carthage comes the self-same voice: "Lama Sabacthana!"—"Oh, Lord my God!"

Life of Joseph the Prophet, by Edw. W. Tullidge, pp. 543-45.

ONE OF THE MOB TESTIFIES

(Note: The Compiler of this book was employed as Forest Clerk on the Gallatin National Forest, Bozeman, Montana, from 1910 to 1916. The *Bozeman Daily Chronicle* published a news item under the date of Jan. 3, 1915, from Clyde Park, Montana, (a town or settlement some 60 miles from Bozeman) which gave the account of an elderly lady who was 100 years of age which verbatim is as follows: "Within a few miles of Clyde Park there lives a woman who has but recently celebrated her 100th birthday—Mrs. Sulvia Whitmar, who lives with her daughter and son-in-law, Mr. and Mrs. Don Gurule, on a ranch on Fall Creek, in the foothills of the Crazy mountains. According to Mr. Gurule, Mrs. Whitmar was born in Illinois on November 15, 1814, and on the 15th of last month was 100 years old, and is still as spry and hearty as are many women 40 years her junior. She does a share of the work about the house and assists in caring for the nine children of her daughter, and insists that she is not an old woman, as the term is generally understood. Mrs. Whitmar declares she knew Abraham Lincoln personally and well in the early days of Illinois, and tells many interesting stories of the early days in the "western" life of that state. She was also a personal friend of the great Mormon prophet, Joseph Smith, and was a spectator in the crowd when the illustrious Mormon met his tragic death at the hands of a mob at Nauvoo, Ill. She insists that she is still good for many years, altho some six weeks past the century mark."

I immediately wrote to Mrs. Whitmar and requested her to give to me in detail all she knew in regard to Joseph Smith and his martyrdom, (copies of all letters being in the files of the compiler.)

I quote but a portion of her letter as follows: (verbatim)

"The day Joseph Smith was killed the teamsters was coming from Carthage, and stoped at grandfather Elsworth's house. And some of them was laughting about the deth of the profit. But one of the fellows spoke and said if you saw wat I saw you would not laugh so much about it, and then he said, I saw a light come from the jail where Joseph Smith was shot and went from the jail into the heavens."

STEPHEN MARKHAM TESTIFIES

Bro. N. B. Lundwall,   Jensen, Utah, Dec. 31, 1938
Salt Lake City, Utah.

Dear Brother:

I have been some time getting started to write a few lines regarding the testimony given to me by my mother concerning the martyrdom of the Prophet Joseph and his brother Hyrum. Grandfather Stephen Markham was with the Prophet in Carthage jail. Just before the shooting he left the jail to get some medicine for Brother Taylor, I believe it was. There were seven of the mob went with him. They had gone but a short distance when the fatal shots were fired. Grandfather turned his horse to go back and the men that were with him guarding him for fear he would get away, stuck their bayonets in his legs till the blood filled his boots and ran to the ground. He testified that there was a light descended from heaven and fell upon the man who made the attempt to cut off the Prophet's head and that he fell to the ground.

My mother was Stephen Markham's oldest daughter, Mary Lucy Markham.

I hope this will be of some value to you. Am glad of having met you and appreciate your acquaintance.

Yours truly,
Joseph S. Dudley
Jensen, Utah, P.O. Box 71

AFFIDAVIT OF CHARLES D. FOSTER

I, Charles Daniel Foster, testify as follows:

I was born on January 5, 1878, in Sunset, Arizona, my father's name being Charles Allen Foster and my mother Josephine Morris Foster. My father was well acquainted with the Prophet Joseph Smith, which acquaintance lasted several years prior to the martyrdom of the Prophet. He was present in Nauvoo when the Prophet made the statement "I am going as a lamb to the slaughter." I have heard father state several times that he was present on the ground when the Prophet was murdered and saw the mob drag his body from under the Carthage jail window after he was shot and saw members of the mob set the body of the Prophet against the well. The leader of the mob asked the others "who will cut his head of?" to which two of the mob stated, "I will cut off his G—d d— head." One of the two raised his sword with the intention of cutting off the head of the Prophet, when a flash of lightning from the heavens struck them both senseless. The mob then fled and left the bodies of the two lying on the ground. To all of the above statements, I solemnly testify my father related to me.   Signed: Charles D. Foster

As witnesses to the above signature we attach our signatures:

Lavora Foster
Earl Foster
N. B. Lundwall

Dated at Eden, Arizona, March 8, 1950.

CYRUS WHEELOCK KNEW THE LIGHTNING FLASH

Note: While at the home of Mrs. Allred, in Spring City, Utah, on August 8, 1951, conversing on the martyrdom of the Prophet Joseph Smith, Mrs. Allred dictated the following statement.

I was born on February 15, 1865, in Spring City, Utah. I was well acquainted with Cyrus Wheelock who lived at Mt. Pleasant, Utah. I have heard Cyrus Wheelock and Orson Hyde in conversation many times, as they would reminisce on their acquaintances and association with the Prophet Joseph Smith. I have heard Brother Wheelock state many times how he was with the Prophet, his duties as a body guard of the Prophet, and of the light that came from the heavens when the mobocrat was making ready as his arm was raised to cut off the head of the Prophet, and how the arm of the mobocrat fell to his side paralyzed. He saw the mob flee in confusion after the martyrdom.

In witness of the truthfulness of the above statements, I hereunto sign my name, on this 8th day of August, 1951.

Signed: Maria J. Allred

Witness: N. B. Lundwall

THE FATAL 27th OF JUNE

(EXCERPTS)

Shortly after five o'clock a noise outside was heard, a cry of surrender, a few musket shots and then a tumult. As planned, the disbanded militia had organized and with faces blackened with powder and mud came up against the jail, two hundred strong. The guard feigned resistance by shooting over their heads. They stormed the prison, some fired from the yard through the windows, and others rushed up the stairs to break into the room. The four men threw themselves against the door, but failed to hold it closed. Guns were thrust in and discharged. A stream of bullets from different directions came pouring into the room.

Hyrum was the first victim. One ball from the door struck him in the face and he lurched back saying, "I am a dead man." Another from the window pierced him as he fell, and two more took effect after he reached the floor. John Taylor, unable to hold the door, ran across the room. A bullet from the doorway struck him in the thigh, and its force would have driven his falling body through the open window, but another ball from outside struck his watch and without wounding him cast his body back into the room. Three more struck him as he lay helpless on the floor. Willard Richards, save a slight wound in the ear, was unhurt.

Up to this time Joseph had not been struck, but he realized he had not long to live. With the same motive that had drawn him from Nauvoo, he sprang to the window, willing to die quickly and thus save his two living brethren. He did not need to jump to the ground, however; two bullets from the door and one from below struck him simultaneously. He fell down at the feet of his murderers with the death cry, "O Lord, my God!"

All the assassins rushed from the jail; the body was set up against a well curb, and Colonel Levi Williams ordered four men to shoot it. *A scantily clothed brutal fellow, coveting the money that had been offered by the Missourians for the Prophet's head, rushed forward with a knife in his hand to gain his trophy. Suddenly a shaft of light from heaven fell down and paralyzed the nearest of the murderers. The rabble and the soldiers ran away in terror, but Williams cried to them for help. Some came back and lifted the helpless bodies of their comrades into a wagon. Then the mob together with nearly all of the inhabitants of Carthage fled from the cursed place.*

For Willard Richards it remained to care for the living and the dead. John Taylor, desperately wounded, was hidden by him in an inner dungeon, and Willard spent the night in watching over the precious remains of the martyrs. Next day he took them to Nauvoo, and the mourning Saints met him on the way. Thousands viewed the familiar features of the two beloved men and wept as they saw them, fallen in the glory of their manhood. Loving hands buried the Prophets secretly and at night, that no unhallowed hands should disturb the sleeping dust.

The mob had fulfilled their threat. They could not reach these men with the law, but they did it with power and ball. In the middle of the nineteenth century Joseph and Hyrum Smith, Prophets of God, died martyrs for the name of Jesus Christ, but as Joseph declared, so it shall be: their blood shall cry from the ground for vengeance.   *Millennial Star,* Vol. 64:411-14.

TESTIMONY OF ORVILLE ALLEN

(GIVEN ON THE 22ND DAY OF JANUARY, 1952, AT THATCHER, ARIZONA.)

I was born on the 21st day of May, 1881, at Taylor, Arizona, my parents being Orville Morgan Allen and Diana J. Allen. I was called on a mission to the Central States on the 6th of April, 1905, and was sent from the headquarters of the mission at Independence, Missouri, to Morgan City, Louisiana, by President S. O. Bennion who was then president of that mission. My companion at the time this narrative deals was Elder Church from Salt Lake City. We labored under the district presidency of Elder Leavitt, in the vicinity of Morgan City and Swevers Port, La. When traveling without purse or script to conference which was held at Kelsey, Texas, we met two old men, 82 and 84 years of age, who were brothers, whose names I wrote in my diary which was later lost. These men lived in the Red Hills of Louisiana, between the two localities mentioned. Neither of them had married and lived alone in the jungles or timbered country.

They testified that they were present at the time of the martyrdom of the Prophet Joseph Smith and were with their people in the mob of from 200 to 250 men. They told us that as they went around the jail to see what was going on, they saw the Prophet Joseph against the well-curb after he had been shot, and they saw a man take the Prophet by the hair of his head with a drawn sword in his other hand. There was a reward of $1,000.00 for the Prophet's head. He raised his sword to strike off the head of Joseph Smith when a flash of lightning from the heavens was seen, the day being bright with no clouds. This so frightened them and the rest of the mob who saw it that they all fled for fear. These two young men (for they were in the neighborhood of twenty years of age) looked back after running a short distance and saw the man whose arm was still raised with the sword in his hand. They continued to travel as fast as they could, anxious to get away from the scene of the murder but the fear remained with them up to the time of our visit with them. They settled in the locality where we found them and still feared the divine punishment that they expected to receive after death, and they asked Elder Church what they should do about it to take away that fear. He told them that they would have to settle it with their God. They feared to die and testified that they had taken part with the mob in killing Joseph Smith and were in full accord with the mob in doing so but after seeing this flash of lightning fear came upon them which was not lessened or removed.

They had seen Elders passing but had never conversed with them and had purposely avoided meeting them. My companion and I passed through the woods and happened to come onto their home. They knew who we were and seemed relieved at meeting us and asked us to return again if we should happen to pass that way but we never returned. They seemed to be very humble after talking to us. They said they knew the mob had killed a man of God because of the fear that always existed in their hearts since the martyrdom. The above incident was one of the strongest testimonies I received concerning the divinity of the mission of Joseph Smith the Prophet, my entire mission being one of many wonderful experiences in the Southern states, while on this mission.

Signed: Orville Allen

In Witness Whereof I hereunto sign my name
and affirm my statement to be true.

Signed in the presence of N. B. Lundwall
Orvil Larson

See Addenda "B"

CHAPTER 11

Comments of Friends and Foes
On the Martyrdom

LETTER OF INSTRUCTION AND INFORMATION
TO THE PRESIDENT OF THE BRITISH MISSION

(Excerpts)

Nauvoo, Illinois, U. S.,
July 9th, 1844.

Elder Reuben Hedlock, Presiding Elder of the Church of Jesus Christ in England, and the Saints in the British Empire.

Beloved brethren, we say to you all, as we say to the saints here, be still and know that God reigns. This is one of those fiery trials that is to try the saints in the last days. * * *

These servants of God have gone to heaven by fire—the fire of an ungodly mob. Like the Prophets of ancient days they lived as long as the world would receive them; and this is one furnace in which the saints were to be tried, to have their leaders cut off from their midst, and not be permitted to avenge their blood.

God has said, "Vengeance is mine; I have not called mine elders to fight their battles; I will fight their battle for them;" and we know, assuredly, that he will do it in his own due time, and we have only to wait in patience and pray for the fulfilment of the promise.

This event is one of the most foul and damnable that ever disgraced the earth, having no parallel in time. Innocent men imprisoned without law, without justice, and murdered in cold blood in the enlightened nineteenth century, in an enlightened country in open daylight.

It will call down the wrath and indignation of all nations upon the perpetrators of the horrid deed, and will prove the truth of the saying, "The blood of the martyrs is the seed of the church." They died for the word of God and the testimony of Jesus Christ.

God has not left his church without witnesses; as in former days, so shall it be in the latter days, when one falls another will arise to occupy a similar station. Our heavenly Father always has had a leader to his people, always will have, and the gates of hell can never prevail against the chosen of heaven.

The murder of Joseph will not stop the work; it will not stop the Temple; it will not stop the gathering; it will not stop the honest-in-heart from believing the truth and obeying it; but it is a proof of the revelations we have received from heaven through him. He has sealed his testimony with his blood. He was willing to die, and desired only to live for the sake of the brethren.

Two better men than Joseph and Hyrum Smith never lived.

Two better men God never made. The memorial of their godly lives is embalmed, printed with indelible ink in the memory of every honest heart who knew their upright walk and conversation; but they are taken away by the hands of assassins, and of the foolish things of the earth God will raise up others to comfort and lead his people, and not one item of his word can fail.

Jerusalem must be rebuilt and Zion must be redeemed, the earth be cleansed from blood by fire, Jesus return to his own, and all who shall continue faithful unto the end shall rest in everlasting peace and blessedness.

We alone, of the Quorum of the Twelve Apostles, are here at this time to write to you, the remaining ten are in the eastern states preaching the gospel, and we expect them soon to return; and as soon as God will, we will write you again.

Proceed onward with all your labors as though nothing had happened, only, preach Joseph martyred for his religion, instead of living, and God will pour out his Spirit upon you, and hasten his work from this time.

Believe not every spirit, but try the spirits; believe not every report, for every false rumor that men and demons can invent is set afloat to gull the world. What we have told you by letter and papers is true, but time will not permit to tell you every particular now.

Be humble, prayerful, watchful, and let not the adversary get any advantage of one of you, and may the choicest blessings of Israel's God rest upon you and abide with you, that you may endure faithful in all tribulation and affliction, and be prepared to be gathered unto Mount Zion, and enter into celestial glory, is the earnest prayer of your brethren in the new and everlasting covenant. Amen.   [Signed] WILLARD RICHARDS,
                                     JOHN TAYLOR.

D. H. C. 7:174-75.

REFLECTIONS ON THE MARTYRDOM

BY BEN E. RICH

Sixty-two years ago, on the 27th of June, just passed, the Prophet Joseph and his brother Hyrum the Patriarch, were martyred at Carthage, Ill. Both of these valiant men had received the revelations of God; both had believed and obeyed His word; both were advocates of the Father and ministers of His divine truth; both declared no doctrine save that which a Christian nation professed already to believe, and which that sacred volume, the Word of God, so clearly defines; both were peaceable, law-abiding men—men of honesty—men of honor—men of integrity—men of God! Both were hated, despised, and abused, not because they were violators of law, but purely because they came in the name of the Lord, filled with His Spirit which discerns the wickedness in the hearts of men and rebukes them for their transgression—because they came with the authority from God to establish His Church in the earth—that Church which Satan has always opposed and so vigorously fought whenever it has been upon the earth; both were in a Christian land; both were citizens of the United States; and yet notwithstanding all this, both were murdered in cold blood at the hands of professed followers of Christ who trampled the Constitution of the United States under their feet in order that the insatiable cravings of their depraved hearts for the blood of innocent men might be gratified.

But that even has passed now and is buried beneath the weight of sixty-two years; and in recalling it at the present time we do so, not because of any spirit of revenge harbored within our breasts, for vengeance belongs to the Lord and He will repay, but because the memories of these divinely inspired men are dear to the hearts of every Latter-day Saint, and because their pains of intense suffering unjustly and cruelly inflicted upon their bodies because of their love for the truth, are forced upon our minds when the anniversary of the day on which they gave their lives for the cause of righteousness comes and goes. * * *

He stands at the head of this dispensation, and some day when the veil of darkness is lifted from the eyes of the world and they are able to see and comprehend the things of God in their true relationship they will then know that June the 27th, 1844, marks the day of the martyrdom of two of God's holy prophets, Joseph Smith, who opened up the greatest of all dispensations on the earth since the world began, and Hyrum the Patriarch, his devoted and self-sacrificing brother.   *Elders Journal*, July 1, 1906.

ATTITUDE OF SAINTS AFTER MARTYRDOM

LETTER FROM WILLARD RICHARDS TO BRIGHAM YOUNG—NAUVOO AFFAIRS, INCLUDING THE MARTYRDOM

(EXCERPT)

Nauvoo, Sunday, June 30, 1844,
6 p.m.

The saints have entered into covenants of peace with the governor and government officers, not to avenge the blood of the martyrs, but leave it with the executive, who had pledged the faith of the state for their safe-keeping. The elders cannot be too careful in all the world, to keep from saying anything to irritate and vex the governor, etc., for at present we must conciliate: it is *for our salvation*. The governor has *appeared* to act with honest intentions; we bring no charge against him—will wait patiently his proceedings in the matter. Let the elders keep cool, *vengeance rests in heaven.*—Yours as ever,   WILLARD RICHARDS.

JOSEPH HAD SUFFERED ENOUGH

BY BRIGHAM YOUNG

He (Brigham Young) then referred to the Missourians when Joseph and others went to jail, snapping their guns at the brethren but they would not go off. The Lord never let a prophet fall on the earth until he had accomplished his work; and the Lord did not take Joseph until he had finished his work, and it is the greatest blessing to Joseph and Hyrum God could bestow to take them away, for they had suffered enough. They are not the only martyrs that will have to die for the truth. There are men before me today who will be martyrs and who will have to seal their testimony with their blood.   *D. H. C.* 7:302.

STORY OF THE MARTYRDOM AS GIVEN BY TWO MODERN PRIESTS OF BAAL

We, by accident, the other day, stumbled on a number of the Jonesborough *Whig*, dated July 24, 1844. The editor, the Rev. William G. Brownlow, is of the true stripe on Mormonism, as the following from his pen will demonstrate:

Death of Joe Smith—Some of the public Journals of the country, we are sorry to see, regret the death of Joe Smith, the Mormon Prophet. Our deliberate judgment is, that he ought to have been dead ten years ago, and that those who at length have deprived him of his life, have done the cause of God, and of the country, good service.

What lead to his death? This question answered properly, and no one will be found to regret his death. By order of Smith and his villainous Council a newspaper press was destroyed on the 10th ultimo, for the reason too, that it did not advocate Mormonism. This was followed by a declaration of Martial Law, and the adoption of other arbitrary measures to the injury and annoyance of other peaceable citizens. These things led to war, and Smith was killed, as he should have been. THREE CHEERS to the brave company who shot him to pieces!

Warsaw Signal, February 19, 1845.
Nauvoo the Beautiful, by E. Cecil McGavin, pp. 152-153.

*   *   *   *   *

The following by Alexander Campbell, the founder of the Campbellite or Church of Christ.

DEATH OF J. SMITH, THE MORMON IMPOSTER. Joseph Smith and his brother Hiram have been providentially cut off in the midst of their diabolical career. They were most lawlessly and mobocratically put to death. But the money-digger, the juggler, and the founder of the Golden Bible delusion, has been hurried away in the midst of his madness to his final account. "He died not as a righteous man dieth." The hand of the Lord was heavy upon him. An outlaw himself, God cut him off by outlaws. He requited him according to his works. He was not persecuted, unless to punish a traitor, a public plunderer, a marauder, be persecution! The killing of Robespierre was not murder. It was the outrages of the Mormons that brought upon the head of their leader the arm of justice. The frenzy of a fanatic cannot make out of the affair persecution. Religion or religious opinions had nothing to do with it. It was neither more nor less than the assassination of one whose career was in open rebellion against God and man. Still the guilt of his death lies upon those who, in violation of the laws both of God and their country, despatched him without even the form of a trial. *Nauvoo the Beautiful,* by E. Cecil McGavin, p. 153.

NEWSPAPER COMMENTS

O.S. Democrat says:

"From all the facts now before us, we regard these homicides as nothing else than murder in cold blood—murder against the plighted faith of the chief magistrate of Illinois—murder of a character so atrocious and so unjustifiable as to leave the blackest stain on all its perpetrators, their aiders, abettors, and defenders."

* * * * *

From the Lee County (Iowa) *Democrat:*

"We also endorse the whole of the sentiments of the St. Louis press, and say it was a premeditated murder, and that the offenders ought to be ferreted out and dealt with according to the strict sense of the law." * * * * *

From the *Illinois State Register:*

"Joseph Smith, the Mormon Prophet, and His Brother, Hyrum. Murdered in Prison."

"The following particulars of the most disgraceful and cold-blooded murder ever committed in a Christian land, is copied from an extra from the office of the *Quincy Herald.* Rumors of the bloody deed reached this city several days ago, but were not believed until Tuesday evening, when there was no further room left for doubt. Next week we will have all the particulars. Every effort will be made to bring the assassins to punishment."

* * * * *

From the *Sangamon Journal:*

"Thus far our news seem to be certain. Rumor says further. that on Thursday of last week, Joe Smith, Hyrum Smith and Dr. Richards were shot by a mob at Carthage. We are incredulous in regard to the truth of this rumor. We cannot think, under the circumstances of the case, the excitement against these men among the anti-Mormons, Governor Ford would have received them as prisoners, to be tried under our laws, had pledged himself for their protection, and then placed them in a situation where they would be murdered. The rumor is too preposterous for belief. We wait with much anxiety to hear the truth on this subject, and this feeling is general in this community."

* * * * *

From the *Missouri Republican:*

"The Murders at Carthage:—A letter from the editor, one from G. T. M. Davis, Esq., and a proclamation from Governor Ford, give all the information which we have been able to collect from the seat of civil commotion and murder in Illinois. They were issued in an extra form yesterday morning, and are transferred to our columns today for the benefit of our numerous readers abroad.

"All our information tends to fix upon the people concerning in the death of the Smiths, the odium of perfidious, blackhearted, cowardly murder—so wanton as to be without any justification—so inhuman and treacherous as to find no parallel in savage life under any circumstances.

"Governor Ford declares his intention to seek out the murderers; and he owes it to his own honor and to that of the state, whose faith was most grossly violated, never to cease his exertions for this purpose.

"The Mormons, it will be seen, were quiet, and not disposed to commit any acts of aggression; their enemies, on the other hand, were evidently disposed to push them to extremities, and to force them from the state."   *D. H. C.* 6:177-182.

*   *   *   *   *

From the *Quincy Herald,* July 10, 1844:

It will probably never be known who shot Joseph and Hyrum —but their murder was a cold-blooded, cowardly act, which will consign the perpetrators, if discovered, to merited infamy and disgrace. They have broken their pledges to the Governor—disgraced themselves and the State to which they belong. They have crimsoned their perfidy with blood.

Nauvoo the Beautiful, by E. Cecil McGavin, p. 154-55.

EXCERPT FROM LETTER OF GOV. FORD TO W. W. PHELPS

The naked truth then is, that most well-informed persons condemn in the most unqualified manner the mode in which the Smiths were put to death, but nine out of every ten of such accompany the expression of their disapprobation by a manifestion of their pleasure that they are dead. The disapproval is most unusually cold and without feeling. It is a disapproval which appears to be called for, on their part, by decency, by a respect for the laws and a horror of mobs, but does not flow warm from the heart. The unfortunate victims of this assassination were generally and thoroughly hated throughout the country, and it is not reasonable to suppose that their death has produced any reaction in the public mind resulting in active sympathy; if you think so, you are mistaken. Most that is said on the subject is merely from the teeth out; and your people may depend on the fact, that public feeling is now, as this time, as thoroughly against them as it has ever been.

Letter dated: Quincy, July 22, 1844.   *D. H. C.* 6:204.

THE PROPHET'S PROMISES REALIZED

By "M. F. C."

My grandfather and his family arrived in Nauvoo from the Isle of Man late in the year 1843. Finding no employment in Nauvoo, grandfather and family removed to Warsaw, he giving his overcoat and grandmother's shawl as security for the loan of four dollars to pay the passage thence. Here they worked hard at brick-making for about six months. My father's journal contains the following:

"By this time there arose a great disturbance about the 'Mormons' throughout the State of Illinois. The little town we lived in was not a whit behind in being excited, and all the inhabitants were ordered to take up arms against the 'Mormons,' Nauvoo, and Joseph Smith. Father, too, was ordered to take up arms against his brethren and sisters. Two armed men came to the house we lived in, and took him by force to the office, where they took names, and offered him a musket, which he refused to accept, saying at the same time, 'Gentlemen, I shall never fight against my brethren—the Saints of Almighty God—no, never!' Those who were walking behind him, when they marched him to their rendezvous, made motions as though they were going to cut his throat. They would not have anything to do with me because I was too young, and told me to go home and take care of my mother. They then ordered us to leave the town within twenty-four hours. We were not able to do so, because we could not procure any conveyance. Father himself was driven late in the afternoon, several miles out of town, at the point of the bayonet. They told him if he ever returned they would shoot him, and appointed a guard that night to see if he came back. He traveled on to Nauvoo, a distance of between twenty and thirty miles. There had been some very wet weather previously, and the creeks were high, so that he was obliged to swim many of the streams during the night. Owing to the current being so swift, he was carried down some of them a considerable distance before he could reach the other side.

"He reached Nauvoo in the morning feeling very fatigued. After resting awhile, and receiving some refreshments, he went to see the Prophet Joseph, told him what had occurred, and that he had left his family to the mercy of the mob, and was afraid they would massacre them. Joseph then raised his hand and said: 'Brother C——, they shan't hurt a hair of their heads. God bless you.' Father then joined the Nauvoo Legion. The guns being all engaged, he procured a pitchfork and marched. * * *

"Father was still in Nauvoo. About 4 p.m., on the 28th day of June, 1844, mother and myself, being in Warsaw, heard cheering and saw men throwing their hats up in the air. I felt like knowing what was the matter, and ran out among them, making my way through the blood-thirsty mob towards the one who was speaking. I soon learned that they had killed Joseph Smith and his brother, Hyrum. The speaker saw me and ordered me home to stop with my mother. Knowing that I was a 'Mormon' boy, a crowd of school boys followed me, being urged on by the mob. They clubbed me all the way home with whatever they could find in the street. I escaped them through a neighboring yard, and got into the house the back way. Soon after I had occasion to go to the river for a pail of water. The mob saw me again, and hired a drunken man, for a large sum of money, to throw me into the river, and drown me. He followed me to the bank of the Mississippi River and as I was stooping to dip up the pail of water, caught me by the back of the neck, and said, 'Now you d—d little "Mormon," I'll drown you.' I asked him why he would drown me, and if I had ever done him any harm? 'No,' he said, 'I won't drown you. I'll be d—d if I do, they may drown you themselves; I've got my pay, you may go home.' By this time, mother heard that the mob was drowning me. I started home with my pail of water, and met her coming to rescue me. Said I, 'Mother, all is right. The Lord is on our side. You know Joseph prophesied the mobocrats should not hurt a hair of our heads. They can't do it.' That evening they put a torch three times to the house we occupied, but it would not burn. During this time the mobocrats of Warsaw were moving their wives and children across the river, so as to be secure from the expected 'Mormon' company. After a few days of excitement and anxiety, a team came for us from Nauvoo, the driver stating that Brother C—had sent him for his family and goods. We were not long in packing up and leaving Warsaw. We arrived in Nauvoo about 3 p.m. the next day. Father was out of town on business, but we met some friends, who found us a house. We got our furniture into it, and felt at home once more, feeling that we were delivered from our enemies, by the power of God."

Considering the times, and the trying position in which they were placed, when bitter animosity in that region was aroused against every man, woman and child bearing the name of Latter-day Saint, and yet escaping without the slightest injury, shows that Joseph was endowed with the spirit of prophecy, and that the Almighty confirmed His words by the direct manifestations of His providence in their behalf.   *Juvenile Instructor*, Vol. 20:223.

THE ARCH MURDERER, THOS. C. SHARP, GLORIES IN HIS CRIME

The spirit of Hancock County seemed to be in harmony with that of the perjured court at Carthage. When the *St. Louis Gazette* called "the men who killed the Smiths a pack of cowards," the editor of the *Warsaw Signal* retorted:

" . . . instead of cowardice, they exhibited foolhardy courage, for they must have known or thought that they would bring down on themselves the vengeance of the Mormons. True, the act of an armed body going to the jail and killing prisoners does appear at first sight dastardly, but we look at it as though these men were the executioners of justice, and their act is no more cowardly than is the act of the hangman in stretching up a defenseless convict who is incapable of resistance. If any other mode could have been devised, or any other time selected, it would have been better; but, as we have heard others say, we are satisfied that it is done, and care not to philosophize on the *modus operandi*."

"Mormonism and Masonry," p. 21, by E. Cecil McGavin

CHAPTER 12

Preparation and Funeral of the Martyrs

MARTYRS LEAVE CARTHAGE FOR NAUVOO

About 8 o'clock on the morning after the murder (the 28th) Dr. Richards started for Nauvoo with the bodies of Joseph and Hyrum on two wagons, accompanied by Samuel H. Smith, who was a brother of Joseph and Hyrum, and a Mr. Hamilton and a guard of eight soldiers who had been sent on that service by Gen. Demming. The bodies were covered with bushes to keep them from the hot sun. Nearly all the people of the city, when they heard the bodies were coming, collected together and went out to meet them; they were under the direction of the city marshal. Besides private citizens there were the City Council, Joseph's staff and the staffs of the other generals of the Legion, and many of the officers of that body. The procession was an imposing one, and the lamentations and wailings of the people, were such as are seldom witnessed or heard. It was as though every person in the assemblage had lost his nearest kinsmen and friends.

When the procession arrived, the bodies were both taken into the Nauvoo Mansion, Joseph's residence. No language that we can use would do justice to the scenes that followed. The heart-rending grief of the families of the deceased and of all who were there was indescribable. But the public was not then admitted to see the bodies. They were told that the next morning they would be exposed to view.

There were about eight or ten thousand people collected together on that occasion. From the frame of the building which stood on the opposite corner to the Mansion they were addressed by Dr. Willard Richards, W. W. Phelps, and two of Joseph's lawyers, Messrs. Woods and Reid, and Col. Stephen Markham. The people were admonished by Dr. Richards to keep the peace. He had pledged his honor and his life, he said, for their good conduct. The other speeches were generally to the same effect. The people resolved with one united voice to trust to the law for a remedy of such a high-handed assassination, and when that failed, to call upon God to avenge them of their wrongs.

The next day it was estimated that over ten thousand persons visited the Mansion to see the bodies of the Prophet and Patriarch. From 8 o'clock in the morning until 5 o'clock in the evening a living stream passed through the doors of the room where they laid in their coffins. A mock funeral took place that afternoon by the boxes which contained the coffins being carried to the graveyard in the hearse. But the bodies were secretly buried that night. This was done to prevent the enemies of the martyrs getting possession of their bodies.

Life of Joseph the Prophet, by George Q. Cannon, *Instructor*, Vol. 15.

THE MOCK BURIAL OF THE PROPHETS

It was a solemn procession wending its way that sultry day in June, from the Mansion House, on Water Street to the public cemetery. As the hearse was drawn from the heart of the city, the funeral of the martyrs was held in the grove near the Temple. There were few dry eyes in the congregation as the dark carriage slowly made its way along Mulholland Street.

Few, indeed, were the ones who knew that the coffins in the carriage contained only bags of sand, for this burial must be as secret as that of Moses, which is thus described: "For the Lord took him unto his fathers * * * therefore no man knoweth of his sepulchre unto this day."

At the city cemetery when the bags of sand were lowered into the graves ostensibly intended for the bodies of the martyrs, strong men wept like children bereft of parents, while hysterical women cried and prayed and fainted; yet the bodies were safely concealed in a darkened closet at the Mansion House, for the bodies of these men were not safe even in the grave. Not only the rigid bodies of the martyrs, but their very graves must be buried to protect them from vandal hands in the night.

The proposed secret burial was known only by a few trusted friends who were pledged to guard the secret with their lives, for the bodies of the martyrs must be shrouded in secrecy and buried in oblivion to prevent vandal hands from profaning the final resting place of these martyred men.*** Fiends from Missouri—their painted cheeks powder burned from the recent bombardment where undisciplined men crowded together, firing promiscously and without careful aim, so eager were they to spill the blood of the prophets—would like to bear in triumph to Governor Boggs the head of Joseph Smith.   *Nauvoo the Beautiful*, by E. Cecil McGavin, p. 160.

THE PROPHET JOSEPH'S SISTER AND BROTHER-IN-LAW TESTIFY

Mr. Fred Salisbury had no hesitation in saying that the bodies of Joseph and Hyrum Smith, while buried secretly and at night soon after the massacre, lie in the exact spot where they were then buried, viz.: in the family burying ground a short distance in the rear of the old mansion house. The bodies were deposited in a brick vault. "When Aunt Emma Smith—Joseph's widow, later Mrs. C. L. Bidamon died in 1875, I think, five of us boys, Fred. Solomon, Don and Alvin Salisbury, and Don Milikin, all her nephews, acted as pall bearers at her funeral. We buried Aunt Emma by the side of the Prophet. Of course there can be nothing left of the bodies of Joseph and Hyrum but dust. I am satisfied that the Prophets were buried there, and that their bodies have never been disturbed." "The reason why the burial was secret," said Mrs. Salisbury, "was from the fact that a large sum of money was offered for the head of Joseph. It was thought best at the time to have the burial private, and both bodies were placed in a brick vault to prevent their being stolen."   *Millennial Star*, 56:549-51.

THE PROPHETS BURIED IN THE NAUVOO HOUSE

In the soft soil of the floorless room beneath the fortress of stone and brick only one story high, busy spades prepared a secret tomb to hide their martyred leaders from vandal hands. Upon the soft, tell-tale carpet of fresh earth forming the floor of the Nauvoo House, beaten paths of footprints were left by the nocturnal visitors who spared the sexton the task of burial. In the gathering darkness they carried the surplus earth to the river and scattered chips of wood and stone about the buried sepulchres so that the spot would not look unlike the surrounding area, thus not arousing the curiosity of the workmen.

Their acts of camouflage were further made complete when the understanding heavens poured down a flood of tears to mingle with those of the sorrowing saints. The procession soon disorganized, each man seeking shelter under his own roof. The privacy of their homes had scarcely concealed the men who knew the secret of the burial, until the weeping heavens deluged the country. When the pounding rain had ceased to fall, there was not a trace of foot prints in the soft soil, the roily rivulets bearing them into the wide stream whose arms feverishly reached across the sandy shore toward the unmarked grave of the martyrs. And thus were interred in a secret tomb not only the bodies of the martyrs, but their graves as well. No visible mounds of earth were left to remind the mourners of the sorrow of the separation.

Nauvoo the Beautiful, by E. Cecil McGavin, pp. 163-64.

BODIES OF THE MARTYRS REMOVED TO THEIR FINAL RESTING PLACE

When the endless chain of time slowly dragged its weary links of days away, numbing the sorrow of the parting and dimming the widows' vision of their slain, it was deemed wisdom to remove the bodies to a safer place of keeping. At the time the early autumn stripped the green leaves from the trees and traded scarred, brown, lifeless vegetation for the fresh foliage of the fields, the thoughts of widows turned, like the season, to scenes of death. It was at this sad season of the year that the widow **Emma** gave birth to her last-born son, thus taking her thoughts back to her martyred husband.

Emma insisted that the bodies be taken to the Old Homestead and given secret burial near the intimate family who slept in the shadow of the old trading post. The spot selected for this unmarked grave was beneath the old Spring House. This small building was simply a canopied cellar within whose moist walls of earth the Smith family had stored their supply of milk, butter, cream, etc., and vegetables during the hot days of summer. This sheltered cellar was so deep and close to the river that its cool walls provided a choice place of refrigeration. In the dead of night a group of pallbearers, fewer in number than when the first burial was made. reverently carried the bodies of the martyrs across the street to the Old Homestead, burying them in the cool basement of the Spring House.

Ten men buried the remains of the martyrs in the basement of the Nauvoo House, while only four men placed the bodies in the secret tomb near the Old Homestead. Before the secret was known abroad, this small structure had been torn down and its cellar compartment filled in with earth, thus doubly securing the mystery of the unknown grave. With the passing of time it became a profound mystery just where the Spring House stood where once the graves were sheltered.

Nauvoo the Beautiful, by E. Cecil McGavin, pp. 164-65.

THE SORROW OF THE PROPHET'S SAINTED MOTHER

After the corpses were washed and dressed in their burial clothes, we were allowed to see them. I had for a long time braced every nerve, roused every energy of my soul and called upon God to strengthen me, but when I entered the room and saw my murdered sons extended both at once before my eyes and heard the sobs and groans of my family and the cries of "Father! Husband! Brothers!" from the lips of their wives, children, brothers and sisters, it was too much; I sank back, crying to the Lord in the agony of my soul: "My God, My God, why hast thou forsaken this family?" A voice replied: "I have taken them to myself that they might have rest." Emma was carried back to her room almost in a state of insensibility. Her oldest son approached the corpse and dropped upon his knees, and laying his cheek against his father's and kissing him, exclaimed, "Oh, my father! my father." As for myself, I was swallowed up in the depths of my afflictions, yet I was dumb until I arose again to contemplate the spectacle before me. Oh! at that moment how my mind flew through every scene of sorrow and distress which we had passed, together, in which they had shown the innocence and sympathy which filled their guileless hearts. *As I looked upon their peaceful, smiling countenances, I seemed almost to hear them say, "Mother, weep not for us, we have overcome the world by love; we carried to them the gospel, that their souls might be saved; they slew us for our testimony, and thus placed us beyond their power; their ascendency is for a moment, ours is an eternal triumph."* I then thought upon the promise which I had received in Missouri, that in five years Joseph should have power over all his enemies. The time had elapsed and the promise was fulfilled.***

On the following day the funeral rites of the murdered ones were attended to, in the midst of terror and alarm, for the mob had made their arrangements to burn the city that night, but by the diligence of the brethren, they were kept at bay until they became discouraged and returned to their homes. ***

Here ends the history of my life, as well as that of my family, as far as I intend carrying it for the present. And I shall leave the world to judge, as seemeth them good, concerning what I have written. But this much I will say, that the testimony which I have given is true, and will stand forever; and the same will be my testimony in the day of God Almighty, when I shall meet them, concerning whom I have testified, before angels, and the spirits of the just made perfect, before archangels and seraphims, cherubims and gods; where the brief authority of the unjust man will shrink to nothingness before him who is the Lord of lords, and God of gods; and where the righteousness of the just shall exalt them in the scale, wherein God weigheth the hearts of men. And now having, in common with the saints, appealed in vain for justice, to Lilburn W. Boggs, Thomas Carlin, Martin Van Buren and Thomas Ford, I bid them a last farewell, until I shall appear with them before Him who is the judge of both the quick and the dead; to whom I solemnly appeal in the name of Jesus Christ. Amen.

History of Joseph Smith, by his mother, Lucy Mack Smith, pp. 324-28.

GRAVES OF THE MARTYRS DESECRATED BY DESCENDANTS OF THE PROPHET JOSEPH

Note: The following is taken from the *Quincy Herald-Whig*, of Sunday, January 22, 1928, copy of which paper is owned by the compiler of this book. The article appeared under the caption: "Bones of Mormon Founders Buried at Scene of Historic Colony. Joseph and Hyrum Smith Graves Found in Nauvoo; Old Mystery Cleared Up." The article is written by Dave Tuffli, *Herald-Whig* staff reporter.)

"Nauvoo, Ill., Jan. 22. Three skeletons, brown with a century's decay, lay in three narrow crypts in a tiny cemetery on the shore of Lake Cooper. Wan, wintry sunlight shadowed the gaunt branches of trees across the strange grave, and sharp gusts of wind stirred the bones in their shallow vaults. A reverent group huddled together as a plaintive voice rose above the ice-muffled requiem of the Mississippi—a minister, pleading for divine guidance. For twenty minutes the voice, quivering with cold at times, intoned a prayer. A cold blast swept "Amen" from his lips, the skeletons were covered, the crypts sealed and a hundred persons hurried to shelter. Such were the final rites Friday for Joseph Smith. Jr., founder of the Church of Jesus Christ of Latter-day Saints, originally known as the Mormon church, and Hyrum Smith, his brother, whose secreted graves were located in Nauvoo by officials of the Church after a six-day search. The bones of Emma Smith, wife of Joseph, were placed beside the skeletons of the brothers.

"Joseph and Hyrum Smith were shot to death by a mob in the Hancock county jail at Carthage, June 27, 1844. Their bodies were taken to Nauvoo and the burial place was kept secret by Emma Smith who feared that enemies might mutilate them. The story of the secret burial was divulged to Frederick M. Smith, of Kansas City, Mo., grandson of the Prophet Joseph Smith, by Frederick Smith's father, Joseph Smith III. The exact location of the grave was not determined until less than a week ago. The bodies have been positively identified, according to officials of the Church of Jesus Christ of Latter-day Saints. The bones were placed in crypts and sealed in a solid block of concrete which will form the foundation for an impressive monument to be erected later. Services held at the sealing of the crypts were simple and brief. Three oblong depressions had been sunk in a base of concrete. After the skulls of both Joseph and Hyrum Smith had been photographed from every angle, the skeletons were assembled on beds of soft material placed in the depressions. The feet lay to the north, and the heads to the south. Joseph Smith, as founder of the Mormon church, now known as the Re-organized Church of Jesus Christ of Latter-day Saints, was placed in the center crypt. To his east was placed Hyrum Smith, his brother, and to the west, the bones of Emma Smith, wife of Joseph, taken from another grave, were laid. * * *

"*Settlement of rumors concerning the location of the bodies of Joseph and Hyrum Smith for all time is the most important significance of the discovery made in Nauvoo a few days ago, according to Frederick M. Smith,* president of the Reorganized Church of Jesus Christ of Latter-day Saints, and J. A. Gardner, publicity director. 'We think it rather opportune that the discovery came at this time,' Mr. Gardner said, 'in view of the fact that in 1930 we are preparing to celebrate the first centennial of the Church. It will have been organized 100 years on April 6, 1930. We are preparing for a great celebration at Independence, Mo., and expect by that time to have the monument over the bodies of Joseph and Hyrum Smith erected at Nauvoo.'

"Frederick M. Smith of Kansas City, now president of the Reorganized Church of Jesus Christ of Latter-day Saints, spoke briefly, eulogizing his grandfather and Hyrum Smith as martyrs to their religion. Then James A. Gillen, member of the Quorum of Twelve Apostles, of Independence, Mo., gave a long prayer. The services were made brief because of inclement weather. The crypts of the three Smiths are located in the old Mormon burial ground, a small enclosed plot located about eight blocks west of the Nauvoo business district, on a peninsula which extends into Lake Cooper, as the Mississippi is known at that point. It is, perhaps, one of the most beautiful spots on the upper Mississippi. Adjacent to the graveyard are the Mansion House, where Joseph Smith was residing at the time he was assassinated; the Joseph Smith home and the Nauvoo house, located to the south of the Smith home, which was to have been a hotel. All of these buildings, though almost a century old, are still standing and have been kept in excellent repair by the church. J. W. Layton, caretaker of the Church of Jesus Christ of Latter-day Saints at Nauvoo, lives in the Mansion House.

"Officials of the Reorganized Church of Jesus Christ of Latter-day Saints, say there is no doubt regarding the identity of the skeletons. The skull of Hyrum, saints say, clearly shows a bullet hole beneath the right eye and to the right of the nose, which biographers and historians claim was the manner in which Hyrum was wounded. Hyrum Smith was leaning against the door of the Hancock county jail to resist forced entrance when a bullet plowed through the door and struck him in the face. The skull is torn away at the point where the bullet is supposed to have struck, and church officials believe this to show the course of the bullet. No bullets were found in the graves, however.

"People of Nauvoo and members of the Reorganized church

apparently have always been certain that the bodies of the two Smiths were located in Nauvoo. *However, officials of the Reorganized church say they have found it necessary to repudiate statements emanating from the Utah branch of the church that the bodies were in Utah. The Utah and the Reorganized church are separate. A breach exists.*

"Frederick M. Smith, now president of the Reorganized church, tells an interesting story of the finding of the bodies. His father, he said, remembered standing by the side of Emma Smith as the bodies were lowered into shallow graves which had been prepared in the bottom of a spring house, standing near the old homestead. The spring house, Joseph Smith III told Frederick, had a brick floor and foundation wall. The bodies would be found in the northwest corner of the place designated, he was told. All of this had been kept a family secret. Emma Smith had kept it so after she allowed two coffins filled with sand to be buried as Joseph and Hyrum Smith, in a Nauvoo cemetery. The spring house rotted and fell away, leaving no mark by which the grave might be found. Attempt to locate the bodies had been discussed often, but other activities prevented until Wednesday, January 11. On that day, W. O. Hand, of Kansas City, engineer, started excavation in the vicinity. He and his men first dug near the water's edge, outside the graveyard enclosure, but met with no success. Then a trench system of searching was devised and after 'a season of prayer,' Mr. Hand and his crew uncovered the bodies on Monday, January 16. The grave of Emma Smith was opened first. It was marked, but the grave stone was removed some distance from the body. From this grave trenches were extended to determine where the ground had been disturbed and finally to the south and west of the feet of Emma Smith the brick walls of the old spring house were struck. Proceeding farther, the men uncovered the remains of two walnut coffins lying side by side, the tops of which had caved in. The wood was nearly dust and gave way as soon as touched. A group of Nauvoo citizens was called in to view the bones in the grave. The bodies were then taken out and put in canvas and the skulls were conveyed to the Mansion House, where they were photographed."

FUNERAL AND INTERMENT OF THE MARTYRS

By B. H. Roberts

When the bodies of Joseph and Hyrum arrived at the Mansion, the doors were closed immediately. The people were told to go quietly home, and the bodies would be viewed the next morning at eight o'clock.

Dimick B. Huntington, with the assistance of William Marks and William D. Huntington, washed the bodies from head to foot. Joseph was shot in the right breast, also under the heart, in the lower part of his bowels and the right side, and on the back part of the right hip. One ball had come out at the right shoulder-blade. Cotton soaked in camphor was put into each wound, and the bodies laid out with fine plain drawers and shirt, white neckerchiefs, white cotton stockings and white shrouds. (Gilbert Goldsmith was doorkeeper at the time).

After this was done, Emma (who at the time was pregnant) also Mary (Hyrum's wife) with the children of the martyred Prophet and Patriarch, were admitted to see the bodies. On first seeing the corpse of her husband, Emma screamed and fell back, but was caught and supported by Dimick B. Huntington. She then fell forward to the Prophet's face and kissed him, calling him by name, and begged him to speak to her once. Mary, (the Patriarch's wife) manifested calmness and composure throughout the trying scene, which was affecting in the extreme. Relatives and particular friends were also permitted to view the remains during the evening.

Saturday 29.—At 7 a.m. the bodies were put into the coffins which were covered with black velvet fastened with brass nails. Over the face of each corpse a lid was hung with brass hinges, under which was a square of glass to protect the face, and the coffin was lined with white cambric. The coffins were then each put into a rough pine box.

At 8 a.m. the room was thrown open for the Saints to view the bodies of their martyred Prophet and Patriarch, and it is estimated that over ten thousand persons visited the remains that day, as there was a perfect living stream of people entering in at the west door of the Mansion and out at the north door from 8 a.m. to 5 p.m., at which hour a request was made that the Mansion should be cleared, so that the family could take their farewell look at the remains.

The coffins were then taken out of the boxes into the little bedroom in the northeast corner of the Mansion, and there concealed and the doors locked. Bags of sand were then placed in each end of the boxes, which were nailed up, and a mock funeral took place, the boxes being put into a hearse and driven to the graveyard by William D. Huntington, and there deposited in a grave with the usual ceremonies.

This was done to prevent enemies of the martyred Prophet and Patriarch getting possession of the bodies, as they threatened they would do. As the hearse passed the meeting ground accompanied by a few men, William W. Phelps was preaching the funeral sermon.

About midnight the coffins containing the bodies were taken from the Mansion by Dimick B. Huntington, Edward Hunter, William D. Huntington, William Marks, Jonathan H. Holmes, Gilbert Goldsmith, Alpheus Cutler, Lorenzo D. Wasson, and Philip B. Lewis, preceded by James Emmett as guard with his musket.

They went through the garden, round by the pump, and were conveyed to the Nauvoo house, which was then built to the first joists of the basement, and buried in the basement story.

After the bodies were interred, and the ground smoothed off as it was before, and chips of wood and stone and other rubbish thrown over, so as to make it appear like the rest of the ground around the graves, a most terrific shower of rain, accompanied with thunder and lightning, occurred, and obliterated all traces of the fact that the earth had been newly dug.

The bodies remained in the cellar of the Nauvoo House where they were buried, until the fall, when they were removed by Dimick B. Huntington, William D. Huntington, Jonathan H. Holmes, and Gilbert Goldsmith, at Emma's request, to near the Mansion, and buried side by side, and the bee house then moved and placed over their graves.

The deceased children of Joseph were afterwards removed and interred in the same place. It was found at this time that two of Hyrum's teeth had fallen into the inside of his mouth, supposed to have been done by a ball at the time of the martyrdom, but which was not discovered at the time he was laid out, in consequence of his jaws being tied up.   *D. H. C.* 6:627-9.

STATEMENT BY B. H. ROBERTS

The above (that is, the "Funeral and Interment of the Martyrs") is from the *Deseret News* of November 25, 1857, published in Salt Lake City. The same historical statement verbatim is found in the *Millennial Star* of August 9, 1862, which was republishing at the time this History from the *Deseret News*. This historical narrative of the burial of Joseph and Hyrum Smith from the two preceding periodicals was published in book form under the title of the History of the Church of Jesus Christ of Latter-day Saints, and includes the above excerpt from the *Deseret News* and *Millennial Star*, in Vol. 6, pages 627-629, so that this has been the continuous history of the burial and burial places of the two martyrs before the people of Utah and all the world.

"In 1884, while writing my *Rise and Fall of Nauvoo*, I visited Nauvoo to secure photographs for illustrating the articles on the above subject which were then appearing in the *Contributor*, a magazine published in Salt Lake City. After photographing the house which was known as the old Smith homestead, and afterwards as the home of Hyrum Smith, I called upon Major Bidamon who at that time was living just across the road from Emma Smith's grave in some rooms raised on the foundations of the Nauvoo House. Mr. Bidamon married Emma Smith some years after the death of the prophet. In the course of the conversation I asked Major Bidamon why Emma Smith was buried out in the yard of the Smith homestead alone, rather than in the Nauvoo cemetery. To this Mr. Bidamon replied: 'She isn't alone; she is buried by the side of her former husband, Joseph Smith and his brother Hyrum.' He then went on to say that a day or two before her demise, Emma Smith called those to her who would likely dispose of her remains, after her death, and directed them to go to the southeast corner of the old Smith homestead, and in a direct line from that corner take twenty-five paces and there dig down and they would come upon a brick vault. She desired that her coffin be placed by the side of that vault. She did not ask for the vault to be opened, but that her coffin might be laid by the side of it, and 'that was done according to her wishes,' said Mr. Bidamon."

"On returning to Salt Lake City from this visit to Nauvoo, I reported this incident to President Joseph F. Smith, the son of Hyrum Smith, and later president of the Church, whereupon Joseph F. Smith stated that this was in exact accordance with information imparted to him by his mother, Mary Fielding Smith, wife of Hyrum Smith. She had stated to him, Joseph Fielding Smith, that at the time that the remains of Joseph and Hyrum were being removed in the night by Emma Smith, from their first place of interment in the basement of the Nauvoo house, she awoke in the night, having a strange presentiment that something was wrong. Some strange thing was either impending or happening, which made her restless and sleepless, and so about midnight she arose from her bed, went about the house and finally outside of it, and soon discovered that something was going on over at the Nauvoo House, and accordingly, on crossing the road she came upon the parties who were removing the bodies of her husband and his brother, under the direction of Emma Smith. Evidently she assented to the removal to which she had been so strangely brought as a witness; and this was the account of that experience which she related to her son Joseph F. Smith, in whose family the incident is a cherished memory.****

"Moreover, Elder S. O. Bennion, president of the Central States Mission of the Church of Jesus Christ of Latter-day Saints, stationed at Independence, Missouri, writing to the president of the Church at Salt Lake City, Utah, under date of January 21, 1928, says:

"Several years ago 'Young Joseph' as he was called (president of the Reorganized church) told me he was going to bring his father's body to Independence, and when I went out to Utah to conference I told President Joseph F. Smith, and President Smith said to me: 'You tell Joseph not to disturb those bodies without letting me know.'"

This message was delivered and there evidently the matter of removing the bodies was dropped by Mr. Fred M. Smith's predecessor.

In view of all of this information representing continuous knowledge by the Church authorities in Utah as to the whereabouts of the burial place of the brothers, Joseph and Hyrum Smith, it will appear to reasonable minds that the effort of sensational "finding" of the skeletons of these men, and the claim of the Utah church authorities being overthrown by such alleged "discovery" is ridiculous and a cheap effort at sensationalism, and the bolstering up of a cheaper claim of "inspirational guidance" in the finding of them, when all along the Reorganized Church branch of the Smith family have known of the location of these bodies as well as the Utah branch of the Smith family has known of it.

In plain terms, the whole procedure of Mr. Fred M. Smith and those associated with him in this business is unwarranted, a cheap bid for a sensation, and for the reputation of being guided by "inspiration" to find the remains of Joseph and Hyrum Smith, when there was no occasion for such "guidance," the location of the bodies being positively known already by Mr. Fred M. Smith, according to his own statement relative to the instruction which his father had given him as to the place where the two brothers were buried before his "engineers and surveyors began the alleged search."

Deseret News, January 31, 1928.

"The remains of the bodies of the Martyrs were re-interred in this cement grave on January 20, 1928, by Frederick M. Smith, the President of the Reorganized Church, after first disturbing the sacred bodies of the Martyrs by taking them to the Mansion House, photographing and measuring the skulls and bones, placing the remains in separate boxed apartments, and then covering deeply with cement.

CHAPTER 13

The Sorrow and Mourning of the Saints

NIGHT OF THE MARTYRDOM

By Apostle Orson Hyde

Twenty-seventh of June, 1844. Eventful period in the calendar of the nineteenth century! That awful night! I remember it well: I shall never forget it! Thousands and tens of thousands will never forget it! A solemn thrill—a melancholy awe comes o'er my spirit! The memorable scene is fresh before me! It requires no art of the pencil, no retrospection of history, to portray it. The impression of the Almighty Spirit on that occasion will run parallel with eternity! The scene was not portrayed by earthquake, or thunderings, and lightnings, and tempests; but the majesty and sovereignty of Jehovah was felt far more impressively in the still, small voice of that significant hour, than the roaring of many waters, or the artillery of many thunders, when the spirit of Joseph was driven back to the bosom of God, by an ungrateful and bloodthirsty world! There was an unspeakable something, a portentious significancy in the firmament and among the inhabitants of the earth. Multitudes felt the whisperings of woe and grief, and the forebodings of tribulation and sorrow that they will never forget, though the tongue of man can never utter it. The Saints of God, whether near the scene of blood, or even a thousand miles distant, felt at the very moment the Prophet lay in royal gore, that an awful deed was perpetrated. O, the repulsive chill! the melancholy vibrations of the very air, as the prince of darkness receded in hopeful triumph from the scene of slaughter! That night could not the Saints sleep, though uninformed by man of what had passed with the Seer and Patriarch, and far, far remote from the scene; yet to them sleep refused a visitation—the eyelids refused to close—the hearts of many sighed deeply in secret, and inquired, "Why am I thus?"

One of the Twelve Apostles, while traveling a hundred miles from the scene of assassination, and totally ignorant of what was done, was so unaccountably sad, and filled with such unspeakable anguish of heart without knowing the cause, that he was constrained to turn aside from the road and give utterance to his feelings in tears and supplications to God. Another Apostle, twelve hundred miles distant, while standing in Faneuil Hall, Boston, Massachusetts, with many others, was similarly affected, and was obliged to turn aside to hide the big tears that gushed thick and long from his eyes. Another, President of the High Priests, while in the distant state of Kentucky, in the solitude of midnight, being marvelously disquieted, God condescended to show him, in a vision, the mangled bodies of the two murdered worthies, all dripping in purple gore, who said to him, "We are murdered by a faithless state and cruel mob."

Shall I attempt to describe the scene at Nauvoo on that memorable evening? If I could, surely you would weep, whatever may be your faith or skepticism, if the feelings of humanity are lodged in your bosom; all prejudice and mirth would slumber, till the eye of pity had bedewed the bier, and the heart had found relief in lamentation. Before another day dawned, the messenger bore the tidings into the afflicted city; the picket guards of the city heard the whisper of murder in silent amazement, as the messenger passed into the city. There the pale muslin signal for gathering the troops hung its drooping folds from the Temple spire (as if partaking of nature's sadness), and made tremulous utterance to the humble soldiery to muster immediately. As the dawn made the signal visible, and the bass tone of the great drum confirmed the call, fathers, husbands, and minor sons, all seized the broken fragment of a dodger, or a scanty bone, for the service that might be long and arduous before their return, or swallowed some thickened milk (as might be the case), and fled to the muster ground; the suspicious mother and children followed to the door and window, anxious to see the gathering hosts emerge from their watch-posts and firesides, where rest and food were scanted to the utmost endurance. The troops continued to arrive, and stood in martial order, with a compressed lip and a quick ear. They waited with deathly but composed silence, to hear the intelligence that mournful spirits had saddened their hearts with during the night. The speaker stood up in the midst, not of an uniform soldiery of hirelings, for they had no wages; their clothing was the workmanship of the diligent domestic—the product of wife and daughters' arduous toil; their rations were drawn from the precarious supplies earned in the intervals between preaching to the states and nations of the earth, and watching against the intrusions and violence of mobs. The speaker announced the martyrdom of the Prophet and Patriarch, and paused under the heavy burden of the intelligence.

But here I must pause; my pen shall touch lightly, as it must feebly, that hallowed—that solemn and ever-memorable hour! The towering indignation; the holy and immutable principle of retribution for crime that dwells eternally in the bosom of God, insensibly impelled the right hand almost to draw the glittering sword, and feel the sharpness of the bayonet's point and its fixedness to the musket's mouth. But the well-planted principle of self-command, and also of observing the order of Heaven and the counsel of the Priesthood, soon returned the deadly steel to the scabbard; and the victorious triumph of loyalty to God, in committing evil-doers to Him that judgeth righteously, and who hath said, "Vengeance is mine, and I will repay," prevailed over the billows of passion; and in the transit of a fleeting moment the holy serenity of the soldiery, depicted by an occasional tear, showed to the angels and men that the tempest of passion was hushed, and wholly under the control of the spirit of wisdom and of God!

The Frontier Guardian, June 27, 1849, Council Bluffs, Iowa.
The Elders Journal, March 1, 1907.

WILFORD WOODRUFF AND BRIGHAM YOUNG
WEEP OVER THE MARTYRDOM

BY WILFORD WOODRUFF

I was sitting with Brigham Young in the depot in the city of Boston at the time when the two prophets were martyred. Of course we had no telegraphs and no fast reports as we have today to give communication over the land. During that period Brother Young was waiting there for a train of cars to go to Peterborough. Whilst sitting there we were overshadowed by a cloud of darkness and gloom as great as I ever witnessed in my life under almost any circumstances in which we were placed. Neither of us knew or understood the cause until after the report of the death of the prophets was manifested to us. Brother Brigham left; I remained in Boston, and next day took passage for Fox Islands, a place I had visited some years before, and baptized numbers of people and organized branches upon both those islands. My father-in-law, Ezra Carter, carried me on a wagon from Scarborough to Portland. I there engaged passage on board of a steamer. I had put my trunk on board and was just bidding my father-in-law farewell, when a man came out from a shop—a shoemaker—holding a newspaper in his hand. He said, "Father Carter, Joseph and Hyrum Smith have been martyred—they have been murdered in Carthage jail!"

As soon as I looked at the paper, the Spirit said to me that it was true. I had no time for consultation, the steamer's bell was ringing, so I stepped on board and took my trunk back to land. As I drew it off, the plank was drawn in. I told Father Carter to drive me back to Scarborough. I there took the car for Boston, and arrived at that place on the Saturday night. On my arrival there I received a letter which had been sent from Nauvoo, giving us an account of the killing of the prophets. I was the only man in Boston of the quorum of the Twelve.

I had very strange feelings, as, I have no doubt, all the Saints had. I attended a meeting on the following day in Boydston's Hall, where a vast number of the inhabitants of Boston and some three hundred Latter-day Saints had assembled. Hundreds of men came to that meeting to see what the "Mormons" were going to do now that their prophets were dead. I felt braced up; every nerve, bone, and sinew *within* me seemed as though made of steel. I did not shed a tear. I went into that hall, though I knew not what I was going to say to that vast audience. I opened the Bible promiscuously and opened to the words of St. John where he saw under the altar the souls of them that were slain for the word of God, and heard them cry, "How long, O Lord, holy and true, dost thou not judge and avenge our blood on them that dwell on the earth?" The Lord informed them that they must wait a little season, until their brethren were slain as they were. I spoke on those words.

Next day I met Brigham Young in the streets of Boston, he having just returned, opposite to Sister Voce's home. We reached out our hands but *neither* of us was able *to speak* a word. We walked into Sister Voce's house. We each took a seat and veiled our faces. We were overwhelmed with grief and our faces were soon bathed in a flood of tears. I felt then that I could talk, though I could not do so before—that is, to Brother Brigham. After we had done weeping we began to converse together concerning the death of the prophets. In the course of the conversation, he smote his hand upon his thigh and said: "Thank God, the keys of the kingdom are here."   *Millennial Star*, Vol. 51, 545-47.

LOCATION OF THE TWELVE AT THE TIME OF THE MARTYRDOM

"Brigham was away with the majority of the Twelve when the martyrdom took place. Two only were in Nauvoo; they were Willard Richards and John Taylor. Both of these were in prison with the Prophet when the assassins, with painted faces, broke into Carthage gaol, overpowered the guards and martyred the brothers Joseph and Hyrum. No pen can describe the universal shock felt among the Saints when the news burst upon them, and sped throughout the United States and Europe.

Brigham Young and Orson Pratt were together at Peterboro, N. H., at the house of Brother Bemet, when a letter from Nauvoo came to a Mr. Joseph Powers, giving particulars of the assassination. The rumor met them first at Salem. Awful as it was to him, the President too well realized that unless the Twelve were equal to the occasion, the Church was in danger of dissolution or a great schism. At best, the Saints must feel for a moment as sheep without a shepherd.

"Those who have followed him in his eventful career, know that Brigham is always greatest on great occasions. He never fails in a trying hour. **** 'The first thing that I thought of,' says the President, 'was whether Joseph had taken the keys of the kingdom with him from the earth. Brother Orson Pratt sat on my left; we were both leaning back in our chairs. Bringing my hand down on my knee, I said, the keys of the kingdom are right here with the Church.'

"The President immediately started for Boston, where he held council with Heber C. Kimball, Orson Pratt, and Wilford Woodruff, relative to their return to Nauvoo. Heber and Brigham remained there a week, awaiting the arrival of Apostle Lyman Wight. During their stay, they ordained, at one evening meeting, thirty-two elders. This act was conclusive evidence that these apostles did not intend to let the Church die.

"As soon as Lyman Wight arrived, the three set out for Nauvoo, and at Albany they were joined by Orson Hyde, Orson Pratt and Wilford Woodruff."

Life of Brigham Young, by Edw. W. Tullidge, pp. 105-07.

PARLEY P. PRATT IS COMFORTED BY THE HOLY SPIRIT

President B. Young and most of the members of the quorum of the Twelve, were then on a mission through the Eastern States, as well as myself. While on this mission, on the 27th of June, 1844, a mob murdered the Prophet Joseph Smith and his brother Hyrum, in a jail at Carthage, Illinois, while Governor Ford had pledged the faith of the State for their protection.

A day or two previous to this circumstance I had been constrained by the Spirit to start prematurely for home, without knowing why or wherefore; and on the same afternoon I was passing on a canal boat near Utica, New York, on my way to Nauvoo. My brother, William Pratt, being then on a mission in the same State (New York), happened, providentially, to take passage on the same boat. As we conversed together on the deck, a strange and solemn awe came over me, as if the powers of hell were let loose. I was so overwhelmed with sorrow I could hardly speak; and after pacing the deck for some time in silence, I turned to my brother William and exclaimed: "Brother William, this is a dark hour; the powers of darkness seem to triumph, and the spirit of murder is abroad in the land; and it controls the hearts of the American people, and a vast majority of them sanction the killing of the innocent. My brother, let us keep silence and not open our mouths. If you have any pamphlets or books on the fulness of the gospel lock them up; show them not, neither open your mouth to the people; let us observe an entire and solemn silence, for this is a dark day, and the hour of triumph for the powers of darkness. O, how sensible I am of the spirit of murder which seems to pervade the whole land." This was June 27, 1844, in the afternoon, and as near as I can judge, it was the same hour that the Carthage mob were shedding the blood of Joseph and Hyrum Smith, and John Taylor, near one thousand miles distant. My brother bid me farewell somewhere in western New York, he being on his way to a conference in that quarter, and passing on to Buffalo I took steamer for Chicago, Illinois.

The steamer touched at a landing in Wisconsin, some fifty or sixty miles from Chicago, and here some new passengers came on board and brought the news of the martyrdom of Joseph and Hyrum Smith. Great excitement prevailed on board, there being a general spirit of exultation and triumph at this glorious news, as it was called, the same as is generally shown on the first receipt of the news of a great national victory in time of war. Many passengers now gathered about me and tauntingly inquired what the Mormons would do now, seeing their Prophet and leader was killed. To these taunts and questions I replied, that they would continue their mission and spread the work he had restored, in all the world. Observing that nearly all the prophets and Apostles who were before him had been killed, and also the Saviour of the world, and yet their death did not alter the truth nor hinder its final triumph.

At this reply many of them seemed astonished, and some inquired who would succeed him, and remarked to me: "Perhaps you will be the man who will now seek to be leader of the Mormons in his stead—who are you, sir?" I replied: "I am a man, sir; and a man never triumphs and exults in the ruin of his country and the murder of the innocent." This was said in the energy of my soul, and by constraint of the Spirit, and a powerful and peculiar accent was thrown upon the word MAN each time it occurred in the sentence. This served as a sufficient rebuke, and all were silent.

Landing in Chicago I found great excitement, and the press had issued extras announcing the triumph of the murderous mob in killing the Smiths. I now hastened on to Peoria, and, staying over night, started next day on foot across the country to Nauvoo— distance 105 miles.

During the two or three days I spent in traveling between Chicago and Peoria I felt so weighed down with sorrow and the powers of darkness that it was painful for me to converse or speak to any one, or even to try to eat or sleep. I really felt that if it had been my own family who had died, and our beloved Prophet been spared alive, I could have borne it, and the blow would have fallen on me with far less weight. I had loved Joseph with a warmth of affection indescribable for about fourteen years. I had associated with him in private and in public, in travels and at home, in joy and sorrow, in honor and dishonor, in adversity of every kind. With him I had triumphed over all our foes in Missouri, and found deliverance for ourselves and people in Nauvoo, where we had reared a great city. But now he was gone to the invisible world, and we and the Church of the Saints were left to mourn in sorrow and without the presence of our beloved founder and Prophet.

As I walked along over the plains of Illinois, lonely and solitary, I reflected as follows: I am now drawing near to the beloved city; in a day or two I shall be there. How shall I meet the sorrowing widows and orphans? How shall I meet the aged and widowed mother of these two martyrs? How shall I meet an entire community bowed down with grief and sorrow unutterable? What shall I say? or how console and advise twenty-five thousand people who will throng about me in tears, and in the absence of my President and the older members of the now presiding council, will ask counsel at my hands? Shall I tell them to fly to the wilderness and deserts? Or, shall I tell them to stay at home and take care of themselves, and continue to build the Temple? With these reflections and inquiries, I walked onward, weighed down as it were unto death. When I could endure it no longer, I cried out aloud, saying: O Lord, in the name of Jesus Christ I pray Thee, show me what these things mean, and what I shall say to Thy people? On a sudden the Spirit of God came upon me, and filled my heart with joy and gladness indescribable; and while the spirit of revelation glowed in my bosom with as visible a warmth and gladness as if it were fire, the Spirit said unto me: "Lift up your head and rejoice; for behold! it is well with my servants Joseph and Hyrum. My servant Joseph still holds the keys of my kingdom in this dispensation, and he shall stand in due time on the earth, in the flesh, and fulfil that to which he is appointed. Go and say unto my people in Nauvoo, that they shall continue to pursue their daily duties and take care of themselves, and make no movement in Church government to reorganize or alter anything until the return of the remainder of the quorum of the Twelve. But exhort them that they continue to build the House of the Lord which I have commanded them to build in Nauvoo."

This information caused my bosom to burn with joy and gladness, and I was comforted above measure; all my sorrow seemed in a moment to be lifted as a burden from my back. The change was so sudden I hardly dared to believe my senses. I, therefore, prayed the Lord to repeat to me the same things the second time; if, indeed, I might be sure of their truth, and might really tell the Saints to stay in Nauvoo, and continue to build the Temple. As I prayed thus, the same spirit burned in my bosom, and the Spirit of the Lord repeated to me the same message again. I then went on my way rejoicing, and soon arrived in Nauvoo, and delivered this message both to the people and friends individually, and in the great congregation. In confirmation that the message was right, I found them already renewing their labors on the Temple, under the direction of John Taylor and Willard Richards, who were members of our quorum, and who were in jail with the prophets when they were murdered — Taylor being wounded with four bullets, and Richards escaping uninjured.

Autobiography of Parley P. Pratt, pp. 368-372.

THE FATEFUL NIGHT OF JUNE 27, 1844

BY MRS. GEORGE A. SMITH

On the evening of the 27th of June such a barking and howling of dogs and bellowing of cattle all over the city of Nauvoo I never heard before or since. I was at Brother David Smith's house. I knelt down and tried to pray for the prophet, but I was struck speechless, and knew not the cause till morning, of course the awful deed was already accomplished, when the spirit refused to give me utterance to prayer the evening before. The next day the bodies were brought and conveyed to the mansion. Here I witnessed the awful scene—the Prophet and Patriarch lying in their gore and thousands of men, women, and children weeping all around.

Juvenile Instructor, 27:471;
Nauvoo the Beautiful, p. 157.

* * * * *

By Sylvia C. Webb: I can remember (I shall never forget) the day when Joseph and Hyrum were assassinated at Carthage. It was the darkest day of my life. No scene before or since has struck such a terror to my heart. Joseph, when living, often patted my head and said, "You're a little Ephraimite." How I loved that man! And I know now even as I knew then that he was a man of God, a true prophet.

The Saints' Herald, March 24, 1915; *Nauvoo the Beautiful*, p. 152.

HOW THE SAINTS MOURNED FOR THE PROPHET JOSEPH

BY FRANKLIN D. RICHARDS

Back in the days when the Prophet Joseph was slain, and the Church was left without him here upon the earth, the whole people mourned—mourned as we have never known how to mourn since.

I want to tell you Saints that felt you mourned when President Young died, when President Taylor died, or now that President Woodruff has departed from us, it is no such mourning as was felt through all Nauvoo, and among all the Saints when the Prophet and Patriarch were slain. It just seemed as if everything around us, even the animals, the trees and the habitations, were clothed in mourning. We felt his absence, because he was to us instead of God. He directed us in everything, taught us in all the great principles that pertain to our salvation and exaltation throughout all this mortal existence and clear into the eternities. Anybody that has the spirit of revelation, and who will read the last revelation that he gave us, cannot help but wonder and admire, and comprehend something of the great mind and capacity of soul that he had acquired during his short experience, in the gospel, of twenty-four years here in the flesh.

Now, when he was taken away, it was the first great and terrible experience in that line, and there was no rule left when the church organization should be perfected. Let me cite you to a few facts in connection with this. When that event occurred, the apostles were all away throughout the United States, on missions, except John Taylor and Willard Richards. They were in prison with the Prophet Joseph. President Taylor was shot nearly to pieces, so that he had like to have died, according to all human appearance. Willard just lost a drop of blood from one of his ears; a ball whistled so near that it broke his skin and let a drop of blood mingle with the others. The Prophet Brigham was in Boston, with Apostle Woodruff. It was a sad and sorrowful time. Immediately the Prophet Joseph was slain, one man and another, and another, who had been taught by him to comprehend some great principles of the Gospel, came to feel so important that one man said, since Joseph was dead there was no man living to whom he owed allegiance. He, therefore, in the greatness of his self-importance, gathered up his family, with a few others, and went away to Texas. Lyman Wight was this man, whose cognomen among the twelve was "the wild ram of the mountain." By and by one of his sons returned to us. Another man, Alpheus Cutler, in the greatness of his experience and self-sufficiency, took his family and some friends and went to a northern state, making a camp of his own, ready to build up a city, a people, a nation, and become a prophet. George Miller, one of the presiding bishops, also started, with a few and went off among the Pancho Indians. Another one, James J. Strang, who thought he had the thing fixed so it had come to stay, went off with a few to Beaver Island, in Lake Michigan, and carried on his operations for a while, till, by and by, one of his followers sickened of him and assassinated him. This is the way these great men, who thought they were somebody, have gone in the strength of their own endowments, feeling themselves as great as Joseph the Prophet. How was it, when the Prophet Brigham came back to Nauvoo, that he realized that the powers of the priesthood and the keys thereof had come down upon him? He went and stood in his place. Sidney Rigdon wanted to become a "guardian" to the church, to guide and lead them till they should see Joseph again. And thus, one after another, these different influences wrought. About this time, too, to fill up the cup and make it run over, and to accomplish the wickedness of the world, a mob got around and forced the twelve, when they got back to Nauvoo, to enter into an agreement with them that they and the people would get up and leave the country. This they did. They made their arrangements, and, as quick as we could finish the temple and get the blessings of the Lord upon us, the Saints started out into the wilderness to find a country as far from civilization as they could.

The Prophet Joseph had a feeling or a premonition of what might be, and we find it on the record of his history that he felt forebodings that he might not stay to see that temple completed. He took the twelve aside—those who were faithful—and he gave them their endowments in a holy place, in a new building that he consecrated for that purpose. He placed upon them the keys, authority and powers which the Lord and the angels had conferred upon him. You recollect that John the Baptist came and ordained Joseph and Oliver to the Aaronic Priesthood. Peter, James and John came and ordained him and Oliver unto the Melchizedek Priesthood— the holy apostleship. In the temple at Kirtland, Moses, Elias and Elijah appeared and conferred upon him the keys of the gathering of Israel, of the Gospel of Abraham, and of the turning of the hearts of the fathers to the children and the children to their fathers. Joseph called the brethren aside and placed all these keys, powers and blessings that he had received upon them. You have heard President Woodruff testify of this, and of the great work and marvelous power thereof. Well, these things bestowed upon the brethren caused some men to become headstrong, and in view of what they knew, they thought they could build up the church unto God, build up the kingdom of God, and stand at the head of it themselves.

While this was going on the powers of the priesthood rested down upon the Twelve Apostles, and President Young always took pains to have a majority of them within reach, where he could arrange for any decisions that he found it necessary to make. He had a great vision, in which Joseph said to us, through him: "Get the holy spirit and keep it." That is a great injunction that is upon us all. If we want to go where these men are, we must get the holy spirit and walk in the light of it. After he and the pioneers had been out here and had found this place for us to come and live in, and then went back to the Mississippi river, in Winter Quarters, the spirit of the Lord, the revelation of the Lord, came upon him. It was about two years and a half, on that occasion, that the Church had been without a first presidency, till the Lord made manifest to them in Winter Quarters, about December, 1847, that the organization should be completed. There being no good place for it, they picked out men and set them to work to build a tabernacle in Kanesville for the conference. At that conference the first presidency was accepted, and, according to the dictation of the revelation, they, Brigham Young, Heber C. Kimball and Willard Richards, were upheld by the unanimous consent and voice and prayers of

God's people. Thus the first great calamity to the Church was remedied, and the fullness of the presidency was again restored.

Millennial Star, 61:147-49.

MEMORIES OF AURELIA S. ROGERS

"It is generally known that our enemies seeing the prosperity of the Saints began to hunt up excuses for serving writs on the leading members of the Church; and that this was the cause of some of the brethren going to prison, while others hid themselves to keep out of their enemies' way, similar to what they have been doing of late years, with this difference, polygamy was not the offense at that time, but hatred toward the Prophet because of the religion the Lord had revealed to him. This persecution lasted until the massacre of Joseph and Hyrum Smith, after which there was comparative peace for over a year.

"Well do I remember the morning after the martyrdom of those noble men. A gloom was cast over the whole city of Nauvoo, men, women and children wept for their departed Prophet and Patriarch. I witnessed the long procession that followed the bodies of our beloved leaders as they were taken to Joseph's Mansion, where they laid in state until the people could take a last look at them and say farewell. My father lifted me thru one of the windows of the Mansion as the doorways were thronged with people, when after viewing the bodies I was passed again and taken home."

Life Sketches, by Aurelia S. Rogers, pp. 31-32.

THE SORROW AND GLOOM ON THE DAY OF THE MARTYRDOM

By LOUISA BARNES PRATT

In the spring of '44, I took up a school in my own house. It was attended with great difficulty, and confusion, being a crowded school in a small room. But it brought me in a little. There were continual hostilities in Nauvoo from either one source or another. Brother Joseph Smith went with his wife to Dixon, an adjoining county, to visit his wife's relatives. Officers from Missouri were lying in wait to kidnap and take him across the river, for which they were to receive a reward. They started with him, called at a public house for the night, *when he made signs to the landlord that he was a free mason.* He was immediately taken out of their custody, the two men were arrested for assault and battery, and brought to Nauvoo in chains. There was great excitement when it was reported that the Prophet was returning, bringing his enemies as prisoners. Lawyer Dixon attended Mr. Smith on his way home; and addressed a crowded assembly in his behalf, while the two prisoners were sitting by his side on the stand. After the exercises, which were exciting in the extreme, Mr. Smith invited, or rather, conveyed the prisoners to his house, took off their shackles, seated them at his table with his wife and mother, treated them as friends instead of enemies. He gave them their liberty. They went to

Carthage and cursed their bad luck in not getting their prey across the river and receiving their booty, so little did unmerited kindness humble their proud hearts.

It was eventually announced that the government of the state had taken up arms against the citizens of Nauvoo; and Joseph Smith was summoned to Carthage to be tried for treason. The governor pledged the faith of the state that he should have a fair and impartial trial. He at first seemed unwilling to go, but being urged by some who had more confidence in the governor's promise, he consented. He was heard to say as he rode on the way: "I am going like a lamb to the slaughter, henceforth it will be said of me, 'He was murdered in cold blood.'" On the morning preceding the murder, the governor rode into Nauvoo with troops, made a speech to the people, in which he railed them in a sarcastic manner for carrying arms.

While the governor was speaking, the report of guns was heard from Carthage. He was in bold terms affirming that Gen. Smith's going to Carthage, according to demand, had saved the city from being burned and the women and children from being put to the sword and perishing by it. The moment the guns were heard, he dismissed the assembly abruptly, jumped on his horse and rode away, as if fearing the people would divine the import and he would be in danger in spite of his troops. He continued his journey, not even stopping in Carthage to witness the bloody deed committed; not halting till he had gone twenty-five miles beyond that place. The brethren went with great speed to the spot, anticipating the tragedy. The citizens were greatly terrified, supposing the exasperated Mormons would burn the town, but so intense was their sorrow, revenge found no place in their hearts. Dumb with anguish, even to profound silence, they laid the dead bodies of the two noble martyrs in a wagon and drove solemnly towards the city where thousands were watching in breathless sorrow for their return.

Such consternation was never known since the rocks were rent, and the sun darkened, when Christ the Lamb was slain! Had the sun and moon fallen from their orbits and left the world in total darkness, it would not have betokened a more irretrievable despoilation! I thought the Church was ruined forever! I rushed into my garden when the news was confirmed and poured out my soul in such bitterness as I had never felt before. The inconceivable cruelty of our enemies!

This was the 28th of June, 1844. At dusk a report came that a thousand dollar reward was offered for the head of the Prophet, and that the mob was at Warsaw, coming across the river! The Legion was called out in the night. Such a tramping of horses was heard, the bass drum beat with astonishing loudness, every blow seemed to strike on my heart, and did really inflict pain, so dreadful was my fear. It was a still night, and the moon was at the full. A night of death it seemed, and everything conspired to make it solemn! The voices of the officers were heard calling the men together and coming in the distance made it fall on the heart like a funeral knell. The women were assembled in groups, weeping and praying, some wishing terrible punishment on the murderers; others acknowledging the hand of God in the event.

I could feel no anger or resentment. I felt the deepest humility before God. I thought continually of his words: "Be still and know that I am God." My children clung to me with great fear. They heard talk of hiding them in case the mob should come in. The question arose, where could we hide them? A deep cellar was suggested, a trap door and carpet overspread. They shuddered at the thought of being concealed in such a place. We concluded to take our chances together and trust in the Lord. I went to bed, but not to sleep. I could hear the men on parade; my whole system was in agitation. I arose in the morning with great prostration and walked my room to and fro.

Later I awakened the children, told them to dress and we would go and see the bodies of our dead leaders. It was the day appointed, and to appearance all the world was there! The Saints had assembled from the settlements abroad through the country. The coffins were placed in a long hall in the Mansion House, a door at each end. The multitude was required to pass through, looking at the corpses as they passed. This occupied the time from early sunrise till dusky evening. The features of Joseph Smith looked natural, but those of Hyrum were terribly marred and disfigured. My second daughter trembled exceedingly at sight of him. I regretted having brought her there to witness the spectacle. The elder one grieved as we all did, but betrayed less excitement. The bodies were conveyed, whither we knew not.

When the solemn event took place, the Twelve Apostles were nearly all absent. They soon returned, and we were all anxiety to know what they would say. President Brigham Young spoke words which pierced my heart like a dagger! Said he, "Had I been here, Joseph should not have gone to Carthage!" The bare idea that any one, or many, had been in fault was terrible to me. Had Joseph given the command, every man, woman and child would have stood in his defense, even to the loss of their own lives. Afterwards brother Willard Richards rehearsed what transpired at Carthage jail. He said everything to console the people; what it was to accomplish a purpose in the Almighty as disposer of events; referred to many remarks of the Prophet Joseph during his confinement, showing that he was aware of his approaching dissolution; of the hymns they sang in prison, and how calm he was.

From that hour I watched for words of comfort, and drank them in as I would an antidote to relieve pain. The enemies stood afar off and wondered; seemed waiting to see if the saints would seek to revenge the wrongs done them. When they found it was not the design of the injured, they again began their aggressions. In the meantime, the work on the Temple rolled on with astonishing rapidity. Everyone seemed inspired with renewed vigor and determination to have the Lord's house completed, and their blessings received, before being compelled to leave the place which was soon anticipated after the tragedy.

There was no lack of evidence in regard to the perpetrators of the bloody deed. I was intimately acquainted with one Miss

Graham, a truthful, amiable girl who was living with an aunt of hers in Warsaw at the time. She testified that the mobbers ate supper at the Hotel where she lived that night on their return from the scene of action, and that she heard certain individuals, calling them by name, boast of their conquest, killing prisoners in jail. One says: "It was my rifle that did the deed;" another, "It was mine." And thus they exulted in the committal of as black-hearted a crime as ever stained the annals of history! Was the testimony heeded by the judges? It was not.

Mormondom's First Woman Missionary, pp. 230-32.

THE LORD PROTECTED THE SAINTS IN NAUVOO

FROM THE DIARY OF ELECTA C. WILLIAMS
SEPTEMBER 1, 1943

The night after Joseph and Hyrum were killed, the mob went to Golden Point to set fire to the city of Nauvoo, and burn the bodies of those martyred. Brother Andrus returned home. He was taken sick while away. All the family were on guard, my husband with the rest. The bass drums were to be beat if any thing alarming should occur before midnight. We heard from the men, saying: "Run, the mob are upon us." The drums were beating violently. The dogs began barking and the cattle looking in every direction. What a night with flashing and vivid lightning and distant thunder in the heavens. Above us we discovered a small cloud. It followed the Mississippi, kept spreading as if to gather the whole waters of that noble river. The mob were marching onward to their destined point of slaughter when the rain began pouring, destroying their ammunition, drenching them to the skin, and killing some of them. The mob was glad to retreat. Thus the Lord on that day fought the battle of the Saints, never to be forgotten by those who were an eye witness of such a scene. The Lord has promised to fight the battles of his people.

Copied at the home of Lettie M. Berrett, Pleasant View, Weber Co., Utah.

THE WAILING OF THE SAINTS AT THE MARTYRDOM

On the 20th of June Brother Joseph sent word to all the apostles to return home immediately; and on the 24th he, with seventeen others, went to Carthage. At this time I was living at Big Mound, an English settlement about eight miles from Nauvoo, and there, while engaged in putting in sod corn I heard of the Prophet's and Hyrum's death. The next morning I started to Carthage with those who went after the bodies. We met them on the road, Dr. Richards having dressed the wounds of John Taylor and started for Nauvoo with Joseph's and Hyrum's bodies.

The wailing of the Saints when they saw the martyrs was terrible. Ten thousand people were addressed by Apostle Richards, who admonished them to keep the peace and trust to the law for a remedy for the awful crimes which had been committed, and if the law failed, to call upon God in heaven to avenge us of our wrongs. The bodies were placed in coffins, the funeral was held, while deep grief filled our hearts and sorrow rested heavily upon us—a stricken

people. The woe of the Saints cannot be described. Our Prophet
and Patriarch dead, only two of the apostles with us and one of
them supposed to be dying, and all this time we were in constant
expectation of an attack by the mob army.

Our enemies were sure now that they had destroyed the gospel
work, but it still lives and will live, for it is the eternal work of
God, and I here bear my testimony that I know that Joseph Smith,
who established it, was a Prophet holy and pure.

Like sheep without a shepherd, we felt lost and bewildered,
and seriously we discussed the question: "Who was highest in
authority? Who held the keys of the kingdom?" On August 6th
the apostles arrived from the East, while we were still uncertain
about choosing a guardian of the Church and it was a great relief
to greet them among us. A council of the priesthood was called and
it was not long before, with the Twelve at the head, we felt that
all things would be managed and directed aright. In the person of
the President of the Twelve, Brigham Young, we knew that a great
character had arisen, to build upon the foundation laid by Joseph
Smith, a kingdom whose equal "there never was in the world."
Now feeling at peace, we pursued our usual work: the work on the
Temple was pushed forward as rapidly as possible.

Life of Christopher Layton, pp. 20-22.

THE POWERS OF DARKNESS PREVAILED

The death of Joseph and Hyrum was a dreadful blow to the
people. They had felt towards Joseph as we imagine the disciples
of Jesus, when he was upon the earth, felt towards him. You
recollect that when the Savior was crucified two of them said: "We
trusted that it had been he which should have redeemed Israel."
They had expected Joseph would live to lead the people until Zion
should be redeemed. They were fully aware of the hatred of the
mob, of the blood-thirsty disposition which Joseph's enemies had
towards him; but he had escaped so many times from their traps
that they hoped he would escape again as he had in times past.
They knew his innocence of every charge brought against him, and
they had confidence that no court could, with the least degree of
fairness, convict him of any wrong doing. The thought of his being
killed by his enemies had not entered into the minds of the majority
of the people, the news of his death, therefore, fell upon them with
stunning and overwhelming effect, and they were almost crushed
by the dreadful intelligence. Oh, how dark and gloomy was that
day at Nauvoo. The night after the murder, and before the word
nad come from Carthage, was one of horror to many. Numbers
arose from sleepless couches to go forth and relate to their neighbor the singular feelings they had through the night. But when
they emerged from their dwellings and heard the dreadful tidings
that Joseph and Hyrum had been slain, that John Taylor had been
desperately wounded and Willard Richards had barely escaped, the
cheeks of all were blanched, and the breath suspended, as they
listened to the tale of horror. It was too horrible to believe that
lives of such purity had been quenched in blood. The wailings and
lamentations of the whole people ascended to heaven on that day.

On the day of the murder of the Prophet and Patriarch, those of the Twelve Apostles who were on missions, as well as other elders, had warnings that something dreadful had happened. They felt cast down and a spell of horror seemed to rest upon them. Some wept without knowing why they should do so, except that they were filled with unaccountable sadness and gloom. The succeeding night was a miserable one to them. When they received the news of the death of Joseph and Hyrum the cause of these feelings was explained, though it was difficult then for several of them to believe that they were dead.

Life of the Prophet Joseph, by George Q. Cannon, *Instructor,* Vol. 14.

I LONG FOR MY REST, SAID THE PROPHET

By Benjamin F. Johnson

"Oh! I am so tired—so tired that I often feel to long for my day of rest. For what has there been in this life but tribulation for me? From a boy I have been persecuted by my enemies, and now even my friends are beginning to join them, to hate and persecute me! Why should I not wish for my time of rest?"

His words to me were ominous, and they brought a shadow as of death over my spirit, and I said: "Oh, Joseph! how could you think of leaving us? How as a people could we do without you?" He saw my feelings were sorrowful and said kindly· "Bennie, *if I were on the other side of the veil I could do many times more for my friends than I can do while I am with them here.*" But the iron had gone into my soul, and I felt that in his words there was a meaning that boded sorrow, and I could not forget them.****

After returning to Macedonia I saw no more of Brothers Joseph and Hyrum, but learned early on June 28th of their assassination. To attempt to delineate the feelings of woe and unutterable sorrow that swelled every heart too full for tears, I need not attempt. I stood up, dazed with grief, could groan but could not weep. The fountain of tears was dry! "Oh, God! what will thy orphan church and people now do!" was the only feeling or thought that now burst out in groans.

I did not go to see their mutilated bodies. I had no wish to look into their grave; I knew they were not there, and the words of Brother Joseph began to come back to me: "I could do so much more for my friends if I were on the other side of the veil." These words—"my friends"—oh, how glad that he was my friend. These thoughts gradually gained the empire in my heart, and I began to realize that in his martyrdom there was a great eternal purpose in the heavens. But we were not able, as yet, to comprehend such a necessity. I could begin now to feel just what he meant, and his words, "do for my friends" to me, were like the promise of Jesus to provide mansions for his disciples that they might be with him always. These things now were my consolation, and when I could begin to rejoice in them, the fountains of my tears began to flow, and I grew in consolation from day to day.

My Life's Review, pp. 97, 102.

CHAPTER 14

The Identity and Trial of the Murderers

AFFIDAVIT OF WILLIAM M. DANIELS

State of Illinois, }
Hancock County, } ss.

On the 4th day of July, 1844, came William M. Daniels before me, Aaron Johnson, a justice of the peace within and for said county, and after being duly sworn, deposeth and saith that on Saturday, the 22nd day of June, 1844, he came to the town of Warsaw, in said county of Hancock, and continued there until the Thursday following, the 27th day of June; that on that morning your affiant joined the rifle company commanded by Jacob Davis; that the lieutenant and ———— Chittenden, Esq., said that as the governor would be absent from Carthage that day, that they would send ten men from each of the two companies to join the Carthage Greys, and kill the two Generals Smith, and if the governor opposed, to kill him too; that among those twenty men were Mr. Houck, a tailor, and Mr. Stephens, a cooper; the rest of the two companies marched towards Golden's Point to the railroad crossing, when they were met by the governor's order to disband all the troops, and Colonel Williams disbanded them.

That then the captains called them to order, saying they had no command over them, but wished them to form in line, which they did; that then Mr. Sharp, the editor of the *Warsaw Signal*, urged by a speech the necessity of *killing the two Smiths*, and a vote was then called who would go and do it.

Captain Davis and about twenty men went home, the residue, eighty-four men, went to Carthage, having six runners ahead to stop the twenty men who had before started for Carthage.

Soon after they started, one of the Carthage Greys met them with a letter, saying it was a most delightful time, the governor had gone, they could now kill Joseph and Hyrum Smith, and must do it quick before the governor returned; that they then turned to the left between the Warsaw and Nauvoo roads, and were not seen again by your affiant till they arrived at the jail in Carthage; that among the names of those who committed the murder at the jail in Carthage, Hancock county aforesaid, on the 27th day of June, 1844, at about 5 o'clock and 20 minutes, was Colonel Levi Williams, of Green Plains precinct, Captain Wires, ———— Chittenden, Esq., of Warsaw. ———— Houck, the tailor, Captain Grovenor, three brothers by the name of Stephens, coopers, ———— Allen, a cooper, all of Warsaw, and a man by the name of Mills, who was wounded in the right arm.

That your affiant would further state that this company before mentioned were painted black; that the guns of the guard at the jail were loaded with blank cartridges; that this was an arrangement entered into by the Carthage Greys, as said the messenger who came to meet said company in the morning.

That your said affiant saw Joseph Smith leap from the window of the jail, and that one of the company picked him up and placed him against the well curb, and several shot him, Colonel Williams exclaiming, Shoot him! Damn him! Shoot him! and further your affiant saith not.   [Signed]   William M. Daniels.

D. H. C. pp. 162-63.

IDENTITY OF THE MEMBERS OF THE MOB

The following letter from Sheriff J. B. Backenstos to Brigham Young, dated June 29, 1844:

ROLL OF CARTHAGE GREYS AND OFFICERS JUNE 27th, A. D. 1844

Robert F. Smith, Captain
F. A. Worrell,
S. O. Williams,
M. Barnes, Jun.
Lieutenants

Guard at the Jail, June 27, 1844

F. A. Worrell, officer of the guard
Franklin Rhodes
William Baldwin
Levi Street, lives near Mendon, Adams county, Illinois
Joseph Hawley, lives in Carthage, Illinois
Anthony Barkman, lives in Carthage, Illinois
Clabourn Wilson, lives in Carthage, Illinois

Balance of (Company of) Greys

Edwin Baldwin, lives near Carthage, Illinois
James D. Barnes, lives near Carthage, Illinois
Marvin Hamilton, lives in Carthage
Ebenezer Rand, lives in Carthage
John W. Maith, lives in Carthage
Thomas Griffith, lives in Carthage
Frederick Loring, lives in Carthage, Illinois
Leyrand Doolittle, lives in Carthage, Illinois
Lewis C. Stevenson, lives in Carthage
Noah M. Rekard, lives in Carthage
Eli H. Williams, lives in Carthage
H. T. Wilson, lives in Carthage

Albert Thompson, lives in Carthage, Illinois
Walter Bagby, left the country, gone to Louisiana, and died
George C. Waggoner, lives 2½ miles north of Carthage
Crockett Wilson, lives 8 miles east of Carthage
Thomas J. Dale, lives 5 miles east of Carthage
Richard Dale, lives 5 miles east of Carthage

The Carthage Greys never numbered more than about thirty, rank and file; during the June mob war, several joined for the time only, who reside at other places, and whose names are unknown to me. The Carthage Greys were nearly to a man parties in the June massacre.

Green Plains

Captain Weir's company of about sixty men

Warsaw

Captain J. C. Davis' company of about sixty men
Captain Wm. N. Grover's company of about sixty men
Captain Mark Aldrich's company of about sixty men, comprising the entire settlement in and about Warsaw and Green Plains, with the exception

of the Walkers, Gillhams, Paytons, Bledsors, Gallahers, Byrrs, Kimballs, Worthens, Summervilles, and Bedells, and the Mormon families who resided in that part of the county at that time.

Those active in the massacre at Carthage—supplied by Sheriff J. B. Backenstos

The leaders of the Hancock mob, and those who took an active part in the massacre of Joseph and Hyrum Smith are—

Thomas C. Sharp, *Warsaw Signal*, Illinois, editor
Colonel Levi Williams, Green Plains, Illinois, farmer
William N. Grover, Warsaw, Illinois, lawyer
Jacob C. Davis, Warsaw, Illinois, lawyer
Mark Aldrich, Warsaw, Illinois, no business
Henry Stephens, Warsaw, Illinois, lawyer
George Rockwell, Warsaw, Illinois, druggist
James H. Wood, Warsaw, Illinois, blacksmith
Calvin Cole, Warsaw, Illinois, tavernkeeper
William B. Chipley, Warsaw, Illinois, doctor
.... Hays, Warsaw, Illinois, doctor
J. D. Mellen, Warsaw, Illinois, merchant
E. W. Gould, Warsaw, Illinois, merchant
Samuel Fleming, Warsaw, Illinois, constable
John Montague, Warsaw, Illinois, no business
Jas. Gregg, Warsaw, Illinois, no business
J. C. Elliott, Warsaw, Illinois, no business
Lyman Prentiss, Warsaw, Illinois, no business
D. W. Matthews, now St. Louis, Missouri, merchant
J. B. Matthews, now St. Louis, Missouri, merchant
Trueman Hosford, Warsaw, Illinois, farmer
Four of the Chittendens, Warsaw, Illinois, different occupations
J. W. Athey, Warsaw, Illinois, no business
Onias C. Skinner, now of Quincy, Illinois, lawyer
Calvin A. Warren, Quincy, Illinois, lawyer
George W. Thatcher, Carthage, Illinois, county clerk
James W. Brattle, Carthage, Illinois, land shark
Alexander Sympson, Carthage, Illinois, land shark
Jason H. Sherman, Carthage, Illinois, lawyer
Michael Reckard, one-half mile west of Carthage, Illinois, farmer
Thomas Morrison, Carthage, Illinois, lawyer
E. S. Freeman, Carthage, Illinois, blacksmith
Thomas L. Barnes, Carthage, Illinois, quack doctor
John Wilson, Carthage, Illinois, tavernkeeper
Edward Jones, 5 miles north of Carthage, farmer
Captain James E. Dunn, Augusta, Illinois, tavernkeeper
Joel Catlin, Augusta, Illinois, farmer, etc.
William D. Abernethy, Augusta, Illinois, farmer, etc.
Erastus Austin, constable, etc.
.... Austin, loafer
Reuben Graves, St. Mary's, Illinois, farmer
Henry Garnett, St. Mary's, Illinois, farmer
F. J. Bartlett, St. Mary's, Illinois, miller
Valentine Wilson, St. Mary's, Illinois, farmer
Sylvester M. Bartlett, editor of the *Quincy Whig*
Major W. B. Warren, a damned villian
Colonel .... Gettis, Fountain Green, Illinois, farmer
Matthews McClaughny, Fountain Green, Illinois, farmer
Nickerson Wright, Fountain Green, Illinois, farmer
John McAuley, Camp Creek Precinct, Illinois, one of the worst men in Hancock
William H. Rollason, Pontusuc, Illinois
John M. Finch, Pontusuc, Illinois
Francis M. Higbee, Pontusuc, Illinois
.... Douglas, Pontusuc, Illinois, schoolmaster
George Backman, one of the Durfee murderers
.... Moss or Morse, one of the Durfee murderers

Jacob Beck, one of the Durfee murderers

Backman lives in Carthage, Moss or Morse, and Jacob Beck have left the country, but expect to return.

The foregoing is a pretty large list; there are others of the smaller fry which I deem unworthy of notice, inasmuch as they were led on through the influence of the leaders, and whiskey. I most cheerfully give you any information in my power in reference to this matter; the only thing that I regret about is, that these things I am fearful will be put off so long that I will not live to see or hear of the awful vengeance which will in the end overtake the Hancock assassins. I have long been of the opinion that forbearance is no longer a virtue, let the guilty be made to answer for their crimes. Let justice be done, and all will be well.

The bloodhounds are still determined on taking my life; I can hear from them every once in a while. I will have to be exceedingly careful this summer, or they will have my scalp. They still act upon the principle that had it not been for me in September last, Worrell and McBradney would not have been killed, and the city of Nauvoo burned to the ground. They want to hold me responsible for everything that was done to put them down in their mob doings last year.

*   *   *   *   *

LIST OF THE MOB AT CARTHAGE ACCORDING TO WILLARD RICHARDS

'William Law	Wm. A. Rollason
Wilson Law	Wm. H. J. Marr
Robert D. Foster	S. M. Marr
Charles A. Foster	Sylvester Emmons
Francis M. Higbee	Alexander Sympson
Chauncey L. Higbee	John Eagle
Joseph H. Jackson	Henry O. Norton
John M. Finch	Augustine Spencer

The foregoing have been aided and abetted by—Charles Ivins and family, P. T. Rolfe, N. J. Higbee.

William Cook, and Sarah, his wife, formerly Sarah Crooks, of Manchester.'

D. H. C.: 142-46.

EVERY STATE OF THE UNION WAS REPRESENTED IN THE MOB

BY BRIGHAM YOUNG

The mob that collected at Carthage, Illinois, to commit that deed of blood contained a delegation representing every State in the Union. Each has received its blood stain. In the perpetration of this great national sin, they acted upon their own free volition which God implanted within them, as much so as if they had been willing to hearken to the advice of the Prophet and his friends when they showed them how to preserve the nation from destruction, how to do good to all, and how to introduce every holy principle that is calculated to bless and exalt a people. But, said they, "We will not hearken to the counsels of this man;" for, like the Jews of old, they were afraid if they let him live he would take away their place and nation. They not only feared the principles which he taught, but they feared the increasing numbers which followed him; they feared that if they let him alone he would incorporate in his religion all the religion there is that is good for anything, or that is according to the Bible, and all the honest, truthful and virtuous of the nation, they feared, would follow him;

and they feared that thereby they would be deprived of their rich emoluments and livings, so they concluded to get rid of him by slaying him. * * * If they had hearkened to the counsel of Joseph Smith, this nation would have had no wars; there would have been no division in the Government, but it would have gone on in harmony and prosperity.   J. D. 12:121.

PREPARATIONS FOR THE TRIAL

Letter written to Josiah Lamborn, Attorney General of Illinois

Review of difficulties attendant upon collection of evidence for the prospective trial of those charged with the murder of the Prophet and Patriarch Joseph and Hyrum Smith.

Sir: We are this evening informed by Mr. Scott that it is your wish as prosecuting attorney vs. the murderers of the Generals Smith that the Mormons should hunt up the witnesses in the case, and that Mr. Murray McConnell had conveyed the idea that there was a committee in the county whose business it was to collect and arrange the testimony against the day of trial and that said committee are supposed to be Mormons, etc. etc.

Now, Sir, in behalf of the Church of Jesus Christ of Latter-day Saints; or, if you choose, the Mormon fraternity, we beg leave to state to you, what has been often reiterated by us, and which is a well known fact, both to our people and the state, viz: that the difficulty causing the pending trials is not between the Mormons and anti-Mormons; nor between the Mormons and the murderers; but it is between the state and the prisoners or offenders.

The facts are, the Messrs. Smiths were murdered while in the charge of the state, relying on the plighted faith of the state for protection, and not in the presence of Mormon witnesses, for the Mormons were not there, but doubtless in the presence of many who were not Mormons.

To show our loyalty to the institutions of our country and preserve peace in the country, as a people, we pledged ourselves to abide the operations of the law as directed by the proper authorities of the commonwealth; and that we would abide the decisions of the court, not taking vengeance into our own hands, (as was then feared by some) or commencing prosecutions, to which we have strictly adhered, and intend still to adhere, that our pledge may be honorably redeemed in the sight of all men, although we have been strongly solicited to enter the field of prosecution, and that, too, by the state or her agents: for instance when Mr. McConnell was engaged in preparation for the prosecution he came to Nauvoo and strongly solicited the Mormons to come out as complainants and assist in procuring witnesses, etc.; but we replied that we had had nothing to do with the affair, and wanted nothing to do with it; and for us to enlist in attempting to bring the murderers to justice, no matter how legal in our movements, it would be construed into a persecution, or a desire to pick a quarrel on our part, which we were and still are determined to avoid, even every appearance of evil, and cut off every occasion of our enemies, or of those who are ready to seize upon any pretext to make us trouble.

We are decidedly for peace, and we ever have been and as the murders were committed while the murdered were in immediate charge of the state, all we ask is, that the state will prosecute the case to final judgment, and redeem her pledge, as we have ours; or if she choose to abandon the prosecution we shall submit peaceably; although, for public good, we would prefer that justice should take place.

We are unacquainted with the statute which suffers indicted murderers to roam at large month after month without arrest; or, after delivery, or surrender, to run at pleasure before trial, and we know not what other similar laws we might come in contact with, and be liable to break to our own endangering or disadvantage, should we attempt to have anything to do with the case in question.

It is reported to us, true or false we know not, that the sheriff of Hancock county and his deputies have been forbidden by the court to act in pending trials, and that the jurors have been discharged without impaneling. If this be true we are unacquainted with the statutes in the case and have nothing to say.

When Mr. McConnell was here last fall, at his earnest solicitation, we collected all the information in our possession and presented the same to him, supposing he would prosecute the case to final judgment. He took minutes at the time and probably has them now, if he has not handed them over, of which you must be acquainted, better than we, and of which we did not preserve minutes: we know of no new information since that period.

We were happy to hear that the trials had been committed to your able charge, and anticipated that you would have made us a visit before the sitting of the court; and we still anticipate that after court you will make us a visit, that we may have the pleasure of a more general acquaintance among our citizens; and we feel confident that such a visit would be highly appreciated by our friend, General Young, with whom we understand you are acquainted.

We shall be ever ready to assist in favoring the ends of right so far as we can do it and not give any occasion of excitement which would be detrimental to public peace.

We are Sir,

Most Respectfully
Your Servts.
[Signed] George A. Smith,
John Smith.

D. H. C. 7:415-16.

THE CHURCH NOT TO PROSECUTE ASSASSINS

'Nauvoo, July 16, 1844.

To Thos. H. Owen.

Sir,—I am sorry that there has been delay which caused your letter to arrive so late to hand, and I feel thankful for the very kind and sympathetic manner in which you express yourself towards us as a people, and shall be very thankful if you will continue your favors to me whenever anything may occur, and you may depend upon my doing the same to yourself.

In regard to the assassination of the Generals Smith, we do not intend to take any action in the case whatever, but leave ourselves entirely in the hands of the governor and the majesty of the law, to mete just and retributive justice in the matter.

You may rest perfectly assured that we never did act on the offensive, or against the law, but shall continue the same course, which appears to have given you so much satisfaction, and act entirely on the defensive, and abide the law.

In haste, sir, I remain yours, etc.,

Willard Richards.

D. H. C. 193:94.

GEORGE D. WATTS' REPORT OF THE CARTHAGE TRIAL

'District Court of Illinois,
Carthage, Hancock County, State of Iillinois,
May 19, 1845.

The Hon. Richard M. Young of Quincy on the bench. The forenoon was spent in organizing. Adjourned at twelve m.

Court met at two p.m.

Colonel Levi Williams, Thomas C. Sharp, editor of the *Warsaw Signal,* Jacob C. Davis, state senator, Mark Aldrich and William N. Grover were held to bail with each other for sureties, in the sum of one thousand dollars each, to make their appearance in court each day of the term; they were indicted for the murder of Joseph Smith at Carthage jail on the twenty-seventh day of June, 1844.

The court decided that their case would be tried on Wednesday morning, May 21st.

Accordingly the sheriff notified the witnesses for both parties to make their appearance on said morning at seven o'clock; the court then proceeded to other business.

Wednesday Morning, May 21st.

Court opened.

The names of the counsel for the defense are as follows: William A. Richardson, O. H. Browning, Calvin A. Warren.

Josiah Lamborn, Esq. for the people.

Colonel Wm. A. Richardson presénted before the court two affidavits drawn out by the defendants to quash the array. The charge of prejudice, consanguinity and partiality was preferred by these affidavits against the county commissioners, the sheriff and his deputies in the arrangement of the present panel of jurors; that their design was to hurt and prejudice the present trial, and thus endanger the lives of the defendants. On these grounds the defendants pleaded for the quashing of the array. After referring to the statute to show the provision made for such a proceeding he submitted to the court.

The attorney for the people then arose and made the following observations, *viz.:* That the doctrine advanced by Colonel Richardson was a novelty to him, as the affidavits of the defendants predicated no charge against the present panel of jurors. either individually or collectively; he showed from the statute that the array could not be quashed upon the above principle, neither did he believe the officers of the county could be discharged upon a mere *exparte* affidavit, but the charges ought to be made and affidavits filed and a trial had before the court. He said it was the first time he had heard of such a proceeding to quash the array, at the same time nothing alleged against it individually or collectively.

He showed that the statute referred to by Colonel Richardson applied to civil and not criminal cases. He could not suffer the idea of having the panel quashed by the discharge of all the officers of the county upon a mere *exparte* affidavit, and that too made by five men indicted for murder. He asked for a precedent in all the experience of this state or any other in criminal cases; he defied them to produce a single case.

Mr. Browning, for the defense, said, that although there had not been a precedent in the United States for such a proceeding, the reason is there has never been a case like this in the United States. He contended that such a proceeding is fully warranted by the English statutes and the statutes of the United States, that in a case like this the county commissioners, the sheriff and his deputies can be discharged, and in their place can be appointed elisors for the purpose of choosing another jury.

The court ruled that the jury be discharged and elisors appointed.

The court then adjourned.

Thursday, May 22nd

The court appointed Thomas H. Owen and William D. Abernethy elisors and they selected a full panel of jurors.

Four panels of jurors were successively called and out of the ninety-six men twelve were selected as a jury satisfactory to the defense.

Mr. Lamborn prosecuted before this jury in a manner which showed clearly to every bystander the certainty of the guilt of the prisoners who were honorably acquitted. Mr. Frank Worrell, who had command of the guard at the jail at the time of the massacre, being summoned as a witness, and being asked by the prosecuting attorney if the guard had their guns loaded with blank cartridges at the time of the attack on the jail refused to answer, assigning as a reason that he could not without incriminating himself.'   *D. H. C.* 421-22.

COMMENTS ON THE VERDICT BY ORSON F. WHITNEY

The trial took place at Carthage, beginning on the 19th of May, 1845. Sixty names had been presented to the Grand Jury of the Circuit Court, as being implicated in the crime, but only nine men had been indicted. * * * One of them, Levi Williams, the leader of the mob, was not only a Colonel of militia, he was also a Baptist preacher, and, of course, an "eminently respectable and conservative" man. Judge Richard M. Young presided at the trial, and James H. Ralston and Josiah Lamborn conducted the prosecution. The defense was represented by William A. Richardson, O. H. Browning, Calvin A. Warren, Archibald Williams, O. C. Skinner, and Thomas Morrison. The panel of the trial jury was as follows: Jesse Griffits, Joseph Jones, William Robertson, William Smith, Joseph Massey, Silas Griffits, Jonathan Foy, Solomon J. Hill, James Gittings, F. M. Walton, Jabez A. Beebe, and Gilmore Callison. The trial lasted until the 30th of May. During its progress, Mr. Warren, of counsel for the defense, argued, it is said, in the course of his plea, that if the prisoners were guilty of murder, then he himself was guilty; that it was the public opinion that the Smiths ought to be killed, and public opinion made the law; consequently it was not murder to kill them. Evidently this wretched piece of sophistry had weight with the jury in making up their verdict.

"In the light of such statements as these, the verdict (not guilty) is easily explained. The jury may have been 'ignorant enough and indifferent enough' in the first place, as alleged; but they doubtless became well enough informed as to the fate that would befall them if their findings failed to please the mob, and were sufficiently interested to provide against the perilous contingency."   *Mormon Prophet's Tragedy*, pp. 89-90.

GOV. FORD'S REVIEW OF THE TRIAL

During the progress of these trials, the judge was compelled to permit the courthouse to be filled and surrounded by armed bands, who attended court to browbeat and overawe the administration of justice. The judge himself was in a duress, and informed me that he did not consider his life secure any part of the time. The consequence was, that the crowd had everything their own way; the lawyers for the defense defended their clients by a long and elaborate attack on the governor; the armed mob stamped with their feet and yelled their approbation at every sarcastic and smart thing that was said; and the judge was not only forced to hear it, but to lend it a kind of approval. Josiah Lamborn was attorney for the prosecution; and O. H. Browning. O. C. Skinner, Calvin A. Warren and William A. Richardson, were for the defense.   *Ford's History of Illinois*, p. 354. *D. H. C.* 7:50.

CORONER'S VERDICT ON MARTYRDOM

(The following appears as a press dispatch, dated, Carthage, Ill., September 11th:

An interesting discovery was made by Thomas B. Griffiths, a pioneer citizen, while hunting among a pile of rubbish in one of the court-house jury rooms. It is the original coroner's verdict on the killing of Joseph and Hyrum Smith at the old Carthage jail, on June 28, 1844. The verdict reads as follows:

"We, the jury, having been duly sworn by George W. Stigoll, coroner of Hancock County, diligently to inquire, and a true presentment make, in what manner and by whom Joseph Smith and

Hyrum Smith, whose dead bodies were found in and at the jail of Hancock County, on the 28th of June, 1844, came to their deaths, after having heard the evidence and upon full inquiry, concerning the facts and a careful examination of the said bodies, do find that deceased came to their deaths by violence, and that the body of the said Joseph Smith has upon it the following marks, to-wit: A bullet wound near the right breast and another in the right shoulder, and that the said Hyrum Smith has the following marks, to-wit: A wound in the throat by a bullet and a wound in the abdomen, inflicted by some person or persons to the jury unknown and which the jury find to be the cause of their deaths."

The document is signed by Wesley Williams, Franklin J. Barlett, Aaron Griffiths, Antony Barklan, George C. Waggoner, Peter Bioan, George Bachman, Thomas Barnett, Elam S. Freeman, John Maherman, Simon Pennock, Samuel Gilpin.

Endorsement: "Verdict of the jury on an inquest upon the bodies of Joseph Smith and Hyrum Smith, filed, October 23, A. D., 1844."

J. B. Backenstoe, Clerk.

The document does not appear to have been filed until four months after the killing and the inquest. There can be no doubt as to its genuineness. It is written on an excellent quality of old style line foolscap, faintly ruled, and is discolored by time.

So far as is known, the only person now living who was on that jury is Mr. George C. Waggoner, of Pilot Grove township. Mr. Griffiths, who found the paper, saw the Smith killing. He was a member of the Carthage Greys, that guarded the jail.

The description of the wounds is so incorrect as to indicate that the document is not genuine. For example, the shot which produced the death of Hyrum Smith struck him in the face. The jurors, however, did not see the remains, which may account for errors in describing the wounds.

Millennial Star, Vol. 52:643-44 (1890).

THE VERDICT GIVEN IN ALL AGES

On Friday, May 30th (1845), the trial terminated, and the prisoners were acquitted in the case of Joseph Smith. This accords with the vote of the city council last July, that when the law failed to atone for the blood of our prophet and patriarch, shed at Carthage on the 27th of June last by a mob, we would refer the case to God for a righteous judgment, and we have never varied from that intention. If those men had been found guilty it would have been a novel case, and a violation of all the rules of the world in all martyr cases before.

The wicked who slew the prophets—boiled the children of Israel in cauldrons, who fried them in pans, who stoned a Stephen, who crucified the Son of God, and who harrassed the Saints to death for sport, or burnt them at the stake, did the laws of the land and its executors ever make the perpetrators atone for that innocent blood? No! alas, no!

We are satisfied to let the dead bury their dead. We ask for even handed justice, a righteous judgment, and we ask for our rights of the powers that be; and then content ourselves as Saints of the living God with the action of those powers, knowing that the judge of all the earth will reward every man according to his work in the day of judgment. The sentence of Jehovah upon Cain for martyring his brother Abel, is a sample for all murderers that have cursed themselves and the earth since — a fugitive and a vagabond in the earth shalt thou be.

The severest punishment upon a guilty conscience is a continual torment in the flesh without satisfying the demands of justice, wiping out the stains of innocent blood, or soothing the cry of widows and orphans to God for vengeance! Again let us say we are satisfied; we will not do wrong because others do. The ghosts that haunt the guilty by night and by day shall never torment us by shedding innocent blood. The blood of the prophets, the tears of the widows, and the weeping of orphan children, let alone the broken faith of a State, and the weakness of law, or even the scars of living witnesses, shall never cry in the ears of the Lord of Sabaoth for vengeance—because we have shed innocent blood, and hid ourselves under the cobwebs of chicanery.

Mormonism was ever above such artifices, being eternal truth; and while we seek peace and salvation, the murderers of Joseph and Hyrum Smith, be they who they may, can rest assured that their case, independent of all earthly tribunals, will be tried by the Supreme Judge of the universe, who has said, vengeance is mine, I will repay. The Mormons do not believe in taking life like the world, knowing that the scriptures say, "No murderer hath eternal life abiding in him."

Calm as a summer's morning; still as the noiseless light that flies from sphere to sphere; and orderly as the worlds roll in their circuits before the Lord, does Mormonism pursue the even tenor of its way—sounding to the nations of the earth good tidings of great joy; continually consoling one another;—with persecutions we are satisfied, with prosperity we are satisfied, yea, with all things we are satisfied when we know that God is satisfied! and from henceforth let all men who drive, despoil, rob, or murder us, do it on the credit of the nation; that if there be any glory in opposing Mormonism, all that act may share in that glory. As for us, we will honour the law, we will honour our country, we will honour virtue, we will honour God. *Millennial Star, 6:41-42.*

THE COURTS OF HEAVEN WILL TRY THE CASE

By the Mother of the Prophet Joseph

She (Lucy Smith) remarked that it was just eighteen years since Joseph Smith the Prophet had become acquainted with the contents of the plates; and then in a concise manner related over the most prominent points in the early history of her family; their hardships, trials, privations, persecutions, sufferings, etc.; some parts of which melted those who heard her to tears, more especially the part relating to a scene in Missouri, when her beloved son Joseph was condemned to be shot in fifteen minutes, and she by prodigious efforts was enabled to press through the crowd to where he was, and to give him her hand; but could not see his face; he took her hand and kissed it; she said, "let me hear your voice once more, my son;" he said, "God bless you my dear mother!" She gave notice that she had written her history, and wished it printed before we leave this place. *She then mentioned a discourse once delivered by Joseph after his return from Washington, in which he said that he had done all that could be done on earth to obtain justice for their wrongs; but they were all, from the president to the judge, determined not to grant justice. "But," said he, keep good courage, these cases are recorded in heaven, and I am going to lay them before the highest court in heaven." "Little," said she, "did I then think he was so soon to leave us, to take the case up himself. And don't you think this case is now being tried? I feel as though God was vexing this nation a little, here and there, and I feel that the Lord will let Brother Brigham take the people away. Here, in this city, lay my dead; my husband and children; and if so be the rest of my children go with you, (and would to God they may all go), they will not go without me; and if I go, I want my bones brought back in case I die away, and deposited with my husband and children."* D. H. C., Oct. 8, 1845, 7:471.

CHAPTER 15

The Prophet Joseph in Zion's Camp

(Excerpts)

BY L. O. LITTLEFIELD

I well remember when the name of Joseph Smith—the Prophet of God, whose destiny was to restore a knowledge of the fulness of the everlasting gospel to the earth at the commencement of the dispensation of the fulness of times—first saluted my ears in this life. I was then a mere boy, perhaps about nine years old.

While playing with my eldest brother Josiah in the dooryard at the home of my parents, some person, whose name has passed out of my memory, came and informed our parents that a strange circumstance had taken place in the western portion of the State of New York, the State in which we then resided. This so impressed my young mind that I ceased to play with my brother and listened to all that was said by the stranger. He related in substance that a young man reported that he had found a record of a people who once dwelt upon this land but had become extinct in consequence of internal wars that occurred in their midst. This record was said to have been engraved upon gold plates, which had been hid in the earth; and that the young man declared that an angel had directed him to the place where they had been concealed for very many years.

This impressed us all as being a very strange rumor, but I do not remember that myself or my parents heard anything additional to satisfy our awakened curiosity, until about two years from that date, after we had removed to the State of Michigan.

We settled in Oakland County, near to the town of Pontiac. Two Mormon Elders came there as missionaries. They were the expounders of a new and very strange religion. My father and mother were members of the Methodist church, but out of curiosity they went to hear them preach and took me with them.

We were a little late in arriving at the place where the meeting was being held, and we heard the speaker's voice distinctly before we reached the house. I have considered it somewhat singular, but it is truly a fact of which I have often spoken, that there was an inspiration or a convincing power which accompanied that man's voice that caused me to feel that he was a good man and was speaking the truth, though I had not distinctly understood a single word that he had uttered. After entering the house I believed every word that Elder Jared Carter, uttered to be the truth. I was convinced, even from the very sound of his voice, and still more confirmed after hearing his doctrines, that what he enunciated was what I have since more fully learned to be the fullness of the everlasting gospel, as was formerly preached by

Christ and His apostles. "Blessed are they who know the joyful sound," saith the Psalmist.

It is sufficient for my present purpose to record here that my parents soon were baptized, together with many others in that section of country. A branch of the Church was organized, over which Elder Samuel Bent was called to preside. This is the man who afterward became well known in the Church and was a member of the High Council in the days of Nauvoo.

During Elder Bent's presidency in that branch of the Church, Elders Hyrum Smith and Lyman Wight came there on a special mission. They had been sent by the Church at Kirtland, Ohio, to gather up as many of the Latter-day Saints as was consistent with circumstances to go up to Missouri to aid the brethren there who had been driven from their homes in Jackson County, and, if possible, accomplish their re-establishment upon their lands in that county, as those brethren were the lawful possessors of those lands, to which they held lawful titles, and from which they had been forcibly ejected by mobs.

I was away from my father's home when I learned of this proposed journey to Missouri. I was impressed with a desire— boy as I still was—to go with that company.

When I returned home I found to my delight that my father was going, and designed to take my brother Josiah and myself with him.

A company of, I believe, eighteen were soon in readiness for the journey. I cannot, from memory, give the names of all who composed the company, but, besides Elders Hyrum Smith and Lyman Wight, I remember Samuel Bent, Lyman Curtis, Meecham Smith, Alanson Colby, Ornon Hoton, Elijah Fordham, George Fordham, Waldo Littlefield, Josiah Littlefield, Lyman O. Littlefield; also three females: Sophronia Curtis, Charlotte Alverd and Sister Hoton, wife of Ornon Hoton.

Our wagons contained our provisions, clothing, bedding, cooking utensils, etc., which, all told, made the loads so heavy that the men had to walk about the entire distance, and the women walked a great portion of the time where the roads were in a condition to admit of their doing so. Our two honored leaders also walked the entire distance.

From our place of starting to the line which forms the western boundary of the State of Michigan was a long distance; but when we reached that we had then to travel across the states of Indiana and Illinois before reaching the Missouri River at Quincy. As this stream, at that point, divides Illinois and Missouri, and as we were all weary and the most of us footsore, we were pleased enough to reach it; and we felt additional joy because of our anticipation of soon joining the main portion of Zion's Camp which was being led by the Prophet Joseph Smith.

This camp—now so celebrated and making so important a portion of Church History—was encamped for a few days' rest at the farm and home where a brother in the Church, by the name of Burget, resided. It was there that our little Michigan company formed a junction with it.

Our company had already learned to love and honor Hyrum Smith because of his dignified and upright course and correct teachings; and we rejoiced that our eager desires to become acquainted with his brother, the Prophet Joseph Smith, were so soon to be realized.

*　　*　　*　　*　　*

Is it any wonder that I, so young in years, should be filled with sensations of intense pleasure and respect for him when I first met him? He was, indeed, more than all this, in my estimation, for I then and there felt, as it were, my whole being absorbed in the conviction and knowledge given me by the divine Spirit of truth, that he was a Prophet of God, raised up in the nineteenth century to restore the gospel that had been discarded by the people of the earth since the Savior was crucified and the prophets and apostles had been slain, or had fallen asleep in death. It surpasses the understanding of the carnal mind to comprehend the force of the testimony which the Spirit of divine truth brings to the minds of the honest in heart when convinced of the truth of the gospel or of the divine mission of God's chosen servants who are sent to deliver a gospel message or perform a work for the salvation and redemption of the fallen sons and daughters of Adam.

He received our little company with manifestations of friendship and joy. The meeting with himself and his brother Hyrum was as might have been expected with two such noble men, united together by natural ties and with souls enlightened by divine influences, the fruits of which was to them the knowledge that God lived and communicated His will from the heavens to them as He had done anciently before the channel of revelation was closed.

The camp had traveled up from Kirtland, Ohio, under a variety of difficulties. The wonder, in the later years of my reflections, has been how the people of the towns, cities and states through which they passed permitted them to pursue their way without interposing force to stop them. It is looked upon by me to this day as being miraculous. God was in it, or they never could have penetrated so many hundreds of miles of the dense population of the United States. Indeed, they were even armed, but only for purposes of self protection, and no intention was entertained to use their arms for aggressive purposes. But why were not the people so jealous of their motive as to deprive them of their arms or turn them back? My emphatic answer to this would be that the camp was not thus hindered because God was in the movement.

Partly for recuperative purposes and to effect a more thorough organization, Zion's Camp was halted at Brother Allred's place, at Salt River. The name of the county I cannot state, but it was no very great distance from the city of Quincy, across the Mississippi River, west. In this work of reconstruction, cleansing and brushing off the dust that necessarily accumulated after many hundred miles of travel, the members of the camp were busily engaged and preparing to continue their march still to the west.

The camping ground presented a city of tents and covered wagons. These were arranged in an order which made them quite convenient for all purposes of passing to and fro for horsemen, carriages or footmen. Visitors were struck with this feature of order, and seemed to look upon the camp as quite a novelty, and the people as being a class used to good order and thriftiness.

The visiting resident citizens at this point, as well as I remember, were by no means unfriendly, but were quite civil and courteous in their deportment towards the members of our company. Brother Allred and family were especially kind and active in making comfortable as many as possible of our large number.

The encampment at Brother Allred's was made, I think, two or three days previous to the arrival of our Michigan company. Our coming had been looked for and now that the junction had been formed, the main and active motive was to prepare for an advance as soon as possible. As I was then so very young I was naturally enough not made acquainted with the intricate or minute order in which the camp was organized for traveling; but I remember that they were classed into messes of tens for purposes of cooking, washing our clothing, eating, sleeping, etc. While there the men were paraded outside of the camp for exercise and instruction. This was an unpleasant feature for me, as I was too young and too small of stature to act with the men. This created within me, as I remember, some lonesome reflections. I sat down upon a rock where the men were passing, the better to observe their movements. While thus seated, the Prophet Joseph Smith, who happened to be passing by in quite a hurry, noticed me. He stepped to where I sat alone. It might have been my isolated position that attracted him. I knew not the motive; but that man, who to me appeared so good and so godlike, really halted in his hurry to notice me—only a little boy. Placing one of his hands upon my head, he said: "Well, bub, is there no place for you?"

This recognition from the man whom I then knew was a Prophet of God created within me a tumult of emotions. I could make him no reply. My young heart was filled with joy to me unspeakable. He passed on and left me in my lonely attitude, for he was then in quite a hurry to accomplish something pertaining to the movements of the men which could not be delayed.

I mention this circumstance as it illustrates a trait of his character, which in after years he has often been seen to exemplify. He was naturally fond of the young—especially little children. He did not like to pass a child, however small, without speaking to it. He has been known to actually cross a street if he saw a child alone on the opposite side, to speak to it or to inquire if it had lost its way.

These little acts of human sympathy were prompted by those innate qualities implanted in his heart which rendered it so easy and natural for him to be ever prompt in administering kindness and rendering aid to all who chanced to move within his accustomed rounds of life. He was not only kind and gentle to the youth, but the aged he treated with the respect due their whitened locks; and their tottering limbs could ever find ready and willing support on his strong arm, ever prompt to lead them to the place where inclination or duty called for their presence.

Thus I have made allusion to my first introduction to an acquaintance with Joseph Smith, the God-chosen Prophet of the nineteenth century. In my estimation he was good and great, and even one of God's noblemen. My subsequent acquaintance with him proved to me that my first estimate of his true character was not too highly formed.

Preparations were rapidly being made for the camp to move upon its westward journey. This required a great amount of care and labor to be performed. Every person was ready and willing to render whatever service Joseph advised, and his wishes were made known with such a good and friendly spirit that none could find a reason to feel anything but satisfied pleasure in pushing forward the necessary preparation.

The camp consisted of two hundred and five persons, all happy, satisfied and hopeful. They felt they were discharging a great duty which they owed both to God and to their brethren who had been by violence dispossessed of their homes and driven from the lands for which they had paid their money and secured legal titles. But we had still to travel a long and weary road which lay, portions of it at least, through a country thickly settled by people who we had reasons to believe were much prejudiced against us and who according to rumor, would oppose our advance when we should reach their settlements. We had but one alternative which was to trust in God and go ahead.

The bugle sounded for prayers night and morning, which service was attended to, not in mass with one person to act as intercessor, but this sacred duty was generally performed in the various tents and wagons according as the brethren were associated together in messes of tens, when some one of that little family would offer prayer for their respective number.

In connection with these seasons of devotion—especially after we had bowed the head and bent the knee in offering our supplications—the sweet singers would sing with the spirit and the understanding, some of the hymns which had been inspired in connection with the great latter-day work. And these hymns were rendered by the faith which the new and everlasting gospel had revived in the hearts of those humble and faithful followers of Christ. In all these seasons of prayer and singing there was felt the power of faith which flowed pure and uninterrupted from the fountain of light. Even the unbelieving strangers who happened to be passing were attracted by these exercises; but the hearts of some were hardened and filled with the spirit of rage and bitterness.

Frequently the leading men of the camp would speak to us and encourage us by their words and testimony concerning the truthfulness of the strange work which God had just brought to light. The Prophet himself frequently spoke to us in a collective capacity, and often with a power and force of utterance that exceeded anything that the members of the camp had ever before heard or seen manifested by mortal man. His inspired mind seemed to commune with, and at times, almost grasp the mind of Deity itself.

Hyrum Smith was much beloved by all the members of the camp for zeal, faithfulness and a straightforward, even course from day to day. His daily deportment was exemplary and whatever he said privately to the brethren or when he talked to them in a collective body, was received with approval and had great influence with them in stimulating them to endure the fatigues of travel with patience. He was a strong support to the Prophet and rendered every service in his power in helping to carry out his counsels and desires.

Men were detailed to stand guard every night to watch our animals and to see that the threats of molestation made occasionally by some of the inhabitants were not carried into effect.

The camp moved forward day after day and the routine of labors that were necessary to be performed was kept up in general good order and punctuality. Nearly every person in the camp had specific duties and labors assigned him. Some were cooks, some drove and took care of the teams; others acted as commissary agents for the various messes, by visiting farm houses and other places to purchase provisions. Persons also were charged with the duty of procuring water for drinking and cooking purposes, while others procured fuel, all to be obtained as speedily as possible when the wagons were halted. We had no drones, and what was very agreeable, none performed these several duties with reluctance; but all were accomplished orderly, with willing hands and cheerful hearts.

The labors and duties that necessarily had to be performed by the members of Zion's Camp, day after day and night after night, were very fatiguing. The large majority of them walked the most of the way. The Prophet was relieved of this task. His duties were such that he had provided himself—extra from his baggage wagons—with a light, open carriage. Frequently he was under the necessity of driving several miles out of the course to be traveled by the main body of the camp, in order to transact business or hold an interview with some of the leading men, in order to allay excitement which here and there existed in opposition to our passing through the country with so large and well-disciplined a force. Often he was under the necessity of taking a few men with him. When there was no business of this character to be attended to, he frequently would take his brother Hyrum or some two or three leading men with him to ride, for the purpose, no doubt, of consulting upon the best and wisest measures to be adopted in order to meet certain difficult circumstances that seemed to menace our advance.

A complication of difficulties seemed to become more and more frequent as we traveled to the west and neared the place of our destination. At times the possibility of reaching the western counties of Missouri seemed dark and forbidding, and had it not been for the firm trust the Prophet and all in camp had in the overruling hand of God, we certainly would have been inclined to abandon all idea of being permitted to pass through the country much nearer to the setting sun. But night after night the prayers of the faithful ascended into the ears of Jehovah to soften the hearts of the people towards us, as we had no design of violence or evil against them or their country. We traveled by faith, and the Lord heard our importunities.

It must have been the 22nd of June, 1834, that we camped at Fishing River, in the State of Missouri, as that is the date of a very important revelation received by the Prophet Joseph Smith. This revelation will be found commencing on page 377 of the third electrotype edition of the Doctrine and Covenants. Persons reading this revelation will obtain authentic reasons why Zion's Camp was started from Kirtland, Ohio, to journey into the western portion of the State of Missouri. The reasons there given are plain and will relieve me of the necessity of trying to give explanations in my own language. I will try, however, to give my readers, as well as I can, an understanding of the scenes that transpired at the place of our encampment, there and in the region round about.

As near as memory serves me it was about 4 o'clock in the afternoon of June 22nd, 1834, that the camp made a halt and camped upon the bank of Fishing River. I am not certain whether the revelation here referred to was received on the very day we reached that point or whether it was received during the following day. I have an impression that this revelation was received the morning after. It will perhaps be sufficient to know that this revelation was received during the time the camp remained at that place.

When we reached Fishing River the day was warm and very pleasant. I think there was not a cloud to be seen in the sky. We found the river in fine condition for fording. The water was reported, by the brethren who went down to it where the road crossed, to be not over knee-deep. Of course, we had plenty of time and might easily have crossed and made our encampment on the opposite shore long before dark; but the brethren felt impressed not to cross the stream at that time. We were soon busy pitching our tents and placing the wagons in position, as was our custom.

While we were building fires and commencing to prepare supper, two or three men rode hastily into camp and commenced a blasphemous tirade about "Jo Smith and the G—d d—d Mormons." They wanted to know what the h—l so many of us were traveling through the county for. They swore that we had got to our journey's end. They declared also that a large force, consisting of several hundred armed men, would be at the ford on the opposite side of the river in a short time, and that our company would all be slaughtered before morning.

The Prophet remonstrated firmly but quietly with them. He tried to calm their excited minds by assuring them that we had nothing but peaceable intentions toward the inhabitants.

I thought the men were intoxicated; but whether this was their condition or not they certainly were very earnest and loud-spoken in their denunciations of the Mormons and "Jo Smith," as they called him. During this parley—entirely unexpected on our part—the entire camp naturally gathered around them. Their position was on the main traveled road, on both sides of which our tents had been pitched. Joseph and a few of the leading men happened to be near the spot where they halted and commenced their angry declamation. I was at the outskirts of the brethren, who were quite densely massed around the rude intruders; but still near enough to note the contrast manifested between Joseph and the brethren and that of the rough, demoniacal appearance of these men as they sat upon their horses and swung their arms uncouthly around to give emphasis to their wicked threats of slaughter.

Joseph maintained his usual dignity of demeanor. They failed to draw from him any angry resentment of words. He firmly and kindly assured them, however, that the remaining portion of our journey would be characterized by the same moderation and justice towards the inhabitants as had been the case all along our route of travel; that we had not asked any aid from the people except we had paid the price asked for what we had obtained; and he intended to pay a just equivalent for all supplies furnished us until our journey was ended. He only asked to travel peaceably through the country as an American citizen, with no intention other than to fully respect the rights of the citizens. He did not quail before them a particle, but took all the pains possible in the short time the men tarried to correctly inform them as to the honesty and justice of our motives.

The men finally reined up their horses and spurred away, still shouting their anathemas to the effect that our company were all to be massacred during that night.

These men were gone just long enough for us to look around a little, when we observed the sky was being rapidly overcast with densely dark and angry clouds. I think we had not all finished eating our suppers, when the rain began to fall in torrents, accompanied with terribly fierce wind. So violent was the wind and torrents of rain that neither our wagons nor tents afforded us protection, and we were quickly drenched and almost unable to stand against the fierceness of the blast. Our condition was indeed critical.

Close by where we were encamped was a large log meeting-house. We had no alternative but to seek shelter within the strong walls of this building. The door was found locked, but the windows were easily raised and we hastily found ingress thereby. Had it not been for that shelter our suffering must have been great—the effects from which might have been fatal to some of us at least.

I have witnessed rain storms in various portions of the earth, but nothing I have ever experienced has equaled that storm in point of the terrible fierceness of the wind and the immensity of water that fell. What added to the destructiveness of the storm were the missiles of hail that were hurled in vast quantities by the currents of wind that rushed and roared through the woods which surrounded our place of shelter, causing the sound of falling trees and massive limbs to add additional terrors to the general clang of the storm.

The vast electric artillery of the expansive firmament seemed to be in a state of rapid combustion, so that night, which otherwise would have been as dark as night could possibly become, was at times rendered so light that we could look far out beyond the swaying trees, and falling and splintered branches hurled along the air and striking the earth with a fury that made us truly thankful for the protecting walls of the strong blockhouse that rendered us secure from the perils of that exciting hour. The elemental phenomena of that night were certainly a strange mixture of hail and rain, light and darkness, alternating in successive motion as if vieing with each other to become champions in the strife.

The heavens above us were so completely lit up by the electric display that the dense and sombrous clouds appeared as ponderous masses floating through luminous areas of glowing light. We looked and gazed through the protecting windows of our place of refuge, and amazement filled our minds as we contemplated the inimitable wonders of the God of nature.

The voice of thunder uttered anathemas against the enemies of truth and righteousness, who were massed with arms across the river, ready at that hour to fall upon us and spill our blood. And that thunder shook the very earth with terrible force, as if threatening to open its caverns and engulf whatever existed upon its surface within the range of that perilous storm. But our trust was in Jehovah, and we looked confidently for His preservation, for we knew, by the faith that the gospel had implanted in our hearts, that the arm of the Eternal Father was stretched out for our preservation.

I cannot relate how our animals fared outside; but the peltings of the rain and hail hurled against them by such fierce wind as blew through that night must have tortured them unmercifully. I understood, however, that they, as much as possible, were placed at the lee side of the wagons and the large building that sheltered us. Nearly everything in our wagons was wet and unfit for use until overhauled and dried.

At length the terrible night was passed and a glorious morning's sun chased away the darkness and revealed for our inspection the fragmentary condition of the woods and fields. A visible change had been wrought by the warring elements. The work of havoc and devastation met the eye in every direction. Trees were uprooted and limbs hurled in great quantities to the earth. But the brightness of the new-born day and the reviving warmth of the June sun re-assured all nature. The birds of the woods hymned their unwritten notes of sweetness and twittered through the branches as if to search out the new disasters that had befallen their wonted resorts.

The brethren also partook of the genial influence. They rejoiced in the morning's effulgence and thanked God that He had preserved them and revived within them an increase of faith in His overruling providences. They took hasty excursions here and there and found the storm had left its destructive mark to an extent that surpassed expectation. From the place of our encampment we heard the roar of water in the river and in a short time some of our men returned and declared that the water in Fishing

River was forty feet deep! When we made our encampment there it was no more than knee deep. What did we understand by this? We understood that the Almighty had sent that storm for the special preservation of Zion's Camp. This was a great truth that was plain to our comprehension and the gratitude we felt to our Heavenly Father was such that melted our hearts with thankfulness.

As soon as we well could we prepared for starting, after partaking of a scanty breakfast. We found the road in many places strewn with limbs and a few trees, some of which we had to remove before we could proceed. Of course the roads were muddy and our progress was anything but rapid. After we had traveled a few miles we came to a friendly family who received us with feelings of humane sympathy. We camped at that place and took time to rest and recover to some extent from the fatigues and exposures of the night. The Prophet Joseph there made a speech to the members of the camp, and, if I remember correctly, a few strangers were present. Joseph spoke almost with superhuman force and clearness. He told us that the storm had been sent by the God of Israel to place a barrier between us and our enemies, to prevent them from falling upon us during the night to massacre us, as the men who rode into our camp the evening before had declared was the intention. We soon learned from the inhabitants that this was certainly in the program of a few hundred men to do, who were posted not far from the ford on the opposite shore.

Could we now have the prophetic declarations made by the Prophet Joseph in his speech at that place they would be far above the value of gold. They were of such import that no man but an inspired servant of Jehovah could have uttered them. I can see him to this day, in memory, as his tall, manly form stood erect and commanding. His face shone with the light of the Holy Spirit, his mild blue eyes fairly sparkled with the fire of the divinity that possessed his being. I can only let that scene live in memory, and thank my Heavenly Father that I heard that mighty man in the days of my youth, when early impressions are not apt to die.

He declared the storm of that night was to be numbered among the manifestations which were to follow in the last days in defense of the house of Israel, scattered among the nations of the earth. He said the fury of elements would yet waste away the wicked, and floods would overflow the river banks and sweep the precious fruits of soil from the possession of those who had labored to mature them. The sea would sweep beyond its bounds and work wonderful havoc, and that earthquakes would shake the earth and cast down the dwellings of those whose hearts rebelled against the everlasting gospel. God would visit the wicked nations with just retribution, for many of them would harden their hearts against the testimony of the humble ambassadors of truth; that the time was nigh when He would have a controversy with the people of the earth, for they would yet shed the blood of His prophets and cast out His people from their borders. These sayings were not uttered in the exact words here written, but this will convey to the reader a portion of the substance of his declarations.

He said also that Jehovah had commanded that journey to be taken and He would protect the members of the camp to their place of destination; that no hand should prosper that should be lifted against them, if they would continue to be united and faithful in walking by the counsel that should be imparted to them from time to time by the influence of the Spirit of the Great Jehovah.

"During our travels," said the Prophet, "we visited several of the mounds which had been thrown up by the ancient inhabitants of this country, Nephites, Lamanites, etc., and this morning I went up on a high mound near the river, accompanied by the brethren. From this mound we could overlook the tops of the trees and view the prairie on each side of the river as far as our visions could extend, and the scenery was truly delightful.

"On the top of the mound were stones which presented the appearance of three altars having been erected one above the other, according to ancient order, and human bones were strewn over the surface of the ground. The brethren procured a shovel and hoe, and removing the earth to the depth of about one foot discovered the skeleton of a man, almost entire, and between his ribs was a Lamanitish arrow, which evidently produced his death. Elder Brigham Young retained the arrow and the brethren carried some pieces of the skeleton to Clay County. The contemplation of the scenery before us produced peculiar sensations in our bosoms; and the visions of the past being opened to my understanding by the Spirit of the Almighty, I discovered that the person whose skeleton was before us was a white Lamanite, a large, thick-set man, and a man of God. He was a warrior and chieftain under the great prophet Omandagus, who was known from the hill Cumorah, or Eastern Sea, to the Rocky Mountains. His name was Zelph. The curse was taken from him, or at least in part; one of his thigh bones was broken by a stone flung from a sling, while in battle years before his death. He was killed in battle by the arrow found among his ribs, during the last great struggle of the Lamanites and Nephites."

Our camp was made at Brother Burget's on the 23rd of June, 1834. Of the night of the 24th of June the Prophet writes:

"This night the cholera burst forth among us, and about midnight it was manifest in its most terrified form. Our ears were saluted with cries and moanings and lamentations on every hand; even those on guard fell to the earth with their guns in their hands, so sudden and powerful was the attack of this terrible disease. At the commencement I attempted to lay on hands for their recovery, but I quickly learned by painful experience that when the Great Jehovah decrees destruction upon any people, makes known His determination, man must not attempt to stay His hand. The moment I attempted to rebuke this disease, that moment I was attacked, and had I not desisted, I must have saved the life of my brother by the sacrifice of my own, for when I rebuked the disease it left him and seized me.

"When the cholera made its appearance, Elder John S. Carter was the first man who stepped forward to rebuke it, and upon this, was immediately seized and became the first victim of the camp. He died about six o'clock in the afternoon, and Seth Hitchcock died in about thirty minutes after. As it was impossible to obtain coffins, the brethren rolled them in blankets, carried them on a horse sled about half a mile and buried them in the bank of a small stream which empties into Rush Creek, all of which was accomplished by dark.

"When they had returned from the burial, the brethren united, covenanted and prayed, hoping the disease would be stayed; but in vain, for while thus covenanting, Eber Wilcox died, and while some were digging the grave others stood sentry with their fire arms, watching their enemies.

"The cholera," he states, "continued its ravages about four days, when an effectual remedy for their purging, vomiting and cramping was discovered, viz.: dipping the person afflicted in cold water, or pouring it upon him. About sixty-eight of the Saints suffered from this disease, of which number thirteen died, viz.: John S. Carter, Eber Wilcox, Seth Hitchcock, Erastus Rudd, Algernon Sidney Gilbert, Alfred Fisk, Edward Ives, Noah Johnson, Jesse B. Lawson, Robert McCard, Elial Strong, Jesse Smith and Betsy Parish."

With regard to the disbanding of the camp Joseph writes: "Early in the morning of the 25th the camp was separated into small bands and dispersed among brethren living in the vicinity."

Our last encampment was made on Rush Creek, in brother Burget's field. It was the ending of a long, arduous and fatiguing journey of over one thousand miles, mostly performed on foot, over roads variegated by dust and mud, and crossing streams of both small and large dimensions.

It being in the warm season of the year, much suffering was necessarily endured by being necessitated, the most of us at least, to walk, unsheltered from the broiling sun. Sometimes, for a little season, we endured both hunger and thirst, but this class of suffering came upon us generally when we were out of the reach of settlements or too far away from the flowing creeks or springs of water. This was our condition sometimes while crossing wide prairies were but sparsely inhabited. But before entering upon districts of country of that description, if we were successful in obtaining the correct information in time, we purchased from the people sufficient supplies of food and filled our vessels with water, which of course prevented, to a considerable extent at least, hunger and thirst.

Sometimes we had met with friends, but often with enemies, who either thirsted for the blood of our leaders or desired calamities should befall us.

As to the genuine character of Joseph Smith as a just and honorable man and an inspired Prophet, estimated among the prophets of early times he is not and will not rank as being inferior to any. This man who led us in Zion's Camp and to whom we all listened with the profoundest convictions that he was inspired by God has been the recipient of all the keys of dispensations held by prophets of old, and the revelations of Jesus Christ declare that those keys shall not be taken from him.   *Instructor*, Vol. 27.

CHAPTER 16

Physical and Mental Sufferings of Persecutors

A MOBOCRAT COMES TO UTAH

Affidavit of William H. Chappell, now residing in Coalville, Summit County, Utah, concerning a member of the mob that killed the Prophet Joseph Smith.

About the year 1892, when I was eighteen years of age (having been born on the 29th of April, 1874), and living in what was then known as East Coalville ward but now known as Cluff ward), an old man by the name of Brooks moved into that neighborhood and lived neighbor to my father, William E. Chappell. This old man had a son by the name of Alf Brooks who was some four years older than I. As I remember, it was a little log house in which he lived. The old man used to come to my father's home, sit on the porch and talk to my father. The conversation turned to pioneer stories and of Joseph Smith the Prophet. On one particular evening after my father had talked about Joseph Smith, the old man Brooks said: "Mr. Chappell, I saw the last bullet shot into the old boy." After Mr. Brooks had gone to his cabin, my father said: "No wonder he is a miserable old soul. If he saw the last bullet shot into Joseph Smith, he was in that mob. If he was in that mob, it has been prophesied that he will suffer all kinds of torment, his limbs shall rot off of his body and he will not have courage to take his own life."

Before this conversation occurred, I had taken no notice of the old man but I had been rather friendly and chummy with his son; but after this conversation I took particular notice of the old man and how he suffered. The old man had a belt which he wore around his waist which the son would take off, then beat the old man with it just to hear him scream and when beating him the son would laugh and profane and seemed to enjoy it. All of this I saw. The old man was crippled and could walk only with the aid of two sticks—one in each hand and without the aid of these he was totally helpless and unable to walk. The cause of this crippled condition was unknown to me. The son would drive the old man up to the coal mine dump about three or four hundred yards from their cabin like he would drive cattle and fill sacks with coal, tie the sacks on the old man's back and drive him back to the cabin. The old man would beg his son not to fill the sacks too full of coal. If he would not go fast enough the son would whip him with his belt which he had taken from the father before going for the coal. They lived in this cabin for some two years and then moved to Coalville, into a house near where the present Beth White hot dog stand is now located. While living here his toes rotted off his feet. Later, a Dr. Cannon, then living in Coalville, and who owned a ranch in Weber canyon about eight miles above Oakley, made arrangements with this old man and his son to start a chicken ranch on Dr. Cannon's premises, onto which the father and son moved. About that time my sister, Elizabeth Chappell, married Thomas Wilde and he owned a ranch adjoining Dr. Cannon's and lived about four hundred yards from where the old man and his son lived. In the spring, Dr. Cannon made inquiry concerning the disappearance of the chickens on the farm and the old man replied that "The skunks had eaten them up." To which Dr. Cannon replied: "You are the biggest skunk."

The son would often leave his father for three or four days and sometimes a week without any food. I was up to my brother-in-law's ranch one fall, in November, when an eight inch snow fell, the weather clearing up in the afternoon, and dropping to zero weather by night. My brother-in-law and I took over an extra quilt and some supper to the old man and also chopped wood which we piled close to the stove so that he could handily keep the fire going during the night without getting out of bed. After returning home later in the night, I heard him screaming. I awoke my brother-in-law and he said: "Don't take notice of him; he always screams like that." When we got up the next morning, we looked towards his cabin and saw that the house was gone. We immediately went to where his cabin had been and found it had burned to the ground during the night. All of the old man's clothes had burned off of him and he was burned all over his body from his feet to the top of his head. He was alive and lay curled up in the ashes of the burned cabin, trying to keep warm. We secured some quilts and with team and sleigh we took him to Peoa where we found the son. The people of Peoa took up a collection which amounted to five dollars, gave it to the son and told him to go to Park City for the particular medicine he was directed to buy. With the money the son bought liquor and became drunk and did not return for four days. The old man died on the fourth day after he was burned, before his son returned. His remains were interred in the Peoa cemetery. The son was ordered out of the country and he left immediately for parts unknown.   Signed: William H. Chappell

State of Utah   }
County of Summit   } ss.

William H. Chappell being duly sworn, deposes and says that the foregoing statement is a true recital of events as they occurred and happened according to his knowledge to which other living witnesses can also testify.

In witness whereof, he has set his hand and signature this 28th day of September, 1948.   Chas L. Frost, County Clerk
in and for the County of Summit, State of Utah.

*   *   *   *   *

Coalville, Utah, November 6, 1948

I, Joseph H. Wilde, was present when my brother, Thomas Wilde and others, took the blankets to the cabin to cover the old man as stated in the above affidavit. The old man was an habitual user of chewing tobacco and upon this occasion my brother had purchased a plug for him and presented it to him. The old man thought it was a revolver that was being shoved towards him and exclaimed: "For God's sake don't shoot me." I was a little boy when these things happened but I can distinctly remember the old man referring to the Prophet Joseph Smith as "old Joe Smith." Although this man was implicated in the murder of the Prophet Joseph, yet the Latter-day Saints who resided in this vicinity were very considerate and brought food and clothing to him, particularly was this true of my brother Thomas Wilde who resided but a short distance from the cabin in which the old man, Mr. Brooks, lived. His son, Alf. Brooks, helped my brother during the haying season and ate dinner at his home when so employed.

Signed: Joseph H. Wilde

Signature witnessed by:
Mrs. Joseph H. Wilde
N. B. Lundwall

THIRTEEN MOBOCRATS MEET A COMMON FATE

Martha James Cragun (who married Isaiah Cox) was born March 3, 1852, in Mill Creek, Salt Lake County, Utah. In October, 1862, they received a call to go to the Dixie country as pioneers and in May Gt. grandfather James Cragun, his wife (Eleanor Lane Cragun) and family started for Dixie. Martha Cox received her schooling there by going to school and working on the side. She started teaching in 1868 and was married Dec. 6, 1869 in the Salt Lake Endowment House by Pres. Daniel H. Wells. She resumed teaching as soon as they returned from Salt Lake City and taught in St. George off and on until the 31st of August, 1881, when she arrived in the Muddy Valley.

FROM DIARY OF J. C. COX

The trustees of the Muddy Valley school had notified me that they expected to open their school September 1st. I was there August 31.*** The next morning after my arrival I visited the trustees at the place where the school house was in course of erection. I introduced myself as their contemplated school "marm." There was Mr. McGuire, the leading trustee, who was a tall Irishman, sitting when I first came up, on a large stone which was to be used as a hearth stone in the building, but who stood up with a pipe with long stem held in his drooling mouth. He removed his hat and scratched his shaggy head while he informed me that it would be three weeks before they would be ready for me.

I asked what preparation was needed for readiness. They said only the finishing of the house and this had only the walls partly up. I looked at Morgan, the second trustee, a great massive form of fat, muscle and bone, whose business it seemed was to haul in the material while Ute Perkins whom I knew as an old St. Georger had the business of putting the mortar and adobies together. I told them if that was all they needed, the school need not wait a day for with such beautiful weather a class seated under the beautiful cottonwood trees by the side of the lovely clear stream could have no better place for learning and if they would assent to it *I* would open school the next morning under the trees. McGuire received my proposition with a doubtful look but that was dispelled when I smilingly told him I could teach all I knew under the cotton-wood trees. So it was arranged. An old man named Roscoe owned a cabin hard by, just across the little creek with a clean hard door yard that reached to the creek bank. Directly across the stream was a level space shaded by three beautiful trees. Here they brought a few of the school desks and Mr. Roscoe loaned me an old table for my use. The pupils hung bonnets and hats on nails driven in the trees, where I also contrived to hang my black board which I had always retained from the time I had it converted from a bread-board for my very first school. That afternoon, Sept. 1st, I registered nine pupils.

An outsider by the name of Logan, the other trustee, living at a place that still bears his name, retained his children—would not send them to be taught by a "Mormon," besides the school house was not being built in the right place as he saw it. The trustees asked me to visit him which I did. He told me he withheld assistance on the house building because it was not placed on the right spot and would not send his children so far to the school and he lived at least five miles away. But he made no reference to the teacher. His tobacco drooling from his mouth and his otherwise stinking person was disgusting and Sister Whitmore and myself soon took our leave. I felt that I had at least one mortal enemy in the valley. He told me also that I would have trouble about getting my pay and told me I had better withdraw and leave the valley. I was not at all frightened.

At a meeting in Saint Thomas (Nevada) called of all the people to consider the wants of the school and the "Mormon" teacher, each citizen was asked to give his mind on the Mormon question—neither Mrs. Whitmore nor myself were invited so we were not present. At this meeting all except Logan decided to sustain me. One man a "Jack Reed" an old man who was respected in the valley, living then in St. Thomas, said in this meeting that he was a member of the mob who martyred the prophet. He was about fifteen years old at the time. He said he took his gun and marched proudly to Carthage and took part in the killing of the two prophets. Mrs. McGuire related to me what he said; then told me also that her own father was one of the mobbers who tarred and feathered the prophet and she told me she thought I was too smart a woman to be a Mormon.

I had my abode with Sister Whitmore. I was expected to help with the work of the house to pay my room. This I did satisfactorily, but it was a difficult thing to find my food. I soon ran out of flour and had to borrow from my friends. I did the milking and cared for the milk for a portion of the milk. It was hard for the folks to find a way to send me supplies. I made arrangement with Sister Whitmore to let me do more work and give me meals. I did some peculiar work. I picked cotton on Saturday and put in one day of work cutting sunflowers.

* * * * *

About the last of September I heard that Jack Reed was very

sick of a strange ailment. He was taken ill in a few days after having made the statement that he took part in the affair at Carthage—but no one had told me of his sickness until I heard it from one of my Indian friends who said he had worms in his flesh. I determined to see him if I could and try to get him to verify the statement he had made at the meeting. The man had no family and Mr. McGuire was his attendant. I asked Mr. McGuire if he would allow Mrs. Whitmore and myself to visit Mr. Reed. He said that Mr. Reed was a sight that no white woman could be allowed to look upon. He was literally eaten alive by worms. His eye balls had fallen out, the flesh on his cheeks and neck had fallen off and though he could breathe he could take nourishment only through an opening in his throat, and said McGuire, "Pieces of flesh as large as my two hands have fallen off from different parts of his body." The sick man's farm was given to the white men who attended him in the first of his ailment. Finally when they could no longer endure the ordeal the Indians were called in to pour water into his throat and give him whatever other attention they could and these received the sick man's bunch of horses for their pay. When he finally passed the Indians carried out the awful remains by the four corners of the blanket upon which he had lain for weeks, and lowered that into the box the white men had prepared. The blanket was tucked in over him and the box quickly nailed up and put into the deep grave as soon as possible. No funeral was held. Beside Reed, Mr. Logan was backed by another man, a lawyer named McGarrigle. I had gathered the idea that this bunch of enemies were heading a petition against me because I was a polygamist. But during Reed's sickness all talk of Mormons seemed to die down. It was not for a long time, some years afterwards, that I learned the cause of the qualm. *One called "Jack Longstreet" became Reed's first attendant in company with McGuire. To these men Reed confessed that his participation in the murder of the Prophets was the cause of his affliction. He said to Longstreet: "It is the Mormon curse that is upon me. I cannot live—I must utterly rot before I die." He said that Brigham Young had pronounced that curse upon all that mob, and he had known thirteen of them to die just as he was dying. But he had lived so long and had passed the unlucky number thirteen, that he thought to escape the curse. He charged his attendants to never do anything against the Mormons, to be their friends, or said he, "You may suffer the Mormon curse." Longstreet related this to Mrs. Emma Huntsman, with whom he often stopped, this confession of Reed's as a warning to her and declared that he himself would not dare to raise a hand against them. I don't think he ever did.*

STATEMENT OF GEORGE E. KING

(Dictated to N. B. Lundwall, at the farm home of Mr. King, near Garland, Utah, on August 4, 1950.)

During the early summer of 1925, I was a graduate student and half-time faculty member of the University of Illinois. As was frequently my practice, I was doing some extracurricular work for a friend at the home of Seth Howe, in Champaign, Illinois. Casually Mr. Howe and I, in conversation, discussed our personal beliefs. He asked me if I was a Methodist, a Baptist, a Presbyterian, a Roman Catholic, and mentioned other faiths but did not ask me if I was a Mormon. I was glad to have the freedom of questioning him, which I would not have had if he had known my belief. At one remark of mine, he stated that my belief seemed to be something like the Mormon belief. As he did not suspect that I was a Mormon, I was able to ask him some questions and obtain answers freely; whereas he would not have volunteered the information he gave me had he known I was a Mormon.

The opening of this conversation was by me asking him: "What do you know about the Mormons?" He replied that he did not know very much about their belief, but stated that his grandmother Howe had once belonged to the Mormon church. Further questioning disclosed the following information: Missionaries during the life of the Prophet Joseph Smith had found the Howe family in one of the settlements in the southern part of Illinois. Mrs. Howe joined the church and desired to go to Nauvoo. Her husband bitterly objected to her gathering with the body of the church. As they had a large family he seemed to feel that if he left home she would not desert the children, which of course proved true; but in his leaving home he joined himself to the mobs which were persecuting the saints. The statement of Seth Howe had a lasting impression on me as he related: "My grandfather was one of the leaders of the mob which murdered Joe Smith." I questioned him further as to what became of his grandfather afterwards. He related that following the assassination of Joseph Smith his grandfather never saw a well day, although he lived for several years afterwards. His condition grew progressively worse and physicians of the day who called to attend him were unable to diagnose it as any known affliction, but his suffering was so intense that he frequently expressed the desire to obtain poison to end it all. His family very carefully kept anything of that nature out of his reach and at his final demise he actually had rotted alive, finally dying in intense agony.

In verification of the above statement, I hereunto sign my name this 4th day of August, 1950.

Signed: George E. King

Witnesses:
Lillian E. King
N. B. Lundwall

A MOBOCRAT ROAMS WESTERN SHEEP RANGES

By Thomas Nichols

In the summer of 1887, I was herding sheep up in Bedue Creek, which empties into the Weber River, just below the lower bridge. One day a little boy about nine to eleven years of age, came to my camp. He was very dirty and shabbily dressed and was very shy.

I noticed he was watching me very closely as I busied myself preparing my dinner. I asked him if he was hungry. He did not answer me, but in a few minutes he went to the creek and went through the motions of washing his hands. When he came back to the camp I looked at him and smiled at him. I then told him I would let him have some soap and a wash basin so he could give his face and hands a good wash. He looked at his hands and smiled at me; took the articles mentioned and ran back to the creek. When he came back to me he was partly clean. When the dinner was ready I asked the blessing on it. The lad looked at me in wonder but as he did not speak a word I gave him a generous supply of fried potatoes, onions, lamb and bread. He ate it very quickly, got up and ran down the creek and was gone. In a few days he came again and made for the creek once more. This time he was not so shy. He gathered wood for the fire and brought water for the camp. He did not say a word until I had given him his dinner. Then he said very quietly, "Thank you." I asked him where he came from. He just pointed down to the river. I asked his name. He said: "Jim," and was gone again. He visited me several times. On one of his visits I asked him if he did not get enough to eat. His reply was: "Sometimes grandpa has some and sometimes he did not. Grandpa snares rabbits and catches fish but mostly his feet hurt him and he did not try." I gave him flour and mutton to take home with him. The next day he came again and asked if I had coffee. "Grandpa wants some and some tobacco." I explained to him that I did not use either one.

I decided that I would visit the grandfather. I found him in an abandoned cabin situated in a grove of aspens. He was not very friendly. The little boy told him I was the man that sent the food to him. Then he came and sat down on a bench outside the cabin. I noticed that he had several bad sores on his face and that his hands were wrapped in rags. I asked him his name but he did not answer. He finally told me he was from the east and had drifted west. I asked him if he was a timber man or a prospector. He said, no. Then I asked him what was his object in coming to Utah and up here in the Weber canyon. He said: "I don't know. I just drifted here and this cabin was empty so I decided to stay a spell." After talking to him in a general way for a while I started to leave. He then asked me to give him some mutton tallow to put on his sores. I said, "Send the boy up and I will give him some." I noticed that the lower part of one ear was gone, a part of the left side of his nose had rotted away, and there were other repulsive sores on his face. He showed me his hands. There was very little solid flesh on them. I expressed my sympathy for him and he said his feet were worse than his hands. I asked him what had caused all this trouble and he replied: "I don't know unless it was a curse God had placed on me." He said some men had told him that was it, because he was with the men who killed Joe Smith, the Mormon Prophet. "I guess that is the main reason I drifted out here; I wanted to know how the Mormons made out without Joe Smith to lead them."

THOMAS FORD

Thomas Ford (Dec. 5, 1800-Nov. 3, 1850), governor of Illinois, was born in Fayette County, Pa. His father was Robert Ford, of a Maryland family. His mother, Elizabeth, was the daughter of Hugh Logue and Isabella Delaney, both natives of Ireland. By a former marriage she was the mother of George Forquer, who by the time of his death in 1837 had risen to be the Jackson leader in Illinois. Robert Ford died in 1803, and the next year his widow removed first to St. Louis, then to New Design in the future Monroe County, Ill. Despite the straitened circumstances of the family, Thomas Ford managed to get a common-school education. Later his half-brother helped him to spend a year at Transylvania University; then with the encouragement of Daniel P. Cook he studied law. After a term of practice in Waterloo, Ill., he set up with Forquer in partnership at Edwardsville, 1825-29, and for the following six years, 1829-35, he served as state's attorney at Galena and Quincy, Ill. On Jan. 14, 1835, he was elected circuit judge by the state legislature, serving until Mar. 4, 1837, when he resigned to become judge of the Chicago municipal court. He was again elected circuit judge, Feb. 23, 1839. When the Democratic general assembly reorganized the state supreme court to swamp a Whig majority, he was elected to the court Feb. 15, 1841, and held office till he resigned to run for governor in 1842. Ford apparently took no active part in politics until 1842. In the latter year the Whig and Democratic nominees for governor, Joseph Duncan and Adam W. Snyder, had long and vulnerable records to defend. The Democratic loss was therefore more apparent than real when Snyder died May 14, 1842. The leaders of the party turned to Ford, and after ten days' entreaty he consented to run. With no chance to gather ammunition for the election on August 1, the Whigs lost to Ford by a vote of 39,020 to 46,507. (T.C. Pease, Illinois Election Returns, 1923, p. 126.) At the end of his term, though he was asked to run against Douglas for the Senate, he resumed the practice of law at Peoria. Unfortunately he was overtaken by tuberculosis, and at his death in 1850 was virtually dependent on charity. His wife, Frances Hambaugh, whom he had married on June 12, 1828, was worn out by nursing him and died a few weeks before him. He left five children for whose financial benefit he had some time before begun his History of Illinois from its Commencement as a State in 1818 to 1847. It was finally published under the auspices of James Shields in 1854.—*Dictionary of American Biography* (N.Y. Schribner's 1931), v. 6, pp. 520-521.

"From this resume of public affairs we turn to Governor Ford's private and domestic concerns. Of his diffidence enough has been said. Ballance [Charles. *History of Peoria,* 1870, pp. 254-55], who knew and was sharply critical of him, draws this picture of his personal characteristics: 'He was a small man with features indicating one from the lower rather than the upper walks of life. His nose was rather sharp and bent a little to one side. He was plain and unpretending in his manners. He was no orator in the common acceptance of the word; but what he said was to the point . . . He reasoned well, not so much by any show of logic as by clever distinct statements. Though his mind was not far-reaching, it was never in a cloud. Whatever he saw, he saw clearly . . . He was not religious in the common acceptance of the word; yet up to his forty-second year he lived as pure a life as any man I know.'

"The qualification is significant, for Ford's 'forty-second' year was the one in which he became governor. The same neighbor and critic relates that during his term in office 'the harpies about the capitol' led him into habits which hastened his death, and which he vainly strove to reform. These statements, if true, shed light upon the conditions, physical and otherwise, attending the writing of the *History*. At the expiration of his term as Governor in January, 1846, Ford retired to his father-in-law's farm to devote himself to this task, and mid-April, 1847, saw it practically completed.

"He had already planned to remove to Peoria to take up anew the practice of law. Peoria was one of the few even moderately sizable cities of Illinois, and Ford's long service as state's attorney and judge in northern Illinois had given him an extensive acquaintance throughout the entire region. Yet the story of his three year's sojourn there is one of unrelieved poverty and defeat, Mrs. Ford, afflicted with cancer, died October 12, 1850 at the early age of thirty-eight. Three weeks later, on November 3, he followed her to the grave.* Left behind were five orphaned children, penniless and of tender years, to face the world as best they might. "To the credit of common humanity, all were taken in charge by considerate townsmen, and reared in homes which were better than their own father could provide. In his closing weeks he had been an object of charity, and his funeral expenses were met by the gifts of a group of citizens."

History of Illinois, edited by M. M. Quaife. Chicago, R. R. Donelley & Sons Co., 1945. v. 1:24-27, *"Historical Introduction."*

RETRIBUTIVE JUSTICE

(INCIDENTS COMPILED BY LYMAN O. LITTLEFIELD)

A testimony published in the latter part of 1874: "A lady was invited to attend a Methodist church at Peoria, Illinois, and noticing a rough box or coffin resting under the pulpit, inquired concerning it, and was informed that it enclosed the remains of the wife of ex-Governor Ford, and was supplied at the public expense. Ford was present, and he looked gaunt and miserable, and his bones appeared ready to pierce through the skin. Two weeks later, the lady attended again, and was astonished to see a similar coffin in the same place. It contained all that was left of Governor Ford, who had for some time lived, and had now died, a pauper. The lady who saw this, though she had left the "Mormon" church, remembered hearing Elder John Taylor say in Nauvoo, that "Governor Ford would live until the flesh would wither from his bones and he would die a pauper."

Also, a few days after the appearance of the above notice, the following account of the tragic fate of Governor Ford's son, Thomas, appeared in print, and may be set down among the many cases where the sins of the fathers are visited upon the children:

"Ford's children, in consequence of his poverty, were adopted

---

*His death was commonly ascribed to tuberculosis. Ballance, however, writing in 1870, firmly insists that his relatively early demise was caused by the bad habits acquired at Springfield. Apparently this means over-indulgence in liquor.

by different citizens, Thomas being taken care of by Hon. Thos. E. Moore of Peoria. The young man served in the army, and afterwards moved to Kansas, where, with an elder brother, he followed various occupations, principally driving large herds of stock from the South.

"Last July he was going to Caldwell and stopped at a ranch for refreshment. Here he was watched by two armed men, and, after proceeding about a mile, was suddenly seized by three men before he could defend himself. They took him for one of the cattle stealers, with which the state was infested, and, in spite of his protestations, prayers and appeals for an investigation, they proceeded to hang him to the limb of a tree. He told them he was the son of ex-Governor Ford, but they laughed him to scorn and refused to examine his papers." *The Martyrs*, pp. 109-10.

THE UNKEPT GRAVE OF THOMAS FORD

Last week an Illinois public man at the state capitol commented on the neglect shown to the grave of one who once was governor of the state and the *Peoria Journal* takes up the subject, describing how the ex-governor's grave, as well as the whole lot, in which rest his wife and youngest daughter, is uncared for. It says that all around it the grass has been carefully mown, and every lot in the vicinity has been kept in good order, but not a single touch has been bestowed upon the lot sacred to the memory of a former governor of the great state of Illinois. The cemetery authorities complained that no money had been given them for the purpose, and neither state nor city, nor any private citizen of state or city had furnished any money. About $60.00 is required as a fund to keep the lot in order. Occasionally there has been talk of raising a subscription for the purpose from the citizens of Peoria, but nobody has taken the initiative. Occasionally it has been proposed to secure an appropriation from the legislature, but no one has felt sufficiently interested to take the matter in charge.

The statement is made that it is proposed to secure such an appropriation at this session; but that meanwhile the cemetery authorities have remained obdurate, and have steadfastly refused to bestow a stroke of work upon the lot. Weeds, tall grass and brush have luxuriated thick and rank within the entire lot to an extent that renders it uncomfortable to walk about in it. Around the lot has grown a thick hedge of evergreen from ten to fifteen feet high, irregular and unkempt — never trimmed. Evergreen trees, higher than the hedge, stand on each side of the entrance. A still taller evergreen spreads its branches wide at the rear of the lot. From some points a glimpse of the top of the monument, erected by the state at a cost of $500, can be obtained, but elsewhere nothing within the hedge is visible. Few people who drive or stroll along the avenue are aware that the remains of a former governor of Illinois reposes there. In such neglect have the people of Peoria allowed Thomas Ford's grave to remain.

Millennial Star, 57:134.

FATE PURSUES FAMILY OF GOV. FORD, ILLINOIS

Peoria, Ill., March 20.—Without the last rites of the Church, and with only four mourners surrounding the grave, the body of Mrs. Anna Davies, who died a pauper in the Deaconess home in Lincoln, Ill., Thursday, was buried here at twilight tonight.

Mrs. Davies was the only surviving daughter of former Governor Thomas Ford of Illinois, who likewise died in poverty.

The spectre of poverty that has beset the family for half a century also found a victim in Mrs. Davies' only daughter, Mrs. Watson of Oskaloosa, Ia., who for weeks before her mother's death sought funds with which to purchase a coffin. Up to the time of Mrs. Davies' death the daughter had been unsuccessful in her quest, but following the demise citizens of Lincoln contributed enough to make possible the obsequies that took place tonight.

It was while under the plighted protection of the state of of Illinois, as represented by Governor Ford, that the Prophet Joseph Smith and his brother Hyrum were murdered in Carthage jail, June 27, 1844. Elder John Taylor, who was with the martyrs at the time and was himself desperately wounded, gave utterance shortly afterwards to a prophecy concerning Governor Ford, the literal fulfillment of which in its utmost detail, is thus recorded.

Newspaper reference indistinct: Sept. 24.

A TRUE PICTURE OF GOV. FORD

By George Q. Cannon

Even after the lapse of nearly thirty-six years, one can not read the history of the last days of Joseph Smith without a feeling of indignation rising towards the miserable creature who acted, at that time, as Governor of the State. *Thomas Ford* is a name that will live in history side by side with that of *Pontius Pilate*. He was an imbecile. A more pliant, short-sighted, weak tool could not have been found, to suit the purposes of the mob, if the country had been searched. He was full of pompous littleness, and the leaders of the mob humored his weak conceit. By this means, they used him, and he was more serviceable to them, without knowing their plans, than if they had explained them to him.

Governor Ford was deaf to all reason. He was surrounded by apostates and the worst enemies of the Saints. On his arrival at Carthage, he had ordered the entire mob into service. He heard their imprecations and their threats, and saw their violence and outrageous conduct; but instead of being disgusted with them, they suited him. He adopted, as the truth, every lie and misrepresentation that the mob circulated. The delegates, whom he wished the Mayor and City Council of Nauvoo to send to him, he treated with great rudeness. When they attempted to make the necessary statements and explanations, he suffered them to be interrupted and insulted by the vile crew who were his companions. Even the communications which they brought were read to him in the presence of these villains, who frequently interrupted the reading by their cursing!   *Instructor*, Vol. 15.

ANOTHER MURDERER'S END

Elder James H. Moyle, writing from the Southern States, in August, 1881, says:

"Bro. W. C. Burton and I met a citizen of North Carolina, named Brown, who claims to be one of the mob that committed the soul-destroying crime of shedding the innocent, unoffending blood of an anointed prophet of God. He says that he lived in Quincy, Illinois, and admits that it was a rich and productive country, but with all its charms he did not seem to have contentment, as he has been wandering from place to place ever since, as though in search of an asylum for a troubled conscience. He is now settled in one of the poorest of poor districts, where he is so situated that he can go no farther, and where he is scarcely able to earn a subsistence.

"During the extremely cold weather last winter, some of his little children were totally destitute of clothing. The neighbors, moved with compassion, collected some old clothes and necessaries of life, and sent them.

"While we should be far, far from despising the poor for their poverty, I cannot help thinking of the saying of the Psalmist: "I have been young, and now am old; yet have I not seen the righteous forsaken, nor his seed begging bread.'

"This man has not been wandering from cruel religious persecution, but, I think, to ease a restless and discontented mind."

The Martyrs, pp. 111-112.

A MOBOCRAT IN EARLY CALIFORNIA HISTORY

Daniel Tyler, in his "History of the Mormon Battalion," in writing of San Diego, says:

"Near the foreigners' burying ground resided a miserable specimen of humanity, who stole and begged from door to door. He was one of the most forlorn of human beings. He acknowledged to having been engaged in the Haun's Mill massacre, and begged our people to forgive him. He claimed to have been one of Fremont's party, and said he had been among the Rocky Mountains for the last seven years."

The following statement is furnished by Brother Joel Parrish, of Centerville, Utah:

"In March, 1877, in company with Elder Charles F. Middleton, I passed through Carthage, Hancock County, Illinois, enroute for St. Louis. We tarried there a sufficient length of time to visit the Carthage jail, where our lamented Prophet and Patriarch, Joseph and Hyrum Smith, were murdered. We visited a Mr. Browning, who then owned and occupied, as his family residence, the old rock building, or jail, where the prisoners referred to were confined. This building was no longer needed as a jail, a new and larger one having been built. Mr. Browning and lady entertained us over night, treated us very kindly, and stated that any of our Elders, passing through, would be welcome to be entertained by them.

"The room where the prisoners were murdered was, at that time, used as a parlor. We were taken therein and shown the arrangement of the room. The bullet hole in the door, made by the fatal ball that struck Hyrum Smith at the left side of the nose, had been filled with putty, but was plainly to be seen. There being a carpet on the floor, we could not see the bloodstains where the murdered Patriarch fell, but we were assured that they were still there. The stains of blood on the walls, also, were obscured, as the room had been white-washed. The jail had been painted and kept in good repair.

"We were asked by Mr. Browning if we would like to see 'the wickedest man in Illinois,' having reference to the notorious Thos. C. Sharp, who was then publishing a paper in Carthage. We replied that we would not object to seeing him without an introduction or being under any necessity of shaking his hand. With this understanding, we went with Mr. Browning to Sharp's office. Sharp was very courteous and polite, and showed signs of wishing to shake hands, a conjunction which we carefully avoided.

"A few years previous to this time, Sharp had been a candidate for office, and while the canvass was in progress, his opponent said, in a public speech: 'Sharp, you know if we had not sworn like h - - l for you, you would have been hung for the murder of the Smiths.'

"One of the Higbees (am not certain whether Chauncey or Francis) then resided fifteen or twenty miles east of Carthage. Mr. Browning stated that a gentleman in conversation with him asked if he ever felt any remorse of conscience for the part he took in the murder of the Smiths, to which Higbee replied: 'If you think I have not, look at my child.' The child referred to was then a young woman, grown, and, strange to behold, the entire left half of her face, on a line with the nose from the forehead to the chin, was one red mass, as if it were fresh blood, warm and dripping. The left arm and hand were also in the same condition. Higbee can see in his offspring the visible mark of God's judgment for his great sin."

Elder Henry G. Boyle says:

"While in California on a mission in the year 1855-56, and laboring on the Russian River, near where Healdsburg now stands, I often heard of an old mobocrat by the name of Kogan, or Cougan, who lived in that vicinity, and who boasted of having helped to murder Joseph and Hyrum Smith at Carthage. He often sent a request to me to visit him and proffered to tell me all about the manner of the death of our Prophet. A few months afterwards I heard that Mr. Cougan was stricken with some very singular disease. So peculiar was his case, that many people came to see him. He grew worse and worse, and lay for three months seemingly at the point of death. He suffered excruciatingly, and constantly prayed to die. He also begged his friends to put an end to his suffering, by taking his life, and even sought an opportunity to commit suicide, but was prevented by those waiting upon him. Many physicians visited him, and declared they never saw anything like his case.

"Many of the people in the neighborhood said: "If such is the end of those who kill the prophets and mob and drive the Saints, then may we be delivered from such a fearful and terrible calamity." *The Martyrs*, pp. 112-114.

ANOTHER MURDERER MEETS A COMMON FATE

North Carolina,
Surry County.

J. Monroe Hiatt, first being duly sworn, deposes and says:
That he is 66 years of age and is and has been a citizen and resident of Surry County, North Carolina all his life, that he is and has been since the organization president of the Mount Airy Branch of the Church of Jesus Christ of Latter-day Saints.

That affiant avers that about the year 1907, District President, Elder John Berrett, of Murray, Utah, requested that he interview the following named persons with reference to their knowledge of facts connected with the participation of Corporal James Belton in the martyrdom of the Prophet Joseph Smith. Accordingly he interviewed these parties and the following is the substance of their statements:

John Wesley Inman, late of Surry County, North Carolina, stated that he was well acquainted with Corporal James Belton and that many times he had heard Corporal Belton state that he took part in the killing of Joseph Smith and that he shot at him, taking as "good aim as he ever did at a squirrel."

Mrs. Bettie Lineback, of Mount Airy, Surry County, N. C., stated that she was a close neighbor of George Belton, son of Corporal James Belton and with Mrs. George Belton visited frequently Corporal James Belton in his home. Corporal Belton was sorely afflicted for several years, his eyes eaten from his head by this disease. Corporal Belton's wife stated that it was with difficulty that she fed her husband, because of his affliction.

Signed: J. Monroe Hiatt.

Sworn and subscribed before me, this the 13th day of August, 1938. Benton Moody,
Notary Public for North Carolina.
(Seal).   My Commission Expires Aug. 12, 1940.

Note: The above affidavit was copied from the files of the Manti Temple, Manti, Utah, August 15, 1951.

*   *   *   *   *

Statement of Arthur S. Haymore on Belton

(Dictated to the Compiler of this book, on Dec. 7, 1951, at Mesa, Arizona.)

I was born in Payson, Utah, on Feb. 1, 1878. My parents were born at Mt. Airy, Surry County, North Carolina, my father, Franklin D. Haymore on Aug. 12, 1849, my mother, Lucinda Adeline Taylor born in 1852.

Father was well acquainted with the Belton family. *James Belton* was a member of the mob that murdered the Prophet Joseph Smith, and after the murder he fled into North Carolina, located there and reared a family.

He was in great poverty and could hardly keep the wolf from the door. When I was visiting that vicinity in 1939, I visited a neighbor of Belton who told me of Belton's illness. He said he died from a cancer in his eye and when his meals were brought to him, the pus from his eye would drop in his plate. He died a horrible death. I asked this neighbor if Belton ever discussed Mormonism or the tragedy of the Prophet's death, and he stated that Belton did not wish to talk about it, that he didn't boast or brag about the martyrdom but was very sorry for what had happened.

I made a special trip to hunt this neighbor up and learn what he might know about Belton.

Statement of Elder James H. Moyle

"In Mt. Airy, Surry Co., N. C., a man named Belton was pointed out to me who claims to have taken a part in the same vile, fiendish crime, and seems to have fared a similar or worse fate, having been taken with something like the palsy. He is disabled for work of any importance, which renders him a perfect object of pity and charity.

"These are the only men I ever saw who claim to be, or bear the name of being connected with those who slew the great latter-day Prophet and Patriarch, Joseph and Hyrum Smith. If these be fair examples of their kind, it certainly looks as though their sins were going before them to judgment."   *The Martyrs*, p. 112.

THE FATE THAT SHOULD HAVE COME TO BOGGS AND ASSASSINS OF THE PROPHETS

"*** We are the supporters of the constitution of the United States, and we love that constitution and respect the laws of the United States but it is by the corrupt administration of those laws that we are made to suffer. If the law had been vindicated in Missouri, it would have sent Governor Boggs to the gallows, along with those who murdered Joseph and Hyrum, and those other fiends who accomplished our expulsion from the States."

Life of Brigham Young, by Edw. W. Tullidge, p. 263.

EX-GOVERNOR BOGGS OF MISSOURI EMIGRATES TO CALIFORNIA

Mr. Burdow, the principal man at the Fort (Laramie) was a Frenchman. He cordially received President Young and his staff, invited them into his sitting-room, gave them information of the route, and furnished them with a flat-bottom boat on reasonable terms, to assist them in ferrying the Platte. Ex-Governor Boggs, who had recently passed with his company had said much against the Mormons, cautioning Mr. Burdow to take care of his horses and cattle. Boggs and his company were quarreling, many having deserted him; so Burdow told that old anti-Mormon that, let the Mormons be what they might, they could not be worse than himself and his men.

"It is not a little singular that this extermination Governor of Missouri should have been crossing the Plains at the same time with the pioneers. They were going to carve out for their people a greater destiny than they could have reached either in Missouri or Illinois—he to pass away, leaving nothing but the infamy of his name.***

"Fifteen miles from Laramie, at the Springs, a company of Missouri emigrants came up. The pioneers kept the Sabbath the next day; the Missourians journeyed. Another company of Missourians appeared. *** The two Missouri companies kept up a warfare between themselves on the route. They were a suggestive example to the Mormons. After they had travelled near each other for a week, on the Sunday following the President made this the subject of his discourse. He said of the two Missourian companies:

" 'They curse, swear, rip and tear, and are trying to swallow up the earth; but though they do not wish us to have a place on it, the earth might as well open and swallow them up; for they will go to the land of forgetfulness, while the Saints, though they suffer some privations here, if faithful, will ultimately inherit the earth, and increase in power, dominion and glory.' "

Life of Brigham Young, by Edw. W. Tullidge, pp. 163-5.

* * * * *

In contrast to the deportment of the above swearing, quarreling, fighting, devils incarnate, read the following history of Saints of God who were hunting a new home, free from the Christian mobocracy of Missouri and Illinois, by Orson Pratt.

"In the spring of 1847, eight of the Quorum of the Twelve, in company with one hundred and thirty-five others, left Council Bluffs on the Missouri River, as pioneers, to explore the great interior of the continent, and find a place suitable for the location of the Saints. We prepared ourselves with astronomical and other scientific instruments of English construction, viz.: One circle of reflection, two sextants, one quadrant, two artificial horizons, one large reflecting telescope, several smaller ones, two barometers, several thermometers, besides nautical almanacs, books, maps, etc. We also invented a simple machine attached to a wagon wheel, by which the whole distance, as well as distance from place to place, were accurately measured. By the aid of these instruments, the latitudes and longitudes of the most prominent places upon our route were obtained, as also their elevations above the sea. Meteorological and geological observations were also taken throughout the whole journey. Geographical descriptions of the streams, rivers, lakes, plains, deserts, mountains, and vales, will also be found interspersed throughout the numerous journals kept by us. Botanical and Zoological observations were not forgotten by the scientific among us; and, indeed, the whole journey was rendered intensely interesting to the lovers of nature. New sceneries, grand and sublime beyond description, were constantly exhibiting themselves to our delighted vision. Mineral springs, caves, and numerous other natural curiosities, were found in abundance, which constantly excited the analyzing and cause-seeking powers of our chemists and natural philosophers."

DEPORTMENT OF MOBOCRATS CONTRASTED
WITH SAINTS OF GOD

From near the first of February to the first of March we were camped on Sugar Creek amid storms, the mercury at one time recording 20 degrees below zero. Yet there was a warm feeling in our hearts for we felt to trust in God. Even in the midst of tribulation, in a stormy winter's encampment, merry songs and happy voices were heard at every camp, and when the weather permitted all ages would join, inspired by sweet music, in the dance. At the signal for prayer, every occupation was suspended, and around the campfire, in wagons and tents, every knee was bowed, and a voice from every circle was raised in gratitude for past and in petition for continued protection.

We left Sugar Creek about the first of March, with snow, sleet, rain and mud, often pitching tents on ground swimming with water and deep with mud. To picture the realities of our journey to Garden Grove, about two hundred miles, is beyond my capacity. One day, in the open prairie, without a road, and ground full of water, our mule's feet, like pegs, could find no bottom and could go no farther. So in the open, treeless prairie we were compelled to stay. The companies had all passed, and we were alone. In the carriage was a small sheet iron stove, but not a stick of wood. The evening was growing cold and snow began to fall. Here was a dilemma. Without fire, and something warm to eat, all would suffer through the night. Seeing no other way I emptied a large, valuable chest, highly prized, split it up with the hatchet, and soon had a warm supper; then in the freezing storm, we crowded into our wagon and remained through the night. Next morning Brother Weatherby went 1½ miles for a green elm pole, which, with a little of the chest, gave us fire for our breakfast. Soon some of the brethren returned to look after and help us, but the ground was now frozen hard enough to bear both wagon and mules. We only needed help to get our wagon wheels out of the deep, frozen mud, in which they had been sunk.

Measles was now in camp, and when its fever was upon our two eldest, the water came so deep into the tent that our beds were soaked. A number of children died, among whom was one of Brother Bostwick's, a little girl about six years of age. Oh! how sorrowful to put her little form, as we did, in a grave half full of water, as no drier place could be found. Yet, with all this, there was hope and cheerfulness in the camp, and perhaps no company of equal size ever journeyed together with less faultfinding or murmuring.   *My Life's Review*, by Benj. F. Johnson, pp. 110-111.

THE FATE OF GOVERNOR REYNOLDS OF MISSOURI

By Wilford Woodruff

Governor Reynolds on one occasion employed men to try and kidnap Joseph and they almost accomplished their designs, but Joseph and some Gentile friends, as well as his brethren, through whom he was rescued, were taken to Nauvoo and released under a writ of habeas corpus. But the governor continued to harass him with writs, and was determined to destroy Joseph. Joseph and the Twelve went before God in prayer, Joseph kneeling before the Lord, offered up prayer, and asked God to deliver him from the power of that man. Among other things he told the Lord that he was innocent before Him and that his heart was heavy under the persecutions he endured. In about forty-eight hours from that time word reached Joseph that Reynolds had blown his brains out. Before perpetrating the deed he left a note on his desk stating, that as his services were not appreciated by the people of the state, he took that course to end his days.

There is another instance that occurs to my mind. A certain man took a stand against Joseph, and endeavored to bring persecution on him. Joseph went to his God and laid the matter before Him, asking to be delivered out of the hands and power of that wicked man. Joseph was a prophet, seer and revelator. He was acquainted with God; he knew the voice of the Spirit when it spoke to him. After offering up his prayer, the whispering of the still small voice came to him, saying: "Wait with patience." The next day that man was taken sick with cholera, and died in a few hours.

J.D., 24:55.

THE REMORSE OF A TRAITOR

Abraham C. Hodge stated that he had some conversation with Robert D. Foster, who told him his feelings on the subject of Mormonism. He said, "Hodge, you are going to the west—I wish I was going among you, but it can't be so, I am the most miserable wretch that the sun shines upon. If I could recall eighteen months of my life I would be willing to sacrifice everything I have upon earth, my wife and child not excepted. I did love Joseph Smith more than any man that ever lived. If I had been present I would have stood between him and death." Hodge inquired, "Why did you do as you have done? You were accessory to his murder." He replied: "I know that, and I have not seen one moment's peace since that time. I know that Mormonism is true, and the thought of meeting (Joseph and Hyrum) at the bar of God is more awful to me than anything else."

D.H.C., 7:513.

FATE OF A CARTHAGE JAIL MOBOCRAT

Sheriff Backenstos arrived in great haste and somewhat excited, said that the mob had driven him from his house in Carthage yesterday, and he went to Warsaw and stayed over night. He soon ascertained that the people were so enraged at him for trying to stop the house-burning that there was little probability of getting away alive, but finally prevailed on an influential mobocrat to escort him out of Warsaw this morning, who came with him about three and a half miles and on leaving cautioned him that if he saw two men together to avoid them for there were deep plans laid to kill him. Soon after he was pursued by a party of the mob on horseback, three of whom took the lead, one of the three had a swifter horse and gained a hundred yards in advance of his party in a short time when his horse stumbled and threw his rider. Backenstos maintained his speed, driving as fast as his horse could go.

The mob took the nearest road to cross his track and on his arrival at the old railroad crossing, the mob were within about 200 yards, they being on horseback and he in a buggy, they had gained on him considerably.

Orrin P. Rockwell and John Redding were refreshing themselves near the crossing as they had been out to bring in some of the burnt-out families who were sick, and on looking up saw Backenstos coming down the hill at full speed, and asked what was the matter. Backenstos replied the mob were after and determined to kill him and commanded them in the name of the people of the state to protect him. Rockwell replied, fear not, we have 50 rounds (two fifteen-shooter rifles besides revolvers).

Sheriff Backenstos then turned to the mob and commanded them to stop, and as they continued to advance raising their guns, he ordered Rockwell to fire; he did so aiming at the clasp of the belt on one of the mob, which proved to be Frank Worrell, who fell from his horse and the rest turned back and soon brought up a wagon and put his body into it.   *D.H.C.*, 6:446.

ACQUITTAL OF SHERIFF BACKENSTOS FOR THE KILLING OF FRANK A. WORRELL

News has arrived that Sheriff Backenstos, who went to Peoria in charge of Henry W. Miller, coroner of Hancock county, and was tried before Judge Purple on the charge of the 'murder' of Frank A. Worrell, was acquitted. The moral atmosphere around the judge was so different, than when at Carthage, that in all his charges and rulings, he appeared like another judge, and as though he had never been afflicted with mobocratic mania.

The jury said if there had been no witnesses only on the part of the state, it would not have required more than two minutes to have made up their verdict.   *D.H.C.* 6:541

THE SUFFERING OF ONE OF THE ASSASSINS

BY MATILDA C. GIAUQUE STEED

After the April Conference in Nauvoo, 1846, Thomas Steed (late of Farmington, Utah) then about twenty years of age, left the city with his uncle John Steed. His last dime was paid to the ferry-boat that landed him to the west bank of the Mississippi River, at Keokuk, Lee County, Iowa. There he found work at unloading boats and received fifty cents the first night, the biggest money he had seen in the United States. He continued this work until he had saved $100.00. He found a home with his cousin Henry Steed, who had married as his second wife Miss Rebecca Reed at Nauvoo. Both were members of the Church, as well as his mother Ann Steed, and the family of James and Caroline Steed, all living at Keokuk. The three counsins had bought jointly a property of eighty acres of woodland and a quarry and worked together at building basements, furnishing their own lime and stone. They now lived on their land in two dwellings.

One cold October morning, in 1846, Thomas went after the two oxen browsing in the Mississippi bottoms and was surprised to find a man whose clothes were white with frost, walking slowly among the trees. "Man, did you spend the night outside? I would have given you a place to sleep in my cabin." "I cannot stay anywhere," was the answer. "Why cannot you?" "I have a farm on the other side of the river, at Warsaw, as good as any farm, but I can't stay in it." "Tell me, why?" "I will tell you stranger: I was in that Smith scrape. Now I can rest nowhere. They prevailed on me to go with them. Would to God I had been a thousand miles away."

Slowly, in the cold, alone and hungry, through the woods of the Mississippi bottoms, this remorseful murderer continued his march. That "Smith scrape," the tragedy of Carthage, was about 28 months past. "I pitied him," said my husband.

HOW SOME OF THE MISSOURI MOBOCRATS MET THEIR FATE

By Andrew Jenson and Edward Stevenson

On the morning of Monday, 10th, (September, 1888) we took a 15th Street cable car to the outskirts of the city (Independence, Missouri) from where we walked in a southeasterly direction to the Big Blue. The reader will remember that it was on this stream the Colesville branch and other Saints located in 1831, and that on the 2nd of August of the year mentioned Joseph Smith the Prophet, and eleven other men, in honor of the twelve tribes of Israel, carried and placed in position the first log for a house as a commencement for the building of Zion in this dispensation. The Big Blue is quite a large but sluggish stream which rises in Johnson county, Kansas, enters Jackson county, Missouri, from the west and then changes its course northward winding through the fields and farms about half way between Kansas City and Independence centers. In going up the hill traveling east, after having crossed the bridge over the Big Blue on the Westport and Independence road (a few hundred feet north of where the ferry over the Big Blue, mentioned in Church history, once was), we turned aside to an old farm house, where we happened on an old Missouri mobocrat, who boasted of having been an enemy to the Mormons for over fifty years. Says he, "I was but a boy when the Mormons were expelled from Jackson county, but, by G-d, I was old enough to shoulder a gun and help drive them out."

We asked him what the Mormons had done to the old settlers which merited so brutal a treatment, and especially wanted him to tell us his own personal experience with them. "O," says he, "they did not molest me, for I was so young, but they did others." He then related how one of the Saints claimed to have received a revelation authorizing him to steal another man's cow, and that the Missourian thus imposed upon retaliated by killing the Mormon, and this was the commencement of the hostilities between the Saints and the Missourians in Jackson county. Of course our knowledge of the true history of the affair prevented us from accepting the statement as true. We did not, however, consider it wise to enter into any argument with him, but proceeded to ask him other questions.

He then informed us that old Col. Pitcher, who took an active part against the Saints in 1833, died about a year ago as a pauper. Not only did he die poor, but during his last days he was shunned and deserted by all. Even his own children neglected to care for him. It went so far that some of the neighbors proposed to take up a subscription in order to raise sufficient means to hire a negro from Kansas City to wait on him until he died; but before the darkey came he breathed his last in the midst of filth and misery. He was once a wealthy man, but during the late civil war his property was burned by the enemy and he was reduced to poverty. Thus he seemed to have received his just due for the cruel part he took in mobbing the Saints and burning their houses in 1833.

It may be proper to state here that nearly every house on both sides of the Big Blue, the very section of country where about 200 houses belonging to the Saints were burned in the beginning of 1834—was destroyed during the guerrilla and bushwacker's campaign of terror in the time of the late civil war. It was a war between neighbors and neighborhoods, and the whole section of country was laid waste, so Mr. Mason informed us. His own house was burned with the rest.

In answer to our inquiry he also told us that Moses Wilson, the old mobocrat general, notoriously known in the Missouri persecutions, died many years ago in Texas as a drunkard, gambler and genuine vagabond, despised by all who knew him.

"What became of Samuel C. Owens who had so narrow an escape from drowning in the Missouri River while fighting the Mormons in 1834," we asked. "Sam Owens," replied Mr. Mason, "why, he was the only man killed in the battle with the Mexicans near the city of Chihuahua in 1846. He had just received bad news from home, informing him that his son-in-law had committed the crime of murder, and Mr. Owens felt so bad about it, that he immediately filled himself with brandy, plunged heedlessly into a hand-to-hand conflict with the Mexicans, during which he was killed, according to his own wish; for he said before starting, that he wanted to go to hell at once, knowing, as he did, that he would have to go there some day anyway." Such was the fate of this old mobocrat, who persecuted the Saints so unmercifully during the Jackson and Clay county troubles.

Mr. Mason, our informant, lives on a farm which once belonged to the Saints. He is seventy-one years of age, and although he was bitter against the Saints, he seemed pleased with being able to point out to us the various bends on the Big Blue, where the humble log cabins of the Saints once stood. At several points there are still remnants to be found of the chimneys and foundations, but not a single house is known to be in existence. The residence of Brother Joshua Lewis, in which the Church held its fifth General Conference, August 4, 1831, crumbled to pieces years ago. That was one of the few buildings not burned by the mob at the time of the exodus, but it was partly torn down. Mr. Mason also told us where the skirmish took place between the Saints and the mob, November 4, 1833, when Andrew Barber and two of the mob were killed.

In alluding to himself the old man, whom we considered a fair sample of many of those who drove the Saints out of Jackson county in 1833, informed us that he had no education. "I can't read a word," said he, "I only went to school three weeks in my life, during which time I got nine lickings and quit."

After we left, Mr. Mason remarked to a neighbor: "They (meaning your correspondents) asked me about these men (alluding to the mobbers), and as I did not want to lie to them I told them the truth. These strangers, even if they were d-d Mormons, possessed one redeeming quality—they were Democrats." On our merits as Democrats he gave us all the buttermilk we could drink and wished us success. * * *

Last evening (Sept. 10, 1888), we were taken in a conveyance, by our friend, Elder George P. Frisbey of the Hedrickite church, to fill our appointment in their meeting house on the Temple lot. Our journey was over rolling land, with fields and forests intermingled, forming a picture worthy of Zion's borders, on which we truly were. Farms containing hundreds of acres of beautiful land, the homes of the Saints more than half a century ago, were pointed out to us; also the residence of the late Col. Pitcher, standing on a hill about four miles southwest of Independence, on the Westport and Independence Road, where the colonel resided for fifty years on a beautiful plantation which subsequently passed away from him. We also learned the fate of another notorious and leading mobocrat, Mr. A. E. Hickman, known as Captain Hickman, once a government surveyor, who took an active part in driving the Saints from their homes in 1833. His possessions were pointed out, and his wealth boasted of as that of a possessor of broad fields. "But," said our informant, "he died in that little cabin on yonder hill in 1882, in the midst of grief and poverty."

THE JAIL WHERE JOSEPH THE PROPHET
REBUKED THE GUARDS

This morning (September 13, 1888) we visited a number of old settlers trying to gather information in regard to circumstances transpiring fifty years ago. We visited the site of the old jail where Parley P. Pratt, Morris Phelps and others were imprisoned from November, 1838, to May, 1839. An old resident told us that he remembered many years afterwards seeing the name of P. P. Pratt on the ceiling of the jail, which was finally torn down and the site is now occupied by a large wagon repairing and blacksmith shop owned by Messrs. Powell & Sons. On the identical spot where the

jail stood is a well from which we drew and drank water in memory
of the past. The jail site is a little more than half a block east of
the northeast corner of the court-house square, on the south side
of the street. We made several inquiries about the old log house,
where Joseph the Prophet and fellow-prisoners were guarded during Judge Austin A. King's trial in November, 1838, and where
Joseph rebuked the guard; but we were unable to find any who
could give us the necessary information. One old settler, Mr. B. H.
Quesenberry, who acted as county clerk of Ray County in 1838,
told us that there were a number of old log houses on the north
side of the court-house square at that time, and it was no doubt
into one of these that the Prophet and his brethren were usherd
on that memorable occasion.

We have also learned that General John B. Clark, the notorious
mobocrat, died as a drunkard in Fayette, Howard county, about
the year 1880, forsaken by his political friends at least. The notorious Austin A. King also died years ago. He was taken sick
very suddenly at St. Louis and died almost immediately. His remains were brought to Ray county for burial. ****

(September 16, 1888). The region around Shoal creek, where
Haun's Mill stood, is much heavier timbered than it was fifty
years ago, and a fine grove of locust trees now covers the site of
old "Mormontown." A resident of Kingston, who yesterday pointed
out to us a number of farms once owned by the Saints, said, that
in going through Caldwell county, he could always distinguish the
old Mormon homesteads from all others. We asked him to describe
to us the difference between Mormon farms and others. "Well," said
he, "nearly every one of the Mormons planted locust trees around
their buildings which was something the Missourians never thought
of doing, and these have now grown and spread, until there are
locusts groves on nearly every farm where the Mormons resided."

Nearly all who participated in the massacre are now dead, or
have moved away, so that their whereabouts, if alive, are not
known. Some of the murderers have died in disgrace and shame,
haunted by their consciences until their last hours. Others have
boasted of their dastardly deeds, until they have been smitten
with sickness and misery, in the midst of which they would curse
God and die.

The notorious Col. Wm. O. Jennings, who commanded the mob
at the massacre, was assassinated in Chilicothe, Livingston county,
Mo., in the evening of Jan. 30, 1862, by an unknown person, who
shot him on the street with a revolver or musket as the colonel
was going home after dark. He died the next day in great agony.
The shooting occurred in Calhoun street, a little northwest of the
present county jail in Chilicothe. Nehemiah Comstock, another
leader of the mob who committed the murders, expired years ago
in Livingston county, as a good-for-nothing drunkard. His mother
was also a drunkard and died a pauper and in the midst of misery
in a Kentucky poor house.

Thomas S. Brockman, one of the principal mob leaders in 1846,
came to a miserable end in Kansas, whither he removed from
Mount Sterling, Adams county, Illinois, after trying in vain to be

elected to office in Hancock county, He was killed during a quarrel, in which he was the attacking party, in 1872. Francis Higbee died in New York, his brother in Pittsfield, Pike county, Illinois. Robert D. Foster went to California and has not since been heard of by our informants. William and Wilson Law are supposed to be alive yet, as they both visited Nauvoo a few years ago, trying to sell their claims on the islands in the Mississippi River, near Nauvoo. All these will be remembered by the Saints as the parties who, more than any others, were the means of bringing about the martyrdom of Joseph and Hyrum. Levi Williams, the principal leader of the Carthage Jail murderers, died at his home in Green Plains, about the year 1858. John McAuley, a notorious mobocrat, died a most miserable death about the year 1872. While lying on his death bed, suffering the most excruciating pains, he told Mr. Morrill, our informant, that if he could only blot out five years of his life (referring to the time he fought the Mormons), he could die a happy man. Mr. Morrill said that a great number of the old mobocrats came to a miserable end, and he did not remember a single one of them who ever amounted to anything after having persecuted the Saints. On the other hand, we heard of several of those who took an active part in defending the Saints who have since occupied various positions of honor and trust. Prominent among them we may mention Mr. Morrill himself, who has always been on the side of justice and right, and took an active part legally in defending a number of the brethren in times of their trouble; he has served ten years as mayor of Nauvoo and several terms in the Illinois legislature.

Our letter would be too long if we should relate what we learned in regard to the Jack-Mormons, the French Icarians, who purchased the walls of the Temple, after the building was burned by the hands of an incendiary, and others who have figured in the history of Nauvoo since the Saints were forced to leave. Suffice it to say that shortly after the exodus and after most of the so-called Jack-Mormons got discouraged and moved to other parts, the population of Nauvoo was reduced to about 300 souls, and property sold for almost a song. To illustrate, we will simply state that a Mr. Reimbold, father of our informant, who came to Nauvoo in 1848, bought a fine two-story house—hewed logs at that—with floors and everything complete, for the sum of $4. The present German population, who have come to stay, have done better than any of their predecessors since the Saints left, but even they cannot make it a place of any importance. No, that is reserved for "others" to do, and even these "others" can not do it till the Lord's time comes.

From letters written by Andrew Jensen and Edward Stevenson, entitled "Infancy of the Church," pp. 56.

A VISIT TO NAUVOO AND TO "SERGEANT WILLIAMS"

BY SAMUEL G. SPENCER

The Mississippi river was frozen over sufficiently to afford the passage of pedestrians. Two gentlemen are running opposition hand sleighs, on which they carry what little express, passengers

or luggage there may be for Nauvoo. I rode on Mr. Reinboldt's
sleigh, himself skating and pushing the sleigh.

In about ten minutes we were across the river. We then took
his conveyance and rode up the rising hill where the once beautiful
town of Nauvoo stood. I could not help the feeling of awe that crept
over me, as house after house was pointed out to me where the
down-trodden, robbed, driven, and murdered servants of God once
lived, among them being the house of the great latter-day Prophet,
Joseph Smith. The houses that are remaining, which the Saints
built, are among the best average buildings of today.

I registered at the Arlington hotel, from Salt Lake City, and
I soon made my business known, and was introduced to an old
gentleman who lived here in the times of trouble, by the name of
Thomas E. Kelley, who received me very kindly and spared no
pains in giving me all the information he could command. We
visited all the houses of note now standing, and I carefully made
note of the history of each, as given by him. He condemned with
the most severe emphasis the way the Mormons had been treated.
He said he was only a boy then, but was eye witness to "Jack-Mormons stealing from parties and hiding it upon the places of Mormon leaders, and then going to the parties whom they had stolen
from and telling them they'd bet the Mormon leaders had them."

I next called at the Nauvoo *Rustler* printing office, and gained
what information I could of the present feeling toward the Mormons. The people here universally acknowledge the mistake of
those who drove the Mormons, and agree that it was one of the
most wicked things that ever happened. With an expressive sigh
they tell of the time when Nauvoo had about 22,000 inhabitants,
while Chicago at that time had 12,000 inhabitants. Nauvoo then,
they are careful to remark, had no saloons; now with about 1,200
inhabitants it has several saloons.

Leaving these people with a kind, interesting feeling towards
the Mormons, I departed for Carthage, having to recross the river
and take train to Keokuk, Ia., and from there to Carthage. I registered at the Grove hotel, made my business known, and was soon
introduced and kindly received by the people. I called at the place
where the Prophet and Patriarch were killed, and found that I had
learned more about the building in a moment's view than I had
ever found out by reading. The place is now used for a dwelling,
and the kind old lady is very hospitable in showing strangers
through the house and giving liberally of her beautiful selection
of flowers. I also secured a piece of stone from the building.

I next called on Sergeant Williams. I found him still bitter in
his epithets toward the man whom he "saw killed." He said: "We
all wanted him killed; we held a meeting the night before and decided to kill him. We loaded our cartridges blank, and agreed upon
the plan carried out." He then continued to say that "Joe Smith
was a bad man; he taught the people to steal. One of his teachings
I remember now was: 'The earth is the Lord's and the fulness
thereof, therefore take whatsoever seemeth you good.' Such doctrine as that would make bad people." So Williams went on. He then
asked me where I was from. I told him from Salt Lake City. He

would not tell me any more, and was seized with such a violent shivering and shaking, that his daughter politely asked me if I would not defer further conversation.

Sergeant Williams, as he calls himself, lives in about the poorest house in Carthage. The forest trees, in their native wildness, remain with the greatest possible dullness, and everything, both within and without, bears the frown of a just God.

I found people in both of these towns who would look at the Views of Salt Lake City, which I had with me, and with moisture in their eyes express: "Surely the Lord is with these people or they could not endure and accomplish what they do."

Millennial Star, 57:123-124.

A MOBOCRAT BURIED IN THE OCEAN

On Tuesday, May 24, 1864, we sailed second cabin on the bark *Onward*, Hempstead, captain. Brother Cluff and I occupied one room with a Missourian named McCarty, said to be suffering with consumption. He was a large, raw-boned man, of a quarrelsome disposition.

One day Captain Hempstead invited us three to have seats on the upper deck with the first-cabin passengers. The reason for this courtesy was soon apparent. Among the cabin passengers were several ministers; and they wanted a little diversion at the expense of the Mormon Elders.

A warm discussion ensued. It was asserted that the Mormons were driven from Missouri and Illinois on account of their thieving and lawless acts. In my defense I challenged the proof of a single dishonest deed, and testified that Joseph and Hyrum were innocent, and that they were murdered in cold blood. Mr. McCarty became angry, and boasted that he helped kill Joseph and Hyrum Smith. I told him then that by his own confession he was a murderer, and that the curse of God was upon him. He would have struck me, but the captain interfered, and made him behave.

About midnight of the 30th of May, I was awakened by McCarty. He was sitting on a stool, in front of his bunk; the full moon shining through the window, giving him a white, ghastly appearance. He told me to get up and get him a drink. I replied that the guard passed the door every five minutes and would wait upon him. He seized a butcher knife, sprang to his feet, and swore he would cut the heart out of me. I was lying in the middle bunk and had but little room in which to move, and nothing with which to defend myself; but I felt I would rather die than do his bidding. I therefore silently asked God to deliver me from his power.

He took one step forward, threw up both hands, and fell backwards. I sprang from the bunk, and raised his head, but the man was dead. Brother Cluff called the guard, who soon brought the captain and the doctor. The latter said he died of heart failure.

In the morning they sewed him up in a canvas, a cannon ball at his feet. I stood by the taffrail, and saw the body slide off the plank; and as I watched it sink into the depths of the ocean, I rejoiced that I had borne a faithful testimony of God's martyred

prophets, and was truly grateful that I had been delivered from
the hands of a wicked man.   *Memoirs of John R. Young, pp. 129-130.*

ANOTHER MURDERER GOES TO HIS REWARD

A telegram from Carthage, Illinois, brings the news that on
the night of Monday, April 9, (1894), Thomas Coke Sharp, editor
and proprietor of the Carthage *Gazette*, died at his home at that place,
from paralysis, from which he had suffered the past three years.
The *Deseret News* gives the following additional information of the
life of this man:

The deceased was the son of a noted Methodist minister, Rev.
Solomon Sharp, of Philadelphia, and was in the 76th year of his
age at the time of his demise. He was a native of New York, having been born at Mt. Holly, September 25, 1818. He came west and
settled in Quincy, Illinois, and engaged in the practice of law.
Shortly afterwards, in the summer of 1840, he moved to Warsaw,
Hancock County. He became associated in business with James
Gamble, and together they purchased from Daniel N. White the
Western World, of which Sharp became editor. A year later the
name of the paper was changed to the *Warsaw Signal*, and for a
number of years it was the only paper published in Hancock County,
outside of Nauvoo. In later years Mr. Sharp became the editor of
the *Carthage Gazette*.

The chief interest of the people of Utah in Thomas C. Sharp
arises from the fact that they and others have had to regard him
as one of the murderers of the Prophet Joseph and the Patriarch
Hyrum Smith, at Carthage jail, June 27, 1844. Perhaps the last
Utah man to visit and converse with him was Sheriff Gilbert Belnap, of Ogden. He stated at the time that Sharp was an invalid,
and his mind impaired. He was non-communicative on the subject
of the assassination, particularly the part he played in it, but
Sheriff Belnap believes that at the time of his visit Sharp would
have told all he remembered if his wife would have allowed it, but
this she would not do. When Sharp came into Hancock County there
was some anti-"Mormon" agitation and he entered into it with
ardor. He was ambitious for political preferment and was wholly
unscrupulous in measures to gain his ends. He published in his
paper the most infamous falsehoods against the Latter-day Saints.
All through those troublous times the columns of the *Signal* were
replete with vicious articles inciting and urging violence toward
the "Mormon" people. Thomas C. Sharp had murder in his heart
then and later availed himself of the opportunity to imbrue his
hands in the blood of innocence. He was denounced by the sheriff
of the county as "a villain of the worst dye." In connection with
his associates he was instrumental in inflaming public prejudice
to the extent that meetings were held, the first of them at Warsaw,
in which resolutions were passed declaring that in the opinion of
those participating the time had arrived when the "Mormons," as
a body, should be driven from the surrounding settlements into
Nauvoo; that the Prophet and his miscreant adherents should then
be demanded at their hands, and if not surrendered a war of ex-

termination should be waged to their entire destruction. Sharp was an ardent advocate of the murderous policy.

This situation was known at the time, as may be seen by the following from the diary of the Prophet Joseph, though the people did not realize the full import of the ominous proceedings. The Prophet says, under date of June 18, 1844:

"About 2 p.m., the Legion was drawn up in the street close by the mansion. I stood in full uniform on the top of the frame of a building. Judge Phelps read the *Warsaw Signal* extra of the 17th, wherein the 'old citizens' were called upon to assist the mob in exterminating the leaders of the Saints and driving away the people."

Thomas C. Sharp was one of the attorneys engaged as prosecuting counsel when the Prophet Joseph and his brother Hyrum were placed under arrest. Knowing that they were innocent of any crime, and that if the case proceeded to trial acquittal must follow, he joined with others in carrying out the mobocratic design. He was a leader in the murderous conspiracy, and conducted the negotiations by which it was arranged that the mob should get possession of the jail unopposed. When the assault took place he was one of the participants. The readers of the *News* will remember that a few weeks ago there was present in this city Col. M. B. Darnell, of Iowa, who was an eye-witness to the shooting at Carthage. A relative of his, a young man who was with the mob, names Sharp as one of the persons who engaged in the actual shooting. He was indicted with others, but all were acquitted by a jury selected, as was well understood by the people then, and as testified to by Col. Darnell from personal knowledge, from among the mobocrats themselves.

No language can make the crime in which Thomas Coke Sharp was a leading participator appear more heinous than it is. He has gone to his final account, where he will receive from a just Judge that reward which his works merit. The people of Utah are satisfied to let the matter rest there. The *News* refers on this occasion to the awful tragedy of June 27, 1844, because it feels it to be a solemn duty to make the record in connection with the passing from mortality of one of the men chiefly responsible for the assassination of the Prophet and Patriarch.   *Millennial Star,* 56:349-350.

THOSE RESONSIBLE FOR THE MURDER OF THE PROPHET JOSEPH SMITH

By Orson Pratt

The word concerning the driving of the people from Illinois, westward to the Rocky Mountains, in the article of the treaty got up by the mobocrats, was that "we must not stop short of the Rocky Mountains, but that we must go beyond them." Were any lives lost in those terrible persecutions, or was it merely property taken away from the Saints, without paying them a cent, in the shape of thousands of acres of land which they had paid the Government for, and comfortable houses? If it had been only our houses

and lands it would have been bad enough; but lives were taken—
innocent men, women and children were shot down. I might go on
and relate some of the circumstances, but I dislike to dwell on the
subject; it is apt to kindle up old nature in one's heart, therefore
I will leave that topic. Suffice it to say that the blood of hundreds
and I might almost say thousands, will be required at the hands
of this nation unless the people repent.

Where is our prophet who translated this book (the Book of
Mormon), that noble youth whom God raised up when only between fourteen and fifteen years of age, Where is that noble boy
to whom God sent His angel, and to whom He gave the Urim and
Thummim, and to whom He entrusted the original golden plates
from which this book was translated. He fell a martyr to his religion under this free Government of the United States. Where is
the Patriarch of our Church, the brother of our Prophet? He too,
was shot down at the same time. By whom? By people who were
painted black, for the occasion, and who boasted of their bloody
deeds in Hancock county, Illinois. Some of them are still alive in
that county, and to this day boast of their bloody deeds in persecuting the Latter-day Saints.

Many scores of our people were wasted away, and their blood
soaks the soil of this great government, crying aloud to the
heavens for vengeance on those who shed the blood of the martyrs,
and who persecuted God's people and sent them forth, as they supposed, to perish in the heart of the Great American Desert. Not
only will they who committed these deeds be brought to judgment,
but those also who stood back behind the screen and said: "How
glad I am, Joe Smith is now dead, the Mormon Patriarch Hyrum
Smith is shot down, and we have killed many of their followers,
men, women and children. They have been driven five times from
their locations and settlements and been robbed of millions of dollars worth of property and we are enjoying it, and it is all right.
Joe Smith ought to have been killed before, long ago."

This seemed to be the feeling of a great many people in the
American nation. They sanctioned the shedding of innocent blood,
if they did not actually shed it themselves, and God will require
it at their hands. Will He require anything at the hands of our
nation, in a national capacity, in regard to this matter? Was it not
within their power to protect us on the lands which we purchased
from the General Government? We did not purchase, to any extent,
land from the Missourians, but we took up land that belonged to
the General Government. We paid our money into that government
land office. Did they protect us in the possession of that land,
which they guaranteed by their deeds to us and our seed or heirs
for ever? They did not. Did they protect us in our citizenship? No,
they did not. Did we appeal to them for protection? Yes, we laid
our case before them. What was their reply? Martin Van Buren,
who sat at the head of the government at that time, said: "Gentlemen, your cause is just, but I can do nothing for you." He saw
the testimony; there was no getting away from it.

Discourse delivered April 10, 1870. *J. D.* 13:136-137.

A MORMON MISSIONARY LEARNS OF
FATE OF MOBOCRATS

Excerpts from daily diary of Alonzo Winters who was a Mormon Elder laboring in Alexandria, Missouri, Nauvoo, Ill, and adjacent territory during the year 1876-1877.

Tuesday, December 6, 1876: Went with Aunt Lucinda to visit a woman, a member of the Church by the name of Herbey. She had been sick for a long time. She told me of two men, residents of Alexandria, that were engaged in the martyrdom of Joseph and Hyrum—John Johnston and a man by the name of Frazier Johnston, the first died a prisoner at the hands of the rebels during the rebellion, perished with the cold. The other, Frazier, still lives here. A man by the name of Bledsaw who is believed to have been in that scrape, and who is known to have been in the mob who drove and plundered the Saints in Nauvoo, froze to death in a corn shock.

Today I listened to some horrid recitals of murders that were committed in Missouri during the Rebellion. In one case where a leading man near here was missing; the Union soldiers arrested twelve peaceable citizens and gave them 24 hours to produce the man or be led out and shot. The man not being found in time, the poor farmers were led out and shot with the exception of one old man with a large family. A noble young man volunteered to save the old man to his family; his offer was accepted, and he was shot in place of the man with the family.

Saturday, December 23, 1876: Spent my time with the family of Mr. Tripp (Alexandria, Missouri) where I was treated very kindly, and heard from him the particulars of the burning of the property that took place during the driving of the Saints from their homes in this country (Lima). Mr. Tripp and his wife who is a sister of Dominius Carter, both stated to me that the principal men who engaged in the mobbing of the Saints from the state of Illinois had come to a miserable end, or they were still suffering with poverty, some of them have been crippled. One broke his back when drunk; some froze to death, and almost without an exception they had come to a miserable end, and in many cases their sufferings were excruciating.

FATE OF MOBOCRAT AT HAUN'S MILL MASSACRE

(Excerpt of letter from George A. Smith and W. I. Appleby to Orson Hyde, written from "Camp of Israel, Muddy Fork, 930 miles from Winter Quarters, Oct. 18, 1849.)

"Many have been the graves we have passed on our journey, some of friends near and dear, others of strangers, that have fallen by the shaft of the destroyer, while journeying over these boundless plains of sage, and mountains of rock, where the buffalo, elk, antelope, bear, ravenous wolf, etc., range undisturbed, except by the red man, or the journeying emigrant.

"Many has been the grave of the gold seeker we have seen, whose bodies have been disinterred by the wolves; and the bones, pantaloons, hose, and other things laying strewed around, with the head board laying near, informing the traveller, who had been buried, where from, the day they died, age, disease, etc. But we have not seen a solitary instance where one of the Saint's tombs, have been disturbed by the wolves. Among the graves of those whose bones lay around their graves, bleaching in the sun, their flesh being consumed by the ravenous wolf, we recognized the names of several noted mobocrats from the states of Missouri and Illinois, who took an active and prominent part in persecuting, mobbing, and driving the Saints from these states. Among others, we noticed at the South Pass of the Rocky Mountains the grave of one E. Dodd, of Gallatin, Missouri, who died on the 19th of July last, of typhus fever. The wolves had completely disinterred him. The clothes in which he had been buried lay strewed around. The under jaw bone was found in his grave, with the teeth complete, being the only remains discernible of him. It is believed he was the same Dodd that took an active part as a prominent mobocrat in the murder of the Saints at Haun's Mill, Missouri; if so, it is a righteous retribution. Our God will surely inflict punishment upon the heads of our oppressors in His own due time and way."

Millennial Star, 12:127.

RENOUNCE MORMONISM AND LIVE

By Brigham Young

I do not acknowledge that I ever received persecution; my path has been kind from the Lord, I do not consider that I have suffered enough even to mention it. But when the words of Governor Lilburn W. Boggs were read by General Clark, with regard to our leaving the state or renouncing our religion, I sat close by him, although I was the very particular one they wanted to get and were enquiring for; but, as kind Providence would have it, they could not tell whether it was Brigham Young they were looking at or somebody else. No matter how this was done, they could not tell. But, standing close by General Clark, I heard him say: "You are the best and most orderly people in this state, and have done more to improve it in three years than we have in fifteen. You have showed us how to improve, how to raise fruit and wheat, how to make gardens, orchards, and so on; and on these accounts we want you; but we have this to say to you, no more bishops, no more high councils, and as for your Prophet," and he pointed down to where Joseph lay, right in the midst of the camp, "you will never see him again." Said I to myself, "May be so and may be not; but I do not believe a word of it." And continued he, "disperse and become as we are."

Do you want I should tell you what I thought? I do not think I will. Renounce my religion? "No, sir," said I, "It is my all, all I have on this earth. What is the world worth as it is now? Nothing. It is like a morning shadow; it is like the dew before the sun, like the grass before the scythe, or the flower before the pinching frosts of autumn. No, sir, I do not renounce my religion. I am looking beyond; my hope is beyond this vale of tears, and beyond the present life. The organization and intelligence God has given me are not to perish in nonentity; I have to live, and I calculate to take such a course that my life hereafter will be in a higher state of existence than the present."   *Millennial Star,* Vol. 52:563 (1890).

THE FATE OF THE MURDERERS OF THE PROPHET JOSEPH

By W. H. RITER

I have respectfully asked what has become of those who drove the Saints from their homes; and the unvarying testimony has been that those who are alive are socially and politically dead. Mr. M. M. Morrill, an attorney in Nauvoo, brother of Senator Morrill, of Maine, who is an old inhabitant of the place, in reply to the above question said: "They are either dead, in the penitentiary, or gone to hell." Palma, the fiend who set the Temple on fire, is now a convict in the penitentiary at Fort Madison. The Rev. Thos. Brockman, commander of the mob forces who expelled the remaining Saints from their homes, in September, 1846, afterwards ran for the office of county clerk for this county. He made his eminent services in expelling the Saints a radical point in his claims upon his party for election. He was defeated overwhelmingly and left the country in disgust. Before leaving, he made a valedictory address to the citizens of Carthage, in which he bitterly complained of the treatment he had received from the citizens of Hancock county in being ungrateful to him for his mighty services rendered in expelling their enemies. During his address he had the flag which waved over his myrmidons laying on the desk before him. He pathetically said, he wished to bequeath the flag to some citizen of Hancock county who would preserve it, and asked who would take the flag. No one made answer for sometime, finally a man, whose name I have forgotten, stepped forward and received that glorious flag (?) which had waved over fifteen hundred brave heads (?) who had succeeded in driving a few defenceless men, women and children from their homes.

Brockman and Col. Williams are both dead, died enjoying the respect of no one as far as I can learn. Col. McCanly, one of the leaders of the mob still lives, but in a state of abject poverty and his faculties are close bordering on idiocy. Tom Sharp still lives; it is said his nose lengthens as he grows in years. The present citizens of Hancock county, as far as I can learn, deprecate the expulsion of the Saints, and none of those engaged in the unholy act ever enjoyed any social respect afterwards—nay more, they were despised by their neighbors and former friends."

Correspondence from Nauvoo, Hancock County, Illinois, The *Deseret News,* Jan. 5, 1870, Vol. 18:48.

THE END OF THE TRAITOR COLONEL GEORGE M. HINKLE

By EDWARD W. STEVENSON

On the 30th of October, 1838, Neil Gillam was at the head of a mob who were disguised as wild Indians. They were painted, and Gillam himself was arrayed as an Indian chief. The mob had been burning houses and driving the Mormons' stock away from their owners, taking prisoners. Colonel Hinkle ordered out a company of militia, about 150 in number, to endeavor to learn the intentions of Gillam and others, who were camping on Log Creek, near Far West. I was one of those under Col. Hinkle and we all were on horseback. We soon learned that their intentions were hostile. A flag of truce in the hand of Charles C. Rich was shot at during the day, and our company was cut off from Far West by a line of battle being formed between us and our homes. Col. Hinkle returned from the front of our line with his military coat off, saying that there were hardly enough of us to allow a mouthful apiece for the numerous hosts before us. He seemed excited and fearfully frightened, and for this and other reasons I have always believed this accounted for his conduct on that occasion. We retreated fifteen miles to Far West, arriving about the time the troops were nearing the city. They were marching with red flags, which were interspersed and mixed up with Gillam's command of painted faces. Our company coming into Far West on the gallop, created quite a sensation, as we were mistaken for the enemy coming in from two different points. We, however, soon proved ourselves to be friends, and were just in time to extend the line already formed in defense of the city. Our adversaries were in the ratio of about ten to one of us, which looked rather serious for a little handful of members of the Church of Jesus Christ of Latter-day Saints.

The Prophet came along after our arrival and said:

"Fear them not. God is for us, and there are more for us than there are against us (meaning the hosts of heaven were on our side.) God and liberty is the watchword," said Joseph. "Fear them not, for their hearts are cold as cucumbers."

Night was fast approaching and flags of truce were passing between the two lines, by which we learned that this formidable army was sent out by Governor Boggs with orders to exterminate us. It was finally concluded not to murder us that night, so the army withdrew until the next morning, when they intended to make a final end of Mormonism. They camped for the night on Goose Creek, one mile away from the city. Thus ended one of the most eventful days of our lives. It fell to my lot to stand guard that night, and the worst confusion and disorder ever witnessed by human beings existed in the enemy's camp. This, with unearthly yelling and howling, produced a real pandemonium very much resembling my idea of hell. A sort of breastwork was constructed during the night made principally of wagons, house logs, etc. A dark and dreary night was that. On the following day, October 31st, we were preparing to meet death, if necessary, rather than surrender our religion to a mob. We trusted in the Lord, however, and a better way was prepared. Col. Hinkle had been communicating with the enemy during the day, and in the afternoon, Joseph Smith and others passed over the breast-works near where I and others were on duty. Col. Hinkle lead the party to meet the enemy, where he betrayed them into their hands. This treachery on his part turned out for the best, for God suffers offences to come, as in the case of Judas, "but woe to him by whom they come."

On the following day, November 1st, 1838, we were marched into a hollow square just outside of the city, where we delivered up about 630 guns, grounded our arms, and advanced to the center of the square, where the small arms and swords were left in a pile. The late Bishop McRae gave six cuts with his sword and a pointer in the ground and left his sword sticking there. We were left without the means of self-defense and at the mercy of a conscienceless set of ignorant, prejudiced people, many of whom, like St. Paul before his conversion, acted as if they were doing God's service in destroying property and abusing the Mormons.

General Wilson, who was one of the mobbers in Jackson county, was in company with Joseph Smith soon after he was condemned to be shot. Joseph asked General Wilson what he had done that he should be treated with such indignity, stating that he had always been a supporter of the Constitution and of good government. Wilson's reply was: "I know it, and that is the reason I want to kill you, or have you killed."

In the public square of Far West, General Clark said in part:

"You must not think of staying here another season or of putting in crops; for, if you do, the citizens will be upon you. If I am called here again in case of non-compliance of a treaty made, do not think that I shall do as I have done now. You need not expect any mercy, but extermination. For I am determined the Governor's orders shall be executed."

"As for your leaders, do not think, do not imagine for a moment, do not let it enter into your minds, that they shall be delivered and returned to you again for their fate is fixed, their die is cast, their doom is sealed. I am sorry, very sorry, gentlemen, to see so many intelligent men found in this situation. Oh, if I could invoke the Great Spirit, the unknown God, to rest upon and deliver you from that awful chain of superstition, and liberate you from those fetters of fanaticism with which you are bound, that you no longer do homage to a man! My advice is that you become as other citizens, lest by a recurrence of these events you bring upon yourselves irretrievable ruin."

It vividly recurs to my mind that at the closing of General Clark's hard talk, Col. G. M. Hinkle also spoke to the large body of Saints, saying:

"I would advise you all to do as I have done, for I have got my hand out of the lion's mouth, and I intend to keep it out hereafter."

It may not be out of place to relate a statement made to me by E. B. Tripp, who authorizes me to use his name, regarding George M. Hinkle, whose hand he said was out of the lion's mouth. Elder E. B. Tripp says:

"In 1852, I lived in Wapelo, Louisa county, Iowa. G. M. Hinkle, a stranger to me, came into my drug store. He introduced himself to me, saying: 'This is Mr. Tripp, I understand. I hear that you

*are going to Utah, and I would like to have a private talk with you.
I am the man who betrayed Joseph Smith and others into the hands
of the mob in Missouri. I am a miserable man, and scarce know
what to do with myself. I would be willing to lay down my life if
this would atone for the sin I committed. What can I do, Mr. Tripp,
for I know Mormonism is true?"*

This is the substance of the conversation as reported by Brother Tripp, who gave him some good advice before he parted with him.
Thomas B. Marsh, then one of the Twelve Apostles, apostatized
during this dark hour of Missouri persecution. I saw him and heard
him speak then, and also when he came to Utah and was rebaptized.
I heard him confess with deep regret, saying:

"Look at my trembling limbs and see the fate of an apostate,
for I am a wreck, but Mormonism is true, and I advise you not to
do as I have done, in my apostasy."

Gen. John C. Bennett, who once flourished in Nauvoo, apostatized because of his iniquities. He died in Polk City, Iowa, a miserable wreck, debased and degraded. When I was in Iowa on a mission I learned of a party who once had a rope around his neck and
over a limb. At that time he barely escaped being hung up like a
dog.   *Reminiscences of the Prophet Joseph, pp. 36-39.*

THE FATE OF JOHN C. BENNETT

John C. Bennett made an affidavit before Daniel H. Wells,
alderman of the City of Nauvoo, "that he never was taught anything in the least contrary to the strictest principles of the gospel,
or of virtue, or of the laws of God or man, under any circumstances,
or upon any occasion, either directly or indirectly, in word or in
deed, by Joseph Smith." When he made this oath he professed to
be anxious to do right. The affidavit was made on the 17th of
May, 1842. On the 25th of that month he was notified that the
First Presidency, Twelve and Bishops had withdrawn fellowship
from him, and were about to publish him in the paper. He begged
them not to publish him in the paper for his mother's sake; he did
this so humbly that the notice was withdrawn from the paper.
The next day he attended a meeting at the Masonic Lodge Room,
and acknowledged his wicked and licentious conduct; he cried like
a child, and said he was worthy of the severest of chastisements,
but he begged that he might be spared. His sorrow appeared so
deep for the moment, or he pretended to have it, that Joseph plead
for mercy, and he was forgiven still.

After this he did not remain long in Nauvoo. As soon as he
got off he commenced circulating every kind of slander and falsehood against Joseph and the Saints. According to his statements
they were unfit to live. While he was professing to be a member
of the Church, and to have great faith in the work, he wrote
several fierce articles about the persecutions which the Saints had
endured in Missouri. He did not publish his own name to these;
but signed them "Joab, General in Israel." After he left Nauvoo,
in writing against Joseph and the Church, he quoted from these
articles. He did this to show the public what a treasonable, blood-

thirsty people the "Mormons" were; but he took care not to tell them that he was the "Joab" who had written the articles.

Bennett published a book filled with the blackest lies about Joseph and the Saints. This created a little excitement, which, however, did not last long. He was despised by every one who knew him, and those who did not know him, but only heard his stories or read his book, looked upon him as a traitor and bad man. For some years before his death he had fits, which were very violent; he also partly lost the use of his limbs and of his tongue. It was difficult for him to make himself understood. He dragged out a miserable existence, without a person scarcely to take the least interest in his fate, and died a few months ago without a person to mourn his departure. And yet there was a time, probably, when he, like many others before and since, thought that if he should apostatize, the work of God would totter and fall! This is the blindness of apostates—the trick of the devil to lead them to do his bidding. He laughs at their folly, and when they can be no longer used by him, he throws them aside and leaves them to their miserable fate.   *Juvenile Instructor*, Vol. 3:111, July 15, 1868.

THE MARTYRDOM PLANNED BY LEADING MEN OF THE NATION

By Brigham Young

When Joseph Smith rose in the majesty of his calling before God, he saw what we are now hearing of through dispatches received from week to week. * * * Joseph rose up and said: "I will save them, if they will let me." He stepped forth like a man and proffered his services to save the nation that is now breaking; and he would have saved it, if they had permitted him. What did they bestow upon him in return? They made a martyr of him. **** They crowned him a martyr of Jesus. They performed an act that secures to him crowns of glory, immortality and eternal lives. They succeeded in shedding his blood and that of the Patriarch Hyrum. They shed the blood of the innocent, and the nation said amen to it. Were they aware of it at the seat of government? I have no doubt they as well knew the plans for destroying the Prophet as did those in Carthage or in Warsaw, Illinois. It was planned by some of the leading men of the nation. I have said here once before, to the astonishment of many of our own countrymen, that there was a delegate from each State in the nation when Joseph was killed. These delegates held their council. What were they afraid of? You and me? No. They were afraid of those eternal principles God has revealed from the heavens; they trembled and quaked at the sound of them. Joseph would have saved the nation from ruin. ****

I have heard Joseph say: "You will see the sorrows and misery of the world and the misery that will be upon this land, until you will turn away and pray that your eyes may not be obliged to look upon it." Said he, "There are men in this council that will live to see the affliction that will come upon this nation, until your hearts sink within you." He did not live here to see it, though he will see it. Can you endure the sight of it, No. Boast not over the misery of your fellow-men. God will fulfil his purposes."

Journal of Discourses, 8:320-321, 325.

*   *   *   *   *

I will tell you another prophecy of Joseph's, of which both Jews and Gentiles are my witnesses. Joseph said that the bones of hundreds of the Missouri and Illinois mobocrats, who drove the Saints from those States, should bleach on the plains, and their flesh should be meat for wolves. Are you witnesses to that, in coming over the plains; Yes, hundreds and hundreds of those characters that started to go to the gold mines, their flesh was meat for the wolves, and their bones are there bleaching today, so far as they have not been buried or entirely rotted away.

Journal of Discourses, 8:357.

RETRIBUTION TO THOSE WHO PERSECUTED

It was prophesied by Joseph the Prophet that the bones of those who drove the Church from Missouri and killed men, women and children should bleach upon the plains. This has been fulfilled. Did they suffer more than the people of God whom they drove from their homes—from their firesides in winter—from their fathers and mothers and friends, and the land of their nativity? Yes, there is scarcely a comparison. Their sufferings in crossing the plains to the gold regions of California have been greater by far than ever the sufferings of the Saints have been in crossing the plains to Utah. These are facts that are present with us. The bones of those who drove the Saints from Independence, from Jackson County, then from Clay and Daviess Counties, and last of all from Caldwell County, from whence they fled into Illinois, have been scattered over the plains—gnawed and broken by wild beasts and are there bleaching to this day, while the Saints who have died on the plains have without an exception had a decent burial where they have died—have had friends to console with and comfort them in their dying moments and to mourn for a season with their bereaved relatives. These comforts and blessings were denied the murderers of Joseph and Hyrum Smith and of scores of the Saints, and they were left in the bitterness of death without a friend and without mercy. They suffered immensely more than did the Saints whom they persecuted; they received that which they sought to bring upon the Saints and that too in good measure pressed down and running over.   Brigham Young, *J. D.* 9:101-2.

THE DEVASTATION OF JACKSON COUNTY, MISSOURI

By Junius F. Wells

I had the pleasure, in the early part of this year (1902) to meet Hon. Leonidas M. Lawson, of New York City, formerly a resident of Clay County, Missouri. Mr. Lawson is a brother-in-law of General

Doniphan, and one night, in the beautiful University Club, a night I shall long remember, he recounted to me many parts of the story here related. He said that his father had told him in his youth of the inhumanity of the Missourians' treatment of the Mormon people, and then he told me of his own visit to General Doniphan, in 1863; of their riding over Jackson County together, and of the incidents related in the following letter, which I requested him to write. Mr. Lawson is a man standing high in his profession, a lawyer of great ability, an orator known in Missouri, New York, and London, a man of world-wide travel and information, whose observations upon affairs and men are of recognized weight and value in the cosmopolitan circle of his acquaintance. It was a pleasure to hear him, without prejudice for or against the Mormons, narrate eloquently the circumstances which he has so briefly, but pointedly, set down in this communication:

New York City, February 7, 1902.

"Mr. Junius F. Wells, New York.

My dear Sir: Responding to your request for a statement concerning the devastation of Jackson County, Mo., permit me to say:

I am preparing a biographical sketch of General Alexander W. Doniphan. It will be remembered that General Doniphan commanded the famous expedition, which during the Mexican War marched from Fort Leavenworth to Santa Fe, and thence to Chihuahua, fighting enroute the Battle of Bracite and the Battle of Sacramento; in this latter engagement his little army of 1000 Missourians was opposed by a Mexican army 4000 strong. In the biography occurs the following interesting passage:

'In the year 1863, I visited General A. W. Doniphan at his home in Jackson County, Mo. This was soon after the devastation of Jackson County, Mo., under what is known as "Order No. 11." This devastation was complete. Farms were everywhere destroyed, and the farm houses were burned. During this visit General Doniphan related the following historical facts and personal incidents:

'About the year 1831-2, the Mormons settled in Jackson County, Mo., under the leadership of Joseph Smith. The people of Jackson County became dissatisfied with their presence, and forced them to leave; and they crossed the Missouri River and settled in the counties of DeKalb, Caldwell and Ray. They founded the town of Far West, and began to prepare the foundation of a Temple. It was here that the trouble arose which culminated in the expulsion of the Mormons from the State of Missouri, according to the command of Governor Lilburn W. Boggs. This was known in Missouri annals as the Mormon War. There were many among those who obeyed the order of the Governor, in the State Militia, who believed that the movement against the Mormons was unjust and cruel, and that the excitement was kept up by those who coveted the homes, the barns and the fields of the Mormon people. The latter, during their residence in the State of Missouri, paid, in entry fees for the land they claimed, to the U. S. Government Land Office, more than $300,000.00 which for that period represented a tremendous interest. During their sojourn in Missouri the Mormons did not practice or teach polygamy, so that question did not enter into it.

'Following the early excitement, Joseph Smith was indicted for treason against the State of Missouri, and General Doniphan

*was one of the counsel employed to defend him, he having shown
a friendly interest in Smith, whom he considered very badly treated.
Joseph Smith was placed in prison in Liberty, Missouri to await
his trial. This place was the residence of General Doniphan. His
partner in the practice of law was James H. Baldwin.*

*'On one occasion General Doniphan caused the sheriff of the
county to bring Joseph Smith from the prison to his law office, for
the purpose of consultation about his defense. During Smith's
presence in the office, a resident of Jackson County, Missouri, came
in for the purpose of paying a fee which was due by him to the
firm of Doniphan and Baldwin, and offered in payment a tract of
land in Jackson County.*

*'Doniphan told him that his partner, Mr. Baldwin, was absent
at the moment, but as soon as he had an opportunity he would consult him and decide about the matter. When the Jackson County
man retired, Joseph Smith, who had overheard the conversation,
addressed General Doniphan about as follows:*

*"Doniphan, I advise you not to take that Jackson County land
in payment of the debt. God's wrath hangs over Jackson County.
God's people have been ruthlessly driven from it, and you will live
to see the day when it will be visited by fire and sword. The Lord
of Hosts will sweep it with the besom of destruction. The fields and
farms and houses will be destroyed, and only the chimneys will be
left to mark the desolation."*

*"General Doniphan said to me that the devastation of Jackson
County forcibly reminded him of this remarkable prediction of the
Mormon prophet.*

Yours sincerely,

L. M. Lawson."

There is a prediction of the Prophet Joseph, not before put into
print, and history has recorded its complete fulfillment.

As a remarkable evidence of its literal and exact fulfillment, I
add the following self-explanatory and interesting letter from Judge
A. Saxey, written in reply to a request for information upon the
subject, and call attention to his use of the almost exact of Joseph's
prophecy, though so far as I know, he has not even heard that such
a prediction was ever made:

Spanish Fork, Utah, August 25, 1902.

Mr. Junius F. Wells, Salt Lake City, Utah.

*Dear Sir: Yours of August 22nd, received. I hardly know how
to write in a letter concerning the subject you inquire about. However, I will give you a little of what I know, and if you can use it,
all right.*

*I enlisted in a Kansas regiment in 1861. During the winter of
1861 and '62, my regiment was stationed at Kansas City, and we
were around in Jackson County a great deal during the winter.
Quantrill was operating in that locality, and we were trying to
catch him. At one time, we surrounded Independence, and arrested
everyone in the town. I can testify that Jackson County contained
more contemptible, mean, devilish rebels than any I came across
in an experience of four years. I had quite a talk with a man I*

arrested who lived on the Blue River, and who was there when the Saints were driven out, but that, I suppose, would be somewhat foreign to your inquiry.

In the spring of 1862, my regiment went south, and it was during that time that "Order No. 11" was issued, but I was back there again in 1864, during the Price raid, and saw the condition of the country. The duty of executing the order was committed to Col. W. R. Penick's regiment, and there is no doubt but that he carried it into effect, from the howl the Copperhead papers made at the time. I went down the Blue River. We found houses, barns, outbuildings, nearly all burned down, and nothing left standing but the chimneys, which had, according to the fashion of the time, been built on the outside of the buildings. I remember very well that the county looked a veritable desolation.

I do not know that what I have written will do you any good, if it will, you are welcome. Of course, I could tell a great deal more than I can write in a letter.   *Respectfully,*
                                                            A. Saxey.

The practice of the guerilla bands of making stealthy, assassin-like, sudden attacks upon the Union troops, from ambush, as they were marching from point to point, and then disappearing, became so intolerable that extreme measures were resolved upon to stop it. These contemplated the destruction of the base of supplies of the marauding parties. It was found that the principal location was Jackson County, where forage for their horses and food for the men, and change of animals and equipment were being secretly furnished, as the opportunity and need of the renegade parties required. Women and children even were frequently discovered contributing to the sustenance and help of these parties. The whole county came to be regarded as a nest-bed of traitors and spies, a refuge for assassins and robbers, whose murderous and uncivilized warfare could not be combatted by the ordinary rules and practices of civilized war, and that must be put down by means that should be effective, however cruel and relentless. This determination led to the issuance of the celebrated "General Order No. 11." which has been more widely published and quoted, because of the manner and thoroughness of its execution, than almost any other order of the Civil War.

"General Order, No. 11
                              Headquarters District of the Border,
                              Kansas City, Mo., August 25, 1863.

"1.   All persons living in Jackson, Cass and Bates counties, Mo., and in that part of Vernon, included in this district, except those living within one mile of the limits of Independence, Hickman's Mills, Pleasant Hill and Harrisonville, and except those in that part of Kaw Township, Jackson County, north of Brush Creek and west of the Big Blue, are hereby ordered to remove from their present places of residence within fifteen days from the date hereof.

"Those who, within that time, establish their loyalty to the satisfaction of the commanding officer of the military station nearest their present places of residence, will receive from him certificates stating the fact of their loyalty and the names of the witnesses by whom it can be shown. All who receive such certificates will be permitted to remove to any military station in this district, or to any part of the State of Kansas except the counties on the eastern border of the State. All others shall remove out of this district. Officers commanding companies and detachments serving in the counties named will see that this paragraph is promptly obeyed.

"2. All grain and hay, in the field or under shelter, in the district from which the inhabitants are required to remove, within reach of military stations, after the 9th day of September next, will be taken to such stations, and turned over to the proper officers there; and report of the amounts so turned over made to District Headquarters, specifying the names of all loyal owners and the amount of such produce taken from them. All grain and hay found in such district after the 9th day of September next, not convenient to such stations, will be destroyed.

"3. The provisions of General Orders No. 10 from these Headquarters will be at once vigorously executed by officers commanding in the parts of the districts, and at the stations, not subject to the operation of Paragraph 1 of this Order, and especially in the towns of Independence, Westport and Kansas City.

"4. Paragraph 3, General Orders No. 10, is revoked as to all who have borne arms against the Government in this district since the 20th day of August, 1863.

"By order of Brigadier-General Ewing.

H. Hannahs, Adjutant."

Prophecies of Joseph Smith and Their Fulfillment,
By Nephi L. Morris, pp. 185-190.

THE JUDGMENTS OF GOD SHALL OVERTAKE THEM

On the 1st of May, 1850, we said goodbye to the old Keokuk. Our outfit consisted of four wagons, heavily loaded, nine yoke of oxen, five cows, two mules and one horse. Richard Cook drove the wagon of Caroline; with his family our contingent was augmented to fifteen. It was a late and cold spring; the ground was very wet. We had much trouble to pull our wagons through the muddy roads. The wheels sometimes would sink down to the hub; and occasionally we had to double the teams to get through the swamps toward Council Bluffs, Iowa. At length we reached the Missouri River and crossed it the 1st of June, 1850, landing at the south side of the Platte. There our company was organized with Milo Andrus for Captain. Our train of emigrants consisted of 56 wagons and five captains of ten. President Orson Hyde organized us and his closing words were: *"If you will strictly observe your prayers morning and evening, keep the Sabbath Day holy, faithfully hold the name of God sacred, and be kind to each other and to your animals, you shall all go safely to the Valleys."* We arrived all well and happy to our destination the 28th of August, 1850, having had one death and one birth. The gold fever prompted many to go to California that summer, by way of the north side of the Platte, so that the feed for animals was all used up. For that reason President Hyde advised us to go along the south side. Some of the gold seekers did take the same route. The cholera broke out among them; they were all around us, before and behind us, although we tried to keep away from them, and many of them died, but our company escaped.

One afternoon our camp stopped earlier than usual. I stole away about two miles to the Bluffs, to see where those people came from who were swept out to such an alarming extent. Such a horrible scene as I beheld I hope never to see again. The graves of the cholera victims were there, with head-boards bearing their names, who were from Missouri; but the hyenas had dug open the graves, dragged the cadavers out and devoured the flesh from their bones; the ravens had plucked out their eyes, and their bloody long skeletons lay stretched out on the ground. That awful sight shocked my feelings beyond expression. I did not take note of their names, unfortunately, but I remembered many were of the mobbers of Missouri, who had so cruelly treated our people. Then I recalled the prophecy of Joseph Smith: *"You shall not die a natural death: the judgments of the Almighty shall overtake you: the wolves shall eat the flesh from your bones and the ravens shall pluck out your eyes."* And I saw it literally fulfilled; but our captain had forbidden us to go to their camps and I dared not mention what I had seen to anyone. I am perhaps the only witness who saw that prophecy fulfilled. This was between Fort Kearney and the crossing of the South Platte.   *Life of Thomas Steed, pp. 14-15.*

THE PROPHET'S FATHER HAD POWER TO BLESS AND TO CURSE

BY PERRIGRINE SESSIONS

(Note: While visiting at the home of Sister Robert Scott, in Rock Springs, Wyoming, on October 13, 1935, Sister Scott dictated the following incident from the diary of her father Perrigrine Sessions.)

In the year 1838, when on my way out of Missouri, near Palmyra, in company with Father Joseph Smith, the father of the Prophet Joseph, and Carlos Smith, his brother, we encountered a heavy snow storm. We halted at a farm house to buy corn and to stay all night. Father Smith asked the owner if we could camp there and buy feed for our animals. He asked: "Are you Mormons?" Father Smith answered: "Yes, we are." He became very angry and said: "Damn you, you can't stay on my property," and with many insulting words and threats we were driven out into the street. Here we stopped and gathered together in the falling snow. Slowly Father Smith removed his hat and with uplifted hands he prayed: "In the name of the Lord whom we serve, let that man be cursed in his basket and in his store, and let this man's name be cut off from under heaven." We all said, Amen.

When I came to travel this same road two years later, this incident was brought fresh to my mind. For behold there was nothing to mark the spot but the ruins of his home burned to ashes; his orchard broken down; his farm a picture of desolation; his wife and three children were burned to death in their home and he at this time was in close confinement for the insane. I saw the power of the priesthood manifested, for at the next farm we were received kindly and given all the comfort and assistance we needed and Father Smith left his blessing on this household as we departed. Here my eyes beheld the fulfillment of his words to the letter as there I looked upon a picture of prosperity and happiness. All this passed and the two neighbors were ignorant of the curse or the blessing placed upon them as we passed on.

THE FATE OF MOBOCRATS

The sad news reached us today of Brother Silas Beckwith being murdered and buried. This Beckwith was one of the Mormon Battalion in the Mexican war, and was, at the time of his death, a worthy member and teacher in the San Juan branch.

I visited his widow and orphans, and spent some hours in the house of mourning. On my second visit I gained and wrote down the following statements pertaining to the history of Joseph Smith:

Mrs. Eunice Corinthia Beckwith, formerly Mrs. Lawn (whose father's name was Joshua Twitchell), was the widow of John Lawn, captain of a company of Illinois militia, of McDonough County, who guarded Joseph and Hyrum Smith in Carthage jail until the morning of the day they were martyred, when himself and company were disbanded by order of Governor Ford, and started for home, leaving the prisoners in the hands of the Carthage Greys.

On taking leave of the prisoners he gave his hand, received Joseph's blessing, and heard him say most solemnly: "Farewell, Captain Lawn; when you and your men leave me my life guard is gone." Previous to this, however, Joseph had read to him the fifty-fifth Psalm, and told him to remember that chapter and read it to his friends when he arrived home. One of the Carthage Greys also read in reply the sixty-first Psalm.

Captain Lawn and his troops had marched about twelve miles towards home when the news reached them of the martyrdom! At this he exclaimed: "Oh that I had known of this massacre, so soon to transpire! I would have remained, and, when the first ball was fired at the Smiths, I would have fired the second through the body of the villain who fired it or died in the attempt."

A man named Townsend, living in Iowa, near Fort Madison, was one of the mob who assaulted and forced in the jail door. The pistol discharged by Joseph Smith wounded him in the arm, near the shoulder, and it continued to rot without healing until it was taken off, and even then it would not heal.

About six months after he was shot Mrs. Lawn saw his arm and dressed it. He was then gradually rotting and dying with the wound. He staid overnight with Mrs. Lawn's father, and groaned through the night without sleeping. He asked the old gentleman what he thought of Joseph Smith being a prophet? He replied that he did not know. "Well," said Townsend, "I KNOW HE WAS A PROPHET OF GOD! And, oh, that I had staid at home and minded my own business, and then I would not have lost my life and been tormented with a guilty conscience, and with this dreadful wound, which NONE CAN HEAL!" He died two or three months afterwards, having literally rotted alive!

James Head, of McComb, was also one of the murderers at the Carthage jail; he was heard by Captain Lawn and others to boast of it afterwards, and Captain Lawn drew a pistol and chased him, but he ran away. He was always gloomy and troubled from the time he helped to murder the Smiths, and frequently declared that he saw the two martyrs always before him! He had no peace.

A colonel of the Missouri mob, who helped to drive, plunder and murder the Mormons, died in the hospital at Sacramento, 1849. Beckwith had the care of him; he was eaten with worms—a large black-headed kind of maggot—which passed through him by myriads, seemingly a half pint at a time! Before he died these maggots were crawling out of his mouth and nose! He literally rotted alive! Even the flesh on his legs burst open and fell from the bones! They gathered up the rotten mass in a blanket and buried him, without awaiting a coffin!

A Mr. ——, one of the Missouri mob, died in the same hospital about the same time, and under the care of Mr. Beckwith. His face and jaw on one side literally rotted, and half of his face actually fell off! One eye rotted out, and half of his nose, mouth and jaw fell from the bones! The doctor scraped the bones, and unlocked and took out his jaw from the joint round to the center of the chin. The rot and maggots continued to eat till they ate through the large or jugular vein of his neck, and he bled to death! He, as well as Townsend, stank so previous to their death, that they had to be placed in rooms by themselves, and it was almost impossible to endure their presence, and the flies could not be kept from blowing them while alive!

These particulars, and many others, were related to me by Brother Beckwith previous to his death, and afterwards by his widow and father-in-law, and others who were conversant with them, and are believed to be correct.

Autobiography of Parley P. Pratt, pp. 474-77, *Millennial Star,* 38:170-1.

THE SLAYERS OF JOSEPH STANDING

Elder George A. Smith, who recently returned home from a mission to the Southern States, was lately furnished by a Tennessee correspondent with some interesting information concerning the members of the Georgia mob that murdered Elder Joseph Standing. Elder Smith kindly permitted the *Deseret News* to make public use of it, and it is as follows:

Ben Clark resides in Georgia, and is poverty-stricken.

John Forssett died a short time after the murder was committed.

James Blair resides in Tennessee and is poverty-stricken.

Newton Nation lives in Arkansas; he has had all kinds of family troubles, and about the same trouble applies to his three brothers, Tom, William and Joe, except the latter, who has paid a small portion of his penalty by losing his eyesight. Joe Nation is supposed to be the one who did the fatal shooting.

Mack McClure and Jeff Hunter, after absolutely failing to make a living at their once happy homes, were compelled to ride the 'blind baggage' to the West.

Andrew Bradley and Jud and Dave Smith are living in Georgia. They are all homeless and make a living by doing odd jobs.

This completes the twelve murderers. *Millennial Star*, 41:582.

FATE OF THE CANE CREEK, TENNESSEE, MURDERERS

By Robert Price

There are in the Southern States at the present time two Elders named Gibbs and Berry. These young men were babes in their mothers' arms when their fathers, together with two other members of the Church, were murdered in cold blood, at the head of Cane Creek, Tennessee. On Sunday morning, August 10, 1884, Elders J. H. Gibbs, William S. Berry and Henry Thompson met at the home of a family of Saints by the name of Condor, where they had purposed holding a meeting with Saints and friends in that district. They knew nothing of the murderous plot that had been concocted by a band of ruffians, who had chosen as their leader a professed minister of the Gospel of Christ, a pretended disciple of the meek and lowly Nazarene. In an unexpected moment a number of masked men rushed in upon the Saints, shot and killed Elders Gibbs and Berry, two members of the Condor family, and seriously wounded Sister Condor. Elder Thompson escaped into the woods, his life being saved by a lady who passed between him and his would-be assassin.

Later Elder Brigham H. Roberts, disguised as a tramp, went to Tennessee, and succeeded in recovering the bodies of the murdered missionaries, and they were brought home to Utah and laid to rest among the people of God. I take the following extract from an editorial published in the *Millennial Star* (Vol. 46) at that time: "It is hard to conceive how a dozen or twenty beings in the human form could be found, in this enlightened age, and in that nation which boasts so much of its freedom and tolerance, so utterly depraved, so devoid of all the finer feelings which are supposed to distinguish the civilized man from the savage, as to deliberately combine for the perpetration of such a crime, even though their victims were ever so unworthy. But how much more difficult to reconcile the thought of their doing so when we know that there was not the slightest provocation for the deed; when we understand that the only fault they could possibly find with their victims was that they believed and taught a religion that was distasteful to them; when we learn that at least one of the assassins was a preacher of religion; when we realize that they chose the Sabbath day for the awful tragedy, and swooped down and mercilessly butchered their victims when they had met for divine worship; Incredibly as these statements appear, they are true—only too true."

I am reminded of this said event by Elder Soren Peterson, while attending the recent London conference. Elder Peterson stated that he followed the remains of one of the martyrs to their last resting place, about twenty-two years ago. Eleven years later, in August, 1895, he, in company with Elder E. S. Larson of Coalville, Utah, visited Cane Creek and preached in the log cabin in which the meeting was held prior to the tragedy. The Condor home had been burned down two months before, but they were told that the blood of the martyrs was there till that time, and that all efforts to erase it had been in vain. David Hinson, the leader of the mob, was killed by James R. Hutson, a half brother of the Condor boys, at the time of the tragedy. The murderers were permitted to go unpunished so far as the law of the land was concerned, but the vengeance of heaven overtook them. Elder Peterson was told by reliable people that Hinson's brother, one of the mob, got into trouble with a man who cut his flesh almost into shreds. So acute was his suffering that he plead with his friends to put him to death and thus end his pain. He said that the reason why he had to suffer thus was because he had assisted in putting to death two servants of the Lord. Before his death his flesh dropped from his bones. All the other members of that notorious gang died unnatural deaths. Four of them became raving maniacs, and died in lunatic asylums.   *Millennial Star*, 68:662-63.

THE CANE CREEK MASSACRE

By Alfred Fuller

(Dictated to the Compiler of this book on December 27, 1951, at Mesa, Arizona

I was born in Harrisburg, Washington County, Utah, on the 21st of October, 1871. My parents were Willis Darwin Fuller and Annie Campkin Fuller. I left home on the 27th of June, 1899, for a mission to the Southern States, and was assigned to the Middle Tennessee conference, in Hickman county. My companion on the following occasion was Elder David C. Shupe, a young man of twenty-two years of age. We visited the northern end of Hickman county, tracting as we went, and as we approached a certain home, the man of the house saw us coming and came out of the house and said: "I know who you are; you are Mormon Elders. Get your grips and come right in this house. You see that little church upon that ridge?" "Yes, sir," we replied. Said he: "Two Mormon Elders came here by the name of John H. Gibbs and William S. Berry. They asked me if I thought it was possible to get permission to preach in that little white church. I told them there had never been a Mormon preach in it; that it was built as a union church, free to the use of all denominations except Mormons; but you might try. I gave the Elders the names of the deacons who had the say of this church. They met the first deacon and asked him if he thought it would be out of order if the truth was once preached in that church, and he said: "No, I would like to hear the truth preached once in that church." Elder Gibbs said: "Well, if you will consent and come out you shall hear the gospel truths preached in their fulness in that church." The man said: "As far as I am concerned I give my consent but you must go and see the others." They called at the homes of the others but they were away from home, which, of course, gave the necessary permission.

Our host who invited us in his home was a little bald-headed school teacher and a member of the Christian church. He said to us: "I used to hold prayer meetings for the Christian church members but since those Elders came here and preached that time I don't hold any prayer meetings. I told our minister that he was absolutely without any authority to preach or baptize or administer any ordinances of the gospel and he had no more authority than the Jews, Protestants or Catholics." Our host further stated: "Do you know, that little Elder Gibbs, if there is such a thing as an inspired man, he was inspired. He had that Bible from Genesis to Revelations on the tip of his tongue. They held six meetings in that little church and each meeting the crowd increased from meeting to meeting until the last meeting when they stood in the aisles. The Elders stayed with me every night. They had dozens of invitations to homes and I just stepped up when one would invite them to stay at their home and say, 'No, sir, I have invited them to stay with me during this meeting period.' He said, 'Do you know that just ten days after those Elders left my home they drifted into Lewis county on Cane Creek and there they were murdered.' "

In going back to our headquarters, we strayed across the line into Lewis county which was out of our assigned territory, as we were desirous of meeting the man where the killing took place which was at the Condor home on Cane Creek. Brother Condor owned 80 acres of land and Cane Creek ran right through his land, where several nice pools were located that were suitable for baptismal purposes. Brother Condor had one son eighteen years of age and a step-son about nineteen or twenty years of age. The post office was two miles north of the Condor home and these boys went every day to the post office for the mail. It was rumored there that ten days away there would be four baptized on Cane Creek on the Condor farm. The postmaster would tell these boys that he heard men say that very morning that there was not going to be any baptisms on that date and at that place. They were not going to permit it. Each day the postmaster would tell the boys that ten or twelve men had said that "there will not be any baptisms. They were not going to stand for it. They were going to take those Elders and whip them with hickory whips until they couldn't stand up, and then haul them out of Lewis county on a wagon." These boys would say to the postmaster when these men made their brags, "that they had better dress their wives in mourning because they are not coming onto our property and take innocent men that have never done any one a bit of harm and mistreat them. No, when you hear them say that once more, you tell them that they had better be careful because this property belongs to us, and those Elders are right at home there. They are not molesting anybody." This went on for seven days. Each day the postmaster would hear more threats from this crowd, who would gather at the post office, and every one of them were drinking.

Brother Condor told us that the leader of the mob held Baptist prayer meetings. This baptismal service was set for two o'clock on the specified day but at ten o'clock on that day about twelve men on horseback, all masked, rode up to the home. All wore guns and most of them had pistols also. They rode up to the gate which was about 100 feet from the house, tied their horses outside the fence, came inside the fence and the leader of the mob walked right into the house, the others remained standing in the yard. Brother Condor said he walked out of the house just as the leader of the mob walked into the house. There was a gun hanging on a rack on the wall. The leader of the mob took the gun off the rack which was across the room from the door, turned to the left in front of Elder Gibbs, pulled his pistol and shot Elder Gibbs twice. Elder Gibbs was sitting in a chair with a hymn book in his hands as they had been singing hymns that morning to Brother and Sister Condor. Both Elders were wonderful singers, Elder Gibbs having a fine tenor voice and Elder Berry a splendid bass voice. They were often asked by their congregations to sing one or more hymns after each meeting.

The leader of the mob then walked out of the house. Elder Berry slammed the door as the leader of the mob went out. The mob could see down the alley way between the houses the son who was in the orchard 150 yards away, who came running to the house at the sound of the shots that killed Elder Gibbs. Not over a minute after Elder Gibbs was shot, the mob started shooting through the door at Elder Berry. About six shots hit him. The son ran upstairs to the window, picked up his gun, and fired one shot which struck the leader of the mob who fell dead just inside the gate. By this time the step-son had reached the window upstairs when six shots hit both of them. Both boys fell right by the window. The mob then put their dead leader on the horse and rode away, after first tying him to the saddle. A stray bullet went through the door of the kitchen and hit Mrs. Condor in the hip, breaking her hip bone which rendered her a cripple for sixteen years.

Brother Condor told us that for two years after the massacre, his red American blood boiled to think that his neighbors, twelve in number, would congregate to murder innocent people. Said he: "I knew every one of them by the horses they rode. The only consolation I had was to kneel down and ask the Lord for strength that I might be able to overcome the feeling of taking the law into my own hands and waylay these men but every time I would ask the Lord to avenge my brothers. One night after two years had passed, the power of God rested upon me and it came to my mind that if these two boys had been in the house ready for the mob, he believed the boys would have killed all twelve of the mob before they could get away. If such had been the case, it would have been the greatest blight on the Church that could have happened because the law would have taken the two Elders, the two boys and myself to jail and we would have hanged for their death. But consolation came to me when I saw the members of the mob drifting toward hell. They were all drinking and visiting the taverns where there were prostitutes and as a result their wives divorced them because they were diseased, for the state law promptly permitted divorces on those grounds. About two years after the massacre two of

these men were in a tavern playing cards and drinking. They
carried their guns all the time. A quarrel came up in this card
game and both raised at the same moment, pulled their guns and
both guns cracked at once, shooting each other through the heart.
All of these mobbers were in the depths of poverty and were vagabonds dressed in rags, and rode pony horses around the country.
All were buried by the county in pauper graves and some of them
died in the insane asylum."

When we started to leave the home of Brother and Sister
Condor, they followed us out of the home, with tears streaming
down their faces, and remarked what a great spiritual feast they
had had during our visit. Their joy was overwhelming as they had
not seen an Elder for about five years. "Won't you promise to
come back to us," they entreated, but our fields of labor did not
permit us to return.

THE GENERAL CAUSE OF APOSTASY FROM
THE CHURCH

BY GEORGE Q. CANNON

Oliver Cowdery, the man who was ordained with Joseph Smith
by angels, and whom you would imagine would of all men in the
Church, next to the Prophet himself, have been firm and steadfast,
left the Church, and the Priesthood, gifts and powers that God gave
to him were given to another. If this man could not stand, who
can expect to stand in this Church? And all who knew his history
know what the cause was. He indulged in impurity; he was un-
virtuous. In consequence of this he lost the Spirit of God and fell
into darkness, and was severed from the Church of Christ. And
he is not alone. I might mention the names of a number who are
distinguished in our history who met with the same fate. The
Lord will not tolerate impurity. No matter what a man may know,
or what testimony he may have, if he commits sin, unless he re-
pents, the Lord will not bear with him. If he does not repent, the
Lord will withdraw His Spirit from him, and leave him to himself.

Millennial Star, 60:164-65.

AN INTERVIEW WITH OLIVER COWDERY

My father, Jacob Gates, while on his way to England, in 1849,
stopped at the town of Richmond, where lived at that time Oliver
Cowdery. Hearing that Oliver was in poor health, and wishing
to renew old acquaintance, as they had been friends in earlier days,
father called on him at his home. Their conversation, during the
visit drifted to early Church history, and to their mutual experiences during the troublous times in Missouri and Illinois. Finally
father put this question to him: "Oliver, I want you to tell me the
whole truth about your testimony concerning the Book of Mormon
—the testimony sent forth to the world over your signature and
found in the front of that book. Was your testimony based on a
dream, was it the imagination of your mind, was it an illusion, a
myth—tell me truthfully?"

To question him thus seemed to touch Oliver very deeply. He answered not a word, but arose from his easy chair, went to the book case, took down a Book of Mormon of the first edition, turned to the testimony of the Three Witnesses, and read in the most solemn manner the words to which he had subscribed his name, nearly twenty years before. Facing my father, he said: "Jacob, I want you to remember what I say to you. I am a dying man, and what would it profit me to tell you a lie? I know," said he, "that this Book of Mormon was translated by the gift and power of God. My eyes saw, my ears heard, and my understanding was touched, and I know that whereof I testified is true. It was no dream, no vain imagination of the mind; it was real."

Then father asked him about the angel under whose hands he received the priesthood, to which he made answer thus: "Jacob, I felt the hand of the angel on my head as plainly as I could feel yours, and could hear his voice as I now hear yours."

Then father asked the question: "If all that you tell me is true, why did you leave the Church?" Oliver made only this explanation; said he, "When I left the Church, I felt wicked, I felt like shedding blood, but I have got all over that now."

Here follows the sworn affidavit of Jacob F. Gates, before Notary Public Arthur Winters, on December 3, 1915, to the truth of the above conversation between Jacob Gates and Oliver Cowdery.   *Improvement Era*, Vol. 15:418-19.

FULFILMENT OF PROPHECY

"You will see the old man go down to the grave in disgrace. He has cast off his political friends, and they cast him off as a thing of naught, and he will become a hiss and a byword."

The prophecy we have quoted, is extracted from a sermon delivered by President Brigham Young in Great Salt Lake City, in the year 1861, and relates to James Buchanan, ex-President of the United States. The fulfilment of prophecy is a theme to which of late we have frequently alluded; but we have never witnessed a more speedy and direct fulfilment of the predictions of the servants of God than in the case of the ex-President.

To convey a correct understanding to others—a proper realization of the judgments of God—we shall quote the testimony of those who have nothing in common with the Latter-day Saints, contained in the *New York Tribune,* and we have no reason to doubt the testimony offered. To enable all classes to better comprehend the great revolution which has taken place in the circumstances of the ex-President, it will be necessary to state, that only five short years have passed since he stood at the head of one of the most promising Republics the world ever saw, wielding a power inferior to that of no potentate or emperor upon the face of our globe. When we consider this, and contrast his present degradation with his former greatness, we are inclined to pity, did we not know that it is a just retribution for the sordid wretch who sold his honor for foreign gold, bartering the blood of innocence for a little of this world's honor, which he enjoyed only long enough to appreciate the height from which he has so suddenly fallen. "Vengeance is mine, saith the Lord, and I will repay." If the Utonians had had the punishing of James Buchanan, they never could have inflicted on him the excruciating torture which has been his, and under which he is still writhing, meted out to him, as it has been, by those very individuals to whose pampered appetites and whims he had pandered, braving the powers of heaven, and trampling under his feet every just law, both human and divine, to gratify the parasites who were sapping the life-blood of the Union. The American people think today it is the nation that has forsaken James Buchanan; in one sense of the word this is true; but can they realize that they are merely instruments in the hands of God in carrying out His purposes?

Why did the nation desert him? They offer us a reason, "The ex-President did not trust the people"; but he did trust them as much as it is possible for a wire-pulling politician, who is today buoyant with hope, and tomorrow lean and sunken almost to despair, to trust his fellowmen. No! it is the curse of an avenging God that rests down upon him, and many generations will pass before that silly old man can emerge from the punishment he so justly merits and is now enduring.

The following sentence uttered by him previous to the desolating war which has partially subsided in the United States, is sufficient to cause his name to be stricken from the scrolls of liberty, and be forever denied a place among the sons of freedom— "Slavery is more sinned against than sinning." God gave all men their freedom, but "Man's inhumanity to man" has crushed millions, not only in the United States, but on the continent of Europe, more especially in Catholic countries; and we can easily trace further east, and say that millions are held in bondage in free and enlightened England. It is, however, not our province to point out the failings and short-comings of any nation in this article, but to hold up to the world another proof that the kingdom of God is established on the earth, and that men can foretell the dealings of the Almighty with the wicked throughout the nations.

Witness the heading of this article, and the following quotation from the New York Tribune—"The last five years must have been full of bitter days to James Buchanan. To live in silence, and retirement and obloquy,—his name the most detested of any name in America; to sit in his home, with the years rapidly bending him to the grave, and feel that, after so much power and honor, and, above all, so many opportunities, he was the most unpopular of Americans,—to feel this and yet to know that he was partly the victim of fate, that after all he had been merely a whirling mariner in a hurricane—the weakest, most muddled, most distracted seaman, it is true, that ever went out upon the salt seas; and that for the life of him he could not tell whether the ship was on her keel or on her beam-ends—that his statesmanship was scribbling and praying, and that he meant to do what was best, even while doing the worst,—to sit and hear nothing but imprecations from a people he had served for fifty years; to be cursed by mothers who had lost their children; to have no friends even among the people of the South, for whom he sacrificed all—this is a retribution more terrible than that of Belisarius wandering in poverty and blindness, or the discrowned Lear on the storm-beaten moor wielding the sceptre of straw."

Here, then, we look upon James Buchanan sinking into a lonely grave—not even a wife or child to mourn over his forsaken bier—standing on the verge of eternity, with not a single ray to lighten his midnight journey; longing for death, and yet starting back in terror when the grim monster appears; wishing to rend the veil, and yet not daring to meet the calm, searching glance of his Creator; dreading the doom which conscience in thunder-tones proclaims for broken laws and mis-spent time—a thing for which we can have pity but which is far too contemptible to despise.

Editorial, *Millennial Star*, Vol. 28:57-59.

FATE OF PERSECUTORS OF MISSIONARIES

(Many dozens of such instances can be compiled and published.)

Elder Bedson Eardley, while traveling in the Norwich conference, England, in June, 1875, held a camp meeting one Sunday near one of the large cities of his district. After the close of the services, seven repentant persons handed in their names and requested baptism. An appointment was accordingly made for the next evening, immediately after the close of a meeting for which arrangements had already been made.

Agreeable to his promise, Brother Eardley proceeded the following evening to the place chosen for the baptism. His converts were ready for him and he had just entered the stream, leading a man by the hand, when a mob came upon the scene with loud shouts and curses. A large, strong man, whom he subsequently learned was a well-to-do blacksmith, emerged from the crowd. He walked to the bank of the creek, which was about four feet above the water in which Brother Eardley was standing, and, with a heavy stick, dealt him a severe blow across the top of the head. So much force was exerted that it appeared as though the skull would certainly be crushed. But, strange to say, the Elder experienced not the slightest pain or inconvenience from the blow—the Lord had protected him. Notwithstanding the cruelty of the blow, he felt no desire to retaliate; for the Spirit whispered, "The Lord will take care of him."

The bitterness of this man did not cease, and it was finally predicted by an Elder of the Church that, as a punishment for his sins, he would be afflicted so that in his agony he would crawl along a wall and seek death but not find it. This prediction was very soon literally fulfilled: The man contracted an incurable disease, and was seen for months crawling along by a wall, vainly seeking death; and he expressed his belief that his affliction was a punishment for having so shamefully treated the "Mormon" Elder.

Juvenile Instructor, Vol. 19:43.

GOD WILL VINDICATE HIS SAINTS

And thus, with the sword and by bloodshed the inhabitants of the earth shall mourn; and with famine, and plague, and earthquake, and the thunder of heaven, and the fierce and vivid lightning also, shall the inhabitants of the earth be made to feel the wrath, and indignation, and chastening hand of an Almighty God, until *the consumption decreed hath made a full end of all nations.*

That the cry of the saints, and of the blood of the saints, shall cease to come up into the ears of the Lord of Sabaoth, from the earth, to be avenged of their enemies.   *D. & C.* Sec. 87.

NONE WILL PROSPER WHO FIGHT AGAINST MORMONISM

By George Q. Cannon

It is a remarkable fact—and I wish you all to pay attention to it, if you have not already done so—that no man prospers who fights against this work. You let your minds reflect upon the days of the past in this Territory, and if you have read the history of the people and ask yourselves, "Where are the men who were distinguished at one time among their fellow-men, who have succeeded in life, who have left a name and a fame behind them who have fought against this work?" I mean a name and a fame that are not beclouded. If their sun was bright, it has gone down in gloom, including Presidents of the United States, including judges, senators, congressmen, and others whom we have had in our own Territory. Where are they? Take it from the beginning, from Brocchus Day and Brandenbury, who came to this land. I have watched them closely. I have been familiar with them—men in Congress and men out of Congress, men of position in the Territory, and men out of position in the Territory—and there is not one that I know of whose example I would like to follow or whose fate I would like to have. So it will be to the end. "No weapon that is formed against thee shall prosper; and every tongue that shall rise against thee in judgment thou shalt condemn." This is the word of the Lord uttered thousands of years ago concerning His work in the last days. It has been fulfilled; and it will be fulfilled. These are blessings that God has given to us, to be delivered, to be strengthened, to be united, to have the love of one another. What is imprisonment? What are trials and difficulties and troubles? What man is there who would shrink from trials or even death if he knew that he had the love of his fellowmen, if he had their affection and their confidence? And this is what we have. We are banded together by indissoluble ties; they cannot be severed; they are stronger than steel. Yes, they are stronger than death.

This people are solidified by the power of God, by the outpouring of the Holy Ghost. God has poured out this great love from heaven upon us. In every land where the Elders go and baptize the children of men, there is a spirit of love descends upon us who are baptized. The Elders have friends who would die for them. An

Elder going to a strange land, when he baptizes those people into the Church and the Spirit of God rests upon them, they uphold him and feel as though they would lay down their lives for him, so great is their love for the man who brings them the Gospel. Who of the Elders that have traveled that do not know this to be true? Who of the Saints that have been baptized abroad that cannot bear testimony to this throughout these mountains?

Millennial Star, Vol. 51:197-198 (1889).

FATE OF RAIDERS OF L. D. S. HOMES

During the days of the "underground" when so many of our leading men were compelled to leave home to avoid spending a term in the penitentiary, our home was under almost constant observation. There were four deputy marshals who were determined to "get" my father. Their names were Steele, Whetstone, Exum, and McClellan. All of these men hated our people and did everything they could to hurt and destroy us. I was but a small boy and was terrified to meet any one of them.

As the years passed by I had occasion to observe what seemed to be retribution that was meted out to these men. Steele went blind and groped his way about Ogden for years, and apparently lived in poverty. He was an object of pity—a pitiable sight. Whetstone was shot and killed in a saloon brawl at 2 or 3 o'clock in the morning. What happened to Exum himself I don't know, but what happened to his son was perhaps as hard for him to bear as anything that might have happened to him. His son was a handsome fellow. He attended the same school I did. As I remember it, he was the only son of his father, and the apple of his father's eye. When he was about ten years old he contracted a disease that seemed to be beyond the ability of the doctors to control. He stopped growing, and turned a sickly yellow color. One leg became stiff as though there were no joint in it. That is as I remember him the last time I saw him.

McClellan moved away from Ogden, and I never knew what became of him. It would be interesting to know.

Robert I. Burton

RESULT OF REJECTION OF THE GOSPEL REVEALED FROM HEAVEN THROUGH JOSEPH SMITH

BY CHARLES W. PENROSE

On the other hand, through the rejection of this Gospel, which "shall be preached to all the world as a witness" of the coming of Christ, the world will increase in confusion, doubt, and horrible strife. As the upright in heart, the meek of the earth, withdraw from their midst, so will the Spirit of God also be withdrawn from them. The darkness upon their minds in relation to eternal things will become blacker, nations will engage in frightful and bloody warfare, the crimes which are now becoming so frequent will be of continual occurrence, the ties that bind together families and kindred will be disregarded and violated, the passions of human nature will be put to the vilest uses, the very elements around will seem to be affected by the national and social convulsions that will agitate the world, and storms, earthquakes, and appalling disasters by sea and land will cause terror and dismay among the people; new diseases will silently eat their ghastly way through the ranks of the wicked; the earth, soaked with gore and defiled with the filthiness of her inhabitants, will begin to withhold her fruits in their season; the waves of the sea will heave themselves beyond their bounds, and all things will be in commotion; and in the midst of all these calamities, the master-minds among nations will be taken away, and fear will take hold of the hearts of all men.

Millennial Star, Sept. 10, 1859.

PROPHETIC FATE OF STEPHEN A. DOUGLAS

On the morning of November 28, 1839, he (Joseph Smith the Prophet) and Judge Higbee arrived at Washington, and on the following day they went to the White House, the residence of the President of the United States. They were soon shown into an upper apartment, where they met President Van Buren and were introduced into his parlor. There they presented their letters of introduction to him. As soon as he had read one of them, he looked upon Brothers Joseph and Higbee with a kind of half frown, and said, "What can I do? I can do nothing for you! If I do anything I shall come in contact with the whole State of Missouri." But the brethren were not to be thus intimidated; they demanded a hearing and constitutional rights, when the President finally promised to reconsider what he had said, and observed that he felt to sympathize with the Saints because of their sufferings. * * *

Van Buren did not make a favorable impression upon Joseph, who describes him as a small man with sandy complexion, ordinary features, a frowning brow and an ill proportioned body; "and to come directly to the point," he adds, "he is so much a fop or a fool (for he judged our case before he knew it), that we could find no place to put truth into him."

After their interview with the President they visited the members of congress from Illinois, and delivered the letters of introduction which they had for them. These members were generally disposed to favor Joseph and the Saints, and this was not without cause. The Saints who had moved to Illinois were numerous, and the men and party in whose favor their votes would be cast at an election would be sure to win, as the two great political parties in the State were about equally divided as to number at that time. The members of Congress knew this, and as politicians it was to their interest to do what they could for the Saints. Consequently they met together and decided, after discussing the subject, that a memorial and petition should be drawn up in a concise manner, and that Judge Young, who was senator from Illinois, should present the same to the Senate. It was expected that the matter would be referred to the proper committee with all the accompanying documents, and be printed. But all of Joseph's exertions, as well as the testimonies, affidavits and other documents which they laid before Congress, failed to have any effect. Neither the President, nor the Senate and House of Representatives would do anything to call the State of Missouri to account for the inhuman wrongs which her people had inflicted upon unoffending free-born American citizens. The Church had appealed to governors and judges, and now, through its President, it appealed to the Chief Executive of the nation, and the Congress, in which every State in the Republic was represented—the highest authority in the land. There was no redress to be obtained from them; nothing further could be done, therefore, but to leave them in the hands of the Lord, who, in his own due time, will plead the cause of His people.

It is interesting to read Joseph's views respecting the men he was thrown in contact with at Washington. "For a general thing," he said, "there is but little solidity and honorable deportment among those who are sent to represent the people; but a great deal of pomposity and show. * * * There is such an itching disposition to display their oratory on the most trivial occasion, and so much etiquette, bowing and scraping, twisting and turning to make a display of their witticisms, that it seems to us rather a display of folly and show, more than substance and gravity, such as becomes a great nation like ours. However, there are some exceptions."

In the latter part of January, 1840, Joseph left Philadelphia accompanied by Brothers Rockwell, Higbee and Foster, and again visited Washington. Sidney Rigdon joined Joseph at Philadelphia, but was still sick, and had to be left there. On his second visit to the capitol Joseph had another interview with President Van Buren who treated him very insolently. He listened very reluctantly to what Joseph had to say, and in reply uttered that sentiment which has obtained such a deservedly widespread notoriety among the Latter-day Saints: "Gentlemen, your cause is just but I can do nothing for you: and if I take up for you I shall lose the vote of Missouri."

Respecting this interview, Joseph remarks: "His whole course went to show that he was an office-seeker, that self-aggrandizement was his ruling passion, and that justice and righteousness were no part of his composition. I found him such a man as I could not conscientiously support at the head of our great Republic." Joseph also had an interview with John C. Calhoun, senator from South Carolina; but his treatment of Joseph was such as very ill became his station. While conversing with him concerning the persecution of the Saints, this renowned statesman said: "It involves a nice question—the question of States rights; it will not do to agitate it." Henry Clay, another prominent senator, whose assistance Joseph also sought, coldly remarked, in alluding to the Saints: "You had better go to Oregon. * * *"

About four hundred and ninety-one persons held claims against Missouri. These Joseph had presented to Congress. These claims amounted, in all, to $1,381,044.51. But they were not all. There was a multitude of similar bills which were to be presented, and respecting which Joseph said: "If not settled immediately, they will ere long amount to a handsome sum, increasing by compound interest."

Becoming satisfied that there was very little use for him to tarry to press the just claims of the Saints on the attention of the President and Congress, he left Washington in company with Brother O. P. Rockwell and Dr. Foster, and started on the homeward journey February 6, 1840.

Brother Elias Higbee stayed at Washington to have further interviews with the congressional committee, and for several years he labored faithfully, introducing additional testimony concerning the Missouri persecution. The committee reported against Congress doing anything about the business; and that redress could only be had in the Missouri courts and legislature.

Wednesday, March 4, 1840, writes Joseph, "I arrived safely at Nauvoo, after a wearisome journey through alternate snows and mud, *having witnessed many vexatious movements in government officers, whose sole object should be the peace and prosperity and happiness of the whole people; but instead of this, I discovered that popular clamor and personal aggrandizement were the ruling principles of those in authority; and my heart faints within me when I see, by the visions of the Almighty, the end of this nation, if she continues to disregard the cries and petitions of her virtuous citizens, as she has done, and is now doing.* * * *

In speaking about the refusal of the government to grant the Saints redress for the wrongs they had suffered, he says: "Since Congress has decided against us, the Lord has begun to vex the nation, and he will continue to do so, except they repent; for they now stand guilty of murder, robbery and plunder, as a nation, because they have refused to protect their citizens and to execute justice according to their own Constitution."

Historical Record, pp. 474, 475, 476, 477.

*   *   *   *   *

In passing through Carthage on his return from a preaching mission to Ramus, May 18, 1843, Joseph dined with Judge Stephen A. Douglas, who was there holding court. After dinner, Joseph, at the judge's request, occupied three hours in giving him a minute history of the persecutions of the Saints in Missouri. The judge listened attentively, and spoke warmly in condemnation of the conduct of Governor Lilburn W. Boggs and the authorities of Missouri, and said that any people who had acted as the mobs of Missouri had done ought to be punished. Joseph, in conclusion, said:

"*I prophecy, in the name of the Lord God of Israel, unless the United States redress the wrongs committed upon the Saints in the State of Missouri and punish the crimes committed by officers, that in a few years the government will be utterly overthrown and wasted, and there will not be so much as a potsherd left for their wickedness in permitting the murder of men, women and children, and the wholesale plunder and extermination of thousands of her citizens to go unpunished, thereby perpetrating a foul and corroding blot upon the fair fame of this great republic, the very thought of*

*which would have caused the high-minded and patriotic framers of
the Constitution of the United States to hide their faces with shame.
Judge, you will aspire to the Presidency of the United States, and
if you ever turn your hand against me or the Latter-day Saints, you
will feel the weight of the hand of the Almighty upon you; and you
will live to see and know that I have testified the truth to you, for
the conversation of this day will stick to you through life."*

Historical Record, p. 514.

ELDER B. H. ROBERTS' PRESENTATION OF FACTS

This prophecy was first published in Utah, in the *Deseret News*
of September 24, 1856; it was afterwards published in England, in
the *Millennial Star*, February, 1859 (Vol. 21, No. 9). In both instances it is found in the History of Joseph Smith, then being published in sections in those periodicals. Stephen A. Douglas did aspire
to the presidency of the United States, and was nominated for that
office by the Democratic Convention, held in Charleston, on the
23rd of June, 1860. When in the convention he was declared the
regular nominee of the Democratic party, "the whole body rose to
its feet, hats were waved in the air and many tossed aloft; shouts,
screams, and yells and every boisterous mode of expressing approbation and unanimity, were resorted to." (See Cooper's *American Politics*, Book 1, p. 86.)

When Mr. Douglas aspired to the presidency, no man in the
history of American politics had more reason to hope for success.
The political party of which he was the recognized leader, in the
preceding presidential election had polled 174 electoral votes as
against 122 cast by the other two parties which opposed it; and a
popular vote of 1,838,169, as against 1,215,798 votes for the two
parties opposing. It is a matter of history, however, that the Democratic party in the election of 1860 was badly divided; and fractions
of it put candidates into the field with the following result: Mr.
Abraham Lincoln, candidate of the Republican party, was triumphantly elected. He received 180 electoral votes; Mr. Breckinridge received 72 electoral votes; Mr. Bell, 39; and Mr. Douglas 12.
"By a plurality count of the popular vote, Mr. Lincoln carried 18
states; Mr. Breckinridge 11; Mr. Bell 3, and Mr. Douglas but 1!"
(See tables in *American Politics*, Book ·7, pp. 22, 26; also *History
of U. S.* by Alexander H. Stephens, p. 559.) Twenty days less than
one year after his nomination by the Charleston convention, while
yet in the prime of manhood—forty-eight years of age—Mr. Douglas died at his home in Chicago, a disappointed, not to say heart-
broken man.

Let us now search out the cause of his failure. Fourteen years
after the interview containing the prophecy had been published in
the *Deseret News*, Mr. Douglas was called upon to deliver a speech
in Springfield, the capital of Illinois. His speech was delivered on
the 12th of June, 1857; and published in the *Missouri Republican*
of June 18th, 1857. It was a time of much excitement throughout
the country concerning the Mormon Church in Utah. Falsehoods
upon the posting winds seemed to have filled the air with the most

outrageous calumny.   Crimes the most repulsive—murders, rob-
beries, rebellion, and high treason—were falsely charged against
its leaders.   It was well known that Mr. Douglas had been on
terms of intimate friendship with the Prophet Joseph Smith; and
was well acquainted with the other church leaders.   He was therefore looked upon as one competent to speak upon the "Mormon
Question," and was invited to do so in the speech to which reference
is here made.   Mr. Douglas responded to the request. He grouped
the charges against the Mormons which were then passing current, in the following manner:

"First, that nine-tenths of the inhabitants are aliens by birth who have
refused to become naturalized, or to take the oath of allegiance, or do any
other act recognizing the government of the United States as a paramount
authority in the territory (Utah).

"Second, that the inhabitants, whether native or alien born, known as
Mormons (and they constitute the whole people of the territory) are bound
by horrible oaths, and terrible penalties, to recognize and maintain the authority of Brigham Young, and the government of which he is head, as
paramount to that of the United States, in civil as well as in religious affairs;
and they will in due time, and under the direction of their leaders, use all the
means in their power to subvert the government of the United States and
resist its authority.

"Third, that the Mormon government, with Brigham Young at its head,
is now forming alliance with Indian tribes in Utah and adjoining territories—
stimulating the Indians to acts of hostility—and organizing bands of his own
followers under the name of Danites or destroying angels, to prosecute a
system of robbery and murders upon American citizens who support the authority of the United States, and denounce the infamous and disgusting practices and institutions of the Mormon government."

Mr. Douglas based his remarks upon these rumors against
the saints in the course of which he said:

"Let us have these facts in an official shape before the president and
congress and the country will soon learn that, in the performance of the high
and solemn duty devolving upon the executive and congress, there will be no
vacillating or hesitating policy. It will be as prompt as the peal that follows
the flash—as stern and unyielding as death. Should such a state of things
actually exist as we are led to infer from the reports—and such information
comes in an official shape—the knife must be applied to this pestiferous, disgusting cancer which is gnawing into the very vitals of the body politic. It
must be cut out by the roots and seared over by the red hot iron of stern and
unflinching law. * * * Should all efforts fail to bring them (the Mormons) to
a sense of their duty, there is but one remedy left. Repeal the organic law of
the territory, on the ground that they are alien enemies and outlaws, unfit
to be citizens of a territory, much less ever to become citizens of one of the
free and independent states of this confederacy. To protect them further in
their treasonable, disgusting and bestial practices would be a disgrace to
the country—a disgrace to humanity—a disgrace to civilization, and a disgrace to the spirit of the age. Blot it out of the organized territories of the
United States. What then? It will be regulated by the law of 1790, which has
exclusive and sole jurisdiction over all the territory not incorporated under
any organic or special law. By the provisions of this law, all crimes and mis-
demeanors, committed on its soil, can be tried before the legal authorities of
any state or territory to which the offenders shall be first brought to trial,
and punished. Under that law persons have been arrested in Kansas, Nebraska
and other territories, prior to their organization as territories, and hanged
for their crimes. The law of 1790 has sole and exclusive jurisdiction where no
other law of a local character exists, and by repealing the organic law of
Utah, you give to the general government of the United States the whole and
sole jurisdiction over the territory."

The speech of Mr. Douglas was of great interest and importance to the people of Utah at that juncture. Mr. Douglas had it in his power to do them a great good. Because of his personal acquaintance with Joseph Smith and the great body of the Mormon people then in Utah, as well as their leaders (for he had known both leaders and people in Illinois, and those whom he had known in Illinois constituted the great bulk of the people in Utah, when he delivered that Springfield speech)—he knew that the reports carried to the east by vicious and corrupt men were not true. He knew that these reports, in the main, were but a rehash of the old exploded charges made against Joseph Smith and his followers in Missouri and Illinois; and he knew them to be false by many evidences furnished him by Joseph Smith in the interview of the 18th of May, 1843, and by the Mormon people at sundry times during his association with them at Nauvoo. He had an opportunity to befriend the innocent; to refute the calumnies cast upon a virtuous community; to speak a word in behalf of the oppressed; but the demagogue triumphed over the statesman, the politician over the humanitarian; and to avoid the popular censure which he feared befriending the Mormon people would bring to him, he turned his hand against them, with the result that he did not destroy them but sealed his own doom—in fulfillment of the words of the prophet, he felt the weight of the hand of the Almighty upon him.

It was impossible for any merely human sagacity to foresee the events predicted in this prophecy. Stephen A. Douglas was a bright, but comparatively an unknown man at the time of the interview, in May, 1843. There is and can be no question about the prophecy preceding the event. It was published, as before stated, in the *Deseret News* of the 24th of September, 1856; about one year before the Douglas speech at Springfield, in June, 1857; and about four years before Douglas was nominated for the presidency by the Charleston Democratic Convention.

Moreover, a lengthy review of Mr. Douglas' speech was published in the editorial columns of the *Deseret News* in the issue of that paper for September 2nd, 1857, of which the following is the closing paragraph, addressed directly to Mr. Douglas:

"In your last paragraph (of the Springfield speech) you say, 'I have thus presented to you plainly and fairly my views of the Utah question.' With at least equal plainness and far more fairness have your views now been commented upon. And inasmuch as you were well acquainted with Joseph Smith and his people, also with the character of your maligners, and did know their allegations were false, but must bark with the dogs who were snapping at our heels, to let them know that you were a dog with them; and also that you may have a testimony of the truth of the assertion that you did know Joseph Smith and his people and the character of their enemies, (and neither class have changed, only as the saints have grown better and their enemies worse); and also that you may thoroughly understand that you have voluntarily, knowingly, and of choice sealed your damnation, and by your own chosen

course have closed your chance for the Presidential chair through disobeying the counsel of Joseph, which you formerly sought and prospered by following, and that you in common with us may testify to all the world that Joseph was a true prophet, the following extract from the history of Joseph Smith is again printed for your benefit, and is kindly recommended to your careful perusal and most candid consideration." . *Here follows the interview with Judge Douglas.*

I have been careful to state in full all the circumstances connected with this remarkable prophecy in order that there might be no question in relation to the prophecy itself, that is, no question as to the prediction preceding the event, and its complete and miraculous fulfillment. And now I have reached the point for the argument.

The prophecy is a fact. Its fulfillment is a fact. God gloriously fulfilled the prediction of His servant Joseph Smith, the prophet. Stephen A. Douglas did aspire to the presidency of the United States. He received the nomination for that high office from a great political party. But he had raised his hand against the Latter-day Saints, the people of the Prophet Joseph Smith; and as a consequence he did feel the weight of the hand of the Almighty upon him; for all his hopes were blasted; he never reached the goal of his ambition; he failed miserably, and died wretchedly, when his life had but reached high noon. Could anything be more clear than that Stephen A. Douglas felt the weight of the hand of the Almighty upon him? But mark you, these calamities came upon him for striking the saints of God in Utah. It was for turning his hand against them that he was disappointed in his hopes, blasted in his expectations, and died heartbroken. And when the Almighty thus vindicated the predictions of his prophet upon the head of this great man, He also did something more—He acknowledged the saints in Utah as His people, the Church in Utah as His Church, and there is no escaping the conclusion.

Under the date of November 27, 1860, Orson Hyde wrote to Judge Douglas, from Ephraim, Utah Territory, as follows:

"Will the Judge now acknowledge that Joseph was a true Prophet? If he will not, does he recollect a certain conversation had with Mr. Smith, at the house of Sheriff Backenstos, in Carthage, Illinois, in the year 1843, in which Mr. Smith said to him, 'You will yet aspire to the Presidency of the United States. But if you ever raise your hand, or your voice against the Latter-day Saints, you shall never be President of the United States.'

"Does Judge Douglas recollect that in a public speech delivered by him in the year 1857, at Springfield, Illinois, of comparing the Mormon community, then constituting the inhabitants of the Utah Territory, to a 'loathsome ulcer on the body politic;' and of recommending the knife to be applied to cut it out?

"Among other things the Judge will doubtless recollect that I was present and heard the conversation between him and Joseph Smith, at Mr. Backenstos' residence in Carthage, before alluded to.

"Now, Judge, what think you about Joseph Smith and Mormonism?" Succession in the Presidency, By B. H. Roberts.

Addenda

Important Note: On pages 290-1, mention is made of the scourge of cholera among the camp. This is in fulfillment of the word of the Lord through Joseph, which is as follows:

"While we were refreshing ourselves and teams about the middle of the day, (June 3), I got up on a wagon wheel, called the people together, and said that I would deliver a prophecy. After giving the brethren much good advice, exhorting them to faithfulness and humility, I said the Lord had revealed to me that a scourge would come upon the camp in consequence of the fractious and unruly spirits that appeared among them, and they should die like sheep with the rot; still, if they would repent and humble themselves before the Lord, the scourge, in a great measure, might be turned away; but, as the Lord lives, the members of this camp will suffer for giving way to their unruly temper. * * *

On the 2nd (July, 1834) I went down near Liberty, and visited the brethren. A considerable number of the camp met me at Lyman Wight's. I told them if they would humble themselves before the Lord and covenant to keep His commandments and obey my counsel, the plague should be stayed from that hour, and there should not be another case of the cholera among them. The brethren covenanted to that effect with uplifted hands, and the plague was stayed." *D. H. C.* 6:80, 120.

THE SELF-INFLICTED FATE OF A MOBOCRAT

"But the tempest of an immediate conflict seemed to be checked, and the Jackson mob, to the number of about fifteen, with Samuel C. Owens and James Campbell at their head, started for Independence, Jackson County, to raise an army sufficient to meet me before I could get into Clay County. Campbell swore as he adjusted the pistols in his holsters. 'The eagles and turkey buzzards shall eat my flesh, if I do not fix Joe Smith and his army so that their skins will not hold shucks, before two days are passed.' They went to the ferry and undertook to cross the Missouri River after dark, and the angel of God saw fit to sink the boat about the middle of the river, and seven out of twelve that attempted to cross were drowned. Thus suddenly and justly went they to their own place by water. Campbell was among the missing. He floated down the river some four or five miles, and lodged upon a pile of driftwood, where the eagles, buzzards, ravens, crows and wild animals ate his flesh from his bones, to fulfill his own words, and left him a horrible looking skeleton of God's vengeance: which was discovered about three weeks after by one Mr. Purtle. Owens saved his life only after floating four miles down the stream, where he lodged upon an island, swam off naked about daylight, borrowed a mantle to hide his shame and slipped home, rather shy of the vengeance of God." *Instructor*, Vol. 27.

PROPHECIES FULFILLED AND YET FUTURE

By Orson Pratt:

O Prussia! the glory and pride of Germany! Why are you thus disquieted? Why are your borders menaced with strong and powerful armies? Why are the fearful terrors of war already upon you? It is because you, through the wickedness of your rulers, and your unrighteous laws, rejected the great message which God sent to you by his faithful servants. You forbid them to deliver the glad tidings of the Gospel in your midst; you ill-treated them, and banished them from your country. If you had repented and turned from all your sins, these great evils with which you are now threatened would have been averted; but alas! it is now too late; that which is decreed upon your devoted land must be fulfilled. As you have rejected the only message which will save you, or any other nation, God has rejected you, and your king and your nobles, and all who sit in high places; and you shall be brought down and humbled; and the days will shortly come that you will cease to be a kingdom; and if you still persist to fight against God and cast out his servants, you shall be utterly overthrown.

O Austria! the stronghold of Catholicism! Why have you so framed your unholy laws, that the light of truth cannot penetrate your country? Why have you effectually shut out all religious liberty from the empire? Why do you imprison those who meet together to read the Bible? Why do you banish the servants of the Most High from your dominions, if they attempt to warn you of your iniquities? Do you vainly flatter yourselves, that God will not call you to an account? Do you suppose that you can measure arms with the Almighty? That you can, with impunity, reject so important a message as the one now sent from heaven? That you can forever revel in your filth, and glory in the abundance of your whoredoms? Your sins have reached the heavens! Your horrible abominations have come up before the face of Him who sits upon the throne, who holds the sword of justice in His own right hand, who disposes of kingdoms and empires according to His will, who executes fierce judgments upon the nations, and none can stay His arm. The great day has come, for mourning, bitter weeping, and sore lamentation throughout all your borders! The young, the middle-aged, the flower of your armies, the pride and boast of the empire, shall be trampled in the dust, and pass away! Woes, fearful desolations, and raging pestilences, will sweep over your guilty provinces, and the end thereof shall be with consuming fire.

Let Saxony be called a desolation, because she persecuted the Lord's servants, and banished the Saints from their midst. Let the kingdoms of Hanover, and Bavaria, and the minor states of Germany be seized with trembling; let their hearts be faint; let sorrow and mourning enter their habitations, and let the angel of death persecute them, because they have, for these many years, thrust the servants and prophets of God into their loathsome prisons, and turned a deaf ear to their humble warnings! Therefore, let their thrones be cast down, and their governments be brok-

en to pieces. O Lord, let not the cries of thine anointed ones come
up before thee in vain. Send forth judgment *unto* victory. Let
the nations who fight against thee, know that thou art God. Arise,
O Lord, and thresh the nations, as with a new, sharp threshing
instrument, scatter them as chaff before the furious whirlwind;
break them to pieces, as potter's vessels, dashed upon the rocks;
and if they continue to harden their hearts against thy Gospel,
blot them out from under heaven, and let them go quickly down
into the pit among the uncircumcised of heart. But let thy kingdom, O God, stand forever, and let thy dominion have no end.

Millennial Star, 28:409-11. (1866.)

By Heber C. Kimball:

Will this land be a land of milk and honey? Yes. Missouri is
cracked up to be the greatest honey country that there is on the
earth; but it will not be many years before they cannot raise a
spoonful in that land, nor in Illinois, nor in any other land where
they fight against God. Mildew shall come upon their honey, their
bees, and their crops; and famine and desolation shall come upon
the nation like a whirlwind.   *J.D.*, 5:93.

* * * * *

An army of Elders will be sent to the four quarters of the
earth to search out the righteous and warn the wicked of what is
coming. All kinds of religions will be started and miracles performed that will deceive the very elect if that were possible. Our
sons and daughters must live pure lives so as to be prepared for
what is coming.

After a while the gentiles will gather by the thousands to this
place, and Salt Lake City will be classed among the wicked cities
of the world. A spirit of speculation and extravagance will take
possession of the Saints, and the results will be financial bondage.

Persecution comes next and all true Latter-day Saints will be
tested to the limit. Many will apostatize and others will be still
not knowing what to do. Darkness will cover the earth and gross
darkness the minds of the people. The judgments of God will be
poured out on the wicked to the extent that our Elders from far
and near will be called home, or in other words the gospel will be
taken from the Gentiles and later on carried to the Jews.

The western boundary of the State of Missouri will be swept
so clean of its inhabitants that as President Young tells us, when
you return to that place, there will not be left so much as a yellow
dog to wag his tail. Before that day comes, however, the Saints
will be put to tests that will try the integrity of the best of them.
The pressure will become so great that the more righteous among
them will cry unto the Lord day and night until deliverance comes.
Then the prophet and others will make their appearance and those
who have remained faithful will be selected to return to Jackson
County, Missouri, and take part in the upbuilding of that beautiful
city, the New Jerusalem.

Deseret News, May 23, 1931. *Prophecy and Modern Times*,
by W. Cleon Skousen, pp. 31-32.

By Brigham Young:

I heard Joseph Smith say, nearly thirty years ago. "They shall have mobbing to their hearts content, if they do not redress the wrongs of the Latter-day Saints. Mobs will not decrease, but will increase until the whole government becomes a mob, and eventually it will be State against State, city against city, neighborhood against neighborhood." Methodists against Methodists, and so on. Probably you remember reading not a week ago, an account of a conference being held in Baltimore, in the course of which they seceded from their fellow-churches in the free States. It will be the same with other denominations of professing Christians, and it will be Christian against Christian, and man against man, and those who will not take up the sword against their neighbors, must flee to Zion.

We are blessed in these mountains; this is the best place on the earth for the Latter-day Saints. Search the history of all the nations and every geographical position on the face of the earth, and you cannot find another situation so well adapted for the Saints as are these mountains. Here is the place in which the Lord designed to hide His people. Be thankful for it; be true to your covenants, and be faithful, each and every one.

I am thankful that we live to see this day, and have the privilege of assembling ourselves in these valleys. We are not now mingling in the turmoils of strife, warring and contention— that we would have been obliged to have mingled in, had not the Lord suffered us to have been driven to these mountains—one of the greatest blessings that could have been visited upon us. *It has been designed, for many generations, to hide up the Saints in the last days, until the indignation of the Almighty be over. His wrath will be poured out upon the nations of the earth. We see the nations steadily driving along to the precipice. The Lord has spoken from the heavens, and He is about to fulfill the prophecies of His ancient and modern Prophets. He will bring the nations into judgment, and deal with them and make a full end of them.* Do you wish to see it done today? Are you prepared for the crisis that will eventually come? No.   *The Deseret News,* Vol. 11, No. 9, May 1, 1861.

By John Taylor:

Were we surprised when the last terrible war took place here in the United States? No. Good Latter-day Saints were not, for they had been told about it. Joseph Smith had told them where it would start, that it should be a terrible time of bloodshed and that it should start in South Carolina. But I tell you today the end is not yet. You will see worse things than that, for God will lay his hand upon this nation, and they will feel it more terribly than even they have done before. There will be more bloodshed, more ruin, more devastation than ever they have seen before. Write it down! You will see it come to pass; it is only just starting in. And would you feel to rejoice? No; I would feel sorry. I knew very well myself when this last war was commencing and could have

wept and did weep, over this nation; but there is yet to come a
sound of war, trouble and distress, in which brother will be arrayed
against brother, father against son, son against father, a scene of
desolation and destruction that will permeate our land until it will
be a vexation to hear the report thereof. Would you help to bring
it about? No, I would not; I would stop it if I could. I would pour
in the oil and the wine and balm and try to lead people in the right
path that will be governed by it, but they won't. Our Elders would
do the same, and we are sending them forth doing all that we can,
selecting the very best men we can put our hands upon—men of
faith, men of honor, men of integrity—to go forth to preach the
Gospel to this nation and to other nations.   *J. D.*, Vol. 20:318.

By the Prophet Joseph:

Yet remember, if the Latter-day Saints are not restored to all
their rights and paid for all their losses, according to the known
rules of justice and judgment, reciprocation and common honesty
among men, that God will come out of his hiding place, and vex
this nation with a sore vexation; yea, the consuming wrath of an
offended God shall smoke through the nation with as much distress
and woe as independence has blazed through with pleasure and delight ***

From Letter of Joseph the Prophet to Senator John C. Calhoun. *D.H.C.*, 6:158.

By Jedediah M. Grant:

One of the marked signs of the last days is the blindness of
the people; we are told they would have eyes and see not, and ears
but hear not, and hearts but understand not. If in the days of
Jesus this was true of the Jews and surrounding nations, it is
doubly so now in relation to the nations with which we are acquainted.

Though the fulfillment of the words of the prophets is clear
and visible to us as the noonday sun in its splendor, yet the people
of the world are blinded thereto; they do not comprehend nor dis-
cern the hand of the Lord. The Saints who live in the Spirit, walk
by the Spirit, and are governed by the counsels of the Almighty,
can see the working of the Lord, not only in our midst * * * but we
let our minds stretch abroad to creation's utmost extent, and we
see the hand of the Lord in all the events of the earth.

We see it in the revolutions of our own continent; we see it
in the scattering and scourging of the house of Israel; in the fading
away of nations, on the right and on the left. * * * We see it in the
preparations of war, and the framing of treaties of peace among
strong nations. The world is in commotion and the hearts of men
fail them for fear of the impending storm that threatens to en-
shroud all nations in its black mantle. Treaties of peace may be
made, and war will stop for a season, but there are certain decrees
of God, and certain bounds fixed, and laws and edicts passed the
high courts of heaven beyond which the nations cannot pass; and
when the Almighty decrees the wicked shall slay the wicked, strong
nations may interfere, peace conventions may become rife in the

world and exert their influence to sheath the sword of war, and make treaties of peace to calm the troubled surface of all Europe, to no effect; the war cloud is still booming o'er the heavens, darkening the earth, and threatening the world with desolation.

This is a fact the saints have known for many years—that the Gods in yonder heavens have something to do with these revolutions; the angels, those holy beings who are sent from the heavens to the earth to minister in the destiny of nations, have something to do in these mighty revolutions and convulsions that shake creation almost to its center.

Consequently, when we see nation stirred up against nation, and on the other hand see other nations exerting a powerful influence to bring about negotiations of peace, shall we say they can bring it about? Do we expect they can stay the onward course of War? The prophet of God has spoken it all, and we expect to see the work go on—and see all things fulfilled as the prophets have declared by the spirit of prophecy in them.

Three days before the Prophet Joseph started for Carthage, I well remember his telling us we should see the fulfillment of the words of Jesus upon the earth, where He says the father shall be against the son, and the son against the father; the mother against the daughter, and the daughter against the mother; the mother-in-law against the daughter-in-law, and the daughter-in-law against the mother-in-law; and when a man's enemies shall be those of his own household.

The Prophet stood in his own house when he told several of us of the night the visions of heaven were opened to him, in which he saw the American continent drenched in blood, and he saw nation rising against nation. He also saw the father shed the blood of the son, and the son shed the blood of the father; the mother put to death the daughter, and the daughter the mother; and natural affection forsook the hearts of the wicked; for he saw that the Spirit of God should be withdrawn from the inhabitants of the earth, in consequence of which there should be blood upon the face of the whole earth, except among the people of the Most High. The Prophet gazed upon the scene his vision represented, until his heart sickened and he besought the Lord to close it up again.

J. of D., 2:146-7.

MEMORIES OF CARTHAGE JAIL
By Franklin D. Richards

"On the noon of Tuesday, the 19th, we left for Jacksonville, 215 miles from Chicago, and the next morning we reached Carthage, in Hancock County. It was to this point that our thoughts had long tended. And the moment that we reached the town we sought out the historical jail. It is now occupied as a dwelling house by James M. Browning, a respectable and courteous man, who has in his time held the office of county treasurer. Today it seems a place of peace. To the casual observer it would possess not even a passing interest. But to us who held the knowledge of the mighty events which had transpired within its walls, of the dark cloud of sin which had rested upon it, and of the mighty martyrdom which had cried aloud to heaven and the ages from its bullet-torn frame — there was something so impressive in its every stone that our hearts were filled with solemnity, and our eyes with tears. We went into the room which had been the prison-place of God's servants previous to the murderous attack. We stood upon the self-same floor which was trodden by the feet of Joseph and Hyrum and John Taylor and Willard Richards on that cruel day of slaughter. We saw the hole in the door made by the bullet which gave Hyrum his mortal wound. We bowed over the spot where he fell exclaiming, "I am a dead man." With chastened feelings, we stood at the door-frame and recalled how President Taylor had interposed his body between the Prophet and his bloodthirsty assailants, and how he had struggled to beat back the guns of the murderers, while discharging a torrent of flames and lead. We leaned from that famous window from which the Prophet jumped or fell, and from which President Taylor was thrown wounded and stricken and tossed back by that providential bullet which struck his watch, shattered it, and cast him upon the floor. We thought of this wonderful interposition of almighty power which saved his life for the great purposes which God has since accomplished through him, and which are yet in store. We retraced our steps down that tragic stairway which had once been crowded with devils in human form, and sought the well where Joseph Smith, the Prophet of God, ended his earthly career. But it is now filled up. The spot, however, is easily discernible. It is now a dainty flower bed, bearing masses of pure and fragrant blossoms. It was sweet to see the spot so hallowed—this ground where Joseph lay stretched in death, "when the fiend approached with a knife to sever the head from his body, and was stopped by a flash of lightning from the heavens." With the remembrance of all these things upon us — recalling the blackness of that hour, the woes of our subsequent wrongs, and then looking at the wondrous condition of the Church today, we were lost in a wilderness of emotions. There was much sadness in this visit, and the memories which it called forth. But there was a compensating sensation of triumph in the thought of the utter powerlessness of mankind — even though calling murder and rapine to their aid, to war successfully against the cause which has within itself the seeds of divine progress."

Contributor, 7:299. *May*, 1886.

L.D.S. CHURCH HISTORIAN RECORDS LIGHT FROM HEAVEN
by Andrew Jensen

Joseph, seeing there was no safety in the room, turned calmly from the door, dropped his pistol on the floor and sprang into the same window from which Elder Taylor had attempted to leap, when two balls pierced him from the door, and one entered his right breast from without, and he fell outward, exclaiming, "O Lord, my God!" He fell partly on his right shoulder and back, his head and neck reaching the ground a little before his feet, and he rolled instantly on his face.

In the instant Joseph fell out of the window the cry was raised, "He's leaped the window!" and the painted murderers on the stairs and in the entry ran out.

Among the murderers outside was a man, barefoot and bare-headed, without a coat, his shirt-sleeves rolled up above his elbows and his pants above his knees; he lifted Joseph up and propped him against the south side of the well curb, which stood a few feet from the jail. Colonel Levi Williams then ordered four men to shoot him. They stood about eight feet from the curb and fired simultaneously. A slight cringe of the body was noticed as the balls struck him, and he fell on his face.

The ruffian who set him against the well-curb, then took a bowie-knife, with the evident intention of cutting off his head, for which, according to reports, a considerable sum of money had been offered by the mob. As he raised the knife, and was in the attitude of striking, a light, so sudden and powerful, burst from the heavens upon the bloody scene (passing its vivid chain between Joseph and the murderers), that they were struck with terror. The arms of the ruffian that held the knife fell powerless; the muskets of the four who fired fell to the ground, and they all stood like marble statues, not having the power to move a single limb of their bodies.

After shooting him, the murderers hurried off in a disorderly manner, as fast as they could. Colonel Williams shouted to some who had just commmenced their retreat, to come back and help to carry off the four men who were still paralyzed. They came and carried them away by main strength to the baggage wagons, and they all fled towards Warsaw.

Historical Record: 7-471

Index

CPSIA information can be obtained
at www.ICGtesting.com
Printed in the USA
BVOW11s0325030218
506823BV00002B/109/P